I Belong to South Carolina

I Belong to South Carolina

SOUTH CAROLINA SLAVE NARRATIVES

Edited by

SUSANNA ASHTON

with the assistance of
Robyn E. Adams, Maximilien Blanton,
Laura V. Bridges, E. Langston Culler,
Cooper Leigh Hill, Deanna L. Panetta,
and Kelly E. Riddle

THE UNIVERSITY OF SOUTH CAROLINA PRESS

#475436740

© 2010 University of South Carolina

Published by the University of South Carolina Press
Columbia, South Carolina 29208

www.sc.edu/uscpress

Manufactured in the United States of America

19 18 17 16 15 14 13 12 11 10   10 9 8 7 6 5 4 3 2 1

Library of Congress Cataloging-in-Publication Data

I belong to South Carolina : South Carolina slave narratives : the lives
of Boston King, Clarinda, "A runaway," John Andrew Jackson, Jacob
Stroyer, Irving Lowery, and Sam Aleckson / edited by Susanna Ashton ;
with the assistance of Robyn E. Adams ... [et al.].
    p. cm.
    Includes index.
    ISBN 978-1-57003-900-3 (cloth : alk. paper) — ISBN 978-1-57003-901-0
(pbk : alk. paper)
    1. Slave narratives—South Carolina. 2. Slaves—South
Carolina—Biography. 3. Slavery—South Carolina—History—Sources.
I. Ashton, Susanna, 1967– II. Adams, Robyn E.
    E185.93.S7I2 2010
    303.3'620922757—dc22
    [B]
                         2009051095

This book was printed on Glatfelter Natures, a recycled paper with
30 percent postconsumer waste content.

CONTENTS

ACKNOWLEDGMENTS

Thanks for research and reference assistance are owed to the library staff at Swarthmore Friends Historical Library, especially Christopher Densmore, who helped trace Clarinda to 1837. Allen Thigpen of Sumter shared very useful information about the history of I. E. Lowery for which I am grateful. The reference and the interlibrary loan specialists at Clemson University Library were patient and obliging throughout the long course of this project, and the scholars at the Maine Historical Society were invaluable in helping trace the history of the anonymous author of *Recollections of a Runaway Slave*.

Drafts of various parts of this work were read and greatly improved by Joe Mai, Mike LeMahieu, Rhonnda Thomas, James Burns, Stephanie Barczewski, Aga Skordzka, and Elizabeth Rivlin. Editorial assistance from Misry Soles, Charis Chapman, Russell Hehn, and Leslie Haines also helped move this project to completion.

This project was made possible by special grants from the College of Arts, Architecture and Humanities at Clemson University. Finally, but most important, the Clemson University–wide program for the pursuit of creative inquiry in the classroom inspired the creation of this special team investigation and made it happen by funding the year-long course and expenses associated with the necessary research and writing.

EDITORIAL METHOD

The goal for editing these texts was simply to make alterations only when helpful to contemporary readers and yet not unnecessarily diminish the tone and historical phrasing particular to these narratives. Silent changes were made in some small instances to remove misleading punctuation and to correct spelling or printing errors that rendered words incomprehensible. Various versions of "Sumpter," "Sumter," "Sumpterville," and "Fort Sumpter" were left as they were in each narrative to reflect the practices of different eras and regions. No changes were made to dialect phrases or words already within quotation marks, nor were capitalization practices altered to reflect contemporary sensibilities. This is particularly notable with the terms "negro," "negroes," "Negro," and "Negroes," which were left precisely as the original printed manuscript read.

In order to convey the significance of the serial reading experience—most important for "Recollections of Slavery by a Runaway Slave," which initially appeared in the *Advocate of Freedom* and later in the *Emancipator,* and also for the memoirs of Boston King, whose narrative was originally published in the *Methodist Magazine*—the installment breaks are indicated. In the case of the Reverend I. E. Lowery, whose memoir consists of an initial serialized narrative published by a friend in conjunction with his own later additions and stories in book form, the complete 1911 edition of the text appears, and thus the breaks in the initial sections of the serialized version are not indicated.

While the lives of Boston King, Clarinda, "A Runaway," John Andrew Jackson, and Sam Aleckson are presented here in their entirety, Jacob Stroyer's narrative and that of I. E. Lowery are trimmed to emphasize their individual life stories and also to focus attention on the narrative thrust of these works. Thus a long chapter of Stroyer's narrative that concerns generalized anecdotes and impersonal recollections of slavery was

excised, as was an appendix assembled by Lowery that excerpts and sum-
marizes newspaper articles, letters, and other documents attesting to
the positive relationships between white and black southerners. Omit-
ting these sections should assist readers in focusing on the compelling
personal testimony these people provide about the South Carolina slave
experience.

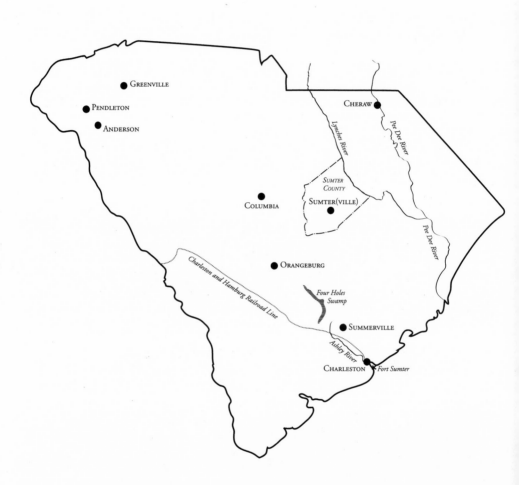

Introduction

—⟋⟍—

In 1846 John Andrew Jackson escaped from a Sumter, South Carolina, plantation. He made his way to the docks of Charleston, where he lurked around the wharves, seeking a northbound boat. Suspicious workers confronted the black man, demanding to know, "Who do you belong to?" Aware that he could not persuasively identify himself as either a freeman or a Charleston slave, Jackson dodged the question by replying simply, "I belong to South Carolina." As Jackson later explained in *The Experience of a Slave in South Carolina* (1862), "It was none of their business whom I belonged to; I was trying to belong to myself."

Jackson's careful words highlight precisely the conundrum this collection seeks to illuminate. While Jackson made it to Boston by hiding in a cotton bale and eventually published his memoir from England, he remained both claimed and unclaimed as South Carolina property. Despite the year-old Civil War, he was a runaway when he wrote, still liable at any time to be seized and forcibly returned to bondage as stolen property under the legal sanction of his nation's fugitive slave laws. Jackson's memoir marked an achievement of self-ownership, to be sure. However, his double meanings could not be fully realized until now, for even a century and a half later John Andrew Jackson remains largely unknown and unclaimed by the public history of South Carolina.

Like almost every memoir by an escaped slave, Jackson's account sought to make the extraordinary suffering of slavery both a collective and a personal horror. When he asserted that he "belonged" to South Carolina he was stating an individual truth, as he had been born a slave in the state. Yet he was cognizant too of the broader issue at hand. He was trying to belong to himself while also trying to belong to a broader South Carolina identity that would not claim him. His family, his labor, and his suffering were not only deeds to self-ownership but also deeds to a collective property—South Carolina. His life narrative, an account of terrible violence and injustice, was a testament to reversing the language of ownership. His narrative staked his claim to "belong to South Carolina," while his life's work went on to assert that, imaginatively at least, South Carolina belonged to him.

Taking Jackson's claim as the title of this collection is part of this project's aim to reinsert seven nineteenth-century slave narratives back into the history of the region and the nation. These stories most certainly belong to the state, but also, as Jackson's narrative demonstrates, they lay waste to any easy notion of belonging or ownership. These narratives and the individuals who recounted them belong to South Carolina only inasmuch as South Carolina belongs to them.

The seven life stories presented here concern the slave experience in all its manifestations: from plantation culture to urban servitude, from sexual exploitation to religious awakening. They depict artisan apprenticeship and brutal fieldwork. The authors of four of these narratives (King, Lowery, Aleckson, and Stroyer) make reference to working with racehorses or even as jockeys when they were children.

These stories tell of daring escapes and equally daring attempts simply to stay put. They both mourn and celebrate the lives of people surviving enslavement. The upstate, central, and coastal regions of South Carolina are all depicted in these tales. Indeed, forced or voluntary migration is a recurring theme in all of these narratives, for many of these individuals crossed townships, states, countries, and oceans—always seeking to define their homes on their own terms.

The culture of slavery in South Carolina was historically distinct from the cultures of slavery elsewhere in the American colonies (and, later, in the American states). South Carolina's semitropical climate and historic ties to the British West Indies, especially the island of Barbados, created a society in which immensely profitable large-scale agriculture demanded a huge labor force working in plantation groups to raise indigo, rice, or cotton, as opposed to the small-scale farm crops that would demand fewer slaves.* Indeed, in 1850 South Carolina's average farm size was the

---

*For a good overview of the astounding profitability of rice and cotton in South Carolina, at least during the eighteenth century and early decades of the nineteenth century, see Walter Edgar, "To Raise Something for Sale," in Edgar, *South Carolina: A History* (Columbia: University of South Carolina Press, 1998), 265–323.

largest in the United States.* Moreover, the expertise of Africans familiar with rice cultivation was much sought after, and South Carolina, more than many other states, imported slaves from areas with shared cultural backgrounds. This fact, in addition to the geographic isolation of large slave populations left to labor in relative isolation on lowcountry plantations, is part of the reason that South Carolina's Gullah communities, with their amalgamation of African and European linguistic and social practices, evolved.[†] While none of the seven individuals featured here identified him/herself specifically as Gullah, the fact that such a unique Creole culture was able to develop at all is another marker of how South Carolina history shaped a world of slavery unlike any other.

South Carolina long had the highest ratio of slaves to free whites of any American colony, and while many slaves fled plantations during the American Revolution, the postwar surge in slave imports more than made up for the difference through the early nineteenth century. South Carolina slave populations grew over the generations, and black codes and legislation passed over the years lessened the chance of any autonomy for slaves to run their own lives. Plantations and farms that came to populate the middle and western, or "upper," part of the state were never as numerous as those in the lowcountry. However, while in 1760 less than one-tenth of the colony's slaves resided outside of the lowcountry, by 1810 almost one-half lived in the middle and upstate regions.[‡]

Charleston was the major port of entry for enslaved Africans brought to the United States, and in the eighteenth century three out of four African-born slaves were brought to Charleston for sale or trade. Although none of the people featured in this collection were born in Africa, at least three did have parents captured from there. Sam Aleckson writes that his great-grandfather came from, "or rather was brought" from, Africa; Boston King describes his father as "stolen away from Africa when he was young"; and Jacob Stroyer, who knew his father well, claims that his father had been born in Sierra Leone before being brought to the Singleton plantation. While Charleston may have represented a warm memory for Sam Aleckson, who felt it was "a grand old city," it was surely

---

*Manisha Sinha, *The Counter-Revolution of Slavery: Politics and Ideology in Antebellum South Carolina* (Chapel Hill: University of North Carolina Press, 2000), 11.

[†]See Daniel C. Littlefield, *Rice and Slaves: Ethnicity and the Slave Trade in Colonial South Carolina* (Baton Rouge: Louisiana State University Press, 1981).

[‡]Larry E. Hudson, Jr., *To Have and to Hold: Slave Work and Family Life in Antebellum South Carolina* (Athens: University of Georgia Press, 1997), 7.

a more danger-fraught and troubled site of memory for at least two of the other authors featured in this collection. John Andrew Jackson and the anonymous author of "Recollections of Slavery by a Runaway Slave" separately made their way to Charleston in order to escape from the South. Smuggled aboard ships leaving the port of Charleston, these two men symbolically reenacted in reverse the harsh and cramped arrival of their forebears. Jacob Stroyer and Sam Aleckson, in contrast, both served the Confederate forces at Fort Sumter and witnessed firsthand the symbolic and strategic importance of Charleston. Thus while Columbia, Greenville, Pendleton, Sumter, and other locations loomed large in the minds of our writers, for many of them, Charleston trumped all others in its urban manifestation of the glory that wealth built on the backs of enslaved people could bring.*

The first detailed accounts we have of North American slave lives are seventeenth- and eighteenth-century criminal confessions transcribed or summarized in pamphlets usually distributed after executions to serve as cautionary tales of sin and repentance. Later in the eighteenth century autobiographies and biographies that were more sophisticated and transatlantic in nature began to surface; these were usually authored by or writen about former slaves who had become sailors or missionaries and framed their life stories as tales of religious or spiritual awakening. Although these eighteenth-century narratives were considerably more sophisticated and nuanced than the criminal tales that had preceded them, and many of them certainly confronted the issue of slavery head-on, these types of slave narrators nonetheless rarely used enslavement as the linchpin of their identity. Even Olaudah Equiano, one of history's great eighteenth-century abolitionists, arguably saw his enslavement in sin as a burden as great as enslavement to man. By the early nineteenth century, however, accounts written by, written with, or written for slaves and former slaves became literary phenomena that only gained momentum as the century progressed. With few exceptions these narratives (primarily from the 1830s to the 1860s) were explicitly composed to raise awareness of the abolitionist cause and to raise money to support former slaves, often by helping them purchase their own or family members' freedom.

While the term "narrative" suggests a work authored solely by one individual, the hazy provenance of so many early slave texts makes such purist

*The most comprehensive overview of what Charleston signified to the black population of South Carolina can be found in Bernard E. Powers, Jr., *Black Charlestonians: A Social History 1822–1855* (Fayetteville: University of Arkansas Press, 1994).

definitions imprecise. As is true with the early narratives in this collection, some were written by the former slaves, some were heavily edited or shaped by abolitionist mentors, some may have been ghostwritten by sympathetic individuals, and others were more in the way of paraphrased interviews. After the Civil War, as literacy spread across the South, many individuals composed life stories with agendas ranging from uplift and inspiration to cautionary and even nostalgic reminiscences. By the early twentieth century the last generation of former slaves put pen to paper and recorded their experiences as youngsters during the antebellum years and, in such witnessing, often provided subtle commentary on the dire state of turn-of-the-century race relations. The South Carolina narratives represented in this collection exemplify those national patterns of how individuals recounted their experiences under slavery through the eras—from bondage as defined by religion to bondage as defined by man, and from freedom from the physical body to freedom of the physical body.

Of the several hundred North American slave autobiographies currently known to exist, only about a dozen are authored by individuals who distinctly identify themselves as South Carolinians.* Of those who seem to consider themselves South Carolinians, few are easily available through mainstream brick-and-mortar publishers, and none have ever been collected together in a South Carolina context. The collection of seven life stories presented here with their intertwined themes doubles the number of South Carolina slave narratives in print.

The first and earliest narrative in this volume is that of Boston King. King tells a remarkable tale of transatlantic triumph and is an invaluable witness to the plight of slaves during the American Revolution in South Carolina.

In November 1775 John Murray, Lord Dunmore, the last colonial governor of Virginia, promised liberty to all slaves escaping from rebel plantations and agreeing to serve the British army. This promise was later clarified and expanded to include women and children. These announcements were not conceived as a great emancipation for any broad philosophical purpose. Rather, they were quite explicitly constructed in an attempt to sabotage the Patriot war effort by forcing slave owners to return

---

*Some extant slave autobiographies indicate that the authors were born in South Carolina or spent brief periods of time there, but the bulk of these life stories reflect the culture of other locales and were thus excluded from this collection. See the afterword in this collection for a further exploration and analysis of this issue.

home from war elsewhere in order to defend their families and property from potential slave uprisings, by bolstering the forces and resources of British troops and, not incidentally, decimating the southern labor force more generally.* The effect of these pronouncements was tremendous, and between eighty thousand and one hundred thousand enslaved people left their plantations during the war. Other estimates are that two-thirds of the slaves in South Carolina alone left their plantations during the war, presumably for the British lines.†

What became of these people? While the overwhelming majority of black people who served the British army in some capacity found no liberty as their reward (indeed, many thousands were shipped back into slavery in the West Indies), a small but remarkable band of individuals did receive their promised freedom from the British.‡ As British forces organized their evacuation from New York, Savannah, Charleston, and elsewhere, they made arrangements for some black Loyalists, whether freemen, former slaves, or slaves of white British Loyalists, to evacuate as well. Thus in the summer of 1783 almost three thousand black Loyalists were given passage, courtesy of the British Crown, to settle in Nova Scotia. Of these three thousand black settlers who landed in Nova Scotia, approximately fifteen hundred chose to establish their own township of Birchtown, named after British brigadier general Samuel Birch, who had authorized the voyages. The black settlers were met with much disappointment and suffering there; promises of deeds to ample farmland were forgotten or deliberately ignored, the white Nova Scotian settlers were wary and even hostile to the influx of cheap competitive labor that the black Loyalists represented, the terrain was rough and rocky, famine was endemic, and the weather was severe. Of the ones who survived that first

---

*James W. St. G. Walker, *The Black Loyalists: The Search for a Promised Land in Nova Scotia and Sierra Leone 1783-1870* (London: Longman & Dalhousie University Press, 1976), 1-3.

†Peter Kolchin provides a summary of statistics on the effects of the Revolution on slavery in South Carolina; see Kolchin, *American Slavery 1619-1877* (New York: Hill and Wang, 2003), 73. Also see Philip D. Morgan, "Black Society in the Lowcountry, 1760-1810," in *Slavery and Freedom in the Age of the American Revolution,* edited by Ira Berlin and Ronald Hoffman (Urbana, Ill.: U.S. Capitol Historical Society by the University of Illinois Press, 1986), 83-142. See also Jim Piecuch, *Three Peoples, One King: Loyalists, Indians, and Slaves in the Revolutionary South, 1775-1782* (Columbia: University of South Carolina Press, 2008).

‡Sylvia R. Frey, *Water from the Rock: Black Resistance in a Revolutionary Age* (Princeton, N.J.: Princeton University Press, 1991), 179-90.

year, many ended up beggars. The situation got even worse when, in July 1784, violent rioting broke out between the white settlers and the black settlers.

The plight of the black Nova Scotians came to the attention of horrified British activists in England, who proposed again resettling the black Loyalists, this time in a free settlement to be located in Sierra Leone. With help from the reformers and also some funding from the British government, the Sierra Leone Company was organized to establish a new British colony in Africa to be populated by former slaves. Boston King, who by this time had become a religious leader of the Birchtown community, agreed to go and was accompanied by twelve hundred other black emigrants, who left from Halifax for Freetown, Sierra Leone, in 1792.

The situation in Sierra Leone was, not surprisingly, a difficult one, and almost immediately upon landing cholera devastated the community, killing many of the black settlers within a few months. The ones who did survive, however, soldiered on, and Boston King's narrative, composed during a brief visit to England in order to further his education so that he might teach school in Sierra Leone, testifies to the optimism amid hardship faced by the wandering slaves who had finally found a home.*

The second tale in this collection also features a person who became a religious leader, but Clarinda's life was circumscribed in very different ways from King's. In addition, although her South Carolina story also testifies to her freedom though Christ, the obstacles that she overcame along the way were entirely different.

Clarinda was born into slavery in 1730 (assuming that she did indeed die in 1832 at the age of 102, as is stated in her story). Her story must have lived on past her death, for the first-known account of her was chronicled well after the Civil War as an inspirational tale of Christianity and faith. Little is known about Clarinda except what seems to have been recounted by Abigail Mott, a prominent Quaker activist who collected Clarinda's brief story and titled it "Clarinda: A Pious Colored Woman of South Carolina" in a book titled *Narratives of Colored Americans*, which was first printed in 1875. Nonetheless, with so few stories of the female experience in slavery known at all and virtually no extant accounts of life for enslaved women in South Carolina, Clarinda's rather mysterious and cryptic account holds an important place in this state's and our nation's histories.

---

*The best and most comprehensive study of these events can be found in Simon Schama, *Rough Crossings: Britain, the Slaves, and the American Revolution* (New York: HarperCollins, 2006).

Although it is the earliest known African American woman's narrative from South Carolina, Clarinda's remarkable story has not been reprinted since the nineteenth century.

Much of what we know about Clarinda's life in bonds can be inferred from the fact that she was described as "A Pious Colored Woman of South Carolina" living decades before emancipation and that she was, to use the careful phrasing of the narrative, "sold under sin." It is possible, of course, that she was not a slave—a small number of free women of color lived throughout South Carolina in the eighteenth century.* However, Clarinda's ensuing story of sin and redemption places her in the depths of an underclass, which suggests that enslavement was at the heart of her experience. She was involved in "almost every species of iniquity" and even learned to play the violin to further "her wicked designs" and lure others into pernicious sin.

After losing a child, Clarinda found her misery led her to God. Her narrative chronicles a deep and emotional engagement with her deliverance. She was inspired to preach, and the narrative speaks of her living in "great poverty" and subsisting at times on "casual charity." The story also refers obliquely to an unnamed person who was in a position to forbid her to hold religious meetings in her home, possibly a master or a religious authority. These vague details do little to clear up her status as free or enslaved but speak instead to the complex cultural interplay of those often less-than-clear conditions. After learning to read, she grew even more expert in the Scriptures and gained many local followers who would come to her for worship and prayer. As this hitherto unknown South Carolina story tells it, a community grew up around her known simply as "Clarinda's People." When she died, her exemplary life became a model for both blacks and whites.

Although not a slave narrative in a strict sense, Clarinda's tale perhaps demonstrates best how the most peripheral and indigent residents of South Carolina are often written out of our history and need to be reinserted in an inclusive sense. Clarinda, whose primary identity seems to come through Christ, rather than slavery, and who renders the usual stuff

*The free black population in South Carolina was largely clustered in urban areas. A recent study dealing with the free people of color in South Carolina is Paul Heinegg, *Free African Americans of Virginia, North Carolina, South Carolina, Maryland and Delaware* (http://www.freeafricanamericans.com/, available online with a useful foreword by Ira Berlin; accessed August 20, 2009). Also see Ira Berlin, *Slaves without Masters: The Free Negro in the Antebellum South* (New York: Random House, 1974).

of nineteenth-century slave narratives subservient to the greater story of her enlightenment, disrupts any easy generalizations we might be tempted to assign the millions of people who were enslaved in South Carolina. People who were enslaved were people first and slaves second. Clarinda's story is a clarion reminder that identities are constructed by how people see themselves, not by how we might see them.

On the opposite end of the spectrum were individuals who understood their bondage in slavery as the overarching force in their lives. The third individual profiled in this volume first told his life story for the abolitionist newspaper *Emancipator* in 1838. His five-part series, "Recollections of a Runaway Slave," is a relentlessly specific testimonial to the violence of slave practices and also to the ways in which plantation culture enabled such violence. Most significantly, though, his narrative illustrates the physical, spiritual, and psychological strategies that enabled the almost incomprehensible survival of many of its victims.

Indeed, the ways in which the system of slavery sought to sever any sense of individual identity is set out almost immediately in this man's narrative when, in his first paragraph, the "Runaway" discusses being whipped as a child. In this passage he notes that the whipping would cut through his skin, although that was not how the masters would describe it. "They did not call it skin, but 'hide.' They say, 'a nigger hasn't got any skin.'" Our anonymous writer was savvy enough to deconstruct the dehumanizing intent of such terms, but even such insights did not fully prepare him for some of the necessary hardening and alienation that enslavement demanded. In later passages he describes in blunt and calm terms being forced to whip a young woman and, quite literally, rub salt into her wounds. Narratives such as this anonymous but desperately individual account demonstrate not only enormous triumphs over unspeakable horrors but also the process by which individuals skinned of their human identities had to reconstruct themselves.

John Andrew Jackson's memoir is the fourth presented here. As outlined in the initial profile of this introduction, his intent upon "belonging" to himself was such a compelling force that it led him not only to a daring escape but also to a career as an internationally prominent lecturer and activist. While Jackson's memoir of 1862 was designed to raise fury and funds, it is also a narrative that reveals much about plantation life in Sumter and the specific economic, cultural, and social practices he observed there. He tells of an underground economy of slaves buying and selling black-market cotton to double-dealing white men. He discusses in detail the murder of a slave by an overseer and how the ensuing legal conflict between the master and the overseer over the "property" loss was negotiated. He paints a complex portrait of issues specific to the region from the point of view of a man who is not recognized as having a stake in such issues. His reconstructed identity as a free man was contingent upon his ability to witness the larger cultural story of his region and his nation.

While the war may have freed the slaves, certain individuals were intent upon moving this nation forward only with a full *awareness* of what had gone before. The fifth memoir of the volume demonstrates such an encompassing sensibility. More so than any of the other narratives in this anthology, Jacob Stroyer's 1885 narrative, first drafted in 1879, was a conscious historical work that thoughtfully confronted and anticipated the growing Reconstruction-era rhetoric that disallowed recollections of a past that included any reference to American slavery as the cataclysmic atrocity it was.

Stroyer felt impelled to write *My Life in the South* to help reconstruct historical memory. He had survived a hard upbringing on the Singleton plantation near Columbia, South Carolina, and although he was trained as a child jockey for the amusement and enrichment of his master, he also toiled in the house and field in often miserable conditions. He had even lived through wounds inflicted by Union soldiers while in service to his Confederate army at Fort Sumter. Despite the fact that he eventually made it north to Worcester, Massachusetts, for religious training and was ultimately ordained as an African Methodist Episcopal minister, he never forgot his experiences back in South Carolina.

Of course, as an author of the postbellum era, Stroyer was not writing as Jackson or the anonymous author in the *Emancipator* had—that is, to reveal the horrors of slavery for the purposes of abolition. Yet he offers no excuses or mitigating explanations for the extensive suffering he carefully chronicles. Rather, Stroyer's goal, as he carefully states at the close of his narrative, is to claim truth in history. Of his own lingering traumas he wrote the following: "But however lasting, I make no complaint against those who held me in slavery. My war is upon ignorance, which has been and is the curse of my race."*

Others recalled South Carolina enslavement in different terms. The sixth narrative in this volume is the Reverend I. E. Lowery's 1911 memoir, *Life on the Old Plantation in Ante-Bellum Days, or a Story Based on Facts by*

---

*This statement closes Stoyer's chapters on slavery in general, which are not presented here. For the full context, see Jacob Stroyer, *My Life in the South* (Salem, Mass.: Salem Observer Book & Job Print, 1885), 83.

the Reverend I. E. Lowery, in which he describes his childhood under slavery in terms nostalgic and even wistful: Lowery's birthplace was, in his words, "a wonderful old plantation" where the labor was so "reasonable" that by working at night, slaves "were enabled to do almost as much for themselves as they did for the white folks during the day." Yet, despite these sorts of observations, he nonetheless hints at more psychologically fraught and tactically complex situations than some of his idyllic stories might reflect. He wryly notes issues such as how slaves were "adepts at giving nicknames to animals, to each other and even to the white folks. But the white folks seldom caught on to the nicknames given to them." Lowery's text suggests that, even under the best circumstances, slaves had their own countertexts to the official stories about slavery.

Overwhelmingly, though, Lowery paints a narrative of slavery in upstate and central South Carolina that engages the human warmth and kindnesses that could occasionally transcend the system of slavery and build genuinely good relations between slaves and their masters. Indeed, in almost incredible terms, Lowery describes "the most pathetic part" of his entire story as "The Breaking Up of the Old Plantation" at the end of the war. The freed slaves, according to Lowery, even went so far as to temper their celebrations and delight at emancipation out of kindly consideration for the hurt feelings of their former owners. The precision and the human dimension of these types of recollections ultimately render even Lowery's most implausible stories persuasive. He forces readers to recognize the complex perspective and nuanced analysis necessary to understanding the complete human experience under slavery.

The deep nostalgia that marks Lowery's text was not atypical for his era and must be understood and valued for its context—as a Reconstruction-era document assembled with goals other than liberation and abolition in mind. Rather than assume that his warmth is due to the false consciousness of identification with his oppressors, or even a facile type of Stockholm syndrome, it is crucial to recognize the incipient cultural pressures that he, as a black preacher in the South, was struggling under simply to keep his community together. After all, according to Tuskegee University statistics, between 1880 and 1929, on average, a black person was lynched every week in the South.* In addition, in the year 1911, the year in which

---

*Lynching statistics were collected by and archived at Tuskegee Institute and have been made available on the Internet in a number of places. One clearly organized site is Lynchings by Year and Race, http://www.law.umkc.edu/faculty/projects/ftrials/shipp/lynchingyear.html. See also Jacqueline Denise Goldsby, *A Spectacular Secret:*

his autobiography was published, over sixty men were lynched in the United States. Lowery's vision of what South Carolina had been and could be was carefully composed within a culture of extraordinary violence. He had a point of view that demanded emphasis on uplift, strategic cooperation, and positive thinking as crucial for salvation, survival, and progress. He clearly believed in slavery as schooling for ultimate civilization and chose to understand it in the way that best suited his worldview.

Of course, not all postbellum slave narratives were marked by such agendas. Sam Aleckson's 1929 memoir, *Before the War and after the Union: An Autobiography,* the final narrative in this collection, is a stunning story of redemption and forgiveness that nonetheless makes no excuses for the injustices the author witnessed. Perhaps most remarkable for our comparison, though, is that Aleckson took up Jackson's notion of belonging to South Carolina and formulated it as follows: "I was born in Charleston, South Carolina in the year 1852. The place of my birth and the conditions under which I was born are matters over which, of course, I had no control. If I had, I should have altered the conditions, but I should not have changed the place; for it is a grand old city, and I have always felt proud of my citizenship." Despite the deprivations of his childhood and the disenfranchisement of his life in the Jim Crow—era South, Aleckson nonetheless felt strongly about claiming citizenship not within the United States at large but specifically within the city of Charleston. He was, in so many words, proud to "belong to South Carolina."

Yet belonging to South Carolina did not mean that he was blind to its crimes. Even sixty-four years after the war Aleckson did not traffic in apologetics. As if responding to memoirs such as Lowery's, he acknowledges that while "there was often a strong manifestation of sympathy" between slaves and slave owners, "there is nothing good to be said of American slavery. I know it is sometimes customary to speak of its bright and its dark sides. I am not prepared to admit that it had any bright sides unless it was the Emancipation Proclamation issued by President Abraham Lincoln." Aleckson's narrative tells of daily life in Charleston during the war and under generally benign owners. He also writes of the interactions of Irish immigrants, working-class whites, house slaves, plantation slaves, soldiers, and how he was pressed into service for the Confederate forces. He notes wryly, "I must admit I wore the 'gray.' I have never attended

---

Lynching in American Life and Literature (Chicago: University of Chicago Press, 2006); Christopher Waldrep, ed., *Lynching in America: A History in Documents* (New York: New York University Press, 2006).

any of the Confederate reunions. I supposed they overlooked my name on the army roll."

Despite his relatively privileged condition as a young slave, in his narrative Aleckson sets about to destroy any easy notions of how slave life operated during that time. He refers to himself as a "Sherman Cutloose," reappropriating with pride the supposedly derisive term used by slaves who had been freed before the war to describe those freed only through the intervention of the Emancipation Proclamation and the Civil War. Aleckson makes it clear that from his perspective no black people were ever truly freed before the war: "I am Persuaded however that all the Negroes in the slave belt, and some of the white men too, were 'Cutloose' by General Sherman." In the end, however, even Aleckson tempers this fierce insight by remarking from the perspective of an elderly man, "But let bygones be bygones."

Aleckson made his way north after the war and writes movingly and humorously of his experiences in Spring Lake, Connecticut, a region he describes as having an overabundance of pie. Yet he ends by reflecting soberly on his own interpretations of "My Country 'tis of Thee," concluding, "I for one, have no fear for the ultimate fate of the Negro. My fears are for the American nation, for, I feel as an American, and cannot feel otherwise." Aleckson in 1929 still felt that South Carolina had effectively repudiated him, and while he might feel as an American before he felt as a Negro, his narrative traces just how caustic his severance from South Carolina was.

The individuals profiled here found a sense of identity through their own experiences, through their own interactions with their families, their friends, their enemies, and their communities. Ultimately their intense individuality reminds us that while they were slaves and South Carolinians, they were first and foremost Boston King, Clarinda, John Andrew Jackson, Samuel Aleckson, I. E. Lowery, Jacob Stroyer, and the nameless "runaway" of the *Emancipator*. It is their legacy as individuals—the sense of them as specific people—that this collection most hopes to depict, for their individuality was the legacy that slavery sought above all to deny them. Sharing these life stories with readers today affirms their value and dignity as men and women who, against all expectations to the contrary, retained a sense of themselves as belonging in some way to the state of South Carolina.

Memoirs of the Life of Boston King, a Black Preacher

—⟋⟍⟋—

Introduction

Susanna Ashton

Slave narratives often tell of harrowing journeys on roads besieged with pa-
trollers and bounty hunters who were eager to seize unaccompanied blacks,
whether free or slaves. Many nineteenth-century slaves escaped by boat or
train or through the woods primarily to avoid the dangers of public roads.
Boston King's account of trekking by foot through Patriot-held territory in
South Carolina in order to deliver a call for reinforcements from a besieged
British encampment reminds us that for eighteenth-century black Carolinians during the American Revolution, the roadside terrors were of a different
sort.*

For Boston King, the dangers of capture by the American rebel forces
were so great that he declined the offer of a horse, preferring to travel almost
thirty miles on foot as the safer option. He wrote, "I expected every moment
to fall in with the enemy, whom I well knew would shew me no mercy."
When he heard a "great noise" on the road, he dove off the path and hid for
his life. Although he eventually made it safely to his destination and delivered the message, "all that I ever received for this service" was "three shillings,
and many fine promises."

While Boston King's entire narrative is characterized by hope and salvation rather than bitterness, this incident of miserly rewards coupled with

---

*For a thorough overview of slaves and the American Revolution, see David
Brion Davis, *The Problem of Slavery in the Age of Revolution 1770–1823* (Ithaca, N.Y.:
Cornell University Press, 1973). Also see Frey, *Water from the Rock*.

fine promises presaged the larger story of what was to become his transatlantic life. Boston King had fled from Richard Waring's South Carolina plantation and served with the British troops in a bold gamble for his freedom.* His story may or may not be an American slave narrative (it is not, for example, included in William L. Andrews's authoritative bibliography of North American slave narratives maintained by the *Documents of the American South* Web project), but it is certainly a transatlantic tale that has its origins in South Carolina. For this reason it offers readers a remarkable perspective on the role of guerrilla warfare in the South.[†] However, more than that, it is a conversion narrative that chronicles his deepening sense of what freedom meant to him.

Following King's repeated displacements makes his search for a spiritual home from which he might never be moved that much more poignant. As he explains regarding trying to convert Africans to Christianity, with their conversion not only would "all pain and wretchedness be at an end," but also they might "enjoy peace without interruption"—surely an appeal that the chronically uprooted King found compelling.

While his father was from Africa, King was born a slave outside of Charleston around 1760 and as a young child worked in Richard Waring's plantation house and tended cattle. As a youngster he had the first in a series of increasingly intense spiritual visions that shaped his life and his memoir. While his first vision led him to acknowledge a true God, it nonetheless left him baffled about where such an acknowledgment should lead. As he wrote, "how to serve GOD I knew not."

At sixteen years of age King was apprenticed to a trade (apparently a master carpenter). King's narrative at this point recounts in detail the hardships inflicted by other apprentices, journeymen, and the master carpenter until King's "proprietor" (most likely Waring) intervened and insisted that young King be better treated. King did not look on these years of apprenticeship

---

*Richard Waring's 526-acre plantation was originally called White Hall, but he changed the name to Tranquil Hill. Made possible by the forced labor of enslaved people, the beauty of the plantation was described by its contemporaries in rapturous terms. See Henry A. M. Smith, "The Ashley River: Its Seats and Settlements," *South Carolina Historical and Genealogical Magazine* 20, no. 1 (January 1919): 50. See also a discussion of the historical gardens and archaeological projects related to the Waring property at http://chicora.org/plantation-garden-archaeology.html.

[†]See William L. Andrews's masterfully assembled scholarly bibliography of North American slave narratives, available at http://docsouth.unc.edu/neh/biblintro.html.

fondly, although his early training in carpentry gave him the skills he later needed to barter for food and to keep him and his wife alive.

As the chaos of war in South Carolina became more intense and in order to escape punishment for having kept a borrowed horse for too long, King fled to the British lines near Charleston. After falling ill with smallpox and receiving some kindness from a British Captain Grey, King aligned himself with the British for some time and traveled with them from one encampment to another. At one point a miscommunication about a hurried decampment meant that King was accidentally left behind, and he was captured by Captain Lewes, who had deserted an American Loyalist militia. King managed to escape back to the British lines and continued to serve Grey and other commanders for another year or two. Eventually King made his way to New York and managed to establish a life as a freeman. He met and married, and he got a job on a pilot boat.

In another unlucky twist, King's boat was captured by an American whaling ship and held in New Brunswick, New Jersey, where British-held areas of New York seemed both tantalizingly close and yet inaccessibly far due to patrolled waterways. Resigned to his fate, King might have let himself be kept in slavery under the relatively beneficent terms of his bondage (he reported that his New Jersey master fed him well and "used me as well as I could expect"). However, King was terrified out of complacency when he witnessed the awful suffering of a teenage boy who, in trying to escape, had been "tied to the tail of a horse" and dragged behind it. Rather than discouraging King from escaping, this horror strengthened his resolve, and King was eventually able to elude the sentinels and guards who watched the river crossings and to make his way to New York and back to his wife.

King survived in New York for three more years. By the winter of 1782, when it became evident that the British forces would soon have to retreat from their strongholds in Charleston, Savannah, and New York as part of their evacuation from the newly established United States, there was great fear among the black Loyalist population—many of whom quite rightly were afraid not only of being taken back into slavery but also of being forced to suffer terrible retribution for their disloyalty.* Many American slaveholders argued that the property clauses in any peace accords would cover the human

---

*The term "black Loyalist" is a problematic phrase inasmuch as it may imply a political allegiance that was more circumstantial than heartfelt. For a thoughtful discussion of this issue by several Canadians who descended from African American refugees who settled in Canada, see http://annapolisroyalheritage.blogspot.com/2008/11/black-loyalists-part-1.html.

beings who had fled from their care. As King wrote, "This dreadful rumour filled us all with inexpressible anguish and terror." The peace accords of 1784 that resulted in the Treaty of Paris went some ways toward calming such fears by agreeing to compensate slave owners for "stolen property," rather than turning over the remaining bands of black Loyalists to their former masters. To this end, the former slaves who hoped to evacuate New York registered with the British in what was called the "Book of Negroes" and were thereby granted travel certificates. Boston King was one of the fortunate few who were recognized with such certificates. He, along with four hundred others, boarded *L'Abondance* for Canada in the summer of 1783.

Although King does not talk about his name in his narrative, at this point he is first identified with the name "Boston King," at least to the British officer who registered his name in the "Book of Negroes." It is true that African and American slave-naming traditions often used place-names such as Boston, and thus it might have been his name from birth. Yet is it not unreasonable to speculate that his name was chosen later, a curious amalgamation of the American city and royalty.* Yet it is not unreasonable to speculate that his name, a curious amalgamation of the American city that had been the hotbed of the rebellion (and which King never indicates having visited) and the title of the monarch who had promised him freedom, was a declaration of sorts. While his first name may well have been the one he was born with and might forever announce his American origins, his second name, which he quite possibly claimed for himself, demonstrated his allegiance to a transatlantic empire and a global promise of liberty.[†]

King discusses some of the initial hardships faced by the black settlers in Nova Scotia, but he also focuses much of his text on his conversion that occurred during this time and how his spiritual growth allowed both him and his community to survive. Despite generous assurances, the settlers had been dropped off in Nova Scotia with little in the way of welcome or support. The

---

*Good studies of slave-naming practices both in general and with attention to the Carolinas are Cheryll Ann Cody, "There Was No 'Absalom' on the Ball Plantations: Slave-Naming Practices in the South Carolina Low Country, 1720–1865," *American Historical Review* 92 (June 1987): 563–96; and John C. Inscoe, "Carolina Slave Names: An Index to Acculturation," *Journal of Southern History* 49 (November 1983): 527–53.

[†]Simon Schama opens his study *Rough Crossings* with a discussion of British Freedom, a man who was part of the black exodus from New York and who later settled in Nova Scotia. No one named British Freedom is listed in the "Book of Negroes," so Schama assumes that the man with this name who is listed on a 1791 petition written in Preston, Nova Scotia, had changed his name after reaching Canadian soil. See *Rough Crossings*, 3–5.

promised farmland did not, on the whole, materialize; when it did, the terrain was rough and rocky. In addition, the weather was harsh and unforgiving. The white settlers were not wholly supportive of the black settlers, and increasing tensions led to violent clashes between them.* While begging and indenturing themselves to white farmers helped some survive, King was forced to leave the settlement for periods of time to find employment in carpentry, fishing, and other tasks. Yet, despite the hardships this community faced, members built churches and built up various spiritual communities and congregations. Increasingly King found himself preaching to his fellow settlers, and over the years he developed a notable following.†

The plight of the black Nova Scotians came to the attention of British abolitionists and activists, who proposed to resettle the black Loyalists, this time in a free territory within Sierra Leone, Africa. In 1792 Boston King, who by this time had established a regular congregation in Preston (which he refers to as "Prestent"), agreed to go. He and his wife were accompanied by twelve hundred other black emigrants who left from Halifax for Freetown, Sierra Leone.

On the voyage King's wife, Violet, became ill and in her weakened state was in no position to survive the fevers and illness that greeted them in Africa.‡ She survived the voyage but died shortly after their arrival. King also became ill but recovered and began working for the Sierra Leone Company and also as a teacher to some of the native Africans. In March 1794 the company paid for him to visit England and study at a Methodist school in order to improve his teaching qualifications. King describes a different kind of conversion during this time. He movingly outlines how his own prejudices against white people were overcome: "In the former part of my life I had suffered greatly from the cruelty and injustice of the Whites, which induced me to look upon them, in general as our enemies; And even after the Lord

---

*What may have been the first race riot in Canadian history occurred in 1784. The details are not entirely clear, but apparently white settlers, angry over the cheap labor of the black settlers and frustrated over any land allocations being directed toward the black Loyalists, rioted. Witnesses reported over twenty houses burned and blacks violently driven out of the town of Shelburne. See Ellen Gibson Wilson, *The Loyal Blacks* (New York: Capricorn Books, G. P. Putnam's Sons, 1976), 91–94.

†James W. St. G. Walker reports that King's Preston Methodist congregation even included a white family; see Walker, *The Black Loyalists*, 73.

‡The fever that ravaged the population was undoubtedly malaria. For statistics about the devastation, see A. B. C. Sibthorpe, *The History of Sierra Leone,* 4th ed. (London: Frank Cass, 1970), 9–10.

had manifested his forgiving mercy to me, I still felt at times an uneasy distrust and shyness towards them; but on that day the Lord removed all my prejudices."

During his two years at the Kingswood school King found time to set down his life story. As is common with slave narratives, it is not entirely clear how much assistance or editorial invention he may have received in the composition of this narrative. He never mentions learning to read or write in earlier parts of his narrative. As he puts it, "I am well aware of my inability for such an undertaking, having only a slight acquaintance with the language in which I write." Nonetheless, despite his discomfort with self-promotion and individualized aggrandizement as not befitting a Methodist congregant, the title of his story clearly declares its origins—it was "Written by Himself."* In 1796 King returned to Africa and taught school in Sierra Leone, along with his second wife, until his death in 1802.

This transcription is based on the original publication of King's narrative. His story was first published in 1798 in four serial installments appearing in the *Methodist* 21 (March 1798): 105–10; (April 1798): 157–61; (May 1798): 209–13; (June 1798): 261–65. Published in London, this magazine was an organ for the Wesleyan Methodists and was intended for distribution in "Preaching-Houses."

—⚭—

MEMOIRS of the LIFE of BOSTON KING,
a Black Preacher.
Written by Himself, during his Residence
at Kingswood-School.
(from *The Methodist Magazine* March, June 1798)

It is by no means an agreeable task to write an account of my Life, yet my gratitude to Almighty GOD, who delivered my affliction, and looked upon me in my low estate, who delivered me from the hand of the oppressor, and established my goings, impels me to acknowledge his goodness: And

---

*For an insightful analysis of King's conversion narrative and an overview of how King's narrative has been framed elsewhere, see Joe Lockard, "The Reluctant Pietist: Boston King and Transatlantic Methodism" (paper presented at a session titled "Slaves and Communities of Faith" at the annual meeting of the Northeast American Society for Eighteenth-Century Studies, October 26, 2007, Dartmouth College, Hanover, N.H.), http://antislavery.eserver.org/news/bostonkingconferencepaper.pdf.

the importunity of many respectable friends, whom I highly esteem, have induced me to set down, as they occurred to my memory, a few of the most striking incidents I have met with in my pilgrimage. I am well aware of my inability for such an undertaking, having only a slight acquaintance with the language in which I write, and being obliged to snatch a few hours, now and then, from pursuits, which to me, perhaps are more profitable. However, such as it is, I present it to the Friends of Religion and Humanity, hoping that will be of some use to mankind.

I was born in the Province of South Carolina, 28 miles from Charles-Town. My father was stolen away from Africa when he was young. I have reason to believe that he lived in the fear and love of God. He attended to that true Light which lighteth every man that cometh into the world. He left no opportunity of hearing the Gospel, and never omitted praying with his family every night. He likewise read to them, and to as many as were inclined to hear. On the Lord's Day, he rose very early, and met his family: After which he worked in the field till about three in the afternoon, and then went into the woods and read till sunset: The slaves being obliged to work or on the Lord's Day to procure such things as were not allowed by their masters. He was beloved by his master, and he had the charge of the Plantation as a driver for many years. In his old age he was employed as a mill-cutter. Those who knew him, say, that they never heard him swear an oath, but on the contrary, he reproved all who spoke improper words in his hearing. To the utmost of his power he endeavored to make his family happy, and his death was a very great loss to us all. My mother was employed chiefly in attending upon those that were sick, having some knowledge of the virtue of herbs, which she learned from the Indians. She likewise had the care of making the people's clothes, and on these accounts was indulged with many privileges which the rest of the slaves were not.

When I was six years old I waited in the house upon my master. In my 9th year I was put to mind the cattle. Here I learnt from my comrades the horrible sin of Swearing and Cursing. When 12 years old, it pleased GOD to alarm me by a remarkable dream. At mid-day, when the cattle went under the shade of the trees, I dreamt that the world was on fire, and that I saw the supreme Judge descend on his great white Throne! I saw millions of millions of souls; some of whom ascended up to heaven; while others were rejected, and fell into the greatest confusion and despair. This dream made such an impression upon my mind, that I refrained from swearing and bad company, and from that time, acknowledged that there was a GOD; but how to serve GOD I knew not. Being obliged to travel in different parts of America with race-horses, I suffered many hardships. Happening one time to lose a boot belonging to the Groom, he would not suffer me to have any shoes all that Winter, which was a great punishment to me. When 16 years old, I was bound apprentice to a trade. After being in the shop about two years, I had the charge of my master's tools, which being very good, were often used by the men, if I happened to be out of the way: When this was the case, or any of them were lost, or misplaced, my master beat me severely, striking me upon my head, or any other part without mercy. One time in the holy-days, my master and the men being from home, and the care of the house devolving upon me and the younger apprentices, the house was broke open, and robbed of many valuable articles, thro' the negligence of the apprentice who had then the charge of it. When I came home in the evening, and saw what had happened, my consternation was inconceivable, as all that we had in the world could not make good the loss. The week following, when the master came to town, I was beat in the most unmerciful manner, so that I was not able to do any thing for a fortnight. About eight months after, we were employed in building a store-house, and nails were very dear at that time, it being in the American war, so that the work-men had their nails weighed out to them; on this account they made the younger apprentices watch the nails while they were at dinner. It being my lot one day to take care of them, which I did till an apprentice returned to his work, and then I went to dine. In the mean time he took away all the nails belonging to one of the journeymen, and he being of very violent temper, accused me to the master with stealing of them. For this offence I was beat and tortured most cruelly, and was laid up three weeks before I was able to do any work. My proprietor, hearing of the bad usage I received, came to town, and severely reprimanded my master for beating me in such a manner, threatening him, that if he ever heard the like again, he would take me away and put me to another master to finish my time, and make him pay for it. This had a good effect, and he behaved much better to me, the two succeeding years, and I began to acquire a proper knowledge of my trade. My master being apprehensive that Charles-Town was in danger on account of the war, removed into the country, about 38 miles off. Here we built a large house for Mr. Waters, during which time the English took Charles-Town. Having obtained leave one day to see my parents, who had lived about 12 miles off, and it being late before I could go, I was obliged to borrow one of Mr. Waters's horses; but a servant of my master's, took the horse from me to go a little journey, and stayed two or three days longer than he ought. This involved me in the greatest perplexity, and I expected the severest punishment, because the gentleman to whom the horse belonged was a very bad man, and knew not how shew mercy. To escape his cruelty, I determined to go Charles-Town, and throw myself into the hands of the English. They received me readily, and I began to feel the happiness of liberty, of which I knew nothing before, altho' I was much grieved at first, to be obliged to leave my friends, and reside among strangers. In this situation I was seized with the small-pox, and suffered great hardships; for all the Blacks affected with that disease, were ordered to be carried a mile from the camp, lest the soldiers should be infected, and disabled from marching. This was a grievous circumstance to me and many others. We lay sometimes a whole day without any thing to eat or drink; but Providence sent a man, who belonged to the York volunteers whom I was acquainted with, to my relief. He brought me such things as I stood in need of; and by the blessing of the Lord I began to recover.

By this time, the English left the place; but as I was unable to march with the army, I expected to be taken by the enemy. However when they came, and understood that we were ill of the small-pox, they precipitately left us for fear of the infection. Two days after, the waggons were sent to convey us to the English Army, and we were put into a little cottage, (being 25 in number) about a quarter of a mile from the Hospital.

Being recovered, I marched with the army to Chamblem. When we came to the head-quarters, our regiment was 35 miles off. I stayed at the head-quarters three weeks, during which time our regiment had an engagement with the Americans, and the man who relieved me when I was ill of the small-pox, was wounded in the battle, and brought to the hospital. As soon as I heard of his misfortune, I went to see him, and tarried with him in the hospital six weeks, till he recovered; rejoicing that it was in my power to return him the kindness he had shewed me. From thence I went to a place about 35 miles off, where we stayed two months: at the expiration of which, an express came to the Colonel to decamp in fifteen minutes. When these orders arrived I was at a distance from the camp, catching some fish for the captain that I waited upon; upon returning to the camp, to my great astonishment, I found all the English were gone, and had left only a few militia. I felt my mind greatly alarmed, but Captain Lewes, who commanded the militia, said, "You need not be uneasy, for you will see your regiment before 7 o'clock tonight." This satisfied me for the present, and in two hours we set off. As we were on the march, the Captain asked, "How will you like me to be your master?" I answered, that I was Captain Grey's servant. "Yes," said he; "but I expect they are all taken prisoners before now; and I have been long enough in the English service, and am determined to leave them." These words roused my indignation, and I spoke some sharp things to him. But he calmly replied, "If you do not behave well, I will put you in irons, and give you a dozen stripes every morning." I now perceived that my case was desperate, and that I had nothing to trust to, but to wait the first opportunity for making my escape. The next morning, I was sent with a little boy over the river to an island to fetch the Captain some horses. When we came to the Island we found about fifty of the English horses, that Captain Lewes had stolen from them at different times while they were at Rockmount. Upon our return to the Captain with the horses we were sent for, he immediately set off by himself. I stayed till about 10 o'clock, and then resolved to go to the English army. After travelling 24 miles, I came to a farmer's house, where I tarried all night, and was well used. Early in the morning I continued my journey till I came to the ferry, and found all the boats were on the other side of the river: After anxiously waiting some hours, Major Dial crossed the river, and asked me many questions concerning the regiment to which I belonged. I gave him satisfactory answers, and he ordered the boat to put me over. Being arrived at the head-quarters, I informed my Captain that Mr. Lewes had deserted. I also told him of the horses which Lewes had conveyed to the Island. Three weeks after, our Light-horse went to the Island and burnt his house; they likewise brought back forty of the horses, but he escaped. I tarried with Captain Grey about a year, and then left him, and came to Nelson's ferry. Here I entered into the service of the commanding officer of that place. But our situation was very precarious; and we expected to be made prisoners every day; for the Americans had 1600 men, not far off; whereas our whole number amounted only to 250: But there were 1200 English about 30 miles off; only we knew not how to inform them of our danger, as the Americans were in possession of the country. Our commander at length determined to send me with a letter, promising me great rewards, if I was successful in the business, I refused going on horse-back, and set off on foot about 3 o'clock in the afternoon; I expected every moment to fall in with the enemy, whom I well knew would shew me no mercy. I went on without interruption, till I got within six miles of my journey's end, and then was alarmed with a great noise a little before me. But I stepped out of the road, and fell flat upon my face till they were gone by. I then arose, and praised the Name of the Lord for his great mercy, and again pursued my journey, till I came to Mums-corner tavern. I knocked at the door, but they blew out the candle. I knocked again, and intreated the master to open the door. At last he came with a frightful countenance, and said "I thought it was the Americans; for they were here about an hour ago, and I thought they were returned again." I asked, How many were there? he answered, "about one hundred," I desired him to saddle his horse for me, which he did, and went with me himself. When we had gone about two miles, we were stopped by the picket-guard, till the Captain came out with 30 men: As soon as he knew that I had brought an express from Nelson's-ferry, he received me with great kindness, and expressed his approbation of my courage and conduct in this dangerous business. Next morning, Colonel Small gave me three shillings, and many fine promises, which were all that I ever received for this service from him. However he sent 600 men to relieve the troops at Nelson's-ferry.

Soon after I went to Charles-Town, and entered on board a man of war. As we were going to Chesepeak-bay, we were at the taking of a rich prize. We stayed in the bay two days, and then sailed for New-York, where I went on shore. Here I endeavoured to follow my trade, but for want of tools was obliged to relinquish it, and enter into service. But the wages were so low that I was not able to keep myself in clothes, so that I was under the necessity of leaving my master and going to another. I stayed with him four months, but he never paid me, and I was obliged to leave him also, and work about the town until I was married. A year after I was taken very ill, but the Lord raised me up again in about five weeks. I then went out in a pilot-boat. We were at sea eight days, and had only provisions for five, so that we were in danger of starving. On the 9th day we were taken by an American whale-boat. I went on board them with a cheerful countenance, and asked for bread and water, and made very free with them. They carried me to Brunswick, and used me well. Notwithstanding which, my mind was sorely distressed at the thought of being again reduced to slavery, and separated from my wife and family; and at the same time it was exceeding difficult to escape from my bondage, because the river at Amboy was above a mile over, and likewise another to cross at Staten-Island. I called to remembrance the many great deliverances the Lord had wrought for me, and besought him to save me this once, and I would serve him all the days of my life. While my mind was thus exercised, I went into the jail to see a lad whom I was acquainted with at New-York. He had been taken prisoner, and attempted to make his escape, but was caught 12 miles off: They tied him to the tail of a horse, and in this manner brought him back to Brunswick. When I saw him, his feet were fastened in the stocks, and at night both his hands. This was a terrifying sight to me, as I expected to meet with the same kind of treatment, if taken in the act of attempting to regain my liberty. I was thankful that I was not confined in a jail, and my master used me as well as I could expect; and indeed the slaves about Baltimore, Philadelphia, and New-York, have as good victuals as many of the English; for they have meat once a day, and milk for breakfast and supper; and what is better than all, many of the masters send their slaves to school at night, that they may learn to read the Scriptures. This is a privilege indeed. But alas, all these enjoyments could not satisfy me without liberty! Sometimes I thought, if it was the will of GOD that I should be a slave, I was ready to resign myself to his will; but at other times I could not find the least desire to content myself in slavery.

Being permitted to walk about when my work was done, I used to go to the ferry, and observed, that when it was low water the people waded across the river; tho' at the same time I saw there were guards posted at the place to prevent the escape of prisoners and slaves. As I was at prayer on Sunday evening, I thought the Lord heard me, and would mercifully deliver me. Therefore putting my confidence in him, about one o'clock in the morning I went down to the river side, and found the guards were either asleep or in the tavern. I instantly entered into the river, but when I was a little distance from the opposite shore, I heard the sentinels disputing among themselves: One said "I am sure I saw a man cross the river." Another replied, "There is no such thing." It seems they were afraid to fire at me, or make an alarm, lest they should be punished for their negligence. When I had got a little distance from the shore, I fell down upon my knees, and thanked GOD for this deliverance. I travelled till about five in the morning, and then concealed myself till seven o'clock at night, when I proceeded forward, thro' bushes and marshes, near the road, for fear of being discovered. When I came to the river, opposite Staten-Island, I found a boat; and altho' it was very near a whale-boat, yet I ventured into it, and cutting the rope, got safe over. The commanding officer, when informed of my case, gave me a passport, and I proceeded to New-York. [To Be Continued]

THE Methodist Magazine, April, 1798
MEMOIRS of the LIFE of BOSTON KING.
Continued.

When I arrived at New-York, my friends rejoiced to see me once more restored to liberty, and joined me in praising the Lord for his mercy and goodness. But notwithstanding this great deliverance, and the promises I had made to serve GOD, yet my good resolutions soon vanished away like the morning dew: The love of this world extinguished my good desires, and stole away my heart from GOD, so that I rested in a mere form of religion for near three years. About which time, (in 1783,) the horrors and devastation of war happily terminated, and peace was restored between America and Great Britain, which diffused universal joy among all parties, except us, who had escaped from slavery and taken refuge in the English army; for a report prevailed at New-York, that all the slaves, in number 2000, were to be delivered up to their masters, altho' some of them had been three or four years among the English. This dreadful rumour filled us all with inexpressible anguish and terror, especially when we saw our old masters coming from Virginia, North-Carolina, and other parts, and seizing upon their slaves in the streets of New-York, or even dragging them out of their beds. Many of the slaves had very cruel masters, so that the thoughts of returning home with them embittered life to us. For some days we lost our appetite for food, and sleep departed from our eyes. The English had compassion upon us in the day of distress, and issued out a Proclamation, importing, That all slaves should be free, who had taken refuge in the British lines, and claimed the sanction and privileges of the Proclamations respecting the security and protection of Negroes. In consequence of this, each of us received a certificate from the commanding officer at New-York, which dispelled all our fears, and filled us with joy and gratitude. Soon after, ships were fitted out, and furnished with every necessary for conveying us to Nova Scotia. We arrived at Burch Town in the month of August, where we all safely landed. Every family had a lot of land, and we exerted all our strength in order to build comfortable huts before the cold weather set in.

That Winter, the work of religion began to revive among us, and many were convinced of the sinfulness of sin, and turned from the error of their ways. It pleased the Lord to awaken my wife under the preaching of Mr. Wilkinson; she was struck to the ground, and cried out for mercy: she continued in great distress for near two hours, when they sent for me. At first I was much displeased, and refused to go; but presently my mind relented, and I went to the house, and was struck with astonishment at the sight of her agony. In about six days after, the Lord spoke peace to her soul: she was filled with divine consolation, and walked in the light of GOD's countenance about nine months. But being unacquainted with the corruptions of her own heart, she again gave place to bad tempers, and fell into great darkness and distress. Indeed, I never saw any person, either before or since, so overwhelmed with anguish of spirit on account of backsliding, as she was. The trouble of her soul brought afflictions upon her body, which confined her to bed a year and a half.

However, the Lord was pleased to sanctify her afflictions, and to deliver her from all her fears. He brought her out of the horrible pit, and set her soul at perfect liberty. The joy and happiness which she now experienced, were too great to be concealed, and she was able to testify of the goodness and loving-kindness of the Lord, with such liveliness and power that many were convinced by her testimony, and sincerely sought the Lord. As she was the first person at Burch Town that experienced deliverance from evil tempers, and exhorted and urged others to seek and enjoy the same blessing, she was not a little opposed by some of our black brethren. But these trials she endured with the meekness and patience becoming a Christian; and when Mr. Freeborn garrettson came to Burch Town to regulate the society and form them into classes, he encouraged her to hold fast her confidence, and cleave to the Lord with her whole heart.

Soon after my wife's conversion, the Lord strove powerfully with me. I felt myself a miserable wretched sinner, so that I could not rest night or day. I went to Mr. brown, one evening, and told him my case. He received me with great kindness and affection, and intreated me to seek the Lord with all my heart. The more he spoke to me, the more my distress increased; and when he went to prayer, I found myself burdened with a load of guilt too heavy for me to bear. On my return home, I had to pass thro' a little wood, where I intended to fall down on my knees and pray for mercy; but every time I attempted, I was so terrified, that I thought my hair stood upright, and that the earth moved beneath my feet. I hastened home in great fear and horror, and yet hoped that the Lord would bless me as well as my neighbours: for the work of the Lord prospered greatly among us, so that sometimes in our class meetings, six or seven persons found peace before we were dismissed.

Notwithstanding I was a witness of the great change which many experienced, yet I suffered the enemy, through unbelief, to gain such advantage over me, that instead of rejoicing with them, and laying hold of the same blessing, I was tempted to envy their happiness, and sunk deeper in darkness and misery. I thought I was not worthy to be among the people of god, nor even to dwell in my own house; but was fit only to reside among the beasts of the forest. This drove me out into the wood, when the snow lay upon the ground three or four feet deep, with a blanket, and a firebrand in my hand. I cut the boughs of the spruce tree and kindled a fire. In this lonely situation I frequently intreated the Lord for mercy. Sometimes I thought that I felt a change wrought in my mind, so that I could rejoice in the Lord; but I soon fell again thro' unbelief into distracting doubts and fears, and evil-reasonings. The devil persuaded me that I was the most miserable creature upon the face of the earth, and that I was pre-destinated to be damned before the foundation of the world. My anguish was so great, that when night appeared, I dreaded it as much as the grave.

I laboured one year under these distressing temptations, when it pleased GOD to give me another offer of mercy. In 1784, I and sixteen persons worked for Mrs. ROBINSON; all of them were devoted to GOD, except myself and two others. The divine preference was with these men, and every night and morning they kept a prayer-meeting, and read some portion of Scripture. On the 5th of January, as one of them was reading the Parable of the Sower, the word came with power to my heart. I stood up and desired him to explain the parable; and while he was shewing me the meaning of it, I was deeply convinced that I was one of the stony-ground hearers. When I considered how many convictions I had trifled away, I was astonished that the Lord had borne with me so long. I was at the same time truly thankful that he gave me a desire to return to him, and resolved by the grace of God to set out afresh for the kingdom of Heaven.

As my convictions increased, so did my desires after the Lord; and in order to keep them alive, I resolved to make a covenant with him in the most solemn manner I was able. For this purpose, I went into the garden at midnight, and kneeled down upon the snow, lifting up my hands, eyes, and heart to Heaven; and entreated the Lord, who had called me by his Holy Spirit out of ignorance and wickedness, that he would increase and strengthen my awakenings and distress, and impress my heart with the importance of eternal things; and that I might never find rest or peace again, till I found peace with him, and received a sense of his pardoning love. The Lord mercifully looked down upon me, and gave me such a sight of my fallen state, that I plainly saw, without an interest in Christ, and an application of his atoning blood to my conscience, I should be lost to all eternity. This led me to a diligent use of all the means of Grace, and to forsake and renounce everything that I knew to be sinful.

The more convictions increased, and the more I felt the wickedness of my own heart; yet the Lord helped me to strive against evil, so that temptations instead of prevailing against me, drove me nearer to him. The first Sunday in March, as I was going to the preaching, and was engaged in prayer and meditation, I thought I heard a voice saying to me, "Peace be unto thee!" I stopped, and looked round about, to see if any one was near me. But finding myself alone, I went forward a little way, when the same words were again powerfully applied to my heart, which removed the burden of misery from it; and while I sat under the sermon, I was more abundantly blessed. Yet in the afternoon, doubts and fears again arose in my mind. Next morning I resolved like Jacob, not to let the Lord go till he blessed me indeed. As soon as my wife went out, I locked the door, and determined not to rise from knees until the Lord fully revealed his pardoning love. I continued in prayer about half an hour, when the Lord again spoke to my heart, "Peace be unto thee." All my doubts and fears had vanished away: I saw, by faith, heaven opened to my view; and Christ and his holy angels rejoicing over me. I was now enabled to believe in the name of Jesus, and my Soul was dissolved into love. Every thing appeared to me in a different light to what they did before; and I loved every living creature upon the face of the earth. I could truly say, I was now becoming a new creature. All tormenting and slavish fear, and all the guilt and weight of sin were done away. I was so exceedingly blessed, that I could no longer conceal my happiness, but went to my brethren and told them what the Lord had done for my soul.

I continued to rejoice in a sense of the favour and love of God for about six weeks, and then the enemy assaulted me again; he poured in a flood of temptations and evil-reasonings; and suggested that I was deceiving myself: The temptation alarmed and dejected me, and my mind was discomposed. Then the enemy pursued his advantage, and insulted me with his cruel upbraidings, insinuating, —"What is become of all your joy, that you spoke of a few days ago? You see, there is nothing in it." But blessed be the Lord, he did not suffer the enemy to rejoice long over me; for while I heard Mr. GARRETSON preaching from John ix.25, "One thing I know, that whereas I was blind, now I see;" the words were so suitable to my experience, that I was encouraged to exercise fresh faith upon the Lord; and he removed every doubt and fear; and re-established me in his peace and favour. I then could say with the Psalmist, "the fear of the Lord is the beginning of wisdom," for I had him always before my eyes, and in some measure walked in the light, as he is in the light. I found his ways were ways of pleasantness, and all his paths were peace.

Soon after, I found a great concern for the salvation of others; and was constrained to visit my poor ungodly neighbors, and exhort them to fear the Lord, and seek him while he might be found. Those that were under convictions, I prayed with them, and pointed them to the Saviour, that they might obtain the same mercy he had bestowed upon me. In the year 1785, I began to exhort both in families and prayer-meetings, and the Lord graciously afforded me his assisting preference.

[To Be Continued]

THE Methodist Magazine, May, 1798.
MEMOIRS of the LIFE of BOSTON KING.
Continued.

The Goodness and Mercy of God supported me in the various trials and exercises which I went through; nevertheless I found great reluctance to officiate as an exhorter among the people, and had many doubts and fears respecting my call to that duty, because I was conscious of my great ignorance and insufficiency for a work of such importance, and as often overwhelmed with grief and sorrow: But the Lord relieved me by impressing upon my mind these words, "I will send, by whom I will send." In the year 1787, I found my mind drawn out to commiserate my poor brethren in Africa; and especially when I considered that we who had the happiness of being brought up in a christian land, where the Gospel is preached, where notwithstanding our great privileges, involved in gross darkness and wickedness; I thought, what a wretched condition then must those poor creatures be in, who never heard the Name of God or of Christ; nor had an instruction afforded them with respect to a future judgment. As I had not the least prospect at that time of ever seeing Africa, I contented myself with pitying and praying for the poor benighted inhabitants of that country which gave birth to my forefathers. I laboured in Burchtown and Shelwin two years, and the word was blessed to the conversion of many, most of whom continued steadfast in the good way to the heavenly kingdom.

About this time the country was visited with a dreadful famine, which not only prevailed at Burchtown, but likewise at Chebucto, Annapolis, Digby, and other places. Many of the poor people were compelled to sell their best gowns for five pounds of flour, in order to support life. When they had parted with all their clothes, even their blankets, several of them fell down dead in the streets, thro' hunger. Some killed and eat their dogs and cats; and poverty and distress prevailed on every side; so that to my great grief I was obliged to leave Burchtown, because I could get no employment. I traveled from place to place, to procure the necessaries of life, but in vain. At last I came to Shelwin on the 20th of January. After walking from one street to the other, I met with Capt. Selex, and he engaged me to make him a chest. I rejoiced at the offer, and returning home, set about it immediately. I worked all night, and by eight o'clock next morning finished the chest, which I carried to the Captain's house,

thro' the snow which was three feet deep. But to my great disappointment
he rejected it. However he gave me directions to make another. On my
way home, being pinched with hunger and cold, I fell down several times,
thro' weakness, and expected to die upon the spot. But even in this situation, I found my mind resigned to the divine will, and rejoiced in the
midst of tribulation; for the Lord delivered me from all murmurings and
discontent, altho' I had but one pint of Indian meal left for the support of
myself and wife. Having finished another chest, I took it to my employer
the next day; but being afraid he would serve me as he had done before, I
took a saw along with me in order to sell it. On the way, I prayed that the
Lord would give me a prosperous journey, and was answered to the joy
of my heart, for Captain Selex paid me for the chest in Indian-corn; and
the other chest I sold for 2s.6d. and the saw for 3s.9d. altho' it cost me a
guinea; yet I was exceeding thankful to procure a reprieve from the dreadful anguish of perishing by famine. O what a wonderful deliverance did
GOD work for me that day! And he taught me to live by faith, and to put my
trust in him, more than I ever had done before.

While I was admiring the goodness of GOD, and praising him for the
help he afforded me in the day of trouble, a gentleman sent for me, and
engaged me to make three flat-bottomed boats for the salmon-fishery, at
1£ each. The gentleman advanced two baskets of Indian-corn, and found
nails and tar for the boats. I was enabled to finish the work by the time
appointed, and he paid me honestly. Thus did the kind of providence
interpose in my preservation; which appeared still greater, upon viewing
the wretched circumstances of many of my black brethren at the time,
who were obliged to sell themselves to the merchants, some for two or
three years; and others for five or six years. The circumstances of the
white inhabitants were likewise very distressing, owing to their great
imprudence in building large houses, and striving to excel one another in
this piece of vanity. When their money was almost expended, they began
to build small fishing vessels; but alas, it was too late to repair their error.
Had they been wise enough at first to have turned their attention to the
fishery, instead of fine houses, the place would soon have been in a flourishing condition; whereas it was reduced in a short time to a heap of ruins,
and its inhabitants were compelled to flee to other parts of the continent
for sustenance.

Next Winter, the same gentleman employed me to build him some
more boats. When they were finished he engaged me to go with him to
Chebucto, to build a house, to which place he intended to remove his

family. He agreed to give me 2£ per month, and a barrel of mackerel, and another of herrings, for my next Winter's provision. I was glad to embrace this offer, altho' it gave me much pain to leave the people of GOD. On the 20th of April I left my wife and friend, and sailed for Chebucto. When we arrived at that place, my employer had not all the men necessary for the fishing voyage; he therefore solicited me to go with him; to which I objected, that I was engaged to build a house for him. He answered, that he could purchase a house for less money than build one, and that if I would go with him to Bayshallow, I should greatly oblige him; to which I at length consented. During our stay at Chebucto, perceiving that the people were exceeding ignorant of religious duties, and given up to all manner of wickedness, I endeavoured to exhort them to flee from the wrath to come, and to turn unto the Lord Jesus. My feeble labours were attended with a blessing to several of them, and they began to seek the Lord in sincerity and truth, altho' we met with some persecution from the baser sort.

On the 2nd of June we sailed for Bayshallow, but in the Gulf of St. Lawrence we met with a great storm, and expected every moment would be our last. In about 24 hours the tempest abated, and was succeeded by a great fog, in which we lost the company of one of our vessels, which had all our provisions on board for the fishing season. July 18, we arrived at the River Pisguar, and made all necessary preparations for taking the salmon; but were greatly alarmed on account of the absence of the vessel belonging to us; but on the 29th, to our great joy, she arrived safe; which was four days before the salmon made their appearance. We now entered upon our business with alacrity, and Providence favoured us with good success.

My employer, unhappy for himself as well as others, was as horrible a swearer as I ever met with. Sometimes he would stamp and rage at the men, when they did not please him, in so dreadful a manner, that I was stupefied like a drunken man, and knew not what I was doing. My soul was exceedingly grieved at his ungodly language; I repented that I ever entered into his service, and was even tempted to murmur against the good Providence of God. But the case of righteous Lot, whose soul was vexed day by day with the ungodly deeds of the people of Sodom, occurred to my mind; and I was resolved to reprove my master when a proper opportunity offered. I said to him, "Dear sir, don't you know that the Lord hath declared, that he will not hold them guiltless who take his Name in vain? And that all profane shall have their portion in the lake that burneth with fire and brimstone?" He bore the reproof with patience, and scarce ever gave me an unkind word; notwithstanding which, he persisted in his impiety, and the men, encouraged by his example, imitated him to the utmost of their ability. Being much grieved with their sinful deeds, I retired into the woods for meditation and prayer. One day when I was alone, and recollecting the patient suffering of the servants of God for the Truth's sake, I was ashamed of myself, on account of the displeasure I felt at my ship-mates, because they would not be persuaded by me to forsake their sins. I saw my folly in imagining that it was in my power to turn them from their evil ways. The Lord shewed me, that this was his prerogative; and that my duty consisted in entreating them, and bearing patiently their insults, as God for Christ's sake had borne with me. And he gave me a resolution to reprove in a right spirit, all that swore in my presence.

Next day my master began to curse and swear in his usual manner. When I saw him a little calm, I entreated him not to come into the boat any more, but give me orders how to proceed; assuring him, that I would do every thing according to his pleasure to the utmost of my power; but that if he persisted in his horrible language, I should not be able to discharge my duty. From that time he troubled me no more, and I found myself very comfortable, having no one to disturb me. On the 11th of August we sailed for home; and my master thanked me for my fidelity and diligence, and said, "I believe if you had not been with me I should not have made half a voyage this season." On the 16th we arrived at Chebucto, and unloaded the vessels. When this business was finished, we prepared for the herring-fishery in Pope's Harbour, at which place we arrived on the 27th of August, and began to set the nets and watch for the herrings. One day as we were attending our net at the mouth of the harbour, we dropped one of the oars, and could not recover it; and having a strong west wind, it drove us out to sea. Our alarm was very great, but the kind hand of Providence interposed and saved us; for when we were driven about two miles from our station, the people on shore saw our danger, and immediately sent two boats to our assistance, which came up with us about sun-set, and brought us safe into the harbor.

October 24, we left Pope's Harbour, and came to Halifax, where we were paid off, each man receiving 15£ for his wages; and my master gave me two barrels of fish agreeable to his promise. When I returned home, I was enabled to clothe my wife and myself; and my Winter's store consisted of one barrel of four, three bushels of corn, nine gallons of treacle, 20 bushels of potatoes which my wife had set in my absence, and the two barrels of fish; so that this was the best Winter I ever saw in Burchtown.

In 1791, I removed to Prestent, where I had the care of the Society by the appointment of Mr. William Black, almost three years. We were in all 34 persons, 24 of whom professed faith in Christ. Sometimes I had a tolerable congregation. But alas, I preached a whole year in that place without seeing any fruit of my labours. On the 24th of Jan. 1792, after preaching in the morning I was greatly distressed, and said to the Lord, "How long shall I be with this people before thy work prospers among them! O Lord GOD! if thou hast called me to preach to my Black Brethren, answer me this day from heaven by converting one sinner, that I may know that thou hast sent me. In the afternoon I preached from James ii.19. "Thou believest that there is one God; thou doest well. The devils also believe, and tremble." Towards the conclusion of the meeting, the divine presence seemed to descend upon the congregation: Some fell flat upon the ground, as if they were dead; and others cried out aloud for mercy. After prayer, I dismissed the public congregation; but many went away with great reluctance. While the Society was meeting, Miss F— knocked at the door, and said, "This people is the people of GOD; and their GOD shall be my GOD." She then desired to be admitted among us, that she might declare what the Lord had done for her soul. We opened the door, and she said, "Blessed be the Name of the Lord for ever, for I know he hath pardoned, my sins for the sake of his Son Jesus Christ. My mind has been so greatly distressed for these three weeks, that I could scarcely sleep; while I was under the preaching all my grief vanished away, and such light broke in upon my soul, that I was enabled to believe unto salvation. O praise the Lord with me, all ye that love his Name; for he hath done great things for my soul." All the Society were melted into tears of joy, when they heard her declarations: and she immediately entered into connection with us, and many others in a few weeks after. From this time the work of the Lord prospered among us in a wonderful manner. I blessed GOD for answering my petition, and was greatly encouraged to persevere in my labours.

The Blacks attended the preaching regularly; but when any of the White inhabitants were present, I was greatly embarrassed, because I had no learning, and I knew that they had. But one day Mr. Ferguson and several other gentlemen came to hear me; speaking the Truth in my simple manner. The gentlemen afterwards told our Preachers, that they liked my discourse very well; and the Preachers encouraged me to use the talent which the Lord had entrusted me with.

[To Be Continued]

THE Methodist Magazine, June, 1798.
MEMOIRS of the LIFE of BOSTON KING.
Continued.

I continued to labour among the people at Prestent with great satisfaction, and the Society increased both in number and love, till the beginning of the year 1792, when an opportunity was afforded us of removing from Nova Scotia to Sierra Leone. The advantages held out to the Blacks were considered by them as valuable. Every married man was promised 30 acres of land, and every male child under 15 years of age, was entitled to five acres. We were likewise to have a free passage to Africa, and upon our arrival, to be furnished with provisions till we could clear a sufficient portion of land necessary for our subsistence. The Company likewise engaged to furnish us with all necessaries, and to take in return the produce of the new plantations. Their intention being, as far as possible in their power, to put a stop to the abominable slave-trade. With respect to myself, I was just got into a comfortable way, being employed by a gentleman, who gave me two shillings per day, with victuals and lodging; so that I was enabled to clothe myself and family, and provide other necessaries of life: But recollecting the concern I had felt in years past, for the conversion of the Africans, I resolved to embrace the opportunity of visiting that country; and therefore went to one of the Agents employed in this business, and acquainted him with my intention. The gentleman informed Mr. Clarkson, that I was under no necessity of leaving Nova Scotia, because I was comfortably provided for: But when I told them, that it was not for the sake of the advantages I hope to reap in Africa, which induced me to undertake the voyage, but from a desire that had long possessed my mind, of contributing to the best of my poor ability, in spreading the knowledge of Christianity in that country. Upon which they approved of my intention, and encouraged me to persevere in it. The Preachers likewise gave us the Rules of the Society, and many other little books which they judged might be useful to us: they also exhorted us to cleave to the Lord with our whole heart, and treated us with the tenderness and affection of parents to their children. After praying with us, we parted with tears, as we never expected to meet again in this world.

January 16, we sailed to Africa; and on the 22nd, we met with a dreadful storm which continued for sixteen days. Some of the men who had been engaged in a seafaring life for 30 or 40 years, declared, that they never saw such a storm before. Our fleet, consisting of 15 ships, were dispersed, and only five of us kept together. We lost one man, who was washed overboard; he left a wife and four children; but what most affected me was, that he died as he had lived, without any appearance of religion. I was upon deck at the same time that he met with this misfortune, but the Lord wonderfully preserved me. After the storm abated, we had a very pleasant passage. But the situation of my wife greatly distressed me. She was exceeding ill most of the voyage; sometimes for half a day together, she was not able to speak a word. I expected to see her die before we could reach land, and had an unaccountable aversion to bury her in the sea. In the simplicity of my heart, I entreated the Lord to spare her, at least till we reached the shore, that I might give her a decent burial, which was the last kind office I could perform for her. The Lord looked upon my sincerity, and restored her to perfect health.

March 6, we arrived safe at Sierra Leone; and on the 27th, my wife caught a putrid fever. For several days she lost her senses, and was as helpless as an infant. When I enquired into the state of her mind, she could give me no satisfactory answer, which greatly heightened my distress. On Friday, while we were at prayer with her, the Lord mercifully manifested his love and power to her soul; she suddenly rose up, and said, "I am well: I only wait for the coming of the Lord. Glory be to his Name, I am prepared to meet him, and that will be in a short time." On Sunday, while several of our friends were with her, she lay still; but as soon as they began singing this hymn, "Lo! he comes, with clouds descending, Once for favour'd sinners slain," &c. She joined with us, till we came to the last verse, when she began to rejoice aloud, and expired in a rapture of love. She had lived in the fear of GOD, and walked in the light of his countenance for above eight years.

About two months after the death of my wife, I was likewise taken ill of the putrid fever. It was an universal complaint, and the people died so fast, that it was difficult to procure a burial for them. This affliction continued among us for three months, when it pleased the Lord to remove the Plague from the place. It was a happy circumstance, that before the rainy season commenced, most of us had built little huts to dwell in; but as we had no house sufficient to hold the congregation, we preached under a large tree when the weather would permit.

The people regularly attended the means of Grace, and the work of the Lord prospered. When the rains were over, we erected a small chapel, and went on our way comfortably. I worked for the Company, for 3s. per day, and preached in my turn. I likewise found my mind drawn out to pity the native inhabitants, and preached to them several times, but laboured under great inconveniences to make them understand the Word of God, as I could only visit them on the Lord's-Day. I therefore went to the Governor, and solicited him to give me employment in the Company's plantation on Bullam Shore, in order that I might have frequent opportunities of conversing with the Africans. He kindly approved of my intention, and sent me to the Plantation to get ship-timber in company with several others. The gentleman who superintended the Plantation, treated me with utmost kindness, and allowed six men to help me build a house for myself, which we finished in 12 days. When a sufficient quantity of timber was procured, and other business for the Company in this place compleated, I was sent to the African town to teach the children to read, but found it difficult to procure scholars, as the parents shewed no great inclination to send their children. I therefore said to them, on the Lord's Day after preaching, "It is a good thing that God has made the White People, and that he has inclined their hearts to bring us into this country, to teach you his ways, and to tell you that he gave his Son to die for you; and if you will obey his commandments he will make you happy in this world, and in that which is to come; where you will live with him in heaven;—and all pain and wretchedness will be at an end; and you shall enjoy peace without interruption, joy without bitterness, and happiness to all eternity. The Almighty not only invites you to come unto him, but also points out the way whereby you may find his favour, viz. turn from your wicked ways, cease to do evil, and learn to do well. He now affords you a means which you never had before; he gives you his Word to be a light to your feet, and a lantern to your paths, and he likewise gives you an opportunity of having your children instructed in the Christian Religion. But if you neglect to send them, you must be answerable to God for it."

The poor Africans appeared attentive to the exhortation, altho' I laboured under the disadvantage of using an interpreter. My scholars soon increased from four to twenty; fifteen of whom continued with me five months. I taught them the Alphabet, and to spell words of two syllables; and likewise the Lord's Prayer. And I found them as apt to learn as any children I have ever known. But with regard to the old people, I am doubtful whether they will ever abandon the evil habits in which they were educated, unless the Lord visits them in some extraordinary manner.

In the year 1793, the gentlemen belonging to the Company told me, that if I would consent to go to England with the Governor, he would procure me two or three years schooling, that I might be better qualified to teach the natives. When this proposal was first mentioned to me, it seemed like an idle tale; but upon further conversation on the subject, difficulties were removed, and I consented. On the 26th of March 1794, we embarked for England, and arrived at Plymouth, after a pleasant voyage, on the 16th of May. On the 1st of June we got to the Thames, and soon after, Mrs. Paul, whom I was acquainted with in America, came to Wapping, and invited me to the New Chapel in the City-Road, where I was kindly received.

When I first arrived in England, I considered my great ignorance and inability, and that I was among a wise and judicious people, who were greatly my superiors in knowledge and understanding; these reflections had such an effect upon me, that I formed a resolution never to attempt to preach while I stayed in the country; but the kind importunity of the Preachers and others removed my objections, and I found it profitable to my own soul to be exercised in inviting sinners to Christ; particularly on Sunday, while I was preaching at Snowsfields-Chapel, the Lord blessed me abundantly, and I found a more cordial love to the White People than I had ever experienced before. In the former part of my life I had suffered greatly from the cruelty and injustice of the Whites, which induced me to look upon them, in general as our enemies; And even after the Lord had manifested his forgiving mercy to me, I still felt at times an uneasy distrust and shyness towards them; but on that day the Lord removed all my prejudices; for which I bless his holy Name.

In the month of August 1794, I went to Bristol; and from thence Dr. Coke took me with him to Kingswood-School, where I continued to the present time, and have endeavoured to acquire the knowledge I possibly could, in order to be useful in that sphere which the blessed hand of Providence may conduct me into, if my life is spared. I have great cause to be thankful that I came to England, for I am now fully convinced, that many of these White People, instead of being enemies and oppressors of us poor Blacks, are our friends, and deliverers from slavery, as far as their ability and circumstances will admit. I have met with most affectionate treatment from the Methodists of London, Bristol, and other places which I have had an opportunity of visiting. And I must confess, that I did not believe there were upon the face of the earth a people so friendly and human as I have proved them to be. I beg leave to acknowledge the obligations I am under to Dr. Coke, Mr. Bradford, and all the Preachers and people; and I pray GOD to reward them a thousand fold for all the favors they have shewn to me in a strange land.

BOSTON KING
Kingswood-School, June 4, 1796

☞ About the latter end of September, 1796, Boston King embarked for Sierra Leone; where he arrived safe, and resumed the employment of a school-master in that Colony; the number of scholars under his care are about forty; and we hope to hear that they will not only learn the English Language, but will also attain some knowledge of the way of salvation thro' faith in the Lord Jesus Christ.

"Clarinda: A Pious Colored Woman of South Carolina" (1875)

—ↀ—

Introduction

Susanna Ashton and Robyn E. Adams

Sexual abuse of women was often represented in traditional slave narratives as a predictable, if horrendous, outcome of a system in which absolute power was accorded one person over another.* In a complex departure from this familiar formulation, the story of Clarinda depicts the protagonist herself leading others down the path of sexual sin. "By her own confession," as our anonymous narrator explains, Clarinda takes responsibility for luring others into sin. And while we might speculate about her own victimhood as a woman who may have been forced into some sort of prostitution, the focus of the narrative is on Clarinda's redemption from her own sins and how she came to faith by ways of much suffering on her part and on the part of others. Clarinda's narrative, therefore, reminds us that notions of guilt and culpability were powerful forces of eighteenth-century ideologies and that how one handled moral failures was a defining feature of one's social validity.

First published in 1837 by the Tract Association of Friends in Philadelphia as *Clarinda, a Pious Coloured Woman of South Carolina, Who Died at the Age of 102 Years*, this narrative offers numerous challenges to our traditional ideas of what American slavery was about and how it was perceived by both the

---

*For a collection of especially useful essays on this topic, see Catherine Clinton and Michele Gillespie, eds., *The Devil's Lane: Sex and Race in the Early South* (New York: Oxford University Press, 1997). See also Nell Painter, *Southern History across the Color Line* (Chapel Hill: University of North Carolina Press, 2002).

white majority of the South and the abolitionists of the North. The nature of the second-person narration as presented here needs to be understood in the context of missionary tracts and Sunday school literature, early nineteenth-century notions of gender roles, and the often hazy line between free blacks and enslaved black people in South Carolina. While this extraordinary early account (the earliest known African American woman's narrative from South Carolina) is a tricky text inasmuch as its provenance is complex and its focus on exemplary spiritual growth is at the expense of details about Clarinda's almost certain bondage, the story of Clarinda nonetheless reaches across the centuries to remind us how historical realities rarely fit into preconceived textual forms.

In the short twelve paragraphs that comprise the life story of Clarinda, she is introduced as a "corrupt heart . . . 'sold under sin,' and involved in almost every species of iniquity." By playing the violin each Sunday and encouraging the mixing of the sexes through dance, she seems characterized as an antithesis to the model Christian as the instigator of moral and social sin. Even as Clarinda was beset with seizures and forced to forsake her music, she continued to model social "wickedness," until the loss of her child caused her to sink into illness and despair. Inspired by spoken biblical scripture, Clarinda's resulting conversion culminated with a divine charge to preach the Gospel, a mission fulfilled with weekly meetings in her home—notably attended by both black *and* white community members. Even after vicious attacks by angry neighbors that left her "head . . . deeply indented with the blows she received," Clarinda persevered in her leadership of "Clarinda's People," ultimately learning to read before her death at the age of 102 years.

As if to echo the relative silence of slave women within the greater slave-narrative genre, the most intriguing and problematic aspect of Clarinda is what we are *not* told about this remarkable life.* While there is a specific reference to her being "sold under sin," Clarinda is never explicitly defined as a slave—a fact that opens up the possibility that she was part of the extremely small number of free blacks in South Carolina in the late eighteenth or early

---

*Of the 296 slave narratives compiled by William L. Andrews on his authoritative "North American Slave Narratives" Web site, only 32 women, or a mere 10 percent, have biographies or autobiographies within the collection. If we examine this population more closely, fully two-thirds of these narratives were published postbellum. See William L. Andrews, "Introduction to the Scholarly Bibliography of Slave and Ex-Slave Narratives," in "North American Slave Narratives" on the Web site titled Documenting the American South, University Libraries at the University of North Carolina at Chapel Hill, http://docsouth.unc.edu/neh/biblintro.html.

nineteenth century. Far more likely, however, is that if she was a slave, that was not seen as a defining characteristic of her life by the narrator (if not by Clarinda herself). Rather, her status as a sinner outweighed any consideration of whether or not she was enslaved, at least as her story was framed by her narrator.

Other details are also tellingly, if frustratingly, vague. No specific geographic references are given, nor are names of white families included that would aid in pinpointing Clarinda among the research of a specific region. Her occupation, for all the discussion of music and dancing, is never precisely articulated. The nature of her actions after being "sold under sin" seems to suggest forced prostitution, which may explain why the author readily notes that Clarinda was taught the violin for "the furtherance of her wicked designs." In addition, the composition and fate of worshipers known as "Clarinda's People" are undetermined and stand as an intriguing testament to the appeal of this religious leader.

The most significant omission of all is the absence of her immediate voice. There are no known sources that contextualize the interview with Clarinda, and her story is told from afar. Our anonymous author may have known Clarinda, but at least one portion is from a thirdhand account. "The person who gives the account of Clarinda's death" does give us some supposed dialogue from Clarinda, but the fact that much of this story seems to be from a viewpoint either once or twice removed forces us to question the validity of Clarinda's "voice."

Yet while the biography of Clarinda focuses on her pious and humble nature, there was something compelling enough about Clarinda's story that warranted her inclusion in a textbook for African American children in the 1830s. In the second edition of *Biographical Sketches and Interesting Anecdotes of Persons of Color,* edited by Abigail Mott in 1837, the story of "Clarinda" provides a female role model profiled alongside Phillis Wheatley and Benjamin Banneker.*

Clarinda's story dovetailed beautifully with the thesis of the 1837 collection: "to encourage virtue and morality in the different classes of society" by showing "the dreadful consequences of that arbitrary power invested in the slave-holder over his fellow being." The target audiences of this textbook were the children at the New York African Free School (a large organization

---

*The editor of this textbook, Abigail Mott (1766–1851), was an important Quaker antislavery activist and was also involved with the Underground Railroad in upstate New York. She was a cousin by marriage to the famous feminist and antislavery activist Lucretia Mott (1793–1880).

founded in 1787 by the New York Manumission Society), who were evidently understood as needing role models in both spiritual and social terms.*

At the end of the narrative about Clarinda a final clue about her legal status is revealed when, even after her heart was freed from the burden of sin, she remained subservient to some unnamed individual who limited the ways she could serve her God. Indeed, as Clarinda lay dying, *"she requested that her people, as she called them, might continue to meet at her house; but this was not allowed"* (emphasis added). Just who was forbidding such meetings is not clear—it could have been another black or white religious leader of a more established church who denied Clarinda pastoral rights, but the emphasis on the house suggests that it was someone who controlled her space, possibly a landlord but most likely an owner who sought to regulate the activities of enslaved people under his control. On her deathbed she was nonetheless answerable to an earthly power.

Of course, regardless of whether she was slave or free, her legacy was in the way she impacted the world in which she lived. "Clarinda's People" continued to meet after her death; her story became a focus of the African Free School textbook, and her story resonates today as a vivid and rare tale of survival coming from the earliest known biography or autobiography of an African American woman in South Carolina.

Rather than offering a host of problems, the text of Clarinda's life introduces new dimensions to the canon of the slave experience. Reminding us that the line between free and enslaved black people was often hazy, the bondage experienced by Clarinda speaks to the opportunities and limitations imposed on all women as well as black people in eighteenth- and nineteenth-century South Carolina. Clarinda's unadorned story also offers a glimpse into millions of slaves' lives that lacked the drama of escape characterizing many of the narratives that made it to the abolitionist publishing houses. Stories such as Clarinda's are nevertheless rich and powerful in their individual claims to the slaves' own humanity.

"Clarinda: A Pious Colored Woman of South Carolina" traces its start to 1836, where it may have appeared as tract 56 in a series issued by the Tract

---

*A good historical and contextual overview of the New York African Free School may be found at the New-York Historical Society, which holds the papers from this organization. See the society's Web site Examination Days: The African Free School Collection, https://www.nyhistory.org/web/afs. See also John L. Rury, "The New York African Free School, 1827–1836: Conflict over Community Control of Black Education," *Phylon* 44, no. 3 (September 1983): 187–97.

Association of Friends in Philadelphia after the last meeting of the year. Officially, tract 56 is listed in the April 12, 1837, annual report and could be found in print for many years afterward. Abigail Mott's *Biographical Sketches and Interesting Anecdotes of Persons of Color* was first published in 1826 by both Mahlon Day Press and the firm of W. Alexander & Son in New York City, and it was intended for use in the African Free Schools of New York City. "Clarinda" was added to the second edition, published in 1837. This edition would be republished four times through 1854. In addition, Clarinda's tract was published in the October 7, 1837, edition of the Quaker newspaper the *Friend* (Philadelphia). In 1875 and again in 1877, under the sponsorship of the estate of Lindley Murray, Mott would seek the assistance of fellow Quaker Mary Sutton Wood in a new version of her work titled *Narratives of Colored Americans,* which was published by William Wood & Co. of New York, owned by Mary Sutton's husband. "Clarinda" appears in this text as well, although the content is targeted for a more general audience.

This version of the text follows that of tract 56 and the version used in the 1837 second edition of *Biographical Sketches*. It contains additional text, beginning in paragraph three with "She was likewise reminded" and closing out the paragraph. There is no reasoning known for this material's deletion in the 1875 edition.

—⚭—

The subject of this memoir was brought up in a state of ignorance unworthy of a Christian country, and following the propensities of a corrupt heart, was, by her own confession, "sold under sin," and involved in almost every species of iniquity. For the furtherance of her wicked designs, she learned to play on the violin, and usually on the first day of the week sallied forth with her instrument, in order to draw persons of both sexes together, who, not having the fear of God before their eyes, delighted like herself, in sinful and pernicious amusements, which keep the soul from God, and the heart from repentance. But even on these occasions she found it difficult to struggle against the Spirit of the Most High.

Often was it sounded in her conscious, "Clarinda, God ought not to be slighted" "God ought not to be forgotten": but these monitions were treated with derision, and in the hardness of her heart would exclaim, "Go, you fool, I do not know God—Go, I do not wish to know him." On one occasion, whilst on her way to a dance, these blasphemous thoughts, in answer to the monitions of conscience, were passing through her mind, and in this frame she reached the place of appointment, and mingled in the gay throng. Whilst participating in the dance, she was seized with fits, and convulsively fell to the ground. From that moment she lost her love of dancing, and no more engaged in this vain amusement. She did not, however, forsake the evil of her ways, but continued her course of wickedness. Thus she went on for about twenty years, when she lost her only child, and was confined for several months by severe illness.

During this period of bodily suffering, her mind was brought under awful convictions for sin: she perceived that the Great Jehovah was a sin-hating and a sin-avenging God, and that he will by no means clear the guilty. She remained in a distressed state of mind for about three months, and when a little bodily strength was restored, she sought solitary places, where she poured out her soul unto the Lord, and in his own good time He spoke peace to her wounded spirit. One day, being thus engaged in earnest prayer, and looking unto the Lord for deliverance, the evening approached unregarded, her soul was deeply humbled, and the night passed in prayer, whilst rivers of tears (to use her own expressive language) ran down her cheeks, and she ceased not to implore mercy from Him who is able to bind up the broken-hearted. While thus engaged, and all this time ignorant of her Savior, something whispered to her mind, "Ask in the name of Christ." She queried, "Who is Christ?" and in reply, these passages of Scripture seemed repeated to her, "Let not your heart be troubled; ye believe in God, believe also in Me." "In My Father's house are many mansions: I go to prepare a place for you, that where I am there ye may be also." "I am the way, the truth, and the life; no man cometh unto the Father but by Me." Being desirous to know whence these impressions proceeded, she was made to believe that they were received through the influence of the Holy Spirit. This remarkable passage was also presented to her mind: "Therefore, being justified by faith, we have peace with God through our Lord and Savior Jesus Christ." She was likewise reminded of several dreams she had formerly had; in one of which a person appeared to her and led her to a place into which she was permitted to look, where she saw "the spirits of just men made perfect," but was informed she could not enter therein. He then gave her a vial and a candle, telling her to keep the vial clean, and the candle burning till He came. She now saw that the vial was her heart, and the candle the Spirit of the Lord. In narrating this circumstance to a friend, she enlarged instructively on the necessity of keeping the heart, since out of it are the issues of life; adding, the eye sees and the heart lusts after the pleasures and possessions of this world, but the crosses of self-denial must be borne; no outside religion will do. She now felt the love of God shed abroad in her heart; the overwhelming burden of sin was removed, and she received ability to sing the praises to the Lord on the banks of deliverance.

Having been thus permitted to see the desire of her soul, she was anxious to learn more of the divine will, and inquired, like the apostle, "Lord, what wilt thou have me to do?" and like him she was commanded to be a witness of what she had seen and heard. Believing she had a commission given her to preach the Gospel, she began to warn the sinful and licentious, that they must crucify the man of sin, or forever forego the hope of salvation. This raised her a host of enemies, both white and colored; she underwent for many years cruelty and persecution which could hardly obtain credence. She bore about on her body the visible marks of her faithful allegiance to the Lord Jesus; yet, while alluding to this, tears filled her eyes, and she said with emotion, "I am thankful that I have been found worthy to suffer for my blessed Savior."

Although living in great poverty, and subsisting at times on casual charity, with health impaired by the sufferings through which she had passed, yet neither promises of protection, accompanied with the offer of the good things of this life, on the one hand, nor the dreadful persecution she endured on the other, could make her relinquish the office of a minister of the Gospel. This office she continued to exercise, holding meetings regularly on the first day of the week, at her own little habitation, where a greater number at times assembled than could be accommodated in the house.

It may be interesting to add some particulars relative to the trial of her faith and the persecution she suffered. One individual in whose neighborhood she lived, who was much annoyed by hearing her sing and pray, offered, if she would desist, to provide her with a home and the comforts of life; but she replied, she had received a commission to preach the Gospel, and she would preach it as long as she had breath. Several ill-intentioned persons one night surrounded her house, and commanded her to come out to them. This she refused to do. After threatening her for some time, they forced open the door, and having seized their victim, they beat her cruelly, so that her head was deeply indented with the blows she received. At another time she was so much injured that she was left nearly lifeless on the open read, whither she had fled to escape from them; but her unsuccessful efforts increased the rage of her pursuers, and after treating her with the utmost barbarity, they left her. She was found after some time, but so exhausted by the loss of blood, that she was unable to walk, and from the effects of the cruelty she did not recover for years. But it may be said of her, that she joyfully bore persecution for Christ's sake.

A man who lived in the same village, being much incensed at the undaunted manner in which she stood forth as the minister of the meek and crucified Savior, swore that he would beat her severely if ever he found an opportunity. One evening, as she was walking home on a solitary road, she saw this person riding towards her; she knew of his intentions, and from his character did not doubt that he would execute them. She trembled from head to foot; escape seemed impracticable, and prayer was her only refuge. As he advanced she observed that his handkerchief fell and was wafted by the wind to a little distance; she picked it up—he stopped his horse, and she handed it to him in a submissive manner; he looked at her fiercely for a moment, when his countenance softened; he took it, saying, "Well, Clarinda," and passed on.

She was not able to read a word till her 66th year, but was in the practice of getting persons to read the Holy Scriptures to her; much of which she retained in her memory with remarkable accuracy. By dint of application, she was at length able to read them herself; and those who visited her in advanced life, found her knowledge of the Scriptures, as well as her growth in grace, very surprising.

When she was one hundred years old, and very feeble, she would, if able to get out of bed, on the morning of the first day of the week, discharge what she thought to be her duty, by conversing with and exhorting both the white and colored people who came to her house, often standing for half an hour at a time. Her zeal was indeed great, and her faith steadfast. She said she often wished she could write, that she might in this way also express her anxiety for the good of souls. Then she would have described more of the exercises of her mind upon the depravity of man by nature and by practice, with the unbounded and redeeming love and mercy of God through Jesus Christ.

The person who gives the account of Clarinda's death says, "I was prevented seeing her often in her last moments; when I did she was always the same: her one theme the love of God to poor sinners, which was always her style of speaking. One day, as I sat by her bedside, she said to me, 'Do you think I am a Christian?' 'Yes,' I answered, 'I do believe you are a Christian.' 'I have tried to be,' she replied, 'but now that I suffer in my body, when I think what an unprofitable servant I have been, I am distressed.' She then wept. 'You know,' I said, 'it is not how much we can do, but what we do sincerely for the love of Christ, that is acceptable.' She seemed comforted, and talked as usual.

"She showed me much affection when I left her, saying 'I shall not live long, my dear—,' and adding a few other words, blessed me, and bid me

pray for her. She had frequently expressed her fears of the bodily sufferings of death, but not accompanied with a dread of eternal death. I asked
her when she was ill, if she now feared to die. She said 'No: this fear was
taken away some time previous to my illness.'"

She requested that her people, as she called them, might continue to
meet at her house; but this was not allowed. I am told they meet sometimes elsewhere, and are called "Clarinda's People." When dying, she told
those near her, to follow her only as she had followed Christ. Her death
occurred in 1832. "Those that be planted in the house of the Lord shall
flourish in the courts of our God. They shall bring forth fruit in old age."

While perusing this remarkable account of "a brand plucked from the
burning," let those who from their earliest years have enjoyed the ines-
timable privilege of access to the Sacred Volume, and various other religious means, seriously consider the blessed Savior's words—"To whom
much is given, of him much shall be required."

"Recollections of Slavery by a Runaway Slave" (1838)

—ɯ—

Introduction

Susanna Ashton and Maximilien Blanton

"Recollections of Slavery by a Runaway Slave" tells the story of a young man who, in the winter of 1837, escaped from slavery near Charleston, South Carolina. While the narrator never identifies himself by name, he more than compensates for that omission by providing the reader with precise accounts of persons, places, and events. These details render his story credible even at its most incredible and violent moments—moments that might otherwise have been seen by skeptical audiences as abolitionist exaggeration. This issue of credibility is at the core, both logistically and thematically, of this harrowing tale of human suffering.

While "Recollections" merits attention in its own right as a gripping narrative, it also represents a specific turn in the construction and reception of slave narratives in the 1830s. This text, which has not been reprinted since before the Civil War, was produced and published in the epicenter of controversies over the accuracy and value of slave narratives. The manner in which this story was shaped was thus at the forefront of new ways by which the very character of slave narratives could be understood.

The facts of the author's life are fairly simple. He claims to have been born near Four Holes swamp, "about 25 miles up in the country from Charleston." Born around 1808, he never knew his parents, his only family being the 125-odd slaves on the Smith plantation, where he would live until he was fourteen years of age. The author guesses to be about twenty years old at the time his narrative was taken down. His life story ends with his escape north. He jumps a train to Charleston and stows away amid cotton bales on a boat bound for Boston. While he says little about his experiences there after finding safety, the fact that his narrative was transcribed by sympathetic activists in Maine suggests that he might have been on his way north to Canada or perhaps to England by the time it was published.

The content of his narrative, however, is anything but simple. "Recollections" offers a grim look at the system of slavery in the South Carolina lowcountry in the early nineteenth century. Its attack on the institution of slavery is made even more compelling by the fact that many of the specific people named were prominent South Carolinians, thus demonstrating that even the most elite South Carolinians were complicit in an intrinsically debased and evil system. Named, for instance, are several members of the state senate, such as Isaac Bradwell and Col. (William) Billy Mellard, who seem to have to some degree shared their slaves, as the narrator was leased to both of them. Other wealthy and important people are mentioned, such as Davy Cohen, son of Mordecai Cohen, perhaps the most influential Jew of Charleston, who owned a vast expanse of land in and around Charleston but who was notable in the narrator's mind for having had a man nearly beaten to death for stealing a few pieces of wood.* The narrator's willingness to accuse so many planters in such specific terms could only have been understood as a challenge to the honor and integrity of southern slaveholders. While "Recollections" testifies to an individual life story, it also reads as a litany of brutality and torture peppered with details so awful and so memorable that the specificity of the names and places mentioned must have been understood as necessary grounding for the rest of the text.

The particular impetus for grounding this story deeply in truth, however, must be understood within the venue and time in which it was published. Facts could never be simple for slave narratives in the antebellum era; there was too much at stake to allow slave testimony to remain uncontested. This focus on substantiating the facts of a slave narrative was especially pertinent during the summer of 1838 due to a scandal that changed the course of the abolitionist strategies in presenting and framing slave narratives as effective tools in their battles. "Recollections" is thus of special historical significance because it appeared at a critical juncture for the abolitionist testimonial

*See a collection of relevant pamphlets reprinted from the *Charleston News and Courier* in Barnett Abraham Elza, *The Jews of South Carolina: From the Earliest Times to the Present Day* (Ann Arbor: University of Michigan Press, 1905), 188. For a good overview of the history of Jews in South Carolina, see Cyrus Adler and Joseph Jacobs, The Jewish Encyclopedia Online, s.v. "South Carolina," http://www.jewishencyclopedia.com/view.jsp?artid=989&letter=S.

and helped pave the way for a new focus on the authentication of fugitives' claims.

Appearing first on August 2, 1838, in the *Advocate of Freedom* and then three weeks later as a series reprinted in the larger *Emancipator,* "Recollections" appeared in the same summer and almost immediately after the first slave narrative ever published by the American Anti-Slavery Society: *The Narrative of James Williams, an American Slave, Who Was for Several Years a Driver on a Cotton Plantation in Alabama.* Various southern journalists challenged the truth of this account, and after reviewing the accusations and the evidence, the American Anti-Slavery Society was forced to admit that "many of the Statements made in the said Narrative were false."* Williams's narrative highlighted the danger that a weekly documented text could be to the abolitionist movement, leading the historian John Blassingame to write, "There were no comparable exposés during the antebellum period."† Indeed, it forever changed the care with which fact checking of slave testimony was carried out.

The Williams scandal was thus played out with public challenges, discussions, and rebuttals in the official organ of the American Anti-Slavery Society,

---

The Narrative of James Williams was ferociously attacked by proslavery newspapers that deemed it false and slanderous due to several contradictions in persons and places. So persuasive was the criticism that our subject's first installment of "Recollections" appeared just seven calendar days before the *Emancipator* printed the arguments about Williams—arguments to which the American Anti-Slavery Society would then retort one month later in the *Liberator,* on September 28, 1838. The episodic exchange of accusations and rebuttals continued. For the specific quotation above, see *Minutes of the Executive Committee of the American Anti-Slavery Society,* August 16, 1838, 92. The full report of the American Anti-Slavery Society was later reprinted in the *Liberator,* November 2, 1938. With the initial publication of "Recollections" in the August 2, 1838, issue of *Advocate of Freedom,* however, the editors anticipated controversy over the narrator's honesty and, in a framing introduction not reprinted in the *Emancipator* version, noted, "We have here merely to express our belief that entire confidence may be placed in the facts, which are there exhibited. So far as the individual himself is concerned, he carries upon his own person the indubitable marks of the truthfulness of his story" (*Advocate of Freedom,* August 2, 1838, 2).

†John W. Blassingame, "Critical Essay on Sources," in Blassingame, *The Slave Community: Plantation Life in the Antebellum South* (1972; repr., New York: Oxford University Press, 1979), 372. For a rich interpretation and discussion of the import of the James Williams scandal, see also Ann Fabian, *The Unvarnished Truth: Personal Narratives in Nineteenth-Century America* (Berkeley: University of California Press, 2000), 79–85, 88–97.

the *Emancipator,* at the same time that the editors decided to run the "Recollections" series. Immediately following up the Williams scandal with the recollections of an anonymous slave was a risky move calculated upon their profound confidence in the accuracy of the story, the truthfulness of the narrator, and confidence in the power such a story could have on even a jaded and skeptical audience.

In "Recollections" the narrator also needed to provide as much hard evidence as he could due to the acutely graphic nature of his stories. In one such instance the narrator tells of a slave rolled "all over the yard in a barrel, something like a rice cask" through which shingle nails were driven from the outside with the slave placed inside. The narrator explains his own horror as his master Bellinger sat "laughing to hear the man's cries" while forcing another slave to roll the barrel or face one hundred lashes himself.

Suffering was not contained to informal plantation discipline. As the narrator recounts it, the institutionalized torture of the "Sugar House" in Charleston also demanded notice, for it too laid waste to any notion of slavery's abuses as being particularized to individual owners rather than being a natural manifestation of the system itself. As our protagonist tells us, he has "heard a great deal said about hell, and wicked places, but I don't think there is any worse hell than that Sugar House." The Sugar House was a prison used specifically for exceptionally miscreant slaves and operated both as a holding pen and more often as a place for owners to "outsource" whipping and torture that they preferred not to have done on their own premises.* In

---

*The Sugar House was a correctional facility in Charleston where slave owners could send their unruly property to, for a fee, "get some sugar." The rationale behind the Sugar House was that conditions were so bad there that slaves would see their masters' tasks as menial and gentle. The Sugar House may have its roots in the American Revolution, when British commander Henry Clinton decided to put all of Charleston's slaves in one location to prevent an uprising. The Sugar House is actually the "workhouse" written about by Robert Mills in his 1826 *Statistics of South Carolina:* "The work house, adjoining the jail is appropriated entirely to the confinement and punishment of slaves." See that quote in more context in Jonathan H. Poston, *The Buildings of Charleston: A Guide to the City's Architecture* (Columbia: University of South Carolina Press, 1997), 392. In 1859 James Redpath published *The Roving Editor; or, Talks with Slaves in the Southern States* (New York: A. B. Burdick), in which Redpath describes the Sugar House with its putrid latrines, treadmills, brine barrels, and whipping posts as "a word of terror to the colored race in South Carolina and the adjoining slave States." Included is an interview by Redpath with Pete Barclay, a man who had survived the Sugar House, and even twenty years after our narrator has described the Sugar House, it sounds much the same (60–61).

punishment for having attempted an escape, the narrator was imprisoned there for three months during the summer of 1837. The threat of being returned to the Sugar House was intended as a deterrent to future escapes, but the memory of it seems to have fueled our narrator's determination to get away, and as we know, he made it north only a few months thereafter.

Although the editors of the narrative went to great lengths to defend the truthfulness of the tale and to defend too the sterling character of the speaker, ultimately the introduction rests on a reframing of the entire debate—as they saw it, the institution of slavery could not be justified on any terms: "In this connection we will repeat what has been so often said and as often overlooked by the pro-slavery party, that the question of the right or wrong of slavery does not turn at all on the treatment of individuals, or the veracity of any fugitives from slavery. Is it right for A MAN to hold A MAN as a slave?" The answer for the author of "Recollections" was agonizingly self-evident.

"Recollections of Slavery" first appeared in the August 2, 1838, *Advocate of Freedom,* a small abolitionist publication sponsored by the Maine Anti-Slavery Society out of Brunswick, Maine.* The *Advocate of Freedom* began publishing under Bowdoin professor William Smyth's direction in March 1838 and appeared semimonthly until 1839, when starting in April it became a weekly, running through 1841.

The editors of the *Advocate* immediately recognized the power of this narrative and indicated that they wanted it to appear in "permanent form," as well as distributed to a wider audience. Thus they passed it along to the *Emancipator* for syndication, and in that newspaper the fugitive narrative was thereafter released in five parts over a period of three months.† The serialization of the text appeared in the August 23, September 13, September 20, October 11, and October 18 editions of the *Emancipator* in 1838.

*For more information on the Maine Anti-Slavery Society, see John L. Meyers, "The Antislavery Agency System in Maine 1836–1838," *Maine Historical Society Quarterly* 23, no. 2 (1983): 57–86. See also *The 4th Annual Report of Maine Anti-Slavery Society with the Minutes of the Anniversary Meeting, Held in Augusta on the 7th of February 1839* (Brunswick, Maine: Thomas W. Newman, 1839).

†The *Emancipator,* an abolitionist newspaper, was first published in 1833. Printed in both New York City and Boston, the paper underwent several name changes. Originally titled the *Emancipator,* the paper had been renamed the *Emancipator and Free American* by December 1841 and maintained that title until March 1844. At that time the weekly paper was dubbed the *Emancipator and Weekly Chronicle.* In October 1845 the original title was reinstated, simply as the *Emancipator,* though this did not last long. By September 1848 the paper had adopted the identity of the *Emancipator and*

The initial text of these "recollections" is composed of an editorial justification for including the graphic nature of the material, vouching for the truthful nature of the narrator, and introducing the circumstances of its composition. This opening preamble was published in the *Advocate of Freedom* on August 2, 1838, and is reproduced here. The text from the narrative proper, also reproduced here, was taken from the *Emancipator's* version published two weeks after the *Advocate of Freedom's* initial publication.

—〰—

RECOLLECTIONS OF A RUNAWAY SLAVE.
[from *Advocate of Freedom*, Spring 1838]

It will not be necessary to call the attention of our readers to the interesting narrative commenced under the above title on our last page. We have here merely to express our belief that entire confidence may be placed in the facts, which are there exhibited. So far as the individual himself is concerned, he carries upon his own person the indubitable marks of the truthfulness of his story. The following communication sent to us with the manuscript, is from a source of the highest respectability, and to our minds is in itself a sufficient voucher, that no pains have been spared to preclude the possibility of mistake or exaggeration. Our friend J. has our thanks for his very acceptable efforts in preparing this affecting exhibition of "slavery as it is." Measures will be taken to give it a permanent form, and a wider circulation than the columns of our paper afford. It is destined, we think, to be a most efficient advocate of the cause of the slave.

MESSRS EDITORS:—I enclose the "narrative of a runaway slave," for which I request a place in your paper. It was taken from his lips by a gentleman of indisputable integrity and fairness, and with the greatest care and caution. The manuscript has been repeatedly read to the young man, and he was cautioned in every instance to state only the simple facts; and after the care that has been taken to correct any mistake or error, into which he may have been led, I believe the "recollections of a slave," are entitled to the confidence of the reader.

It is not necessary to inquire into the actual hardships and cruelties of slavery, in order to form a right judgment of the system. Whoever is at all

---

Free Soil Press. However, this change was particularly short lived, lasting only from September to November 1848. Following this alteration, yet another title for the paper was adopted, the *Emancipator and Republican,* which lasted from November 1848 until at least December 1850.

acquainted with the propensities of man, or the history of the world, must know that whenever one man has absolute power over other men, there will necessarily result from the exercise of that power, cruelty and oppression. Hence, in order to ensure the execration of slavery, abolitionists do not think it proper generally to enter into the details of the system—to show that the whip and other instruments of torture are in common use, or that marriage is not allowed among slaves; but they prefer to dwell mainly upon the thing itself—upon that relation from which these evils spring, for the purpose of showing its injustice and inhumanity. Still, it is considered not improper sometimes to tear away the covering of this great prison-house and exhibit slavery to the life, that its practical, every-day characteristics may be seen—that the world may see some of its thousand enormities—that it is, in truth, "the habitation of cruelties." If the short history of this individual can furnish so dark a catalogue of oppression and suffering, who can compute the amount of sufferings and woe, endured by all the slaves in this FREE country through successive generations?—But there is no one to keep the record of the black man's wrongs. A.

Text reproduced from *The Emancipator,* August 23, 1838
(Installment #1)
From the Advocate of Freedom.
RECOLLECTIONS OF SLAVERY.
BY A RUNAWAY SLAVE.

No attempt has been made to impart interest to the following narrative, by remodeling it in more forcible language or refined style than it was clothed with as it fell from the lips of the narrator. My sole object has been to let him tell his own story. I have, therefore, as nearly as possible, given his own words.

Still, one thing is lacking;—that earnestness—that depth of feeling which gave it life, as it was uttered by one, who himself had seen all and felt much of the reality. Divested of this perhaps, it will appear dull and repulsive. I am aware that excepting the account of his escape, there is not a gleam of light—not even a bright shade through the whole of it. Let none, on this account neglect it. IT IS TRUE; and they who are the subjects of the cruel system here partially delineated are lying wounded and bleeding at our very door. There was no *poetry* in the bruises of the man who fell among thieves between Jerusalem and Jericho. It was no pathetic tale of distress, that lured the good Samaritan from across the way, but the simple sight of a bleeding brother. *"He bound up his wounds, pouring in oil and wine."* "Go and do *thou* likewise."

J.

July, 1838.

Narrative.

I was born in South Carolina, at a place called "Four Holes" about 25 miles up in the country from Charleston. My father was an outland man. He died when I was very small and I can just remember him. My mother died when I was a baby. I am about twenty years old and have been a slave all my life. I was owned by a widow woman named Smith till I was about fourteen.

As long ago as I can remember, I worked 'round the house in company with about 20 little boys and girls. We worked in the potato patch and cotton patch, and sometimes at the cotton gin; grubbed ground, pulled up roots, raked up chips and threw them on the log heap to burn; and rainy days we worked in the garden and cleared up the trash in the yard. As soon as children get old enough to walk about, they always set them to do something or other. Mistress was very strict, and if we did not do every thing exactly to please her we were sure to get a whipping. An old man whipped us on our bare flesh with hickory switches. A schoolmaster named Cleeton boarded with her, and used to bring home a great many of them and put them in the chimney to dry. He called them "nice switches to whip the little niggers with." A good many of us were entirely naked and the rest had nothing on but shirts. I never wore any clothes till I was big enough to plough. When they whipped us they often cut through our skin. They did not call it skin, but "hide." They say, "a nigger hasn't got any skin."

Mistress had a little daughter named Jane, and she used to send her out to the old cotton house to watch us, and see if we were working smart. She crept along and peeped through the chinks, and if she saw us laughing and talking or a little merry, though we were about our tasks, she would say, "Ah, I see you idle, I shall go and tell ma." Then we would beg and say, "Pray don't tell this time, Missy Jane," but she always did. It pleased her mightily to have us whipped.—An old woman cooked for us when we were so small. We had two meals a day, one at morning and one at noon. They never gave us anything at night. Sometimes mothers would stint themselves and save a piece of ash cake to give to their children at night. This is all they can do for them.*

* To the question, "Do not mothers sometimes teach their children!" he replied, "No, sir, they *can't,* for they have nothing to teach; they don't know anything themselves."

When I got a little older I was sent into the field to work under a driver. Children, when very young, are made to go there in droves. The driver shows them the first year what is to be done, and after that they have to manage for themselves. Then, if they don't do their task they get a whipping just like the rest. In some kinds of work we didn't have a task, only we had to keep along together, and the one that lagged behind was whipped.

While my old mistress owned me she hired me out several times. The first master who hired me was Col. Billy Mallard. He lived on Dean Swamp. I worked for him about two years. His overseer, named Tom Galloway, was all the time cutting and slashing among us. We used to be afraid of him as death. Sometimes five or six of us would be at work, and when we saw him coming with his whip we would tremble, for if everything was not exactly right, we knew we should be whipped. He would cut among us all, without stopping to enquire who was in fault. Children sometimes get so frightened that they run away when the overseer is coming.

There was a little girl, named Margaret, that one day did not work to suit the overseer, and he lashed her with his cow-skin. She was about seven years old. As soon as he had gone she ran away to go to her mother, who was at work on the turnpike road, digging ditches and filling up ruts made by the wagons. She had to go through a swamp, and tried to cross the creek in the middle of the swamp, the way she saw her mother go every night. It had rained a great deal for several days, and the creek was 15 or 16 feet wide, and deep enough for horses to swim it. When night came she did not come back, and her mother had not seen her. The overseer cared very little about it, for she was only a child and not worth a great deal. Her mother and the rest of the hands hunted after her that night with pine torches, and the next night after they had done work, and every night for a week, and two Sundays all day. They would not let us hunt in the day time any other day. Her mother mourned a good deal about her, when she was in the camp among the people, but dared not let the overseer know it, because he would whip her. In about two weeks the water had dried up a good deal, and then a white man came in and said that "somebody's little nigger was dead down in the brook." We thought it must be Margaret, and afterwards went down and found her. She had fallen from the log-bridge into the water. Something had eaten all her flesh off, and the only way we knew her was by her dress. She was lying on the sand-bed, and her hair was all buried in the sand. Her mother cried when we found her, but in a little while got over it.

One day one of the women was planting turnips. She had to sow in rows very regular; but the ground was rough, and when Mallard came by he saw she was scattering the seed. He told her the Devil was in her because she wasted the seed, and if she did not do better, when he came back from the house he would make her. When he came back she had not done any better, and he snatched up a root and knocked her down and kicked her, and then sent a man called Tennant to the house for a whip. Mallard whipped her till he was tired, and then Tennant whipped her. He was so mad he did not stop to tie her up, but beat her about on the ground, and every once in a while hit her with the butt end of the whip. They whipped her till she could not scream.

Mallard had a Guinea man who could not understand a word of English, nor understand anything that was said. When the driver whipped him he did not beg like the rest. We always have to say, "Please massa," "Do massa." Master said he would teach "the —— nigger to beg." Then they told him what to say, but he did not understand. He was tied up by his wrists, and they kept beating him till they were tired. They then went into the house to drink and left him hanging there. While they were gone, a woman named Sarah went to him and tried to make him understand how to beg. She said, "Only say '*do massa*'—and they'll stop whipping."—When they came out they tried a new plan. They took him down and lashed him to a log, and master stood on one side and the driver on the other. They whipped him with cowskins till they cut a great gash in his side that they had to sew up. All the sound they could get out of him was a kind of grunt,—"ugh," "ugh." The next day he went into the woods and stayed five weeks before he was caught.

The next man that hired me of mistress was Elias Road, of Wasmasow. I lived with him one year, and was then hired for three years by Isaac Bradwell, a little short man with one eye living near the 35 mile house on the State road from Charleston. While I worked with him I fared better than with any master before or since. In the winter time, when they killed their hogs, we had a hog's head cut in two every day, and boiled till it came all to pieces. We used to go to the house with our gourds in the morning, and again at noon, and get two sticks full of hominy pudding dropped into each; then we made a hollow in the middle of it and had it filled up with soup. I never got but two meals a day all the time I was a slave. If we wanted any thing at night we had to steal it. We used to steal potatoes from Brad-well for supper.

While with him I had frequently seen a very rich planter named Ned Broughton pass his house going to Charleston, on horseback, before great six-horse wagons, loaded with cotton and indigo. He owned a great deal of River Swamp and made great crops. He punished his slaves by putting them into a long box just large enough to hold them, and then screwing a board made to fit into the box down on to them. The board had a hole in it for them to breathe through.

Wm. Smeth, at the twelve mile house, hired me next. I stayed with him one year. He afterwards moved on to the Rail Road. He had a neighbor named Bellinger, on the Dorchester road. One day master sent me to his plantation on an errand, and I saw a man rolling another all over the yard in a barrel, something like a rice cask, through which he had driven shingle nails. It was made on purpose to roll slaves in. He was sitting on a block, laughing to hear the man's cries. The one who was rolling wanted to stop, but he told him if he didn't roll him well he would give him a hundred lashes. Bellinger is dead now.

Another of Smeth's neighbors was named Monpay. He was a Frenchman, and lived at Goose Creek. He was a very bad man. We could hear his whip going regularly every morning. He used to lock his slaves up over night, when they did not do their tasks, and whip them before they went to work in the morning. There was on his plantation a low squat tree, with limbs stretching out close to the ground, and his common way of punishing was to lash his slaves by the hands and feet, face down, to the limbs of the tree, and then cut up their backs with a cowskin. I have seen the blood spattered on the tree when I have been over there on Sunday.

When I was about 14 years old, all the slaves belonging to mistress were shared among her children. They made a large dinner and got together a great many people from the plantations all about. After dinner they gathered us into the yard and divided us into five lots. They made five rings on the ground, and put 25 or 26, large and small, into each ring. Then the appraisers shifted some from one lot to another till they were about equal. It took them till night to get through. After all was fixed they drew for us with pieces of paper. The lot I was in fell to the oldest son. I lived with him five years. He lived at Bethel, Sumterville District, 8 miles from Sumterville. He was the oldest son, and was named Alfred. His wife was Rebecca Singleton before marriage. She was the most spiteful woman I ever saw, and very cruel to the house servants. When she went into the kitchen and found the cook woman had not got every thing exactly to her mind, she struck her and beat her about the head with the tongs, or a knife, or anything she could get hold of.

One day when I was watering the horses at the well near the kitchen, I heard a great noise, and in a few moments the cook woman Lucinda, came out with her head all bloody, so that you could not tell whether she had hair or not. Her head was all gashed up with a knife. When mistress found her head was bleeding all over the kitchen she sent her out to wash it off.— Bob Bradford of Sumterville once jabbed a fork into a cook-woman and broke off the prong in her head, and his man Harry afterwards helped paddle her. I went there for salt, flour, coffee and sugar, and was there when he did it.

Mistress was sick a good deal, and when she could not go down into the kitchen she made the servants stand by her bed while she whipped them with switches. When master went to the fields he would bring home sticks the size of a broom stick for her to crack the house people's heads with. Once when I was raking up grass in the yard, Mr. Smith was lying in the shed, playing with his little boy. Mistress came down into the kitchen and asked the cook if she had been all this time getting dinner and not got it done yet?—told her it was half past 12 o'clock and that she had been lazy. Then she began to beat her over her face and head, and made her hold her hand down all the time. Her husband laid there playing and calling out "beat her with the butt, Rebecca." Mistress beat her till she was tired and then threw down the stick and cried because she couldn't whip any more. Her master went in and knocked her about, and told her, "you — bitch, I'll see if I can't have my dinner by 12 o'clock." The house stood very high, and he pushed her out of the door over the steps and kicked her in the yard, and then made her go in and finish cooking.

Almost every day mistress had some complaint to make to master against one or another of the house servants. He had a place fitted up in the lumber house on purpose to whip them in. There was a long table there, and a hogshead on purpose to lash them to while the overseer whipped and paddled them, and whenever she complained he ordered them to be carried right straight to the whipping house.—One day, Edith, the house girl, was sent into the yard with a basket to get some eggs. Mistress's little girl was with her.—In coming back she stumbled a little and knocked the child down and broke one of the eggs. When mistress heard it she flew into a violent rage, and beat her over the head till her face was all swelled up. This did not satisfy her, but when master came home she told him that Edith had been abusing the little girl. He ordered me to take her right away to the whipping house and get her ready for him to whip her. When he came out he scolded at me for not doing it right. He made me take off all her clothes and tie her on to the table. Her hands and feet were bound fast, and he then put a rope 'round her neck and bound her close down so that she could not stir in any way. When he had done this he went into the house and got something to drink, and then came out with his cowskin and whipped her till her skin was all cut up, and there was a puddle of blood on the floor just as if a hog had been killed. He then took a paddle and paddled her on top of that almost to death, and made me wash her down with brine. The brine is to keep the raw flesh from putrifying, and to make it heal quick. They mix it very thick and rub it in with corn husks.

Smith had a place in the woods for whipping his people. We cut down saplings for stakes and drove them into the ground. The distance was measured by making a man lie on the ground and straighten out his arms and legs as far as he could.

The cook woman had a little child that was treated very cruelly. Mistress would never have it in the kitchen while she was cooking, so she had to put it in a basket and leave it out doors. It stayed there all day long, and sometimes its mother would not be able to go to it all day, because mistress hurried her so fast from one thing to another. When we came home to feed the horses and mules at 12 o'clock we would move it into the shade. It was very dirty, and at last the worms got into it and it died. When it was very sick, mistress asked what was the matter with that little nigger brat?— They told her it was dying for want of attention. Then she let its mother take it into the kitchen and tend it. It died when she was getting breakfast.

The infants of the slaves are always neglected. Their mothers take them into the field in the morning, slung on their backs, and carry a cradle on their heads made from a hollow tree. They put them in this and set them in the shade, and if they hear them cry ever so much they cannot go to see what is the matter. When they go to suckle them they sometimes find them covered with ants, and sometimes the snakes get at them and bite them. [To Be Continued]

The Emancipator, September 13, 1838 (Installment #2)
From the Advocate of Freedom.
RECOLLECTIONS OF SLAVERY.
BY A RUNAWAY SLAVE.
Continued from Emancipator No. 121.

One of master's slaves was named Monday. He was a Guinea man. His language was very broken, so that we could hardly understand him. He was one day taken sick, and told the overseer, but he said it was all sham and that he was deceiving to get rid of work. They would always say, "nigger isn't sick, till he's got the fever." When we complained they would send for us to come to the house, and then they felt of us, and if we had not got the fever, they said it was all sham,—that "nigger had been eating dirt,"—and then they sent us straight off to the field, and we had to do our tasks the same as though nothing was the matter.—Monday said he was full of pain, but because he hadn't the fever they made him work, hoeing and planting, and pulling up cotton stocks for about a week. When it was Sunday he went to see his wife on another plantation, and was so sick that they brought him home in a cart. Then they began to take care of him and give him physic. After that, it was only two or three days before he died. They put him into the "lumber house," an old building without any door to keep the cold air out, and gave him some straw for his bed, and an old blanket to cover him. I and another boy took turns in watching him by night. It was my turn the night he died. I fell asleep, and was waked by a noise made by Monday who was rolling upon the floor as if he was in great pain.—He kept all the time groaning and muttering something to himself. All I could understand was *"I want to go to father over the water."* He said this a great many times. I dragged him back to his straw, and when I had fixed him I went to sleep again. I did not think he was so near dying.— When the horn sounded in the morning, I went to him, and asked him how he felt. He did not answer, and when I touched him, I found he was dead. I told the overseer and we nailed some rough boards together for a coffin and buried him.

When master was first married he lived with old Mrs. Singleton, his wife's mother, and took care of her plantation. In rainy weather the slave women have some cotton weighed out for them to spin, and it is weighed when they return it, to see if they do not keep any part back. One day Mrs. Singleton said to her son William, "What's the reason Lucy's cotton does not hold out, as much as Hannah's and Affa's? I think she steals it and stuffs it into the cracks of her house, or knits it." He said he would go and see. He went and found her in the potato patch, and told her to bring out her broaches for him to see. He weighed them and found they fell short. Then he told her to cross her hands, but she was frightened, and instead of doing so, began to beg him not to whip her. He had a horse whip in his hand at the time, and struck her in the face with the butt-end of it, and knocked her eye out. We always have to cross our hand the first thing, when they call us out to whip us, or they beat us over the head and almost kill us. Lucy screamed that her eye was out, but he did not seem to notice it at all. He kept a beating because she held her hand to her eye, instead of doing as he wanted.—At last when he found her eye was out, he sent her to the house to have something done for it. His mother told her it was her own fault that her eye was out. It would teach her to cross her hands another time.

Mr. Smith sold me to Davy Cohen, a Jew who lived on Ashley River, about 12 miles from Charleston. He was very rich and some years made such great crops of rice that he was not able to sell it all, and stowed it away in his barns. He raised besides a great quantity of hog meat, but he would not eat any himself nor let us have any. Sometimes we would steal a hog and carry it into the fields and roast it, and share it, and then hide it in the ground and get it as it was wanted. We stole only four in the two years I lived with him. He was in the habit of walking about at all hours of the night to find out who stole wood, or turnips, or hogs, or any thing else. One time he found out that an old man, named Peter, had been stealing wood down by the river. He took it and hid it in the woods, calculating to carry it off the next Sunday. Every Sunday five or six of us had to row the boat-load of wood to Charleston to market. We started at midnight so as to get there by breakfast time Sunday morning. Master rode in his chaise and got there early to sell it. Sometimes instead of wood we carried water-melons, and ducks, and eggs, and had a good boat load of all kinds of fruit and other things. People do a great deal of marketing in Charleston on Sunday. Our boat was always loaded Saturday evening, and Peter's plan was to put the stolen wood on top of master's, and throw it off in some back place in town, and sell it when he found a chance. There were only five or six sticks of it.

When master missed his wood, he took ten of the slaves and carried them to the camp, and after he had whipped three or four of them, Peter's boy got frightened and informed against his father. They carried Peter to his hut, and tied him up so that his feet could not touch the ground, then tied his feet together and put a great log between them, to keep him stretched tight. Then they whipped him till he fainted twice in the rope. They did not leave off whipping him till midnight. One of the men that kept the door said he "guessed Peter would have to be buried the next day, master whipped him so much." They always say "a nigger is not whipped to do him good, unless he faints." They say "cut into him; a nigger hasn't got any feeling;—there's no feeling in a nigger's hide;—you must cut through his hide to make him feel!"

After they had done whipping Peter, they gave him a dose of salts and put him in the stocks, down in the cellar, where it was so dark, you could not see your hand before you. When any one is put in the stocks a chain is put around his neck with a padlock on it, and the end of it is fastened to a beam of the house. His feet are put into holes between two pieces of wood, which are then bolted down close to his ankles,—his hands are tied, and he has to lie down on his back, without being able to move any part of his body except his head. Sometimes slaves are kept in the stocks two or three weeks, and whipped twice a week, and fed on gruel, because they run away or steal.

Slaves have to go to the fields after being whipped, when their skin is so cut up that they have to keep all the time pulling their clothes away from the raw flesh. Sometimes they are so bad off that they can't wear any clothes on their back at all, and have no dress but a piece of cloth tied around their bodies. In this case, they have to put boughs on their heads and shoulders to keep away the flies. A great many of them never have a hat, and the sun and rain will turn their hair all brown or red, just like flannel. We were allowed one pair of shoes in a year. They were given to us in the winter, but we used to keep them till summer, for the heat was worse than the cold. The sand was so hot that if we buried an egg in it in the morning, it would be cooked by ten or eleven o'clock, and our feet got all blistered and burnt up if we went without shoes. If we carried water with us into the fields, we dug deep holes and buried it, to keep it cool. Our houses were nothing but pole pens, built square, and covered with pine and cypress bark, without any floor. In wet weather the rain would beat in upon us, the same as though we were out doors. When we got a chance, we brought home boughs and laid them on the roof, but the rain still came in. We had no beds but hay or grass, or clapboards, and some-times no covering but our old clothes, made into patchwork. If they ever gave us a blanket, we had to make it last four or five years. Often we did not have beds at all, but slept in the ashes. We built our fires in the mid-dle of the house, and never moved the ashes, so that there was a great heap, and when we came home we prepared our ash-cake, and put it into the hot ashes to bake, and then laid down there ourselves and slept till the horn blew in the morning. Then we got up and brushed the ashes off, and took our cake or potatoes and went straight to work.

When I lived with Cohen I was hostler, but had to work in the field besides. When they wanted to go anywhere in the carriage, they called me and made me pull off my old rags, and put on the clothes which they had in the house.

One night towards the last of the week, our allowance was gone and we were very hungry.—So I and two others went into the musk-melon patch

and took three or four melons apiece. The next day they measured our
tracks and then measured our feet, and whipped some of us, till one told
who did it. There was a man and woman besides me. The man's name was
Reuben. They carried the man into the woods, where they had four stakes
driven into the ground, and stretched him out and fastened him there.
The driver whipped him for a long time. Afterwards they washed him
down with brine and then put him in the stocks. I was tied 'round a log.
They tied me as close as possible with strings round my neck and hands
and feet.—They put a cap on my head and drew it down closely over my
face. It covered my whole face, and was tied under my chin, and was not
taken off till the whipping and washing were all over. After whipping I was
put into the stocks. They tied the woman up to a tree, and made her hug
'round it. She was whipped more than I was, though I was whipped badly
enough. They put her into the dungeon, a dark hole under the house.

The same driver whipped us all. After he was done he complained that
he was tired. All drivers are black men, and slaves. They have to do as the
overseer says, or they will get whipped themselves. They live in houses
apart from the rest. Their business is to blow the horn in the morning for
us to get up, and then drive us all day to get as much out of us as they can.
They get praise when we do a good day's work, and that makes them drive
us harder and cut and lash us, so as to make us do as much another day.

The morning after our whipping, we all had to go to work, as if nothing
had happened. I was so sore I could hardly do anything. I had to leave my
row and go off over the fence a great many times, and towards night, when
I saw I could not get my task done, and knew I should be whipped again, I
made for the woods, and at midnight went as far as I could down the country. I there fell in with some more runaways, who had a camp in the swamp,
and stayed with them till I was caught. It is very common for slaves to run
away into the woods after being badly whipped. They are forced to, for
they cannot do their tasks, and so they have to stay in the woods till they
get well. Sometimes they stay there five or six weeks till they are taken, or
are driven back by hunger. I have known a great many who never came
back; they were whipped so bad they never got well, but died in the woods,
and their bodies have been found by people hunting. White men come in
sometimes with collars and chains and bells, which they had taken from
dead slaves. They just take off their irons and leave them, and think no
more about them. They keep a great many hounds on purpose to hunt
runaways. They call them "nigger dogs." Alfred Smith had about fifty of
them. They teach them to run colored people when they are pups.—They
used to make me run off a good ways, when I was very small, and then

send the pups on my tracks. I thought it was fine sport. Sometimes they called the hands from the field and made them run 'round the house and climb trees, with the dogs after them. They cooked every day a great pot of hominy for them, and the victuals left from master's table was always given them. When I have passed them in the yard eating a good piece of meat, I have often wished that I was a dog, they seemed so much better off than we.

I have been hunted by the hounds a great many times. The only way to do when I heard them coming was to go across water and put them off the scent, and then climb a high tree in the thickest part of the swamp where the overseer can't come. If the hunters could see us they would shoot us.— They don't think any more about shooting a nigger than a dog. It's all one thing. I have seen several shot. One evening about dusk when I lived with Mallard, I was going into the fields to do something, and I saw a runaway named Jack, belonging to Mr. Finkley at Four Hole Swamp. He was crossing the field with a bag on his back. Tom Galloway, our overseer, had been out hunting squirrels, and was just coming back with his gun. When he saw Jack, he squat behind a tree and waited till he got near, and hailed him, and told him to stop. He did not stop, but run, and just as he was jumping the fence, overseer fired, and he fell about twenty yards from the fence. He said "O'we," three or four times and died. When the overseer came home he said he met somebody's runaway nigger, and let him have what there was in his gun. The black people that night made a hole, and lined it with boards, and buried him.

When I was living with Alfred Smith, a man belonging to Caleb Williams of Pocatalago, Sumterville District, stole pears from the pear house. The door was not very strong and he lifted it off the hinges. The first time Williams missed pears, he knew that some of the niggers must have stolen them. A little while afterwards, he was hunting out in the woods for deer in company with master. I was riding behind them on a mule, and heard what they said. He said, "Smith, what is the best way to do, when niggers take to breaking into houses to steal?" Master told him he "thought it was the best way, to watch himself, because watchmen sometimes sleep." He said "I've got a fellow that I mean to put a load of shot into some night, for I know it's he that steals. He's the biggest rogue I've got." That same week, about Saturday night, he killed him. He told my master afterwards that he watched with his window open, and he heard the door creak, and got up, and saw him. He fired at him with buck shot. He said he did not mean to kill him, but only meant to put the shot into his legs.

While we stayed in the swamp we lived in a camp of bushes and trees. We laid in the thicket all day, and rambled and plundered all night long. After we had been there two or three weeks, two of us ventured out one day a little ways to hunt for plums. It was very hot, and we were tired, and towards the middle of the day we went to the brook to drink, and laid down by a log and fell asleep. Master's overseer and another man were out to hunt for niggers, and they came upon us before we knew it. The other man was waked by the noise they made, and sprung up and run, but they fired and shot him down. The shot hit him in the middle of his back. The noise of the gun startled me. I jumped up, but when I saw them so near me I did not run. They tied him on to a horse, and tied me and made me walk before the horse, back to the plantation. When they got there, the man seemed almost dead. They had to lift him off the horse. Master went to his hut and beat him about his head with his walking stick.

They took me and gave me a bad whipping. It was then almost noon. They gave me a task, to pound out a bushel of rice in a mortar, and I got it done about sun down. I felt mighty bad that night. I could not sleep. I went to the mill house to grind my corn for the next day, and I just stood up and leaned my head against the corner of the house, and ground and nodded all night. My flesh was all cut up, and I was too sore to lie down. When the horn sounded in the morning I had just enough corn ground to last me.

The mill in which we ground our corn was made of stones about as large as common grindstones, and was turned by hand. I used to carry my corn there in a calabash and spread my shirt under it to catch it as it fell. Many of the slaves did not know how to set the stones to make them grind right. They would just crack the kernels, but were glad enough to get it in that way. They do not always have so great a convenience for preparing their food, though all the masters that I lived with had one.

All the time I was a slave, except the little time I worked with Isaac Bradwell, and a few weeks on the railroad, the slaves had a regular allowance of food given them the first of the week, and that was all they got without stealing. One week we had four quarts of corn, the next a peck of sweet potatoes, and the next four quarts of peas. They never gave us anything else, not even salt, though on some plantations they do get a little salt now and then. Some get a gill a month. We were not able to make the allowance last more than four or five days, and we had to steal for the rest of the time. I did not think it was wrong to steal enough to eat. I thought I worked hard to raise it, and I had a right to it. Every night, after coming from the field, we had to prepare our victuals for the next day. Some would parch their corn; some boil it, when they could get anything to boil it in, and others would grind it, and make it into cakes which they baked in the ashes. We gathered dry branches on our way home for our fires. We buried our dough in the hot ashes and left it till morning, and then washed it in the brook before eating it. I have often come from the field tired, and thought I would sleep a little, before preparing my cake, and have not waked till the horn blew in the morning; then I had to catch up my raw corn and hurry away to the field. We never had but two meals a day, one in the morning and one at noon, and were allowed about fifteen minutes to each, except in harvest time, when we did not get so much. They always cleared and planted as much land as possible in the spring, and in autumn hurried us, to have it all harvested. Then they used to drive us so hard that some of the hands could not stand it. They would faint away and drop down in the fields. Some of them would go to the brook to drink, and after stooping down they could not get up again, but died there with their faces in the water. A great many died in that way.

I have sometimes been so faint from hard work, and from eating green and raw food, that I had to go over the fence and sleep. I could not go on with my work any way. When I came back the driver would say, "What you gone so long over the fence for? You're lazy." Then I would tell him I was so weak I couldn't work; but he said it "was no concern of his; I must tell Buckra. While I was in the field he must make me work," and then he would whip me. If a slave goes into the field he must do his task. If he does not, the driver whips him, because he will have the task done at any rate. I used to get my full share of whipping. All the scars on my back were made in that way.*

*Some of the scars are the size of a man's thumb, and appear as if pieces of flesh had been gouged out, and some are ridges or elevations of the flesh and skin. They could easily be felt through his clothing.

The scar under my eye was made by Alfred Smith. He struck me with a cane, because I did not stretch up close enough to the tree when I was tied up to be whipped.

I ran away from Cohen because he whipped me. A black man stole some hog meat and hid it for his wife under his house. The overseer, in searching about after stolen things, found it, and then whipped me to make me tell who put it there, because they thought I knew. As soon as they had done, master sent me to get the mules, but I kept right on into the swamp;

I never came back. I went off to Four Holes and stayed some days in the woods 'round Bradwell's plantation, where my sister lived, before I could get a chance to speak to her. At last I hid near the field where she was hoeing and got close to her row, and when she came along I contrived to let her know I was there. After a while we got a chance to talk together, and she told me that Cohen had offered 50 dollars for me, and said she wished I would get some of the hands to ask Bradwell to buy me. She thought he would be willing to. I stayed about there nearly a month, talking with the people every night. One drizzly night when I was in the mule lot among the slaves, a man named John Strutts dodged 'round the corner of the fence, and hid behind the mules, so that I could not see him, and then he called to me and told me to stand still till he tied me. After he tied me he took me to his house and kept me till next morning, and then carried me to the Sugar House in Charleston. As soon as we got there they made me strip off all my clothes, and searched me to see if I had anything hid. They found nothing but a knife. After that they drove me into the yard where I stayed till night. As soon as master's father, Mordecai Cohen, heard that I was caught, he sent word to his son, and the next morning master came. He said "Well, you stayed in the woods as long as you could, now which will you do,—stay here, or go home?" I told him I didn't know. Then he said if I would not go home willingly I might stay there two or three months. He said "Mr. Wolf, give this fellow fifty lashes and put him on the tread mill. I'm going North, and shall not be back till July, and you may keep him till that time." He said this just to make me say I would go back with him, for he had no intention of going to the North. As soon as Cohen turned his back, Wolf whistled, and two drivers came, and he told them to put me in the rope.

When they had got me fixed in the rope good, and the cap on my face, they called Mr. Jim Wolf, and told him they had me ready. He came and stood till they had done whipping me. One drew me up tight by the rope and the other whipped, and Wolf felt of my skin to tell when it was tight enough. They whipped till he stamped. Then they rubbed brine in, and put on my old clothes which were torn into rags while I was in the swamp, and put me into a cell. The cells are little narrow rooms about five feet wide, with a little hole up high to let in air.

I was kept in the cell till next day, when they put me on the tread mill, and kept there three days, and then back in the cell for three days. And then I was whipped and put on the tread mill again, and they did so with me for a fortnight, just as Cohen had directed. He told them to whip me twice a week till they had given me two hundred lashes. My back, when they went to whip me, would be full of scabs, and they whipped them off till I bled so that my clothes were all wet. Many a night I have laid up there in the Sugar House and scratched them off by the handful.

[To Be Continued]

The Emancipator, September 20, 1838 (Installment #3)
From the Advocate of Freedom.
RECOLLECTIONS OF SLAVERY,
BY A RUNAWAY SLAVE.
Continued.

In a few more weeks master came and asked if I was ready to go home now, I told him I "didn't know." The truth was, the sugar house was worse than the plantation, but I would not tell him so. When he found I was stubborn, and would be likely to run away again if he took me out, he said he would keep me there till the speculators came along in the fall. Pretty soon I grew sickly, and when he say how poor I was, and thought I should not live till fall, he set me up to vendue. They bid 670 dollars for me, but he would not sell me for that. He said he would have his price, or I should stay in the sugar house till I died. Afterwards a good many came to see me. They felt of me and said I was thin. Master kept me there a few days longer, and then sold me to John Fogle for 700 dollars. I cost him twelve hundred. It was in June, 1837, when he sold me.

I have heard a great deal said about hell, and wicked places, but I don't think there is any worse hell than that sugar house. It's as bad a place as can be. In getting to it you have to go through a gate, in a very high brick wall. On the top of the wall, both sides of the gate, there are sharp pointed iron bars sticking up, and all along the rest of the wall are broken glass bottles. These are to keep us from climbing over. After you get into the yard, you go through a gate into the entry, then through a door of wood and an iron door, chained and locked together, so as both to open at the same time. The lower story is built of stone of great thickness,—and above, brick. The building is ceiled inside with plank. Away down in the ground, under the house is a dungeon, very cold, and so dark you can't tell the difference between day and night. There are six or seven long rooms, and six little cells above and six below. The room to do the whipping in is by itself. When you get in there, every way you look you can see paddles, and whips, and cowskins, and bluejays, and cat-o'-nine tails. The bluejay has two lashes, very heavy and full of knots. It is the worst thing to whip with of any thing they have. It makes a hole where it strikes, and when they have done it will be all bloody.

In the middle of the floor are two big sills, with rings in them, fastened to staples. There are ropes tied to the rings to bind your feet. Over the sills is a windlass, with a rope coming down to fasten your hands to. This rope leads off to the corner of the room, and there are pegs there to tie it to, after they have got you stretched.

Slaves are carried there to be whipped by the people in the country four or five miles round, and by all the people in the city, and the guard men carry there all the runaways they take up. Some would want their niggers whipped with the cowskin and paddled on top of that, and some with the paddle alone, because the paddle blisters and peels the skin all up. They wet the paddle, and then rub it in sand, and every time they hit with it, the skin peels off just the same as you peel a potato. When it gets well it will be right smooth, and not in knots as when whipped with the cowskin. Some would want their niggers whipped with one thing and some with another, and some wouldn't care how they were whipped, so they got it.

Mr. Wesley or Wesler was the keeper while I was there, and Mr. Wolf was the clerk. As soon as a slave was brought to be whipped, Mr. Wolf whistled, and two drivers came. If it was a man, they fixed him in the rope themselves, but if a woman they called a woman to do it. When she had got her fixed she let them know, and they went in to whip her. Both men and women were stripped entirely naked, except a small piece of cloth round the body, and a cap was drawn over their face. Mr. Wolf always went in to see that they were stretched tight enough, and to count the lashes. As soon as they had given enough he stamped. You may hear the whip and paddle there, all hours in the day. There's no stopping. As soon as one is loosed from the rope, another is ready to be put in. Some days they have so many brought to be punished that they don't get through till late at night. It's just the same on Sunday as any other day—there's no difference. It's going on all day long. Some people carry their slaves there themselves, and some send them with a letter to the clerk. As soon as he reads it, he whistles for the drivers, and has them tied in the rope. The clerk is a mighty bad man; he never cared what he did with any of us. One morning he beat one of the women over the head with the shovel, because she did not do her sewing.

Mrs. Wolf keeps the women at work, sewing for her all the time, and she used to tell Mr. Wolf that he ought to give them one or two cuts more than the law says, to make them work better.

Widow women, every week, brought their slaves to be whipped. Some went away and left them, and some went into the whipping room and stayed till it was over. They would say, "how does that feel? Which had you rather do, have that, or mind your business?" A young woman once came and brought three to whip and one to sell. Elizabeth, about 17 or 18 years old, was one brought to whip. She was an Indian girl, with straight black hair. She was a seamstress, and dressed in pretty good clothes. Sancho laid on as hard as he could. She screamed and hallowed in the rope, and Wolf said, "Can't you stop that woman's mouth, Sancho?"—then he pulled the cap close down to her chin. Sancho was the best driver they had, because he could whip better. He whipped slow, and waited after striking till they turned round, and then struck again.

They once tried to make a driver of me. A Frenchman brought his girl to be whipped, and they called me to do it. I whipped so fast it did not suit Wolf, and he began to whip me. Then I had to stop. The Frenchman took the whip and gave her three or four cuts, and said he should like for her to have ten cuts more. Wolf called up Sancho and made him finish, and I rubbed her down with salt.

Some of the women who were carried there, were very much frightened, and fretted a great deal, and got down on their knees and begged "do, massa, forgive this time, and I will serve missa well." Master would say, "you bitch, you've got the devil in you, and I'll get it out." I never knew one carried away without being whipped 20 or 30 lashes.

Our only food was dry hominy. It was given to us every day at 11 o'clock. Some of the speculators gave their hands salt fish, and we used to beg the liquor it was boiled in, and were glad enough to get it.

I was in the sugar house about three months. All the time I was there, the rooms were so crowded at night, that the children had to lay on top of the others and sometimes the men. We laid on the floor in two rows, with our heads to the wall, leaving a path between our feet just wide enough to walk in. All the rooms were crowded in this way, and the cells were full too. A driver watched in each room, and three or four in the yard. It was so hot and close that we almost smothered. We sweat so, that in the morning the floor would be right wet, just as though water had been thrown on it.

The speculators sometimes stopped there with their droves of slaves. They carry the children in a wagon, behind, throw in naked one on top of another, just like pigs. When they stop, they sometimes find one or two smothered.—John Fogle, who bought me of Cohen, was a Dutchman, and lived in Orangeburg district. He had but few slaves, and no overseer. He was among us all the time, cursing and scolding. He either laid out our tasks himself or made his sons do it. He had two sons at home, one 12 years old, the other 17. His slaves were three women, one old man, one boy about six years old, and me. He did not trouble me when I first went there, but he was beating the women all the time. The women are always beat worse than the men. The more they whip the men, the more likely they are to run away into the swamp, but the women don't run away so much.

We all worked together in the field. The old and young always have to work alike. Each one is made to do as much as he can. I have seen old men and women so bent down that they have to lean on a stick with one hand, while they hoed with the other. At night they could not carry home their crop themselves, but waited in the fields till some of the younger ones went back to help them. When they get so feeble they can hardly walk, they are set to tend sheep, with a boy to run after the stray ones. Fogle was a drunkard. He once bought a barrel of spirit at Midway, and came home and was drunk all the time. He had no learning; he could neither read nor write. When he sold corn, his sons always marked it down. If we wanted a ticket to go to meeting he went to them. Sometimes they would not give us any, but would curse us and drive us off.

I have lived with a good many masters, but never found any who cared to let their slaves go to meeting, or who talked with us about religion. Until I came into the free States a few months ago, I did not know any thing about God or the Bible. The planters used to curse God, when it rained in harvest, or when the hail cut off their crops, or any thing happened that did not please them. That was all I heard of Him. I never knew any body to preach to slaves but once. When I lived with my old mistress at Four Holes, two free colored men came out by night and preached. One of them could read, and the other only prayed. The patrol found it out and went among them, and caught the preachers, and tied them up, and gave them a bad whipping. They gave one of them more than a hundred lashes. He was whipped so bad that he could not get away for two days. They told them they were "going about putting the devil into the rest of the niggers, and that if they ever came back they would put a load of shot into them." One of them went to Charleston, and the other went away up the country and we never saw them again.

Sometimes a white preacher, when he meets a slave on the road alone, stops and talks with him if nobody is in sight. He takes a book out of his pocket and reads, and tells him about a wicked place that he will go to when he dies, and be burnt up if he does not mind master and mistress.

If any body is looking they don't dare to say a word. I never heard them tell about heaven.

The ministers hold slaves as well as others and treat them just the same. They do not often live where their slaves are, but have a plantation in another place. One minister lived near Billy Mallard's on Dean Swamp. His name was Jenkins. We could hear his people halloo when they whipped them. He had more than fifty slaves at work, besides little children too young to work. He stopped every Sunday at master's as he went to meeting, and they all went along together. I never heard him preach. He was an old gray haired man. His hands used to come over to our plantation to beg salt. We sometimes got a little from the kitchen when it was left after cooking.

Stephen Williams, another minister over Dean Swamp, preached at Harry meeting-house. He had a man called Jess who was in the habit of running away. He said he meant to break him of running away, or kill him. He said the last whipping he gave him, the ants did as much good as the whip did. He had him tied down to a great ant's nest and they stung him while he whipped. Jess was not broken, but afterwards somebody shot him in the woods.

[To Be Continued]

The Emancipator, October 11, 1838 (Installment #4)
From the Advocate of Freedom.

RECOLLECTIONS OF SLAVERY.

BY A RUNAWAY SLAVE.

Continued from No. 139.

All the people I lived with, except Davy Cohen, used to go to meeting. Sometimes they gave us a ticket to go, and sometimes not. Some masters won't let their slaves go hardly at all. They whip them, if they ask them for a ticket. When I could not get a ticket, I would steal away after master had gone and get in back of the meeting house, and then just before meeting broke up, would steal away again and run a round-about way down by the branch, and get home before the rest. The slaves never go into the meeting house, except a few who have the care of children. The rest stay out back, and sometimes there are seats built there for them to set on. As soon as meeting is done, the patrol comes right up and asks for tickets, and all who have not got any are tied on the spot to a tree and whipped. I never could understand what the minister was preaching about. I heard a mighty hollowing and that was all. I knew a woman once who was whipped for praying. The overseer used to creep round behind the camp at night to listen and find out what we were talking about. He heard the woman praying, and in the morning she was whipped for it.

They do not like to have any kind of seriousness in the slaves. *They do not want them to think.* If they see one of them looking sober they tell him to be merry. They say he is hatching up some kind of deviltry. They used to say so to me, for I never could laugh and joke as the rest did. I never saw a slave who could read. They would not let us touch a book, but whipped us for that as much as anything.

If we hated master ever so much, we did not dare to show it, but we must always look pleased when he saw us, and we were afraid to speak what we thought, because some would tell master. I knew that I was wronged, and I have laid many a time and thought how to get revenge, but something always said "don't do it." We had heard a little about a free country. A man called Sailor Jack once came among us, and told us that there were no slaves in his land; but we did not believe him, and some of the slaves got angry, when anything was said about it. They would say it was all a lie. That we were made to serve Buckra, and that was what we had got to do all our lives, and our best way was to bear it as well as we could. They said it only made us unhappy to keep talking all the time about freedom, and that if there was any free country, Buckra's land was so big we could never get there, so the best way was to say no more about it. I did not really believe there was any free county, till two days before I left slavery.

I lived with Foyle three months. He did not whip me but once, but was constantly whipping the women. He tied them up and called his oldest son to help him. They whipped with a cowskin, and sometimes with hickory rods. He used to get great bunches of these rods and hang them up in his house to dry, and then take five or six at a time and wear them out, and send for more. He would whip till he was tired and then sit down on a stump, and when rested begin again. His son-in-law came over from his plantation to help him whip me. He was very strong, and could strike harder than the old man. They used the brine on me and on the women. A few days after whipping me he hired me out to the contractors of the Hamburg and Charleston Rail Road. There they were, cutting and slashing all the time. Every hour in the day we could hear the whip going. They did not use brine there. After we were whipped we had to go straight back to our work. They did not care whether we got well or not, because we were other people's niggers.

They had a great many hands repairing the road; some of them women. Their business was to wheel dirt up on to the road on skids, in some places fifteen or twenty feet high. It was very dangerous business. Some-times the wheelbarrow would slip and they fall down. Two women fell; one broke her arm, the other only fainted. They bled the last and in an hour they made her go to work again.* A great many wheelbarrows were bro-ken, and two or three carpenters were constantly at work close by, mak-ing new ones. They employed a great many little boys and girls to throw chunks in the road, and we covered them up with dirt. Some of them wheeled dirt in little wheelbarrows, up the skids. They had no task, but were kept at work all day. A little girl fell off and was hurt badly. They sent her home to her master. There was hardly a day that some of the slaves did not get crippled or killed. There were more killed there than at any other place I ever worked at. On the State road a great many died, but nothing near so many as there.

> *This part of the narrative was corroborated incidentally, in con-versation with a gentleman who had traveled extensively in the southern states. He remarked that the place that he had seen slaves treated the worst, was on the Rail Road from Charleston to Ham-burg. He saw women nearly naked wheeling loads of dirt up on to the road from pits by the road side, on planks about a foot and a half wide. If they lost their balance, they would fall from ten to twenty feet.

I worked there about two months, digging pits and wheeling, and taking up old rails and laying new ones. I began about seventy miles from Charles-ton, and worked up towards the city twenty miles. A white man marked off and showed us what to do and we did it. Our task was to dig a pit ten feet by twelve, and three deep, and roll the dirt up on to the road. The women had the same task as the men. The pits were not close to the road but some ways off. There were a great many camps for the slaves, about ten miles apart, scattered all along the road.

I was whipped while there three times. The last whipping I got was very bad, because I did not finish my pit, though I worked hard to get it done. It is always the way, that if a slave tries ever so hard to finish his task, and tires himself almost to death, he is sure to get a whipping if he leaves only a little piece, or if a few straggling weeds are left, or if it is not done exactly to please the overseer. They tie him up by his hands, and put a pole be-tween his legs to make his skin tight, and give him twenty or thirty lashes. The tighter they stretch him the more the whip gashes. The slaveholders are all the time contriving punishments. They go round to each other's plantations to find out how they manage. All they talk about when they meet, is, what crops they get, and how they manage their slaves. They say "such a one gets great crops, he treats his negroes so and so." It would take me a long time to tell about all the different kinds of punishment I have seen. Some of them tie the slaves up by the heels with their heads down, and set a pile of corncobs on fire under them, and, after it has burnt a little while, put out the flame and leave them there to smoke. John Cross used to do this, but Monpay followed it up more than any.

Nobody can tell how badly the slaves are punished. They are treated worse than dumb beasts. Many a time I have gone into the swamp, and laid down and wished I was a dog, or dead. The house servants are not treated any better than the rest. Some mistresses when they give them cloth, will not let them make it into gowns or frocks to cover their arms and shoulders, but make them just tie it on with strings, so that they may be fair for whipping.—I have seen pretty tight times, but it's all over now I am free. I am mighty happy now. I am so glad, I can't sleep at night for thinking of it. The people here are different from what they are in Carolina. I like them a heap better. They look different, and act and talk different. There they all look pale and sickly. They don't work, but have every thing done by slaves. All the women do is to read, or play with the children, or sing and make music and go to balls and parties. The men hunt, and race horses. Some of them never had the sun shine on their skin. They wear great broad hats, and never step out of the house without an umbrella. If they are only getting out of a carriage to go into a meeting house, they have the umbrella spread. If they go out into the fields and stand under a tree awhile and look at us, their lady will say, "what do you go out in the hot sun for, and get all tanned up?—you've got a good overseer and driver, let them look after the niggers."

[To Be Concluded]

The Emancipator, October 21, 1838 (Installment #5)
From the Advocate of Freedom.
RECOLLECTIONS OF SLAVERY.
BY A RUNAWAY SLAVE.
Concluded.
Escape from Slavery.

The day after I was whipped so bad on the railroad, I found I should not get my task done, and knew I must be whipped again. It was almost night. And the overseer had left the road for a few minutes to go down to the camp. I was on one side of the road by myself, and the rest of the hands were all busy digging their pits on the other side. When nobody was looking I threw down my spade, and crouching down, slipped away towards the woods as fast as I could. If I had not gone that moment I could not have got away at all. After I had run a little way I got behind some mounds and brush, that hid me, and then stopped and saw that I was not missed, for they all kept on with their work. Then I ran into the woods. After staying there till midnight I thought of a way to escape. My object was to get to Four Holes. I had a sister there, at Bradwell's and I thought perhaps her master would buy me. I knew I could not be worse treated than I was on the rail road, I hoped to fare better.

When it was very dark, and all still, I went back to the road and crept along to the rail road cars, which always stop at "Midway" over night. I found the people were away, and went to the hind car and got in among the cotton. They do not stow the bales close, but just throw them in, and leave chinks and holes between. I drew the curtains together and crawled down between the bales. In the morning they fired up and started off, and never thought that I was there, I knew all the way to Charleston, and when we got pretty near the city, I jumped off close by some woods. I fell down when I jumped, but it was sandy and did not hurt me much. I then went through the woods by a round-about way into town.

When there, I went to the tavern where I used to stop, when I carried eggs and peaches and other things to market. That night and every night while I stayed in Charleston, I slept on some hay under a shed in the tavern yard. The next day I went down to the stevedore's stand and waited there with the rest of the hands to get work. By and by a stevedore came along and asked if I wanted to work. I told him yes. He said come along, and I followed him on to the wharf, and worked with a good many others in stowing away cotton in a vessel.

I had no money to get victuals; so when the rest went to the cook-shop I would go along with them, and just as they got there, slip away and go back to the vessel. I then got acquainted with the steward, and every day he used to give me something to eat. It was Tuesday when I got into Charleston, and I stayed there till Saturday night. One day in going from the cook-shop to the vessel, I was walking along among the bales of cotton on the wharf and saw something shining on the ground. I did not know what it was, but picked it up and put it in my pocket. It had a chain to it and some marks on it. That night, when we were all at work, the policeman came on board the vessel with a paper in his hand and said, "Holloo, have you got any run-away niggers here?" The stevedore said "no,—no runaways in this lot." Then the police man said he must see *badge.* So he made them all show badge. When he came to me, I took the thing that I had found out of my pocket, because I saw it looked just like the rest. I was very much frightened, because I did not know as it would do, but he looked at it and said it was right, and then I felt mighty glad. If I had not had that badge I should have been carried straight to the sugar house.

One day while I was eating with the steward he said to me, "how much of your wages do you have to give to master?" I told him "all." He said it was not so where he came from. There the people are all free. When he told me this I began to think that there was a free country, and to wish that I could get there. The next time I saw him we talked about it again. Then he asked me what I would give him to carry me to the free country. I told him "two months' wages." I told him so just to see what he would say, for I had not at that time a single cent. He said, "well, he thought he could carry me, but he did not want any pay for it," and then he was going on to tell me how to manage, but the hands got back and we had to stop talking. Next meal time we talked again, and he told me just what to do. He said the vessel was all loaded and would sail next morning. That day was Saturday, and he told me that after I knocked off work and had got my pay, I must stay about there till it was dark and all the people in the ship were asleep and that he would wait for me. He said he had got a place made to hide me in, and that if I was sure not to cough, or make any noise, he thought he could get me away safe.

When it was dark, I crept along on the cotton bags on the wharf towards the vessel. I got pretty near and saw some men standing there smoking cigars, and so I stooped down and waited till they went away. When it was all still I went to the vessel. The steward heard me make a little noise and said "who's there?" I told him "me;"—then he said "well,—make haste,—get up quick." I got up as fast as I could and he opened the scuttle and told me to jump down, and crawl away back and not make the least noise. Then he put down the scuttle and I crowded in between the bales, through a little narrow place, where I could hardly get my head in, and I went away back till I got to a place where there was a little more room,—but *there* there was not room to lie down or sit upright, and I could move round only a very little.

In the morning the steward came down and stopped up all the chinks by jamming wood into them, so that nobody could see me. Everyday he used to bring me water in a bottle and a cracker, and sometimes bread with raisins in it. When I came on board I offered him the money which the stevedore paid me, but he said he did not carry me away for the sake of money, and I should want it myself when I got to the free country. I told him I should not and that he must take it. Well, he said he would take it, and buy with it something good for me to eat.

We were four weeks in getting to Boston. I laid in that hole three weeks without going out or even seeing the light, only when they lifted up the scuttle to get wood. Then I could see the men through the chinks. I was very sick all the time, and once when the steward asked me how I felt, I told him "mighty bad, I thought I should die and never get to the free country." I expected to die, but I didn't care, I had rather the vessel would sink than I should be carried back to slavery. Every little while, steward told me that I should be in the free country in a week, but when I found we did not get there I began to think he was deceiving me.

When we had been out about two weeks I felt very cold, and he said we were coming into a cold country, and I must squeeze as close to the cotton bags as I could to keep myself warm, and he would try if he could find an old blanket, or anything to put over me. The next time he came he brought a jacket and told me to wrap it round my feet, but this did not make me much warmer. All the clothes I had on were thin, and I thought I should freeze. The place where I was became very dirty, and I suffered dreadfully. Sometimes the vessel would be rocking and pitching so that it seemed as though my feet were up and my head down; but it was all nothing to what it would be to go back to slavery.

One night after I had been there about three weeks, the steward told me to come out, and set a little while with him. He said they were almost to Boston, but had to wait for the wind. I crowded out, but my strength was so nigh gone that when I got up through the scuttle I could not stand. I sat with him till his watch was almost over, and then had to go back again. I went up so, two nights. I saw lights on shore, and he told me that that was a free country, but not the place that we going to. In three days the wind was fair, and I stayed in my hole till we got to Boston. When I heard we should be there in a day or two I was so glad that I did not want to eat, and I left the crackers that he brought me, there in the hole.

At last he told me we were there, but must lie still till night, and he would let me out. About nine o'clock he said the people were away, and I might come out. I was so weak I could hardly walk. He then went with me up into the street and then stopped me and said, "now, my friend, I have brought you so far, safely, and that is all I can do for you: go down this street and inquire for a boarding house for colored people, and some of your colored friends will tell you what to do." He shook my hand and said "God bless you," and went back to the vessel. I saw him next day working on board the vessel, but did not get a chance to speak to him. I have not seen him since and do not know his name.

After he left me, I went along holding on by the houses, and when I had got down the street a good ways, I met a colored man and asked him where the boarding house was. He asked me if I was a sailor, I told him not much of one, but that I had just come from a ship. He said "I understand it all." He knew from my dress and the cotton on my head and clothes, that I was a runaway. He carried me to a boarding house, and the next day to ——, who gave me some warm clothes. He sent me into the country, to stay with some colored people. I am now as well situated as I wish to be, and have no fears of being carried back to slavery.

Having brought these "Recollections" to a close, it is proper now to present the attestation of the Advocate of Freedom, to the credibility of the narration. It is all that we know about it, but we should place the greatest reliance on the integrity and cautious judgment of the conductors of that paper. In this connection we will repeat what has been so often said and as often overlooked by the pro-slavery party, that the question of the right or wrong of slavery does not turn at all on the treatment of individuals, or the veracity of any fugitives from slavery. Is it right for A MAN to hold A MAN as a slave?

Recollections of Slavery, & c.

We give on our last page, the conclusion of the interesting story, which has occupied a portion of our space for a few weeks past. A few immaterial errors have been discovered by a close re-examination of the subject of the narrative, which will hereafter be corrected. The leading and material facts may however, we think, be relied upon with implicit confidence. At least such is the unhesitating opinion of all, who like ourselves have had the opportunity personally of questioning the narrator in respect to them. So far as the whippings and scourgings are concerned of which he so frequently speaks, the evidence on his own person is so strongly marked, as to satisfy, we presume, the most skeptical. It is intended to publish the narrative soon, in a pamphlet form, with such additions, corrections, notes, &c. as will best fit it for more general circulation. It may be made, we think, a very efficient plea for the slave, and our friends we hope will aid us in the effort to send it forth.

Should the narrative, through the medium of our paper, as by this time it may possibly have done, or in any other way, fall under the eye of any at the South, disposed to set up a claim for this piece of property, which has unceremoniously moved off, and became so suddenly changed into a thinking agent, abundantly able to take care of itself, we advise them to pocket the loss at once, with as good grace as they may, and to take no thought for its recovery. For, 1st. It is now in the possession of its right owner, and had better therefore remain where it is. 2. It has been so changed by its transfer to the North, as to make it a very unsafe thing on a southern plantation; for it has already very much increased its knowledge of geography, and has become somewhat initiated into the dangerous mysteries of reading and writing, and withal has learned to talk about liberty in strains fearfully contagious. 3. All attempts to recover it will be unavailing, and the expense therefore of the effort might as well be saved.

We wish our friends could all have the opportunity we enjoyed of hearing the story of this fugitive from the blessings of the patriarchal institution, from his own lips. It would not be necessary again, for one year at least, to exhort them to active, self-denying effort for the slave. The scarred back of the victim attesting the truthfulness of his story, his privations and sufferings in the house of bondage, the perilous escape, as he would tell of them—the joyful exclamation "but it is all over now, I am *free*, I am FREE!" would send a thrill through their hearts, that they would not forget to their dying hour, and lead them, as it led us, to repeat before High Heaven the vow, never to relax their efforts, until the whole system of vile oppression and wrong, by which millions of such are crushed in our land, is uprooted and destroyed. We wish that the doubters in immediate emancipation, might have the same opportunity. A mere thing, a mere chattel personal so suddenly changed into a man, thinking, reasoning, working too, just like other men—it is indeed wonderful. If any reliance can be placed on a single instance, this would seem to prove pretty conclusively, that if all the rest of like goods and chattels at the South, were at once, in the twinkling of an eye, to undergo the same transmutation, it would be for the benefit of all the parties concerned. The quiet deportment, the cheerful performance of labor under the stimulus of wages, the joyful use of free limbs, the content that all day long rests on the brow of the fugitive might lead them at least to examine with candor the mass of other evidence by which the great truth is now demonstrated, that the best preparation for freedom is to set the slave immediately free. We wish that such cases were more generally seen and known. It would awaken thousands, who are now folding their arms in sloth, to generous effort for the bleeding slave.

The Experience of a Slave in South Carolina, by John Andrew Jackson (1862)

—ɯ—

Introduction

Susanna Ashton and Deanna L. Panetta

When John Andrew Jackson heard of Mack English's death, he realized that it was an opportunity to reevaluate God's plan. English, a brutal man slated to inherit Jackson, was now out of the picture, and for the first time Jackson could view his future with some hope. English's death renewed Jackson's conviction that God loved him, and this thought inspired Jackson eventually to flee his bondage. He wrote, "I, myself, was willed to that tyrant, but God had willed me to myself." Jackson believed that he was fated to be in control of his own life, and Mack's death only solidified his conviction that it was God's intention for all slaves to be free.

Born in Sumter, South Carolina, Jackson grew up on the English family plantation. After giving a brief account of his parents' history, Jackson begins his narrative with several instances of harsh treatment he received and witnessed during his time as a slave, a rhetorical decision that sets the tone for the rest of Jackson's story. He quickly dissuades any preconceived notion of women as less complicit in the horrors of slavery than men by painting a chilling portrait of his mistress and her family. As he puts it, "The sight which most delighted her eyes was to see a slave whipped," and one of her daughters grew up to murder Jackson's sister by having her whipped to death. Through his narrative Jackson was intent upon exposing the horrors of slavery, and these barbaric portraits of female behavior serve his story by illustrating the long reach of slavery's hold on southern society.

Just as with his focus on female cruelty, Jackson took pains to note that some of the greatest evils of slavery could be found in the most unlikely of places. He describes, for instance, members of the English family and their in-laws, Quakers who, in spite of their religious affiliation, were, as Jackson phrases it, "equal to the devil himself." Similarly, he tells of a circuit-rider preacher who not only seduces or rapes a slave but also compounds the deed by paying her with a counterfeit dollar. As Jackson queries, "If the pastors do such a thing, what will the masters and their sons do?"

The most compelling part of Jackson's narrative may be his escape, which he describes in a manner both persuasive and particular in its accounting for details. He mentions that mental illness had struck his owner, declaring, "my master had just then gone out of his mind," a situation that allowed Jackson greater freedom about the plantation. After trading some chickens for a pony from another slave, Jackson took advantage too of the three-day Christmas holiday to flee the plantation. He made it all the way to Charleston, some "150 miles" he says, and immediately began to look about for a vessel he might board and thereby escape to the North. After being refused aid by a suspicious sailor, Jackson eventually managed to stow away on a ship headed north by hiding between two cotton bales. He arrived in Boston on February 10, 1847, overcome with emotion. He "thanked God that I had escaped from hell to heaven, for I felt as I had never felt before—that is, *master of myself,* and in my joy I was as a bouncing sparrow."

In Boston, Jackson found various forms of employment, all the while saving money in the hope of buying his family back in South Carolina out of slavery. A letter he sent inquiring of this possibility reached his owners, who then sent an agent to Boston in pursuit of him. Fortunately, by the time the agent arrived in Boston, Jackson had already moved to the town of Salem, Massachusetts, and was thus able to elude capture. Jackson reports, however, "Just as I was beginning to be settled at Salem," the passage of the Fugitive Slave Act of 1850 made his situation even more perilous, and he decided again to flee. He tells of meeting with Harriet Beecher Stowe, who assisted him in escaping to Canada. In New Brunswick, Canada, Jackson married a second time and became acquainted with antislavery activists, who arranged for him to travel to the British Isles in the spring of 1857 in order to solicit contributions to purchase his family. There Jackson and his new wife met with Scottish and British clergy, who vouched for him with the many testimonials accompanying this narrative. Alerted to the compelling nature of his witness, antislavery activists sponsored Jackson on a lecture circuit and helped him publish his book. Jackson and his wife lived in London until the end of the American Civil War. Only then was he able to return to South Carolina, where he lived out his days.

Readers of this narrative, particularly those familiar with accounts written for or sponsored by antislavery societies, may find it to be reminiscent of other well-known narratives by runaways, for it features many of the stock ingredients often found in slave accounts. Jackson's story includes conventional figures and scenes such as a merciless master, a husband and wife torn apart, and a fateful escape to the North. Nonetheless, Jackson's story is more than a predetermined tale of woe crafted using a formula contrived by his abolitionist mentors. His tale is populated by specific individuals and locales, and even when he is reciting the most formulaic of anecdotes, he crafts them with pathos, humanity, and emotional honesty that render his narrative on equal footing with the most influential slave narratives of the nineteenth century.

Not unlike Frederick Douglass, who famously denounced slavery as an institution that created evil, Jackson too saw the institution of slavery as fostering cruelty in the hearts of innately good people.* Jackson, however, took it a step further. He argued that not only was slavery a breeding ground for inhumanity to man, but it was also a stage on which any propensity to evil could be played out. "Slavery produces a full exhibition of all that is vile and devilish in human nature," he stated.

Jackson's dark portrait of human nature is somewhat mitigated, however, by his inclusion of slave songs at the end of his tale. While former slaves not infrequently appended the texts of spirituals or slave songs to the ends of their life stories, this was most commonly done with little commentary or analysis. Jackson, cognizant of the sophistication and cultural import of these songs, presents them with his own analysis and commentary.† While Jackson acknowledges, for example, that songs often provided bondsmen with a rhythm to coordinate their fieldwork, he also takes pain to argue that the structural shaping of the songs reflects an appreciation for narrative and imagination that is often denied to slaves. Slave songs were, as he understood

---

*A fuller explanation of Douglass's abolitionist philosophy can be found in James Oakes, *The Radical and the Republican: Frederick Douglass, Abraham Lincoln, and the Triumph of Antislavery Politics* (New York: W. W. Norton, 2007). See also Nathan Irvin Huggins, *Slave and Citizen: The Life of Frederick Douglass* (Boston: Little, Brown, 1980); and William S. McFeely, *Frederick Douglass* (New York: Norton, 1991).

†For an imaginative approach to the breadth of the development and legacy of slave music, see Shane White and Graham J. White, *The Sounds of Slavery: Discovering African American History through Songs, Sermons, and Speech* (Boston: Beacon Press, 2005).

them, often snatches of hymns overheard and misunderstood but reshaped and reinvigorated in spiritual form. He accounts for this phenomenon by remarking that "probably the reason for the number of repeats, is because they have no books allowed them; and indeed . . . on hearing a single line sung by white people, these poor slaves cannot prize it too much, as is shown by their singing it over and over." Jackson's subtle reading of how these songs worked (he notes, for example, that a "hallelujah" grammatically misplaced in the middle of a line is necessary because of the emotive energy behind it) demonstrates how, in his larger story of his life, he sought to weave together the story of all bondsmen and how their humanity shaped their world.

Jackson's narrative is filled with detailed accounts about aspects, even logistics, of the slave trade that were commonly known but not always well documented. He includes references to the complex maneuvering of the black-market slave economy, for example, in which white people illegally sold and traded with slaves and in which slaves traded and sold things among themselves. He describes with chilling precision the technical details of torture instruments (paddles with gimlet holes designed to raise blisters, for example, and whips entwined with wire) and differing methods of abuse. He even tells of the agonizingly ironic court case between his cruel mistress and her overseer, Burl Quiney, who angered her for having whipped one of her slaves to death *without her permission*. While it is not clear how and if Jackson was literate enough to have composed his life story independently, it is nonetheless obvious that the relentless emphasis on specific testimony was intended to convince all readers that he spoke truth that demanded notice, action, and righteous reverence.

The Experience of a Slave in South Carolina was originally published in 1862 by Passmore and Alabaster Press. Printed in Finsbury Square, London, this publication followed John Andrew Jackson's speaking tour in the British Isles.

—⚉—

John Andrew Jackson
The Experience of a Slave in South Carolina
PREFACE

In aiming to arrest the attention of the reader, here he proceeds to the unvarnished, but our true tale of John Andrew Jackson, the escaped Carolinian slave, it might be fairly said that "truth was stranger than fiction," and that the experience of slavery produces a full exhibition of all that is vile and devilish in human nature.

Mrs. Stowe, as a virtuous woman, dared only allude to some of the hellish works of slavery—it was too foul to sully her pen; but the time is come when iniquity should no longer be hid: and the evil which Wilberforce and Clarkson exposed, and of which Wesley said it was "the sum of all human villainies," must now be laid bare in all its hellish atrocities. The half has not yet been told; but appalling as are the statements made, yet when the fiercest organized effort to extend the monster of evil of North-American slavery is being made, every patriot is called on to sympathize over the woes and sufferings of human kind, and plead for freedom and liberty.

Cowper long ago told his fellow-countryman that

"Skins may differ, but affection
Dwells in white and black the same."

Therefore, kind reader, we ask your sympathy, while you peruse some of the iniquities perpetrated upon a suffering race, and that too often by men and women calling themselves Christians, and using a religious cloak to screen their monstrous, foul, and cruel acts.

Shrink not, gentle reader, when those fearful atrocities are brought before your notice. Such narratives as Jackson's are wanted to arouse the people. The evil is afar off, and interested parties say, "Don't believe it; it is false, or it is exaggerated." Not so; the worst cannot be told. You cannot speak out, or tell a fraction of the horrid scenes enacted, where every child and feeble woman is at the brutal mercy of brutalized man; where marriage is a fiction, and five millions of people live practically in a state of unrecognized whoredom and polygamy.

Would that English mothers and English daughters could feel as they out for those whose virtue and honor, whose life and liberty, may be purchased by any libertine wretch, who has the "almighty dollar" in plenty in his pocket. Let us but think of our sisters, our wives, our children, and thank God with them that

"I was not born a little slave
    To labor in the sun;
    To wish I was but in my grave,
    And all my labor done."

Many an English reader, knowing that every year we pay a million of money as interest for the twenty million by which the freedom of West Indian slaves was purchased, and spend nearly another million to keep down the slave trade of America, Cuba and Brazil, are very earnest in declaring their abhorrence of American slavery, and, like the *Times*, finds fault with President Lincoln's government for not putting an end to slavery by proclamation, thinking that our British hands are quite clean. But they forget the share that England has had in the bondage of the human race. Liverpool and Bristol for years was the seat of the African slave trade; and, once upon a time, G. F. Cooke, the actor, on the boards of a Liverpool theatre, when displeased with his audience for hissing him, turned fiercely on them, and told them that Liverpool was paved with blood of the negro slaves; and in 1862 it is not quite clear of the same, vide the *Nightingale Slaver.*

Three hundred years ago Sir John Hawkins procured the first cargo of negroes from the coast of Guinea, and took them to Hispaniola, and so profitable was his trip that a new expedition was soon prepared, of which Queen Elizabeth shared the profits. This royal patronage of the slave trade was further extended under other reigns, and, on the 10th of December, 1770, our good King George issued a proclamation under his own hand, commanding the Governor of Virginia, "upon pain of the highest displeasure, to assent to no law by which the importation of slaves shall be in any respect prohibited and obstructed."

Before we then heartily condemn the United States, let us remember that when they would not have slavery, it was forced upon them by the English Government.

When in 1645 the ship of one Thomas Keyser and James Smith brought a cargo of negroes to Boston, they were heavily fined and compelled to return those negroes again to Africa. Noble men were they of Massachusetts; and despite the Irish and rowdy elements of Boston and Portland, yet noble men are they at the present hour. There the fugitive slave has liberty and protection.

Virginia, long the battle ground of freedom during the old war, as well as the new one, often spoke out nobly against slavery. Her patriots, like Jefferson, though himself a slaveholder, yet steadily resented the influence of that growing evil. At that time, Franklin spoke through the press, and memorials from all the States were sent to King George. The king was inexorable; and while the English judges declared that when a slave set his foot on the soil of England he was free, yet the monarch stood in the path of humanity and became the pillar of the American Slave Trade.

England gave America slavery. England, by the use of her cotton, has mainly helped to continue it; and let but English sympathy be withdrawn from the South, and soon slavery there must fall. It lies with Christian men and women to expose its evils, denounce its cruelties, lay open its horrors, and spare not its infamous immoralities. Truly there is a God that judges the earth. There is wanted fact upon fact to enlighten the English public, when its *leading papers* palliate and excuse the atrocities of the South. They would ignore the existence of four million out of the twenty who live and breathe beyond the Atlantic under the stars and stripes. Christian England should stand up to a man opposed to those who would kill every slave found with arms in hand, or away from his master's plantation; who have no scruples in brutalizing, burning, flaying, flogging, scourging, and shooting the wives and daughters of their runaway slaves.

Every sickening brutality is practiced upon the hapless men and women, without hope of any redress; surely these injustices cry to heaven for vengeance. How long, Lord, how long. Stonewall Jackson may, with the courage and piety of a Cromwell, but without his rightful cause, carry the war into Maryland, and Pope and M'Clellan be driven back to the Free States; but yet with one burst of freedom, even Dr. Mackay shall re-echo from Washington to the "Times" of tomorrow, his favorite phrase:

"There's a good time coming, boys,
Wait a little longer."

The day of escape from bondage will come to all, as it has to some; and surely their cry will be heard, and the refrain so long sung by the negroes of the South:

"O let my people go,"

be answered from heaven, perhaps even with a slaughter as great as that of the "smart Egyptians," when they came onward with all the panoply of their chariots and horsemen to the Red Sea, there to sing amid the waters. Then sang Miriam:

"Sound the loud timbre o'er Egypt's dark sea,
Jehovah hath triumph'd, his people are free."

W.M.S.
September 20, 1862.

CHAPTER I
My Birth and Training

I was born in South Carolina. My grandfather was stolen from Africa. My father learned the African method of curing snake bites, and was in consequence, called Dr. Clavern. My mother's name was Betty. I had five brothers and five sisters. Of these, two brothers and two sisters were dead when I left the plantation. My earliest recollection was of my mistress, whom I feared above all persons, as she used every means in her power to spite me. The reasons for this was as follows: When I was about ten years old, her son and I were digging for hickory root to amuse ourselves with, when he, seeing that I was obtaining mine quicker than he, kicked me on the nose, upon which I wiped the blood upon him. He ran and informed his mother, who whipped me on my naked back to console her son, till the blood ran down. After that, she always hated not only me but my family, and would even stint my mother's allowance; and since then, I had many whippings through her influence.

My mistress had four daughters, viz.: Anne, Eliza, Jane, and Martha. Of Anne, the eldest, I knew but little, as she married when I was very young, and went to another plantation. Eliza, the next, was the worst of the three. She used to whip me almost as much as my mistress. Of Jane, the next, I also knew but little, as she married a minister named Brailly, when I was very young; but, as far as I know, she was the best of the three. Martha, the youngest, was very bad. I will give a specimen of her abilities. One day, as she was returning from a walk in the garden, she saw my youngest brother, William, walking in the yard, and, from pure mischief, she picked some horse nettles, and, coming up to him (he was quite naked), began to sting him with them, and, as he ran away, she ran after him, and kept up with him, stinging him on the sides and back, till at last he fell down through pain; nevertheless, she kept on stinging him, without any intermission; at last he got up and began running, and by that time I got up to him (I was about ten years of age, and he being between five and six), and I cried out to him, "Run faster, William, run faster," whereupon she turned upon me, and I being able to run faster than she, I escaped her, and by that means my brother William effected his escape. When William got home, he was covered with large lumps all over his body. When she was married she had my sister whipped to death. The circumstances were as follows:

My sister was religious, and perhaps it stung her conscience, or it might have been for some other reason; but, at all events, she ordered my sister to leave off praying, and as she discovered my sister did not obey her commands, she asked her husband, Gamble McFarden (a member of Salem Brick Church, who was, if possible, worse than herself, and she was a member also) to give her a hundred lashes, and he took her and hung her up by the hands to the beef gallows (an apparatus on which they hang oxen when they skin them), called his negro slave Toney, and ordered him to give her a hundred lashes, and he commenced beating her incessantly; he then remonstrated with his master, because she fainted, and his brutal master (who, though a member of a Christian church, was notwithstanding, equal to the devil himself) coolly ordered him to bring a pail of water and throw over her, to revive her; and when she came to, he ordered him to continue, which Toney did; but at length made a pause, and told his master that he had given her fifty lashes, but the brutal answer was, "Give me the whip, and I will give her the other fifty," which he did. She died at the end of three weeks, leaving two children, a boy and girl, who, with my father, I now hope to buy. My mistress also had four sons: James, Robert, Thomas, and Mack. James English, a member of Brick Church, was as bad as any of them; he was married when I was little. I worked on his plantation once, driving oxen, and I will relate what I saw there. A slave named Jack was taken sick while working on the plantation, and he laid himself down in the fence corner. When his master came, he saw him lying down, and he told him to get up immediately and go on working. Jack replied, "O massa, I'm so sick." "Get up immediately, you lazy varmint," replied his master, and he commenced whipping him till he got up; but as soon as his master was off that field, he lay down again. The slaves, seeing his master returning, told him he had better get up, as master was coming, but he could not, and when the master returned he began to whip him again; but seeing he could not get up, he went to the house and brought a tumbler-full of castor oil, and forced him to drink it, and then he said, "Now get up, you rascal, or I will whip you," and made him continue his work; but his conscience smote him, and he sent for a doctor, and upon his certificate allowed him to return home. I cannot leave off without relating another incident about him. On one occasion there were a hundred negroes to be sold, and James English went to buy. Among the negroes to be bought there was one named Willis; when he was put on the block, and the bidding began, James English began to bid, and Willis, seeing him bidding, jumped down from the auction-block. The auctioneer said, "Why do you jump down, you rascal?" He replied, "Because that man (pointing at James English) is bidding for me." "Why do you not want him to bid for you?" "Cause he's the baddest massa 'tween this an' hell fire." This scene was repeated twice, but James English at length bought him; and he went towards the plantation till within three miles of it, when the negroes of another plantation again told him that there was not a worse master in the whole district. His fears returning, afresh, he fled to the woods, but hunger compelled him to return. When he got back he was put into irons, and taken out next morning and hung up, and received a hundred lashes;

and when the stripes were partially healed, they gave him twenty-five lashes every other morning as long as they thought he could bear it.

Afterwards, James English was taken ill, but such were his savage propensities, that he got out of bed and dressed himself, took his whip and went into the cotton field, and commenced quarrelling with a slave named Old George, on a plea that he did not pick cotton fast enough. I will repeat his words: "Never mind, you old rascal, when I get better I'll give you sixty lashes—never mind, you old rascal you." But from that time he began to get worse, and went home and sent for the doctor, Mr. Miller. The following conversation then took place: "Doctor, I am very sick. Can you help me?" The doctor, after feeling his pulse, replied, "I can't save you." "Why, doctor?" "You have mortification in the head." He did not believe this, and sent for Dr. Hainsworth. When Dr. Hainsworth came, he said also, "I can't save you; you will die in a few days." His terror on hearing this announcement was extreme. He prayed the doctors to save his life, but in vain. In five days that terrible hour drew nigh, and his agony and death struggles were such that he required to be held down. Thus ended the life of a member of a Christian church. When the tidings of his death reached the negroes, they were overjoyed, and especially Willis, who went round to every hut, and shook hands with every negro, saying, "How d'ye do, brudder, de devil is dead an' gon' to hell, an' Old George got clear of his sixty lashes." Of Robert, the next brother, I knew nothing, as he died very young. Thomas, the next, was, if possible, worse than James. He was also a member of Mount Zion Chapel. He was articled to a lawyer. While studying the law, he used to whip the negroes on the plantation exceedingly. I will give you an instance of it. He had just bought a new whip, and wished to try it, and, seeing me go by, he called me and told me to bring him some water to wash his hands in. I went and got it as quickly as possible. When I brought it to him, he said, "You have been too slow, now pull off your jacket," and he then commenced whipping me, having first shut both doors, but I pushed open one of them and ran. I was then between ten and twelve year of age. He ran after me, and soon caught me, and whipped me again till the blood ran. When a young man, he went to Tennessee and married. The lady's name was Livinia. At his marriage his father gave him twelve negroes. He had then a son names West, and after ten years he returned to South Carolina. His father bought him a plantation five miles from his own, and gave him another slave girl as a nurse for his boy. The boy was very cross, and his mother asserted that the girl pinched the baby, which was not true. This girl was continually being whipped upon that false accusation, so that at length she ran away and went back to her old plantation. But the master tied a rope round her neck and sent her back to his son, who immediately ordered two flat irons to be put on the fire, and had her laid down on a log, and made three negroes, by the names of Frank, Save, and Peter, hold her down. He then took the first iron and pressed it to her body on one side; and when he removed it the skin stuck to it. He repeated the same with the other iron, on the other side of the body. She then left him, and started that night for the old plantation: her pain was so great that she was all night going that little distance. The old master, on seeing the burns, declared that she should not go back any more. The following conversation took place when Thomas came to see his father: "Thomas, did you burn this girl so?" "Yes, pa, I did, because she ran away." "Well, you shan't have her any more." But, in this case, Thomas was a true son of his father, and the old proverb remained unshaken, viz., "The chip off the old block don't fall far from the stump." About this time he became a minister. He preached his first sermon in Mount Zion Chapel, and the negroes flock to hear him, and were so overjoyed to think that now he had experienced true religion, he would be more merciful to them, but he was the same devil still. He owned a slave whose name was January, who could not pick cotton as fast as the other negroes. For this reason, this minister of religion gave him from twenty-five to one hundred lashes, and fifty blows with the paddle, which so frightened the negro that he ran away into the woods; but was caught, and again whipped, and put into the stocks, and was taken out every other morning, and received twenty-five lashes for a time, and then put to work with a lock and chain around his neck. At that time, his son West was overseer and whipping the negroes for his father. At the time I left slavery he often whipped the slaves severely. In the Southern States of America, any negro found out at night after nine o'clock, without a pass, is liable to be taken up and receive thirty-nine lashes; and it is a common amusement for young men to go out at night in parties patrolling. This minister, Thomas English, one night joined a party, and they came upon a slave named Isaac, on Dr. Grag's plantation, and they gave chase, but he outran them, and this minister was leading them on, shouting at the top of his voice, with horrid oaths, "Catch the rascal." We will now pass on to Mack, the youngest brother, he was worse than either of the others, and was the one who kicked me when I was digging for hickory root. He had not finished his schooling, before he was put to oversee his father's plantation. He used to whip the slaves more than his father. Among the atrocities which he committed, he knocked my mother down with the butt of his whip, while I stood by feeling as if I had been struck myself, when he

suddenly turned round and said, "Go on with your work, you —— rascal."
His whip spared neither old nor young. This youth ordered every negro
to pick one cwt. of cotton each day—which was almost impossible for
them to do—and on their not representing that amount of cotton at the
machine, he gave them from twenty-five to fifty lashes each; so that during the cotton-picking season, the place was filled with screams of agony
every evening. There was a slave named Isaac, who could not pick cotton
so fast as the others, and the consequence was, that he was flogged every
night by this youth. This tyrant was going to give him fifty lashes again one
evening, on the scaffold where they weigh the cotton, about ten feet high;
and Isaac jumped down in the dark on a snaggy stump and ruined his
feet, and could not work for more than a month. He used often to call the
negroes up at midnight to screw cotton, and to move fences in the sweet
potato fields.

The time of killing hogs is the negroes' feast, as it is the only time that
the negroes can get meat, for they are then allowed the chitterlings and
feet; then they do not see any more till next hog-killing time. Their food
is a dry peck of corn that they have to grind at the hand-mill after a hard
day's work, and a pint of salt, which they receive every week. They are only
allowed to eat twice a day. Mack English once tied down a slave named Old
Prince, and gave him one hundred lashes with the whip, and fifty blows
with the paddle, because he could not work fast enough to please him. A
slaveholder named Mr. Wilson died in debt, and my master bought two of
his slave girls, named Rose and Jenny. Jenny was forced to have Adam who
was already married; also her sister Rose was married to March, before
she came on our plantation. Mack English, having turned a wishful eye on
Rose, wrapped himself up in his big cloak, and went to the nigger-house
in the night, and called a slave named Esau, and told him to tell Rose to
come to him, as he wanted her. She sent back to say, "I'm nursing my baby
and can't come." "Go and tell her I don't care about her baby, she must
come," answered Mack, "and if she does not come, I'll give her twenty-five
lashes tomorrow morning." "Go and tell him, Esau, my husband will be
coming, and I can't come," answered she. The next morning he tied her
up and cut her naked back all over; the further particulars are too revolt-
ing to tell.

We will now relate his death. He went with his father one summer to
the White Sulfur Springs. There he was taken ill, and death took place
in five days. His death-bed was a scene of heartrending agony. He swore,
and he cursed, he shrieked "Murder! Murder!! Murder!!! Pa, you stand
here and see all these doctors hunching and punching me. Murder!

Murder!!" Then, as he expired, he shrieked with fearful agony, "God to blast." This I heard from Old Bob, the carriage driver, who was his nurse till his death. The following conversation I overheard when his father returned: "Wife, our son is dead and gone to hell." "Hush! Hush! Talking so before the niggers." "Well, he is; he died cursing and swearing." Just then, Mack's playmate, named Davey Wilson, entered and inquired for him. "Your playmate is dead and gone to hell," was the answer he received. His wife immediately replied, "Hush! Hush! Shut your mouth, you old fool. What are you telling him that for?" Davey Wilson went and told his mother, who told the minister, Mr. Reed, of Mount Zion Church, who preached a sermon to the young people about his death. After that, none of the English's family attended Mount Zion Chapel. When he went to the White Sulfur Springs, I prayed that I might never see him again, and thus was my prayer signally answered. I remembered when he and his father both whipped me at the same time, about sunrise, on my naked back, and then made me work till twelve o'clock without eating anything. I also remember that when he was going to the springs, he said, "When I get back, my father will give me the Creek Swamp plantation and fifty niggers, and then I will buy a cowhide whip, well corded, five feet long, and I'll make all the niggers take Ephraim by force, and tie him to an oak tree and I'll make Adam give him one of the hardest hundred lashes that ever man put on nigger." I, myself, was willed to that tyrant, but God had willed me to myself. Surely the words of the Psalmist came true in this case: "They search out iniquities; they accomplish a diligent search; both the inward thought of every one of them, and the heart, is deep. But God shall shoot at them with an arrow; suddenly shall they be wounded."

CHAPTER II

Reminiscences of My Old Master

We will now speak about my old master, the father of those whom I have spoken of in the above chapter. He was originally a Quaker in North Carolina, United States, but he came to South Carolina and married a lady who had a few slaves. He then set up a liquor store on the Creek Swamp plantation, where he sold to the white people in the daytime, and at night traded with the slaves. He told the slaves round about to steal cotton and bring it to him, and he would give them whiskey for it; but if their masters caught them, they were not to say that they were bringing it to him. The consequence was that some slaves brought one cwt. to him, for which he gave them one gallon of whiskey. The cwt. of cotton was worth fourteen dollars, or about £2 18s. 4d. in English money, and the gallon of whiskey was worth one dollar, or about 4s. 2d.; but the slaves did not know this, and so they were cheated. Others who brought a half-cwt., yet received half a gallon, and so on. This he continued for a long time, until for fear of being betrayed, he put a stop to it. This method of getting rich is very common among the slaveholders of South Carolina. He afterwards became very rich, and owned two plantations, where he hired different overseers to whip his niggers, and he himself whipped them too. He used to work them till nine o'clock at night, and in the winter season he blew the horn at midnight, and put them to killing hogs, and cutting down pine trees, and threshing wheat and oats. He also had a mill on a "branch" and on the other side there is a Church called the Rock Church; he and other masters, made their slaves go to hear the Rev. Mr. Glen preach on such texts as "Servants obey your masters," "Thou shalt not steal," and "He that knew his master's will and did it not, shall be beaten with many stripes." But, after a while, Mr. Glen did not insist sufficiently on that doctrine, and therefore, they drove him away, and different "circuit riders" took his place. These circuit riders are a rascally set. The following is an instance of their wickedness: one of them, as he was riding along the road by the cotton fields where the slaves were working, saw a female slaved named Matilda, who pleased him, and he told her to meet him at such a place. She did so; and when he had accomplished his vile purpose, he gave her a dollar, which turned out to be a bad one. He often preached at St. Luke's Church on Lynch's Creek. If the pastors do such a thing, what will the masters and their sons do? But, to return to my master; he could not bear any one of the negroes to finish his task before sunset; if any did, he would set them such a heavy task next day, that it would be impossible for him to finish it, and then he would give him fifty lashes, which sometimes would cause him to fly to the woods; and when he returned, he would receive one hundred lashes, and fifty blows with the paddle.

A negro woman of the plantation called my mother names, and thereupon my mother and this woman went to fighting; and when my master heard of it, he tied my mother up and gave her ninety lashes, but did not touch the other woman, (called Nancy) as she was his favorite; and there was my mistress looking on and saying, "That's right, put it to her, cut her all to pieces." Among other things, the mule I had to plough with was a very vicious one, and used sometimes to kick the plough out of my hands. Once, as the mule was kicking, my master came into the field, and said that I spoiled the mule; he then at once tied me up and gave me fifty lashes. One morning, as he was going to whip me again, I started off for the swamp, and he set five dogs after me, and said, "Suboy! Suboy! Catch him!" When the dogs came level with me, I clapped my hands also and said, "Suboy! Suboy! Catch him!" as if both my master and I were in chase of a fox or hare ahead of us, and, upon that, the dogs went before me and were soon out of sight, and so I got away. About this time, my master went to the White Sulfur Springs, and hired a man named Burl Quiney, to oversee the plantation during his absence. There was a nigger-driver named Old Peter. Mrs. English told Burl Quiney that he should give the first slave that he took up to whip a pretty good hiding to scare the whole plantation, for that they were a set of niggers never conquered by any overseer that had ever been there. She said so, supposing that I or another slave named Isaac—whom she hated as much as she did me—would be first to be made an example of. But it turned out differently. The task of Old Peter, the nigger-driver, was to see that all the negroes had their proper tasks. When Burl Quiney rode along, he noticed one of the females and said, "Peggy, you shall not do so much work as the rest of the girls today." So he moved the stake back, so that she should do only three tasks instead of four—the allotted quantity of each slave. This was done that she should have time to meet him in the evening. After a time, Old Peter coming along and seeing the stake moved, enquired, "Who moved that stake?" "Massa Burl Quiney," said Peggy, "because I have the cows to milk." Old Peter answered, "Massa makes you do as much as the rest, so I'll move the stake back." When Burl Quiney came back that way and found the stake moved back again, he asked Peggy who moved it. "Uncle Peter," said Peggy. "How dare he move a stake from where a white man put it? Where is he?" said Burl Quiney. "At the other end of the field," replied Peggy. He then rode up to him and said, "Peter, haul off your jacked, sir! How dare you move that stake?" "Massa always makes that girl do as much as the rest," replied Old Peter. Now, the example was to be made of Old Peter, the favorite slave of my mistress. He cut his back with a lash in which wire was interwoven. That evening, old Peter went to the house, and told his mistress that Burl Quiney had cut his back to pieces, because he told Peggy to do as much as the other slaves. "Did he want her to do less?" enquired Mrs. English. "Yes, ma'am." "What for?" "I don't know," he said. But still, old Peter *did* know, but dared not tell his mistress. When Burl Quiney went to supper, Mrs. English said to him, "Mr. Quiney, I did not mean that you should whip Old Peter!" "You made no distinction, madam, but told me that the first one I took up to whip I was to make an example of, to frighten the whole plantation." Next morning, when the horn was blown, Burl Quiney looked anxiously for Old Peter, intending, to give him another whipping for telling his mistress what he did; but he did not make his appearance. So Burl Quiney hastened down to the nigger-house, and there he found Old Peter lying sick from the effects of the whipping of the previous day. Burl Quiney then said, "Peter, did you not hear the horn blow?" "Yes, sir, but I am sick!" "Out with you, sir, or I'll make you sicker than that before I have done with you." So he hauled him out, and kicked and beat him all the way to the field. When he got him there, he said, "Now sir, haul off your jacket, and I am going to give you one hundred lashes!" The old man would not. He then kicked him in the stomach several times, and knocked him down with the butt end of his whip, and said, "Now, cross your hands, sir." And he kicked him, and he cried out to the slaves, "Run here, this man is going to kill me!" The slaves immediately surrounded him; but Burl Quiney seeing them do so, said "Why do you come round me? Go off to your work!" And he ran off a short distance; but we all surrounded him again like blackbirds, and would not go away, because we thought we should frighten him from the old man. Old Peter's daughter went to her mistress, and told her to come and stop Burl Quiney from beating papa; and as she was coming, the slaves cried out to her, "Come on quickly, missus; Burl Quiney is going to kill Uncle Peter!" She answered, "What can I do? Go away from there, you niggers, that man will have you all hung and burnt!" Then, Burl Quiney tied his hands and tied him to a tree, and gave him one hundred lashes; then he ordered him to do his duty, but the poor old nigger-driver was unable. Two slaves, named Isaac and Prince, took him on a hand-barrow to the nigger-house; but Burl Quiney went down and ordered him into the field. He was forced out by the cowhide. When he got to the field, he lay down, and Burl Quiney whipped him up, and again made him discharge his duties; but he lay down again, and was again whipped up with a horrid oath. At twelve o'clock, the horn was again sounded for the negroes to go home to breakfast. But, to return to Old Peter; he was carried home on a mule to the nigger-house, never again to come out of it. He died three days after. A coroner's inquest was held upon the body, and also a post mortem examination and Dr. Gray found that one of his bowels was ruptured. The injury returned the following verdict: "Burl Quiney, overseer to Mr. English, did willfully cause the death of the deceased by whipping with the cowhide." But Burl Quiney answered, "Yes, gentlemen, but Mrs. English was the cause of it." Mrs. English exclaimed, "You are a liar, sir!" The Rev. Thomas English here said, "Sir, if you say that man was the instigation of your killing that old nigger, you are a liar, and the truth is not in you!" Burl Quiney was then committed to jail; and on taking him to Sumterville prison, all three mounted, Burl Quiney having a much better horse than either of the other two. When, therefore, Quiney bade the others "Good night," he put spurs to his horse and was soon out of sight. During the inquest, Thomas English said, "Let this be an example to you niggers;" but I (Jackson) said in my mind, "No, let it be an example to you and your mother."

CHAPTER III

My Mistress

My mistress was a native of South Carolina; she was mean to everybody but her own family; she used to say that the bran flour was too good for the slaves to eat. The sight which most delighted her eyes was to see a slave whipped. John Durant had a large plantation of slaves on Lynch's Creek, which he willed to John Ashmore, his nephew. The uncle was drunk one night, and it was understood that John Ashmore tied a silk handkerchief round his uncle's neck and strangled him, in order to take possession of the property, which he did. He took liberties among the female slaves. Three brothers of the deceased, Alex Durant, Davy Durant, and Dr. Durant, believed that John Ashmore had murdered their brother, and they sued him for the property. The lawsuit was progressing when I left, and some of the negroes were sold to carry it on; but it is most likely John Ashmore won it, as he engaged the best lawyer in Sumterville, named Lawyer Moses. I bought of one of the slaves, who was leaving, a little sow pig, for which I gave three yards of cloth, and took it to Wells' plantation, where my wife lived, and she raised it there and it increased to twenty pigs. My mistress found out that my wife had some hogs; one of the slaves informed me. "Is it Jackson's wife?" said she. "They are his hogs then, and he feeds them on my plantation." She then called my mother: "Old Bet, where does Jackson get food for his hogs?" "They live on the acorns, ma'am." "You are a liar, they feed on my corn," said she; "I will order Ransom Player (the overseer) to give him one hundred lashes and kill all his hogs, the unlawful rascal." He killed one, but I hid the others until I sold them, but I was forced to sell them against my will. A poor man named Daniels determined to get these hogs by stratagem. He asked me what I would take for them, and he told me he would give me twenty dollars. We killed some out of the drove, and for those which were left he offered me thirteen dollars; but I did not sell them for a long time because I knew he would not pity me. He told me if I did not sell them to him, the first time he caught me when patrolling, he would whip me; but I did not mind that either; but when my mistress kept tormenting me about them, I told

Daniels he might have them for thirteen dollars, to get rid of the fuss. He said, "Well, you must bring me a written permission to sell them, before I can buy them." I said, "My mistress hates the Daniels family and won't give me a permission." "Well, Jack, get your wife Louisa to get an order from her owners." My wife got it, so I went one evening, as I was afraid he was not going to give me the money, and said, "Now Mr. Daniels, if you have the thirteen dollars ready I have the order." He replied, "Well, let me see it." "No, you put the money in my hand first." Daniels replied, "No, I can't do that until I see the order." "Well, if you don't give me the thirteen dollars will you give me the order back?" He said, "Yes." "But have you the money with you?" "Oh! Yes," replied Daniels. I then handed him the order. He then read it, and said, "Well, this is as good in my pocket as ten dollars. Now, Jackson, if you interfere with those hogs I'll prosecute you—they are my hogs now." "But you promised to give me the thirteen dollars." "Ah! by George I haven't got it." "Why, you told me you had." "Well, so I have if you can change a one hundred dollar bill." "But I have no money, I thought you were going to give me some, and then fearing you wouldn't I wanted the money first." Now, these Daniels were considered to be great liars. They were once had up before the magistrate for stealing Alex Durant's long-tailed sow; they were tried and sentenced to be whipped in the same manner as a slave; but Lawyer Moses got him out of it. But, to return to the hogs they were about to steal from me. Daniels told me to bring my wife Louisa, and he would pay her, which I did. He then put us off, telling us to come next week, and so on, week after week, till we found out it was no use, for he did not intend to pay us. The last time I went, on going to the gate, the dogs were barking furiously, and the old father came out, and said, with a horrid oath, "Who is that?" "It's me," said I. "What do you want?" "I have brought Louisa for the money." "Well," said he, "my son ain't at home." I stood there in the dark, when the son came out and said, "Where is she?" I said, "Here I am." "Have you got your wife with you?" "Yes." "Well, I ain't got the money yet." We went away sorrowfully; he never paid us a cent of the money.

My mistress's expressed opinion was this, "Never to give the niggers any meat; for where she was brought up a dry peck of corn and a pint of salt was all that was allowed to niggers per week." My master, her husband, did as she said, so that we were often on the verge of starvation. Nevertheless, she had a favorite dog, which she called "Old Rip," of the mastiff breed, which she continually fed with meat that we would give anything to possess. She would tie the female slaves, who did the domestic work, to trees or bedposts, whichever was handiest, and whip them severely with a

dogwood or hickory switch, for the slightest offence, and often for nothing at all apparently, but merely for the purpose of keeping up her practice. She would also make her daughters whip them, and thus she brought
up her children in the way they should not go, and in consequence, when
they were old they did not depart from it. Through her my mother got
many a hundred lashes. Since my escape I heard of the death of my mother.
My mistress had two household gods, viz., her bunch of keys, in which she
manifested a peculiar interest, and her brandy bottle, which she consulted
with a frequency which was most alarming, especially when she was drunk
it was her invariable practice to attack the cook (one Ann Dolly) most
unmercifully with the broomstick.

CHAPTER IV
My Youthful Days

My first employment was that of a scarecrow in the corn fields. I was
driven into the field at the earliest dawn of day, and I did not leave the
field till sunset. My food was a cake made by mixing Indian meal with
water and a little salt, and which was then baked in the ashes. This I had
to take to the field to subsist on during the day. When I was older I had to
manage the plough. Being young, I had not sufficient strength to hold the
plough steadily; in consequence of which, my master used to follow me
from end to end of the field, beating me over the head with a cowhide. On
our way across the field one of the leashes happening to touch the mule,
it kicked the plough from my hands, for which my master stripped me
totally naked, and beat me till my back was covered with blood. My brothers, and indeed, all of my age shared the same fate with me. The horses
were usually turned out at night into the field, and it was my duty to bring
them home before daylight. The horses, however, apparently anxious to
escape the hard work imposed on man and beast alike, had hid themselves
in a wood which abounded with rattlesnakes. This caused me great fear as
I was barefooted. After a hard hunt I succeeded in finding them. However,
on my arrival home, I was tied up and beaten severely by both my master
and son at the same time. I was also ox-driver, and in that capacity, I was
sent to Wilson's Steam Saw Mill for planks, on various occasions. When
the account was rendered, my master was surprised at the number of
planks he had used, and to escape paying for the whole, he declared that
I had fetched the planks for myself, which was a diabolical falsehood. I
wanted no planks, and had I wanted them, I should not have got them in
that way, as I should have been sure to have been found out. Nevertheless,

to carry conviction that his word was true, he took me before Mr. Wilson's house, and stripped me, and gave me fifty lashes.

About this time, I fell in love with a slave girl named Louisa, who belonged to a Mrs. Wells, whose plantation was about a mile off. Mrs. Wells was a comparatively kind mistress. Shortly after, I married Louisa. Do not let the reader run away with the idea that there was any marriage ceremony, for the poor slaves are debarred that privilege by the cruel hand of the fellow-man. My master was exceedingly angry when he heard of my marriage, because my children would not belong to him, and whenever he discovered that I had visited my wife's plantation during the night, I was tied up and received fifty lashes. But no man can be prevented from visiting his wife, and the consequence was, that I was beaten on the average, at least every week for that offense. I shall carry these scars to my grave. My wife had two children, one of whom died. But we were soon separated, as her owner removed to Georgia, and we were parted for ever.

Our clothes were rags, and we were all half naked, and the females were not sufficiently clothed to satisfy common decency.

I will now refer to the "American Camp-Meeting," which is held in tents, and is a gathering of both black and white Methodists for worship and prayer. It is continued day by day for a week; but the blacks can only attend during Saturday night and part of Sunday, having to be at work again early on Monday morning. These meetings are infested by a set of white people, who are libertine scoundrels, and attend for the purpose of seizing and carrying off by force, for their own vile purposes, the most beautiful slave girls they can see. On the father's interfering to save their daughters, they only receive a shower of blows on the head with hickory sticks. I often saw this with my own eyes, and not daring to say a word. One of these wretches, John Mulder by name, having seized a negro's wife, on their way to the camp-meeting, and threatening the husband's life with a pistol, was knocked down senseless by the enraged husband with a stick. In consequence of which, a Lynch law was made that no negro should carry a stick. It is no wonder that this is the case, for "If the blind lead the blind, they will both fall into the ditch;" and the Methodist ministers there are notorious for their villainy. As an instance of the truth of this, I may mention the case of the Rev. Thomas English, of whom we have already spoken, and indeed I could give many instances too vile to speak about. It was the custom among them when conducting the Lord's Supper, to have the white people partake first, and then say to the negroes—"Now, all you niggers that are humble and obedient servants to your masters can come and partake." The negroes said among themselves "There is no back kitchen in heaven;" but if they had been overheard, they would have been whipped severely. I fear this case will be an example of the truth of our Lord's saying, "The first shall be last and the last first."

We were now put to picking cotton. This is not so pleasant a job as might be imagined. The whole field is covered with "stinging worms," a species of caterpillar. At the setting of the sun each slave had to bring one hundred weight of cotton, which many of the weaker slaves could not do. In consequence of this, each night there were two hours' whipping at the "ginning house." The masters would not even allow them their usual night's rest. They made them pack cotton before daylight, and as soon as twenty bales were packed they were sent off to Charleston. The cotton plant is planted in April or May, and the cotton is picked out of the pods in August. The heat of that month raises large bumps on the slaves' backs; besides, the frequent infliction of the whip and the lash is almost intolerable. One slave, named "Old Prince," because he could not do sufficient work, was continually being beaten. On one occasion, he received fifty lashes, and fifty blows with the paddle—a paddle is a board six inches broad, and eight inches long, with twelve gimlet holes in it; each of these holes raised a blister every time a blow was inflicted, which rendered it extremely painful—in a few days the skin all peeled off his lacerated body. At this time we were under the control of Burl Quiney, who murdered Old Peter, as related before. He also murdered four negroes belonging to James Rambert. Wherever he was overseer, he succeeded in murdering one or more negroes. He used to make the negroes shuck corn till past midnight, and they had to rise with the sun next morning to their day's work. They are not allowed a change of clothes, but only one suit for summer, and the perspiration is so great that they smell rank; thus they are robbed of comfort and cleanliness by the cruelty and avarice of their masters. They wear no shoes, and they had to work in "the New Ground," a place infested by snakes and scorpions, and they were often bitten by snakes, while 6,000,000 of lazy white men are riding about calling negroes lazy, whilst they are the laziest.

CHAPTER V
My Escape

A slave on a neighboring plantation had a pony; it being discovered by his mistress, she ordered the overseer, the Rev. P. Huggin, to kill it. Meanwhile, I went in the night and purchased it of the slave with some fowls. As my master had just then gone out of his mind I could keep it with greater impunity, so that at length I went to a camp meeting on it. My mistress' grandson saw me on it, and told Ransom Player, the overseer, and my mistress ordered him to give me one hundred lashes, and to kill the pony. When he attempted to tie me I resisted and fled, and swam across a mill pond, which was full of alligators, and so escaped the whipping. I went to work next day, and kept a look out for them. My mistress hearing of it, said to the overseer, Mr. Player, "You can't whip that nigger yourself, wait till Rev. T. English, and Mr. M'Farden, and Mr. Cooper, are here, and then you can catch him in the barn." The last two were her sons-in-law. I kept the pony hid in the woods till Christmas.

We all had three days' holiday at Christmas, and I, therefore, fixed upon that time as most appropriate for my escape. I may as well relate here, how I became acquainted with the fact of there being a Free State. The "Yankees," or Northerners, when they visited our plantations, used to tell the negroes that there was a country called England, where there were no slaves, and that the city of Boston was free; and we used to wish we knew which way to travel to find those places. When we were picking cotton, we used to see the wild geese flying over our heads to some distant land, and we often used to say to each other, "O that we had wings like those geese, then we could fly over the heads of our masters to the 'Land of the free.'" I had often been to Charleston—which was 150 miles distant from our plantation—to drive my master's cattle to market, and it struck me that if I could hide in one of the vessels I saw landing at the wharfs, I should be able to get to the "Free country," wherever that was. I fixed, as I said before, on our three days' holiday at Christmas, as my best time for escape. The first day I devoted to bidding a sad, though silent farewell to my people; for I did not even dare to tell my father or mother that I was going, lest for joy they should tell some one else. Early next morning, I left them playing their "fandango" play. I wept as I looked at them enjoying their innocent play, and thought it was the last time I should ever see them, for I was determined never to return alive. However, I hastened to the woods and started on my pony. I met many white persons, and was hailed, "You nigger, how far are you going?" To which I would answer, "To the next plantation, mas're;" but I took good care not to stop at the next plantation. The first night I stopped at G. Nelson's plantation. I stopped with the negroes, who thought I had got leave during Christmas. Next morning, before day, I started on for the Santé River. The negro who kept that ferry, was allowed to keep for himself all the money he took on Christmas day, and as this was Christmas day, he was only too glad to get my money and ask no questions; so I paid twenty cents, and he put me and my pony across the main gulf of the river, but he would not put me across to the "Bob Landing;" so that I had to wade on my pony through a place called "Sandy Pond" and "Boat Creek." The current was so strong there, that I and my pony were nearly washed down the stream; but after hard struggling, we succeeded in getting across. I went eight miles further, to Mr. Shipman's hotel, where one Jessie Brown, who hired me of my master, had often stopped. I stayed there until midnight, when I got my pony and prepared to start. This roused Mr. Shipman's suspicions, so he asked me where I belonged to. I was scared, but at length, I said, "Have you not seen me here with Jesse Brown, driving cattle?" He said, "Yes, I know Jesse Brown well. Where are you going?" I answered, "I am going on my Christmas holiday." This satisfied him. I was going to take a longer holiday than he thought for. I reached Charleston by the next evening. There I met a negro, who allowed me to put my pony in his master's yard, his master being out of town at the time. It is the custom there, for the masters to send their slaves out in the morning to earn as much money as they can, how they like. So I joined a gang of negroes working on the wharfs, and received a dollar-and-a-quarter per day, without arousing any suspicion. Those negroes have to maintain themselves, and clothe themselves, and pay their masters two-and-a-half dollars per week out of this, which, if they fail to do, they receive a severe castigation with a cat-o'-nine-tails. One morning, as I was going to join a gang of negroes working on board a vessel, one of them asked me if I had my badge? Every negro is expected to have a badge with his master's name and address inscribed on it. Every negro unable to produce such badge when asked for, is liable to be put in jail. When I heard that, I was so frightened that I hid myself with my pony, which I sold that night for seven-and-a-half dollars, to a negro. I then bought a cloak from a Jewish lady, who cheated me, and gave me a lady's cloak instead of a man's, which, however, answered my purpose equally well. I then got seven biscuit-loaves of bread, and a bottle of water which I put in my pocket, and I also bought a large gimlet and two knives. I then found I had over ten dollars left of what I had earned. I then went to the wharf early in the morning with my cloak on, and underneath all my rattletraps. A few days previously, I had enquired of a mulatto negro, for a vessel bound for Boston. I then went on board and asked the cook, a free negro, if his vessel was bound for Boston? To which he replied, "Yes." "Can't you stow me away?" said I. "Yes, "said he, "but don't you betray me! Did not some white man send you here to ask me this?" "No." "Well," answered he, "don't you betray me! for we black men have been in jail ever since the vessel has been here; the captain stood bond for us yesterday and took us out." "What did they put you in jail for?" said I. "They put every free negro in jail that comes here, to keep them from going among the slaves. Well, I will look out a place to stow you away, if you are sure no white man has sent you here." So I went the next morning to ask him to redeem his promise. I went on board, and saw him lighting a fire in his galley, so I said to him, "Now I am ready for you to stow me away." "Walk ashore, I will have nothing to do with you; I am sure some white person sent you here." I said "No, no one knows it but me and you." "I don't believe it," said he, "so you walk ashore;" which I did. But as I looked back, I saw him go into the galley again and shut the door, so I went on board the vessel again, and crept stealthily on tiptoe to the hatch. I stood there fearing and hoping—fearing lest the cook should come out of the galley, and hoping that the mate or captain would come from the cabin, and order me to take off the hatch. Presently the mate came out of the cabin, and I asked him if I should take off the hatch. He, thinking that I was one of the gang coming to work there, told me I might. So I immediately took off the hatch, and descended. The gang soon came down; they asked me, "Are you going to work here this morning?" I said, "No." "Aren't you a stevedore?" I said, "No." "I know better, I know by that cloak you wear. Who do you belong to?" I answered, "I belong to South Carolina." It was none of their business whom I belonged to; I was trying to belong to myself. Just then they were all ordered on deck, and as soon as I was left, I slipped myself between two bales of cotton, with the deck above me, in a space not large enough for a bale of cotton to go; and just then a bale was placed at the mouth of my crevice, and shut me in a space about 4-ft. by 3-ft., or thereabouts. I then heard them gradually filling up the hold; and at last the hatch was placed on, and I was left in total darkness. I should have been stifled for want of air, but by the providence of God, a board in the partition between the sailors' sleeping place and the hold where I was, was broken out, so that the air came through there. Next morning, I heard the sailors singing their farewell songs, and soon after, the vessel began to rock from side to side. I then began to feel that I was indeed, now upon my journey from slavery to freedom, and that I soon should be able to call myself FREE, and I felt so happy, and rejoiced so in my heart; but all these feelings were rudely stopped by a feeling of sickness, and the more the vessel went, the sicker I got, till I felt as miserable as I was happy before. I then began to bore with my gimlet, and after a long time, I was able to bore two holes in the deck with great labor, through which I could see the sailors passing and re-passing overhead. By this time I found that my water was exhausted, and I began to feel all the horrors of thirst. I felt that

I could with pleasure have drunk the filthiest water in my native swamps. I cast my eyes up through the gimlet holes and saw the stars, and I thought that God would provide for me, and the stars seemed to be put there by Him to tell me so; and then I felt that He would care for me as He did for Jonah in the whale's belly, and I was refreshed. Next morning I saw through the holes, a man standing over them with his arms folded, apparently in deep thought, so I called out, "Pour me some water down, I am most dead for water." He, however, looked up instead, and persisted in examining the rigging, apparently thinking the voice came from there, so I cut a splinter and pushed it through the hole to attract his attention; as soon as he caught sight of it, he ran away and called to the captain, "Run here, cap'n, there is a ghost aboard!" The captain came and knelt down and examined the holes, and asked me how I came there? I said, "I got stowed away." He asked me if some white man did not stow him away to get him in trouble? I assured him he was mistaken, as I stowed myself away. The cook said, "Cap'n, there was one wanted me to stow him away at Charleston, but I would not." "Cook, you should have told me that," said the captain. "Boys, get the chisel and cut him out." As soon as I was out, I saw the cook preparing to wash his hands, and I seized upon the water and drained it to the last drop. It was nearly half-a-gallon.

The vessel continued her journey to Boston. The captain persisted that some white man had placed me there to get him into trouble; and said he would put me into the first vessel he met, and send me back; however, he met no vessel, and we gradually approached Boston. At last the pilot come on board, and I was sent into the forecastle to prevent his seeing me, and we soon arrived at Boston. At nine o'clock on the evening of the 10th of February, 1847, I landed at Boston, and then indeed I thanked God that I had escaped from hell to heaven, for I felt as I had never felt before—that is, master *of myself*, and in my joy I was as a bouncing sparrow. Three sailors names Jim Jones, Frank, and Dennis, took me to the sailor's boarding-house, kept by one Henry Forman, Richmond-street, and I became his servant, and worked for him, and received my board as payment. About June I left him, and went to Salem, and worked for James Brayton, Samuel Pittman, and many others, in the tan yards. I received a dollar-and-a-half per day, out of which I saved one hundred dollars in the course of a year, which I put in the savings bank. I used often to work at sawing wood during the night, and it did not seem such a hardship as when I did the same in South Carolina. Why? Because I felt that I was free, and that I worked because I wished; whilst in South Carolina I worked because my master compelled me. This *fact* is, in my mind, more satisfactory than twenty theories, as to the superiority of free labor over slave labor. When I was a slave we were employed the whole of the day in breaking and hauling home the corn, and then when night came on we were not allowed to snatch an instant's sleep until we had shucked the whole of the corn brought in during the day; so that it was generally between one and two o'clock in the morning before we were allowed to rest our weary bodies. As soon as dawn appeared we were roused by the overseer's whip, for we we were so exhausted that the horn failed to rouse us as usual; and then we would discover that the rats had actually eaten a part of our feet. As the slaves are not allowed boots or shoes (except for a short time in the winter), the combined action of the frost at night, and the heat during the day, harden the feet; so that the outside skin at last cracks, and is very painful to the negroes. This outside skin is called "dead skin," as the slaved cannot *feel* the rats eating it until their teeth touch the more tender part of the feet. During the day, that part of the foot which has been skinned by the rats is very tender and causes great pain. The presence of rats in our houses brought venomous snakes, who frequented them for the purpose of swallowing the rats, and who sometimes bit the negroes, and then my father's power of curing snakebites was called into play. On one occasion there was a sale of slaves near, and a man came to the auction to purchase a slave girl. He fixed on one who pleased him, and took her into a neighboring barn and stripped her *stark naked,* for the purpose of examining her, as he would a horse, previous to buying her. The father and mother of the girl were looking through the window and keyhole and various crevices, with many other slaves, who saw all that passed. He ultimately purchased her for his own vile purposes, and when he had had several children by her, sold both her and her children. Marriage in the slave States among the slaves is absolutely "Nil." There was on one plantation, a slave about thirty years of age and six feet high, named Adam. He had a wife on a neighboring plantation belonging to Mr. Hancock. My master bought a young slave girl about fourteen years old, named Jenny Wilson, and he then ordered Adam to leave his present wife and take Jenny. Adam, after having some hundreds of lashes for obstinately persisting in loving his wife, at last consented, but not so Jenny, who was in love with me and I with her. But she was at last compelled to obey her master by the bloody cowhide. My master served nearly all his male slaves in the similar manner. One of his slaves, however, named Abraham, was unusually obstinate, and would not give up his wife. At last my master, in despair, sent him to his son-in-law's plantation, Gamble M[c]Farden, who was an inveterate drunkard, and who murdered my sister Bella, as related elsewhere. He ordered Abraham not to go up to see his wife any more; but Abraham loved his wife too much to be parted from her in that manner, so he went fifteen long miles once every fortnight, on the Saturday night, for the pleasure of seeing his wife for a short time. He was found out, and whipped to death by that drunkard Mr. M[c]Farden. My brother Ephraim did not escape; he was compelled to leave his wife and marry the house girl.

But I am wandering. While I was at Salem, I heard from Mr. Forman, that Anderson, my old slave-driver, had called for me. I will give some incidents that will illustrate his character. He was brought up among the negroes, and was so familiar with negro habits, that he possessed unusual facilities for getting them into trouble. He was hired for the purpose of subduing me and another slave named Isaac, but fortunately my escape saved me from experiencing his tender mercies.

In the adjacent swamp there was an abundance of wild turkeys, the sight of which greatly tantalized the negroes, as they had no gun to shoot them with. On one occasion my father, old Doctor Clavern, had made a pen to catch the wild turkeys with. This soon came to the ears of Anderson, and he immediately sought out my father, and accosted him with "Old Doc. Clave., where is your turkey pen?" "In the swamp, massa." "Tell me where it is? Turkeys are too good for niggers." "I can't exactly tell where it is, massa." "Then I will find out and destroy it; for turkeys are too good for niggas." He fully carried out his threat; for soon afterwards he discovered the pen, and destroyed it. When he next met with my father, he said, "Old Doc. Clave., does you catch turkeys now?" "No, massa Anderson; somebody spoil my pen." "Twas I spoiled it, you rascal, so that you should not catch turkeys any more." This may serve to show his badness of disposition. On another occasion, I had made a fish trap in the stream which ran through the swamp. Anderson heard of it, and organized a party to proceed to the swamp, and search for it. After a long search they succeeded in discovering it, and took all the fish out, and destroyed it, for the simple reason that "fish was too good for niggers." Owing to his having been brought up among negroes, he was perfectly familiar with their peculiarities of dialect, &c. If he suspected that any negroes had fresh meat, obtained as narrated above, he would sneak to the nigger houses in the dead of night, and say, in their peculiar manner, "Brudder, ope' t' door; I want to 'peak to you for a minnit." This would deceive the negroes, and they would open the door, expecting to see another negro, when, to their amazement and confusion, it would be "Neddy Anderson," as he was called. "O you rascals!" he would say, "you got fresh meat here; you steal it;" and next day they would have so many lashes for daring to eat meat, or whatever it might be. He was accustomed to be hired to whip negroes, and he used to revel in this (to him) delightful occupation. He would sneak about during the night, for the purpose of catching negroes wandering from their plantations, so that he might have the pleasure of whipping them. I heard since my escape, of my mother's death, and that she died under him. I therefore cannot but conclude that my mistress, who hated her, incited him to whip her in particular, and that, horrible to think of, she must have died under his lash. I believe, also, that my youngest brother, Casey, must have fallen a victim to his cruelty; for I have heard of his death also, and that Anderson had given him some severe whippings. Had I sufficient space I could fill a volume with instances of his wickedness and cruelty. But, to proceed—he was so anxious to catch me that he followed me to Boston—at least, I believe, from the description given by Mr. Forman, that it was he; but fortunately I had gone to Salem, which is 15 miles from Boston. Mr. Forman did not tell Anderson where I was, but merely told him that there was no such person as Jackson there. Anderson said, "I know better, here is the letter he wrote home, wishing to know what he can buy his father and mother for, and I now want to see him." This incensed the sailors, who said, "Here are the slave-hunters, hunting for niggers," and drove them from the house. Mr. Forman wrote to me at Salem, to warn me not to come to Boston, as they were hunting for me there. I remained at Salem, and worked in the tan yard there, turning the splitting machine, until I had saved one hundred dollars. Since my escape I have saved about one thousand dollars of my own earnings, for the purpose of purchasing my relatives. I was in correspondence with some gentlemen in America, through my friend the Rev. C. H. Spurgeon, for that purpose, when the present war interrupted and broke up my hopes and plans. If this war obviates the necessity of buying my people, by freeing the negroes, (as I hope and pray to God it will, and as I believe it will) I shall then, if God pleases, devote my money in building a Chapel in Canada, for escaped slaves; or wherever my old fellow-laborers are located. Though "absent in the body," my whole heart is with my fellow-sufferers in that horrible bondage; and I will exert myself until the last of my relatives is released. On one occasion I saw my brother Ephraim tied up and blindfolded with his own shirt, and beaten with fifty lashes before his own wife and children, by a wretch named Sam Cooper, because he was falsely accused of having stolen a yard of bagging. Fathers! Think of being tied up and stripped before your wife and children, and beaten severely for nothing at all; and then think that it is a daily, nay, hourly, occurrence in the slave states of America, and you will begin to have some idea of what

American slavery is. But to proceed with my life. Just as I was beginning to be settled at Salem, that most atrocious of all laws, the "Fugitive Slave Law," was passed, and I was compelled to flee in disguise from a comfortable home, a comfortable situation, and good wages, to take refuge in Canada. I may mention that during my flight from Salem to Canada, I met with a very sincere friend and helper, who gave me a refuge during the night, and set me on my way. Her name was Mrs. Beecher Stowe. She took me in and fed me, and gave me some clothes and five dollars. She also inspected my back, which is covered with scars which I shall carry with me to the grave. She listened with great interest to my story, and sympathized with me when I told her how long I had been parted from my wife Louisa and my daughter Jenny, and perhaps, for ever. I was obliged to proceed, however, and finally arrived in safety at St. John's, where I met my present wife, to whom I was married lawfully, and who was also an escaped slave from North Carolina. I stayed there some time, and followed the trade of whitewasher, and at last I embarked for England. When I arrived at Liverpool, I proceeded to Scotland, where I met with true friends of abolition. I lectured in most of the Free Churches there, including Dr. Candlish's, Dr. Guthrie's, and Mr. Alexander Wallis's. I lectured twice in Dr. Candlish's Church. I then proceeded to Aberdeen, where I lectured to crowded audiences; and I then fell in with more friends, until I met with the Rev. Mr. Barker, of Huddersfield, who directed me to the Rev. C. H. Spurgeon, who received me and my wife into his Church as members, and who has been my firm friend and adviser ever since. I am now only anxious for the war to end with freedom to the oppressed (for I firmly believe that will be its ultimate issue), and then I will revisit the old scenes of oppression, and read the Bible to those to whom it has long been a sealed Book. May God hasten this happy consummation.

CHAPTER VI

American Butterfly and Slavery

A bad man called Old Ben Calo, who was nearly seven feet high, used to go about ditching for different slaveholders, far too lazy to work on his own plantation in the Pine Woods. On one occasion, he wanted me to steal from my master a bushel of corn for him, which I refused to do. This annoyed him very much, and, in the course of time, he came to my white people and told them that he saw me the night before on a horse, and that he believed me to be trading with Tom Hancock. This he did to gain their favor. They then asked him how he knew it was me. "I know it was him," he replied. "It might have been a white man," said they. "No; I am sure it was Jackson, for I waited some time for him to return on this side of the branch. After I had started to go home, I heard a noise on the horses' feet coming behind. As he approached, I gave him the road, and ordered him to stop; he disregarded this and galloped by. I then pulled the trigger of my gun three times to shoot him, but it would not fire, because he bewitched it." Foolish man—if what he said was true—God alone preserved my life that night. Ben Calo is not the only man who acts so deceitfully; there are scores whom I might mention. One more instance I will mention here of a man named Squire Sanders; he lived in South Carolina, Sumter District; he had been in the habit for a long time of trading secretly with slaves, which trading he, of course, found very profitable; and he encouraged them to steal cotton, corn, etc. He was at least suspected of having received stolen property. Thereupon, James Laws and another slaveholder, at once hit on the following plan to find him out: they placed a basket of cotton on the head of one of their own slaves, named Job. Previous to this, however, a negro from the same plantation, named Alex, ran ahead on purpose to inform Squire Sanders that his master was coming that night to test his honesty, and begged him not to purchase anything, of any slave that might come to him. "Well, my boy," said the Squire joyfully, "if I find this to be true, I will make you a present of five dollars." Between ten and eleven o'clock, Job arrived, followed at a distance by his master on horseback. The dogs began to bark, and Squire Sanders came out to enquire what was the matter. "Who's that?" he asked. "James Law's Job," was the answer. "What do you want?" "I have some cotton for you." "Have you got an order from your master to bring me cotton this time of night?" "No, sir," said Job. "How dare you bring me cotton here without an order? Go along back, and to-morrow I will see your master about this." James Law then returned, convinced in his own mind that the Squire was an honest man, and did not trade with slaves. And Alex received his five dollars. So the Squire went on trading as usual; but he adopted the plan of having the cotton taken to one of the negro-houses, and received by Abraham, a negro. This I know to be the truth.

American Butterfly

The character of the slaveholder, is to work his slaves very hard so that they may not get up in the night to raise an insurrection, or carry off cotton or corn to other masters who trade with slaves at night. "The harder we work them," say they, "the sounder they will sleep until we blow the horn to put them to work next day." The butterfly, and bumble bee, and the mosquito-hawk, fly from blossom to blossom to blossom through the cotton fields, enjoying the glorious liberty which is denied to the slaves. A circumstance occurred in the cotton fields, during a very heavy thunderstorm, which I think is worthy of notice here. The thunder and lightning was terrific, frightening the most hardened. One old negro sinner named Munday, who was ploughing in the field, and who was swearing fearfully, was struck dead by the lightning.

The lightning once burnt a space of ground in the cotton fields, and nothing afterwards ever grew on that spot.

We will now turn to the hawk and the owl. The hawk snatched away chickens from the hen during the day, and the owl steals them at night, yet the slave is not allowed to have a gun to shoot them. I went one Sunday to see my old aunt, and I came back through my master's pasture, three miles in length and about the same in width, killing snakes and scorpions as I went along, until I came up to a region where the great storm—which we call a hurricane—had torn up the pine trees by the roots. On one of these trees there was a large head, which frightened me; it had large dreadful-looking eyes, which turned as I walked on. I afterwards discovered this to be an owl, not able to fly; but the head was quite as large as a full-grown owl's. I succeeded in killing this, but not until I had a sharp fight with the old ones, who were overhead, and who followed me quite half a mile, knowing I had taken their young one. The slaveholders live upon their slaves just as the hawk and owl live upon the hen and chicken.

The Methodists and Independents hold slaves, as also do the Baptists.

CHAPTER VII
The Negro Songs

I fear that this chapter will prove to many rather uninteresting; but at the same time, there are many who, I am quite sure, would wish to know what *are* the songs with which the negroes beguile their leisure hours. The following is one of them, and a great favorite among the negroes.

A SPIRITUAL HYMN

"O Sheperd, wha' thou bin all day,
O Shepherd, wha' thou bin all day,
O Shepherd, wha' thou bin all day,
You promised my Jesus to mind these lambs,
And he pays you at the coming day.
O children, he pays you at the coming day,

O children, he pays you at the coming day,
O children, he pays you at the coming day,
O Shepherd, the lambs all gone astray,
O Shepherd, the lambs all gone astray,
O Shepherd, the lambs all gone astray,
You promised my Jesus to mind these lambs,
And he pays you at the coming day.
O children, he pays you at the coming day,
O children, he pays you at the coming day,
O children, he pays you at the coming day.
Did you ever see such a carriage roll,
Did you ever see such a carriage roll,
Did you ever see such a carriage roll,
And it rolls like judgment day.
O children, it rolls like judgment day,
O children, it rolls like judgment day,
O children, it rolls like judgment day.
The fore-wheel roll by the grace of God,
The fore-wheel roll by the grace of God,
The fore-wheel roll by the grace of God,
And the hind-wheel roll by faith.
O children, the hind-wheel roll by faith,
O children, the hind-wheel roll by faith,
O children, the hind-wheel roll by faith.
It roll for me and it roll for you,
It roll for me and it roll for you,
It roll for me and it roll for you,
And it roll for the whole world round.
O children, it roll for the whole world round,
O children, it roll for the whole world round,
O children, it roll for the whole world round.
My Jesus he put on the long white robe,
My Jesus he put on the long white robe,
My Jesus he put on the long white robe,
And he sail thro' Galilee.
O children, he sail thro' Galilee,
O children, he sail thro' Galilee,
O children, he sail thro' Galilee.
He sail for me and he sail for you,
He sail for me and he sail for you,

> He sail for me and he sail for you,
> And he sail for the whole world round.
> O children, he sail for the whole world round,
> O children, he sail for the whole world round,
> O children, he sail for the whole world round."

This hymn is a great favorite with the slaves, and is sung by them while they clap their hands to keep time. Probably the reason for the number of repeats, is because they have no books allowed them; and indeed, they cannot read, and therefore, on hearing a single line sung by the white people, these poor slaves cannot prize it too much, as is shown by their singing it over and over.

The following is a favorite hymn of the poor negroes in the dusk of eventide, or on the dark night, after work:

> "We shall hear the trumpet sounding
> 'Fore the break of day,
> We'll take the wings of th' morning,
> And fly away to my Canaan land,
> Bright angels shall come to bear my soul
> To my rosen, rosen* Lamb."

*rosen, probably a corruption of risen.

This hymn was often to me a sweet solace after a hard day's work under the horrible tyranny of slavery. It used to refresh us to think that heaven was so near, and that soon we should be there.

The following is perhaps, not quite so intelligible as the previous one:—

> "Oh, me an' my wife we'er hand in hand,
> And all our children in one band—
> They honour the Lamb.
> Oh, silver slippers on my feet,
> We'll slip and slide thro' paradise,
> And honour the Lamb."

It must be remembered that these hymns are composed of fragments of hymns, which we had heard sung at the meeting-houses and camp-meetings of the white men. Under these circumstances, it is indeed wonderful that they are as intelligible as they are. A few more may, perhaps, be acceptable to the reader. This one we used to sing when in some such spirit as was David of old, when he indicated that interesting Psalm, beginning "Truly God is good to Israel." (lxxiii.)

> "Old Satan told me to my face
> He'd drag my kingdom down;
> But Jesus whispered in my ears
> He'd build it up again.
>
> CHORUS
> Oh, we'll walk and talk 'bout Jesus,
> Glory, hallelujah!
> Oh, we'll walk and talk 'bout Jesus,
> Glory to my soul."

We used to sing this when we had seen the wicked in high places, and the servants of God suffering injustice. But when we had sung this we considered the end, and saw that they were set in slippery places. Our hymns were all we could get of real spiritual food, and yet they were blest by God to the conversion of many, and to the building up of his saints. "Truly out of the mouths of babes and sucklings hath he perfected praise."

After we had sung one of these songs, we would kneel down, and one of us would offer prayer, and then we would spring up and strike up a new song—one of joy and gladness:—

> "Oh, what a happy day
> When the Christian people meet,
> They shall meet to part no more.
> Tracks I see and I'll pursue
> The narrow way to heaven I view,
> Jesus, my all, to heaven is gone,
> He whom I fix my hopes upon.
>
> CHORUS
> Oh, what a happy day, &c., &c."

It will be seen more particularly from the foregoing, that the negroes compose their songs chiefly from snatches of hymns which they hear sung by the white people, interpolated, it is true, with now and then a line of the original. Judge them not harshly, gentle reader, for their plagiarism, if such it may be called, for were you in their position, we doubt if you could do better.

As perhaps these slave songs may be interesting to the reader, I will give two or three more, with which I will conclude:—

> "I want to go where Moses gone,
> Glory, hallelujah!

> I want to go to the promised land,
> Glory, hallelujah!
> Sweet milk and honey overflows,
> Glory, hallelujah!"

These lines would be repeated with great energy, the hallelujah being sometimes in the middle of the line, or in its legitimate position; thus:—

> "I want to go, hallelu', hallelu',
> Where Moses gone, hallelu', hallelu', hallelu."

The following may show our feelings with regard to death

> "Death, O death, O where are you going?
> Oh hallelu', hallelu', hallelujah!
> I'm coming for some of your souls,
> Oh hallelu', hallelu', hallelujah!"

We feared not death, but would rather welcome it with songs, for we, ignorant as we are, felt that we should receive the "Crown of Life."

It is remarkable to notice that, although the poor negroes are but very little acquainted with the Sacred Scriptures, yet the Almighty, apparently to show man the futility of attempting to keep the mind of his fellow-man in ignorance of Him, has imparted to the poor despised one a species of subtlety in acquiring religious knowledge, which may appear to those who are not personally acquainted with the fact, extraordinary and impossible. If God so honor the negro, and if He works for his deliverance from bondage as He has been doing, ought we to be idle? Surely if we stand calmly by, and see our brother murdered, shall not we be guilty of his blood? Some have blamed "Abolitionists: for over-zealousness; but surely no one could be too zealous for the destruction of a system which works, or can work, as described in these pages. "Let us be up and doing, for the night cometh when no man *can* work."

> "Oh, early in the morning,
> Early in the evening,
> Then we'll shout glory, glory, in my soul.
> Old fathers, can't you ride and tell?
> Bless the Lord, we'll rise and tell,
> Then we'll shout glory, glory, in my soul."

This the slaves sing to keep time while picking cotton in the field under the burning sun; soon after, the whiplash falls on their backs by their drunken masters and overseers, till the blood runs down. And still they say that the slaves are better off than the working people in free countries, which is as big a lie as ever was told.

A man by the name of Stevondecause, in South Carolina, kept a store-house at the cross road, over the mill branch. There he sold liquor and other things to the white people at daytime; he enticed the negroes to steal at night cotton and corn, and other things, for which he gave them liquor and one thing or another; and he steals it from them by not giving them what it is worth, and tells them to go and steal more, and not let their masters see them. And when he got rich enough to buy niggers himself, he stopped trading with the others. He went across Black River Swamp, where he bought plantation, and was one of the worst masters that ever lived. He was afraid to let any of his niggers leave his plantation at night, and told them if they did he would whip them; and why, because it takes a rough to catch a rough, and he is afraid they will steal his cotton, as he got other masters' niggers to steal for him to make him rich. Mr. Neddy Anderson, and William Miles, and Stevondecause, are very bad men—more like beasts than men—they used to go about all the plantations on Sunday nights, and frighten the negroes that used to come together to hold prayer-meetings, chasing them here and there, and whipping as many as they could catch without a pass. Mr. Anderson spends a great deal of his time in plaiting whips to whip the negroes with; my mistress hired him as overseer to come and flog all the negroes, and me in particular, after Christmas, because I had a black pony. But she gave us three days at Christmas, and I have not been home since; for I and the pony gave them leg-bail for security, and thank God, got safe to a free state.

Two negroes were being taken away from their families in chains to the new countries, on the way there, the master stopped for dinner at one of the planter's houses, while the slaves were fastened to a tree. After dinner, he sent for his horse to be brought. The horse would not let the slave put the bridle on him, he bit at him. "Master," said the slave, "I can't catch your horse, he bites." "Oh, well, I'll go." He went, and said, "What are you about, sir?" and rubbing him down behind, and lifting one of his hind feet, the horse kicked his brains out. The slaves were then let loose and sent back.

The Rev. Mr. Reed, minister of Mount Zion Church, South Carolina, when his wife wanted him to whip her slave girl, he said, "I can't, I am a minister of the gospel." "Well, other ministers whip their niggers and you can whip yours, too." "No, I can't." "Well, I will send her to Mr. Sam. Wilson, and have her whipped." So she sat down and wrote a few lines, and she called her slave girl to her and said, "Here, Madam Manda, take this letter to Mr. Wilson." which was five miles from her house. When he broke open the letter, he read, "Please give the bearer fifty lashes on the bare back, well put on." The girl looked astonished, and thought she had committed some crime, and said, "Please massa, don't whip me, mistress gave me this letter to give to you." He said,

"I don't care, I am going to give you fifty lashes."

After she was flogged, she returned to her cruel mistress, who examined her back, and said, "Right good for you; I'm glad, I long wanted you whipped." A drunken slaveholder, by the name of Old Billy Dunn, whipped one of his negroes to death, and dug a hole in the field, and threw him in without coffin or anything of the kind, just as dogs are buried; and in the course of time, the niggers ploughed up the bones, and said, "Brudder, this the place where Old Billy Dunn buried one of his slaves that was flogged to death."

I, John Andrew Jackson, once a slave in the United States, have seen and heard all this, therefore I publish it.

ANTI-SLAVERY SONGS

FLIGHT OF THE BONDMAN,

DEDICATED TO WILLIAM W. BROWN

And Sung by the Hutchinsons.

BY ELIAS SMITH

AIR—Silver Moon.

From the crack of the rifle and baying of hound,
Takes the poor panting bondman his flight;
His couch through the day is the cold damp ground,
But northward he runs through the night.

CHORUS

O God, speed the flight of the desolate slave,
Let his heart never yield to despair;
There is room 'mong our hills for the true and the brave,
Let his lungs breathe our free northern air!
Oh, sweet to the storm driven sailor the light,
Streaming far o'er the dark swelling wave;
But sweeter by far 'mong the lights of the night,
Is the star of the north to the slave.
O God, speed, &c.
Cold and bleak are our mountains, and chilling our winds,

But warm as the soft southern gales
Be the hands and the hearts which the hunted one finds,
'Mong our hills and our own winter vales.
O God, speed, &c.
Then list to the 'plaint of the heart-broken thrall,
Ye blood-hounds go back to your lair;
May a free northern soil soon give freedom to *all*,
Who shall breathe in its pure mountain air.
O God, speed, &c.

THE BEREAVED MOTHER.
Air—Kathleen O'More.
Oh, deep was the anguish of the slave mother's heart,
When called from her darling for ever to part;
So grieved that lone mother, that heart-broken mother,
In sorry and woe.
The last of the master her deep sorrows mock,
While the child of her bosom is sold on the block;
Yet loud shrieked that mother, poor heart-broken mother,
In sorry and woe.
The babe in return, for its fond mother cries,
While the sound of their wailing together arise;
They shriek for each other, the child and the mother,
In sorrow and woe.
The harsh auctioneer, to sympathy cold,
Tears the babe from its mother and sells it for gold;
While the infant and mother loud shriek for each other,
In sorrow and woe.
At last came the parting of mother and child,
Her brain reeled with madness, that mother went wild;
Then the lash could not smother the shrieks of the mother,
Of sorrow and woe.
The child was borne off to a far distant clime,
While the mother was left in anguish to pine;
But reason departed, and she sank broken-hearted,
In sorrow and woe.
O list ye kind mothers, to cries of the slave;
The parents and children implore you to save;
Go! rescue the mothers, the sisters and brothers,
From sorrow and woe.

THE YANKEE GIRL.

She sings by her wheel at that low cottage door,
Which the long evening shadow is stretching before,
With a music as sweet as the music which seems
Breathed softly and faintly in the ear of our dreams.
How brilliant and mirthful the light of her eye,
Like a star glancing, out from the blue of the sky
And lightly and freely her dark tresses play
O'er a brow and a bosom as lovely as they.
Who comes in his pride to that low cottage door—
The haughty and rich to the humble and poor?
'Tis the great Southern planter—the master who waves
His whip of dominion o'er hundreds of slaves.
'Nay, Ellen, for shame! Let those Yankee fools spin,
Who would pass for our slaves with a change of their skin;
Let them toil as they will at the loom or the wheel,
Too stupid for shame and too vulgar to feel.
But thou art too lovely and precious a gem
To be bound to their burdens and sullied by them—
For shame, Ellen, shame!— cast thy bondage aside,
And away to the South, as my blessing and pride.
O come where no winter thy footsteps can wrong,
But when flowers are blossoming all the year long;
Where the shade of the palm-tree is over my home,
And the lemon and orange are white in their bloom.
O come to my home, where my servants shall all
Depart at thy bidding and come at thy call;
They shall heed thee as mistress with trembling and awe,
And each wish of thy heart shall be felt as a law.
O could ye have seen her—that pride of our girls—
Arise and cast back the dark wealth of her curls,
With scorn in her eye which the gazer could feel,
And a glance like the sunshine that flashes on steel:
"Go back, haughty Southron! thy treasures of gold
Are dim with the blood of the hearts thou has sold;
Thy home may be lovely, but round it I hear
The crack of the whip and the footsteps of fear!
And the sky of thy South may be brighter than ours,
And greener thy landscapes, and fairer thy flowers;
But, dearer the blast round our mountains which raves,

Than the sweet sunny zephyr which breathes over slaves
Full low at thy bidding thy negroes may kneel,
With the iron of bondage on spirit and heel;
Yet know that the Yankee girl sooner would be
In *fetters* with *them*, than in freedom with *thee*!"

THE SLAVE SONG
AIR—Dearest May.
Now, freemen, listen to my song, a story I'll relate,
It happened in the valley of the old Carolina State:
They marched me to the cotton field, at early break of day,
And worked me there till late sunset, without a cent of play.

CHORUS
They worked me all the day,
Without a bit of pay,
And believed me when I told them
That I would not run away.

Massa gave me a holiday, and said he'd give me more,
I thanked him very kindly, and shoved my boat from shore
I drifted down the river, my heart was light and free,
I had my eye on the bright north star, and thought of liberty.

They worked me all the day,
Without a bit of pay
So I took my flight in the middle of the night,
When the sun was gone away.

I jumped out of my good old boat and shoved it from the shore,
And traveled faster that night than I had ever done before;
I came up to a farmer's home, just at the break of day,
And saw a white man standing there, said he, "You are run away."

They worked me all the day,
Without a bit of pay,
So I took my flight in the middle of the night,
When the sun was gone away.

I told him I had left the whip, and baying of the hound,
To find a place where man was man, if such there could be found,
That I heard in Canada, all men were free
And that I was going there in search of liberty.

They worked me all the day,
Without a bit of pay,
So I took my flight in the middle of the night,
When the sun was gone away.

YE HERALDS OF FREEDOM.

Ye heralds of freedom, ye noble and brave,
Who dare to insist on the rights of the slaves,
Go onward, go onward, your cause is of God,
And he will soon sever the oppressor's strong rod.
The finger of slander may now at you point,
That finger will soon lose the strength of its joint;
And those who now plead for the rights of the slave,
Will soon be acknowledged the good and the brave.
Though thrones and dominions, and kingdoms and powers,
May now all oppose you, the victory is yours;
The banner of Jesus will soon be unfurled,
And he will give freedom and peace to the world.
Go under his standard, and fight by his side,
O'er mountains and billows you'll then safely ride;
His gracious protection will be to you given,
And bright crowns of glory he'll give you in heaven.

TESTIMONIALS IN FAVOUR OF JOHN ANDREW JACKSON, A FUGITIVE SLAVE

"I am very happy to say that Mr. Jackson is a member of my Church, and is well worthy of all confidence and regard.
April 12th, 1860.C. H. SPURGEON."

"We, the undersigned, bear testimony to the truth of Mr. Jackson's statements, being satisfied regarding these either by personal investigation of his case, or by the evidence of those who have done so, and on whose veracity we can depend. The credentials he carries with him are attested by parties of the very highest respectability in Edinburgh. We therefore commend him to the kind sympathies of every friend of the slave, not only on account of his exposure and denunciation of slavery in general, but his very laudable object of raising funds to procure the deliverance of his father and two children of a murdered sister from bondage.

MEREAMLER WALLACE, Minister, East Campbell Street N. P. Church, Glasgow.
WILLIAM BRUCE, Minister, U. P. Church, Edinburgh.

WM. GRAHAM, Minister, Newhaven.

ROBT. NELSON, Deacon, St. John's Free Church.

THOS. NELSON, Printer, etc.

W. J. DUNCAN, Banker."

"18, Coates Crescent,
Edinburgh, 7th May, 1857.
Mr. Jackson, on producing what seemed to me sufficient testimonials, and particularly to strong one from Mrs. Beecher Stowe, was allowed to deliver two lectures in my Church. These lectures were, I have no reason to know, very creditable to him. I have no doubt of his being entitled to countenance and support in his laudable undertaking.

THOS. CANDLISH, D.D.,
Minister of Free St. George's.

JAMES GRANT, 7, Gilmore Place."

"Resermere Presbyterian Manor,
Loanhouse, Edinburgh, 18th May, 1857

From testimonials produced by Mr. Jackson, given by Mrs. Beecher Stowe and others, I was convinced of the truth of his case, gave him the use of my Church for public lectures on two occasions, and felt happy in affording him hospitality for two nights. From all I have seen and heard, it gives me pleasure to testify my conviction that he is entitled to cordial sympathy and encouragement in the laudable object he has in view—the deliverance of some relations from that state of bondage from which he himself has in the good providence of God escaped.

I can cordially unite with the above, from

WM. ANDERSON, Minister of the gospel.

DAVID GUTHRIE, Minister of the Free Church, Tibetson."

"Glasgow, October 15, 1857.
At a meeting of the Joint Committees of the 'Glasgow New Association for the Abolition of Slavery,' the certificates of John Andrew Jackson, a fugitive slave, having been examined and considered satisfactory, it was unanimously agreed to vote him two guineas towards the object of his mission.

JOHN SMITH, Treasurer."

"J. A. Jackson having called on me and shown his testimonials, I took him to a lady, Miss Griffith, who was visiting this town on anti-slavery business, and who has resided several years on America. She examined him very closely, and was fully satisfied that his representations of himself are correct. I believe implicit reliance may be placed in his truthfulness and honesty.

RICHD. SKINNER,
Minister of Ramsden Street Chapel,
March 25th, 1858.   Huddersfield."

Samuel Fessenden, a gentleman well known in the United States, with whom Mr. Jackson lived some time, gave him this character:—

"This may certify that I have known Mr. John Andrew Jackson more than five years; I believe him to be a reliable man for integrity and truth. His history, which is very thrilling, may be relied on, as he relates it. He is anxious to redeem his father and two children of a sister in slavery. He has a claim on your sympathies.

SAMUEL FESSENDEN."

"Boston, April 3oth, 1856
Be it known that we know John Andrew Jackson, a colored man, to be industrious and honest; said Jackson worked in Salem, Mass., having worked for us at different times during the years of 1847–8–9, and 50. We further state that we believe said John Andrew Jackson was formerly a slave, and that his word may be relied upon, as we think him a man of integrity and truth.

SAMUEL HIGBEE, North Street.
JOHN GILMER."

"Be it known to whom it may concern, that I went with the above John Andrew Jackson and saw Mrs. Foreman, in Richmond Street, Boston, and she fully corroborated his statement in reference to his being a slave; also said her son had been on board the vessel, and seen the spot where the said John Andrew Jackson was cut out, according to his statement; I would further add, that I know the above gentlemen, Samuel Higbee and John Gilmer, to be men of character and highly respectable, and that their statement may be fully relied upon.

G. W. COCHRANE, 60 & 70 Read St."

Mr. Jackson lectured twice in the Rev. Mr. Candlish's Church, Edinburgh, when the rev. gentleman took the chair; he also lectured in almost all the Churches in Edinburgh and Glasgow, and he lectured all the way through to London, where he still continues to lecture on slavery, and endeavors to bring in the gospel of our Lord Jesus Christ; he is now waiting to see how the conflict in America will end; and if it please God that the slaves get their freedom, his intention is to go and preach the gospel among them as long as he lives.

I am happy to say, that since writing the foregoing, President Lincoln has issued his proclamation, that "On January 1st, 1863, all slaves within any State, or part of a State, the people whereof shall then be in rebellion against the Federal Government, shall be then, thenceforward, and for ever *free.*"—J. A. J.

PASSMORE & ALABASTER, Printers, Wilson Street, Finsbury.

My Life in the South, by Jacob Stroyer (1885)

—⁓—

Introduction

SUSANNA ASHTON AND KELLY E. RIDDLE

When he was fourteen years old, Jacob Stroyer was sent along with a team of other slaves from his Sumter County plantation to serve with the Confederate army at Fort Sumter.* During the time he spent at the fort in 1864, Stroyer witnessed the death knells of the army that defended the system that had encircled his childhood in pain, destruction, and cruelty. He wrote that "the nearer the war approached its close the less the slaves had to do, as the masters were at the end of their wits what to do." Despite the irony of being forced to fortify the defenses of the Confederacy, Stroyer writes of the pride he and his fellow slaves took in being in military service and of the admiration this service would win them on their home farms. He also writes that the work at Fort Sumter and Sullivan's Island was easier than that

---

*For more information on the role that slaves, willingly and unwillingly, played in the Confederate forces, see Alexia J. Helsley, "South Carolina's Black Confederates," in *Black Confederates,* compiled by Charles Kelly Barrow, J. H. Segars, and R. B. Rosenburg (Gretna, La.: Pelican, 1995). See also Dwight T. Pitcaithley, "In Search of a Useable Past: Neo-Confederates and Black Confederates," in *Slavery and Public History,* edited by James Oliver Horton and Lois E. Horton (New York: New Press, 2006), 187–212; and Charles Kelly Barrow, J. H. Segars, and R. B. Rosenberg, eds., *Forgotten Confederates—an Anthology about Black Southerners* (Atlanta, Ga.: Southern Heritage Press, 1997). Also useful is Arthur W. Bergeron and Richard M. Rollins, eds., *Black Southerners in Gray: Essays on Afro-Americans in Confederate Armies* (Redondo Beach, Calif.: Rank and File Publications, 1994).

demanded at home and that the slaves had far more free time. According to Stroyer, the move from plantations "filled our cup of joy." His assertions that the time he spent in the war was relatively good demonstrate a determination to depict hope and happiness somehow sustained in a life broken by slavery. This forces the reader to consider what his standards for relatively good might have been, for his war account is rift with tales of violence, terror, and injustice. No matter how good life may have been on Fort Sumter, he lets his readers know that black slaves who were severely injured in combat "were put into boxes, with pieces of iron in them, and carried out a little away from [Fort] Sumter and thrown overboard." Direct and unsentimental, Stroyer makes it clear that he and his fellow slaves prayed ceaselessly for the Union to win the war.

Stroyer's lengthy narrative is divided into three chapters that reflect his resolve to use his life story in the service of others and ultimately to refashion his sense of national identity. The first part consists of family history. The second part focuses on anecdotes of slave life in South Carolina more generally; only one section of that chapter relating specifically to his sister is included here. The third part returns to Stroyer's experiences during the war. His final coda, "The Great Conclusion," ends not with his own personal migration to the North but rather with a vision of Columbia in the spring of 1865 as emancipated slaves praised God for their deliverance beneath the Stars and Stripes. As Stroyer saw it, liberty rendered them Americans anew.

Stroyer's childhood was full of hardships but was perhaps more stable and happy than many others depicted in slave narratives, for among other advantages, he was able to sustain a relationship with his parents (although raised offsite from them in what he describes as an enormous plantation nursery). His father, whom Stroyer describes as a slave from Sierra Leone, was purchased by Col. Dick Singleton and brought to the large Singleton plantation, twenty-eight miles southeast of Columbia. There he met the woman who was to be Jacob Stroyer's mother, Chloe.

Stroyer was born in 1849, and his account of his earliest days on Singleton's summer seat is generally bright. Known by Singleton's slaves as the "sand hill" and situated four miles from the plantation, the summer seat was the seasonal residence of slave children judged too young to work. Stroyer shared his "sand-hill days" each summer with between 80 and 150 children, who were looked after by three or four women too old to work on the plantation and several older boys sent as leaders. Stroyer describes the processes undergone by the slaves in preparation for visits by the master and mistress: the children were washed and clothed in their best, "but before this was done, the unsuccessful attempt was made to straighten out our unruly wools with some small cards, or Jim-Crows as we called them." These visits, alternating with long periods of neglect, his harsh treatment by his fellow slave Gilbert, and the consistent diet of mush, are the only complaints about a life that Stroyer otherwise describes as "very pleasant."

As he became older, however, he was removed from the sand hill, and his life took a dramatic change for the worse. He had developed an interest in horses from an early age, as his father cared for the plantation's horses and mules. Singleton thus allowed Stroyer to work alongside his father and train as a child jockey, an occupation that abruptly ended when Singleton died and his widow sold the plantation's racehorses the year after Stroyer's first races. That one year, however, made an impression on young Stroyer and marked a dark shift in his situation. Though he loved working with horses, the brutality he experienced at the hands of Boney Young, his white trainer, traumatized Stroyer during his childhood. When Stroyer complained of his first beating at the hands of Young, his father helplessly admitted, "'I can do nothing more than to pray to the Lord to hasten the time when these things shall be done away: that is all I can do.'" After this brutal beating, Stroyer's father urged his son to go on with his work even while in pain. His mother tried to defend her son and consequently received a severe beating at the hands of the groom as well. Stroyer writes that "the idea first came to me that I, with my dear father and mother and the rest of my fellow negroes, was doomed to cruel treatment through life, and was defenseless." Depicted over several pages in which the family's struggle against the situation is expressed, Young and a black groom repeatedly torture Stroyer, once almost to the point of death, in an effort to subjugate him. Stroyer's depictions of his parents' reactions—his father's impotent grim stoicism and his mother's heartbroken grief—reveal the havoc inflicted on traditional family relationships by the institution of slavery.

Soon after Stroyer was removed from the stables and returned to field-work, the Civil War broke out. Although he was only thirteen years old, Stroyer's master sent him as part of a plantation tithe to work for the Confederate army. In what may be the most unique contribution of this narrative, Stroyer gives an account of his war experiences and of the coastal fighting as seen from the point of view of slaves invested in their own survival more than in the Confederate cause. This truly renders his narrative a remarkable historical document.

The poignant proximity of the Union forces and, indeed, the proximity of the black Union soldiers to the enslaved black Confederates are demonstrated by his stories of slaves desperately escaping their Confederate captors and swimming under fire to Union fortifications. Similarly he sketches out how slaves were intentionally exposed to Union bombardment in order to shelter the white Confederate soldiers.

After a severe injury from a Union shell, young Stroyer was removed to a hospital in Charleston, where he was treated only after having identified himself as belonging to the Singleton plantation. Returned to the now only haphazardly supervised plantation, he lived there until the end of the war, at which point his career became focused on religious training. In his brief account of his actions after the war, he states that he studied in Columbia and Charleston and in 1870 made it to Massachusetts, where he studied at "evening schools" before getting enough money to attend Worcester Academy for two years.* He became licensed as a minister of Worcester's African Methodist Episcopal Church and later ordained as a deacon in Newport, Rhode Island. Stroyer finishes this part of the narrative by sharing his goal to complete his theological studies at Talladega College in Alabama, which he planned to finance with proceeds from the sale of his narrative.†

The final part of his narrative returns to the writer's time in service to the Confederacy, in particular his forced labor on the coastal fortifications of South Carolina. Slave men erected batteries, mounted guns, and repaired forts. Some more fortunate slaves, such as Stroyer, were given lighter physical duties; they worked as messengers and waited on officers. In a tone similar to that of John Andrew Jackson's reflections about his experiences with the Confederate forces, Stroyer writes about the fervent activity of battle and the extraordinary luxury of more free time than plantation tasks usually allowed. While it is well known that black soldiers in Northern regiments not infrequently learned to read during their wartime service, Stroyer recounts studying while under fire in the service of the Confederate army: "I carried my spelling book with me, and, although the northerners were firing upon us, I tried to keep up my study." Stroyer tells of the immense pride the slaves took in being in military service, albeit with the Confederate forces.

As the memories of a child slave—Stroyer was only sixteen years old when he was freed by the end of the Civil War—the episodes that comprise Stroyer's narrative show both his development as a normal boy and the

*See Bill Ringle's article about Stroyer in "History of Worcester Academy: Influential Alumni," http://www.worcesteracademy.org/about/history/detail.asp?newsid =58684.

†Talladega College was founded in Alabama in 1867 for the education of freed men and women. See "The History of Talladega," http://www.talladega.edu/index/history.

ways in which his enslavement corrupted this natural growth. He includes memories typical of any other small child alongside horrific anecdotes that, with seeming artlessness, are folded into his story. Stroyer's narrative displays that, though he grew up in a remarkably stable environment with two parents and characterizes his childhood years as "very pleasant," the psychological toll of enslavement still followed him and helped construct his memories of his experiences.

Jacob Stroyer's story was first published as *Sketches of My Life in the South, Part I* in 1879 by Salem Press in Massachusetts. The work was originally designed as the first part of a two-volume autobiography, but the second part was never printed. *Sketches* was later reprinted in 1885 as *My Life in the South*. The 1885 edition, which is reproduced here, is thirty-two pages longer than that of 1879, and Stroyer used this additional length primarily to recount in more detail what became chapter 3 about his Civil War experiences.

—⚬⚬—

Entered according to Act of Congress, in the year 1879, by JACOB STROYER, in the office of the Librarian of Congress, at Washington, D.C.

THIRD EDITION.

MY LIFE IN THE SOUTH.

By

JACOB STROYER.

NEW AND ENLARGED EDITION

SALEM OBSERVER BOOK AND JOB PRINT

1885.

INTRODUCTION.

Salem, August 4, 1879.

I have read the manuscript from which this little work by Rev. Mr. Stroyer is printed and found it both interesting and instructive. It is in simple style and words, the autobiography of an emancipated slave, born and raised on an extensive plantation in central South Carolina, the owner of which had on his own several plantations, nearly 500 negroes of varying shades of complexion, all becoming free men by the Proclamation in 1864. The writer, now (1879), minister of the African Methodist Episcopal Church in this city, tells of his own severe training and experience, of some of the customary ways of owners and of slaves—of the severity of plantation discipline, and of the burdens of a life of involuntary servitude.

Hints are not wanting that the importation of slaves was not, in the time of the author, wholly discontinued.

The hope of Mr. Stroyer is that he may be able, by the sale of his work, to raise means to enable him to add to an education already attained with very great difficulty and long and patient toil and waiting, his whole object being to devote his services and attainments to the good of his race.

HENRY K. OLIVER.
August 13, 1879.

In this book Mr. Stroyer has given us, with a most simple and effective realism, the inside view of the institution of slavery. It is worth reading, to know how men, intelligent enough to report their experience, felt under the yoke. The time has come when American slavery can be studied historically, without passion, save such as mixes itself with the wonder that so great an evil could exist so long as a social form or a political idol. The time has not come when such study is unnecessary; for to deal justly by white or black in the United States, their previous relations must be understood, and nothing which casts light on the most universal and practical of those relations is without value to-day. I take pleasure therefore in saying that I consider Mr. Stroyer a competent and trustworthy witness to these details of plantation life.

E. C. BOLLES.

CITY OF SALEM, MAYOR'S OFFICE,
November 5, 1884.
This is to certify that since the year 1876 I have known Rev. Jacob Stroyer, as a preacher and minister to the colored people of this city. He is earnest, devoted and faithful.

He is endeavoring by the sale of this book to realize the means to enable him by a course of study, to better fit himself as a minister to preach in the South.

I most cheerfully commend him in his praiseworthy efforts.
WM. M. HILL, *Mayor.*

CITY OF SALEM, MASS., MAYOR'S OFFICE
January 20, 1885.
Such tales as Mr. Stroyer's are now no longer required to enlighten the community and show the few lights and many shadows of American slavery. We may be thankful that the subject has now simply an historical interest.

Although it does not possess the dramatic incidents of Mrs. Stowe's famous story, it has the advantage of being a true sketch of Southern life. It is a simple, readable production, and shows what education will do for the race.

Mr. Stroyer will do good work among his people, and deserves encouragement and support.

ARTHUR L. HUNTINGTON, Mayor.

Mr. Stroyer's book is a setting forth in a fresh and unique manner of the old and bitter wrongs of American Slavery. It is an inside view of a phase of our national life which has happily passed away forever. Although it concerns itself largely with incidents and details, it is not without the historical value which attaches to reliable personal reminiscences. The author has made commendable progress in intellectual culture, and is worthy of generous assistance in his effort to fit himself still more perfectly for labor among his needy brethren in the South.

E. S. ATWOOD.

PREFACE.
THIRD EDITION.

The author, in presenting the third edition of his book to the public, would take occasion to thank his patrons for the very liberal manner in which they have appreciated his efforts. When the work was first projected, the necessity for another edition was not thought of; but the unexpected favor which the work has met at the hands of those interested in the author and his object, has constrained him to offer a second and now a third edition of this little story of the trials and sufferings of himself and his once oppressed brethren, to their kind consideration.

J. S.

CHAPTER I

My father was born in Sierra Leone, Africa. Of his parents and his brothers and sisters I know nothing. I only remember that it was said that his father's name was Moncoso, and his mother's Mongomo, which names are known only among the native Africans. He was brought from Africa when but a boy, and sold to old Colonel Dick Singleton, who owned a great many plantations in South Carolina, and when the old colonel divided his property among his children, father fell to the second son, Col. M. R. Singleton.

Mother never was sold, but her parents were; they were owned by one Mr. Crough, who sold them and the rest of the slaves, with the plantation, to Col. Dick Singleton, upon whose place mother was born. I was born on this extensive plantation, twenty-eight miles southeast of Columbia, South Carolina, in the year 1849. I belonged to Col. M. R. Singleton, and was held in slavery up to the time of the emancipation proclamation issued by President Lincoln.

The Children

My father had fifteen children: four boys and three girls by his first wife and eight by his second. Their names were as follows: of the boys—Toney, Aszerine, Duke and Dezine; of the girls—Violet, Priscilla, and Lydia. Those of his second wife were as follows: Footy, Embrus, Caleb, Mitchell, Cuffey and Jacob, and of the girls, Catherine and Retta.

Sand Hill Days

Col. M. R. Singleton was like many other rich slave owners in the South, who had summer seats four, six or eight miles from the plantation, where they carried the little negro boys and girls too small to work.

Our summer seat, or the sand hill, as the slaves used to call it, was four miles from the plantation. Among the four hundred and sixty-five slaves owned by the colonel there were a great many children. If my readers had visited Col. Singleton's plantation the last of May or the first of June in the days of slavery, they would have seen three or four large plantation wagons loaded with little negroes of both sexes, of various complexions and conditions, who were being carried to this summer residence, and among them they would have found the author of this little work in his sand-hill days.

My readers would naturally ask how many seasons these children were taken to the summer seats? I answer, until, in the judgment of the overseer, they were large enough to work; then they were kept at the plantation. How were they fed? There were three or four women who were too old to work on the plantation who were sent as nurses to the summer seats with the children; they did the cooking. The way in which these old women cooked for 80, and sometimes 150 children, in my sand-hill days, was this:—they had two or three large pots, which held about a bushel each, in which they used to cook corn flour, stirred with large wooden paddles. The food was dealt out with the paddles into each child's little wooden tray or tin pail, which was furnished by the parents according to their ability.

With this corn flour, which the slaves called mush, each child used to get a gill of sour milk brought daily from the plantation in a large wooden pail on the head of a boy or man. We children used to like the sour milk, or hard clabber as it was called by the slaves; but that seldom changed diet, namely the mush, was hated worse than medicine. Our hatred was increased against the mush from the fact that they used to give us molasses to eat with it, instead of clabber. The hateful mixture made us anxious for Sundays to come, when our mothers, fathers, sisters and brothers would bring something from the plantation, which, however poor, we considered very nice, compared with what we had during the week days. Among the many desirable things our parents brought us the most delightful was cow peas, rice, and a piece of bacon, cooked together; the mixture was called by the slaves "hopping John."

The Story of Gilbert

A few large boys were sent yearly to the sand-hill among the smaller ones, as guides. At the time to which I am referring there was one by the name of Gilbert, who used to go around with the smaller boys in the woods to gather bushes and sticks for the old women to cook our food with.

Gilbert was a cruel boy. He used to strip his little fellow negroes while in the woods, and whip them two or three times a week, so that their backs were all scarred, and threatened them with severer punishment if they told; this state of things had been going on for quite a while. As I was a favorite with Gilbert, I always had managed to escape a whipping, with the promise of keeping the secret of the punishment of the rest, which I did, not so much that I was afraid of Gilbert, as because I always was inclined to mind my own business. But finally, one day, Gilbert said to me, "Jake," as he used to call me, "you am a good boy, but I'm gwine to wip you some to-day, as I wip dem toder boys." Of course I was required to strip off my only garment, which was an Osnaburg linen shirt, worn by both sexes of the negro children in the summer. As I stood trembling before my merciless superior, who had a switch in his hand, thousands of thoughts went through my little mind as to how to get rid of the whipping. I finally fell upon a plan which I hoped would save me from a punishment that was near at hand. There were some carpenters in the woods, some distance from us, hewing timber; they were far away, but it was a clear morning, so we could hear their voices and the sound of the axes. Having resolved in my mind what I would do, I commenced reluctantly to take off my shirt, at the same time pleading with Gilbert, who paid no attention to my prayer, but said, "Jake, I is gwine to wip you to-day as I did dem toder boys."

Having satisfied myself that no mercy was to be found with Gilbert, I drew my shirt off and threw it over his head, and bounded forward on a run in the direction of the sound of the carpenters. By the time he got from the entanglement of my garment, I had quite a little start of him. Between my starting point and the place where the carpenters were at work I jumped over some bushes five or six feet high. Gilbert soon gained upon me, and sometimes touched me with his hands, but as I had on nothing for him to hold to, he could not take hold of me. As I began to come in sight of the carpenters, Gilbert begged me not to go to them, for he knew that it would be bad for him, but as that was not a time for me to listen to his entreaties, I moved on faster. As I got near to the carpenters, one of them ran and met me, into whose arms I jumped. The man into whose arms I ran was Uncle Benjamin, my mother's uncle. As he clasped me in his arms, he said, "Bres de Lo, my son, wat is de matter?" But I was so exhausted that it was quite a while before I could tell him my trouble; when recovered from my breathless condition, I told him that Gilbert had been in the habit of stripping the boys and whipping them two or three times a week, when we went into the woods, and threatened them with greater punishment if they told. I said he had never whipped me before, but I was cautioned to keep the secret, which I had done up to this time; but he said he was going to whip me this morning, so I threw my shirt over his head and ran here for protection. Gilbert did not follow me after I got in sight of the carpenters, but sneaked away. Of course my body was all bruised and scratched by the bushes. Acting as a guide for Uncle Benjamin, I took him to where I had left my garment.

At this time the children were scattered around in the woods, waiting for what the trouble would bring; They all were gathered up and taken to the sand-hill house, examined, and it was found, as I have stated, that their backs were all scarred. Gilbert was brought to trial, severely whipped, and they made him beg all the children to pardon him for his treatment to them. But he never was allowed to go into the woods with the rest of the children during that season. My sand-hill associates always thanked me for the course I took, which saved them and myself from further punishment by him.

Master and Mistress Visiting

When master and mistress were to visit their little negroes at the sand-hill, the news was either brought by the overseer who resided at the above named place, and went back and forth to the plantation, or by one of master's house servants, a day ahead. The preparation required to receive our white guests was that each little negro was to be washed, and clad in the best dress he or she had. But before this was done, the unsuccessful attempt was made to straighten out our unruly wools with some small cards, or Jim-Crows as we called them.

On one occasion an old lady, by the name of Janney Cuteron, attempted to straighten out my wool with one of those Jim-Crows; as she hitched the teeth of the instrument in my unyielding wool with her great masculine hand, of course I was jerked flat on my back. This was the common fate of most of my associates, whose wools were of the same nature, but with a little water and the strong application of the Jim-crow, the old lady soon combed out my wool into some sort of shape.

As our preparations were generally completed three-quarters of an hour before our guests came, we were placed in line, the boys together and the girls by themselves. We were then drilled in the art of addressing our expected visitors. The boys were required to bend the body forward with head down, and rest the body on the left foot, and scrape the right foot backward on the ground, while uttering the words, "how dy Massie and Missie." The girls were required to use the same words, accompanied with a courtesy. But when Master and Mistress had left, the little African wools were neglected until the news of their next visit.

Our sand-hill days were very pleasant, outside of the seldom changed diet, namely the mush, which we had sometimes to eat with molasses, the treatment of Gilbert, and the attempt to straighten out our unruly wools.

I said that my father was brought from Africa when but a boy, and was sold to old Col. Dick Singleton; and when the children were of age, the Colonel divided his plantations among them, and father fell to Col. M. K. Singleton, who was the second son.

On this large plantation there were 465 slaves; there were not so many when it was given to Col. M. R., but increased to the above stated number, up to the time of emancipation.

My father was not a field hand; my first recollection of him was that he used to take care of hogs and cows in the swamp, and when too old for that work he was sent to the plantation to take care of horses and mules, as master had a great many for the use of his farm.

I have stated that father said that his father's name in Africa was Moncoso, and his mother's Mongomo, but I never learned what name he went by before he was brought to this country. I only know that he stated that Col. Dick Singleton gave him the name of William, by which he was known up to the day of his death. Father had a surname, Stroyer, which he could not use in public, as the surname Stroyer would be against the law;

he was known only by the name of William Singleton, because that was his master's name. So the title Stroyer was forbidden him, and could be used only by his children after the emancipation of the slaves.

There were two reasons given by the slave holders why they did not allow a slave to use his own name, but rather that of the master. The first was that, if he ran away, he would not be so easily detected by using his own name as by that of his master. The second was that to allow him to use his own name would be sharing an honor which was due only to his master, and that would be too much for a negro, said they, who was nothing more than a servant. So it was held as a crime for a slave to be caught using his own name, a crime which would expose him to severe punishment. But thanks be to God that those days have passed, and we now live under the sun of liberty.

Mother

Mother's name was Chloe. She belonged to Col. M. R. Singleton too; she was a field hand, and never was sold, but her parents were once.

Mr. Crough who, as I have said had owned this plantation on which mother lived, had sold the plantation to Col. Dick Singleton, with mother's parents on it, before she was born.

Most of the family from which mother came, had trades of some kind; some were carpenters, some were blacksmiths, some house servants, and others were made drivers over the other negroes. Of course the negro drivers would be under a white man, who was called the overseer. Sometimes the negro drivers were a great deal worse to their fellow negroes than were the white men.

Mother had an uncle by the name of Esau, whom master thought more of than he did of the overseer. Uncle Esau was more cruel than was any white man master ever had on his plantation. Many of the slaves used to run away from him into the woods. I have known some of the negroes to run away from the cruel treatment of Uncle Esau, and to stay off eight or ten months. They were so afraid of him that they used to say that they would rather see the devil than to see him; they were glad when he died. But while so much was said of Uncle Esau, which was also true of many other negro drivers, the overseers themselves were not guiltless of cruelty to the defenseless slaves.

I have said that most of the family from which mother came had trades of some kind; but she had to take her chance in the field with those who had to weather the storm. But my readers are not to think that those whom

I have spoken of as having trades were free from punishment, for they were not; some of them had more trouble than had the field hands. At times the overseer, who was a white man, would go to the shop of the blacksmith, or carpenter, and would pick a quarrel with him, so as to get an opportunity to punish him. He would say to the negro, "Oh, ye think yourself as good as ye master, ye—" Of course he knew what the overseer was after, so he was afraid to speak; the overseer, hearing no answer, would turn to him and cry out, "ye so big ye can't speak to me, ye ——," and then the conflict would begin, and he would give that man such a punishment as would disable him for two or three months. The merciless overseer would say to him, "Ye think because ye have a trade ye are as good as ye master, ye ——; but I will show ye that ye are nothing but a nigger."

I said that my father had two wives and fifteen children: four boys and three girls by the first, and six boys and two girls by the second wife. Of course he did not marry his wives as they do now, as it was not allowed among the slaves, but he took them as his wives by mutual agreement. He had my mother after the death of his first wife. I am the third son of his second wife.

My readers would very naturally like to know whether some of the slaves did not have more than one woman. I answer, they had; for as they had no law to bind them to one woman, they could have as many as they pleased by mutual agreement. But notwithstanding, they had a sense of the moral law, for many of them felt that it was right to have but one woman; they had different opinions about plurality of wives, as have the most educated and refined among the whites.

I met one of my fellow negroes one day, who lived next neighbor to us, and I said to him, "Well, Uncle William, how are you, to-day?" His answer was "Thank God, my son, I have two wives now, and must try and make out with them until I get some more." But while you will find many like him, others would rebuke the idea of having more than one wife. But, thanks be to God, the day has come when no one need to plead ignorance, for master and servant are both bound by the same law.

I did not go to the sand-hill, or summer seat, my allotted time, but stopped on the plantation with father, as I said that he used to take care of horses and mules. I was around with him in the barn yard when but a very small boy; of course that gave me an early relish for the occupation of hostler, and I soon made known my preference to Col. Singleton, who was a sportsman, and an owner of fine horses. And, although I was too small to work, the Colonel granted my request; hence I was allowed to be numbered among those who took care of the fine horses, and learned to ride. But I soon found that my new occupation demanded a little more than I cared for.

It was not long after I had entered my new work before they put me upon the back of a horse which threw me to the ground almost as soon as I had reached his back. It hurt me a little, but that was not the worst of it, for when I got up there was a man standing near with a switch, in hand, and he immediately began to beat me. Although I was a very bad boy, this was the first time I had been whipped by anyone except father and mother, so I cried out in a tone of voice as if I would say, this is the first and last whipping you will give me when father gets hold of you.

When I had got away from him I ran to father with all my might, but soon found my expectation blasted, as father very coolly said to me, "Go back to your work and be a good boy, for I cannot do anything for you." But that did not satisfy me, so on I went to mother with my complaint and she came out to the man who had whipped me; he was a groom, a white man master had hired to train the horses. Mother and he began to talk, then he took a whip and started for her, and she ran from him, talking all the time. I ran back and forth between mother and him until he stopped beating her. After the fight between the groom and mother, he took me back to the stable yard and gave me a severe flogging. And, although mother failed to help me at first, still I had faith that when he had taken me back to the stable yard, and commenced whipping me, she would come and stop him, but I looked in vain, for she did not come.

Then the idea first came to me that I, with my dear father and mother and the rest of my fellow negroes, was doomed to cruel treatment through life, and was defenseless. But when I found that father and mother could not save me from punishment, as they themselves had to submit to the same treatment, I concluded to appeal to the sympathy of the groom, who seemed to have full control over me; but my pitiful cries never touched his sympathy, for things seemed to grow worse rather than better; so I made up my mind to stem the storm the best I could.

I have said that Col. Singleton had fine horses, which he kept for racing, and he owned two very noted ones, named Capt. Miner and Inspector. Perhaps some of my readers have already heard of Capt. Miner, for he was widely known, having won many races in Charleston and Columbia, S.C., also in Augusta, Ga., and New York. He was a dark bay, with short tail. Inspector was a chestnut sorrel, and had the reputation of being a very great horse. These two horses have won many thousand dollars for the colonel. I rode these two horses a great many times in their practice gallops, but never had the opportunity to ride them in a race before Col. Singleton died, for he did not live long after I had learned so that I could ride for money. The custom was, that when a boy had learned the trade of a rider, he would have to ride what was known as a trial, in the presence of a judge, who would approve or disapprove his qualifications to be admitted as a race rider, according to the jockey laws of South Carolina at that time.

I have said that I loved the business and acquired the skill very early, and this enabled me to pass my examination creditably, and to be accepted as a capable rider, but I passed through some very severe treatment before reaching that point.

This white man who trained horses for Col. Singleton was named Boney Young; he had a brother named Charles, who trained for the colonel's brother, John Singleton. Charles was a good man, but Boney our trainer, was as mean as Charles was good; he could smile in the face of one who was suffering the most painful death at his hands.

One day, about two weeks after Boney Young and mother had the conflict, he called me to him, as though he were in the pleasantest mood; he was singing. I ran to him as if to say by action, I will do anything you bid me, willingly. When I got to him he said, "Go and bring me a switch, sir." I answered, "yes, sir," and off I went and brought him one; then he said, "come in here, sir;" I answered, "yes, sir;" and I went into a horse's stall, but while I was going in a thousand thoughts passed through my mind as to what he wanted me to go into the stall for, but when I had got in I soon learned, for he gave me a first-class flogging.

A day or two after that he called me in the same way, and I went again, and he sent me for a switch. I brought him a short stubble that was worn out, which he took and beat me on the head with. Then he said to me, "Go and bring me a switch, sir;" I answered "Yes, sir;" and off I went the second time, and brought him one very little better than the first; he broke that over my head also, saying, "Go and bring me a switch, sir;" I answered, "Yes, sir," and off I went the third time, and brought one which I supposed would suit him. Then he said to me, "Come in here, sir." I answered, "Yes, sir." When I went into the stall, he told me to lie down, and I stooped down; he kicked me around for a while, then, making me lie on my face, he whipped me to his satisfaction.

That evening when I went home to father and mother, I said to them, "Mr. Young is whipping me too much now, I shall not stand it, I shall fight him." Father said to me, "You must not do that, because if you do he will say that your mother and I advised you to do it, and it will make it hard for your mother and me, as well as for yourself. You must do as I told you, my son: do your work the best you can, and do not say anything." I said to father, "But I don't know what I have done that he should whip me; he does not tell me what wrong I have done, he simply calls me to him and whips me when he gets ready." Father said, "I can do nothing more than to pray to the Lord to hasten the time when these things shall be done away; that is all I can do." When mother had stripped me and looked at the wounds that were upon me she burst into tears, and said, "If he were not so small I would not mind it so much; this will break his constitution; I am going to master about it, because I know he will not allow Mr. Young to treat this child so."

And I thought to myself that had mother gone to master about it, it would have helped me some, for he and she had grown up together and he thought a great deal of her. But father said to mother, "You better not go to master, for while he might stop the child from being treated badly, Mr. Young may revenge himself through the overseer, for you know that they are very friendly to each other." So said father to mother, "You would gain nothing in the end; the best thing for us to do is to pray much over it, for I believe that the time will come when this boy with the rest of the children will be free, though we may not live to see it."

When father spoke of liberty his words were of great comfort to me, and my heart swelled with the hope of a future, which made every moment seem an hour to me.

Father had a rule, which was strictly carried out as far as possible under the slave law, which was to put his children to bed early; but that night the whole family sat up late, while father and mother talked over the matter. It was a custom among the slaves not to allow their children under certain ages to enter into conversation with them; hence we could take no part with father and mother. As I was the object of their sympathy, I was allowed the privilege of answering the questions about the whipping the groom gave me.

When the time came for us to go to bed we all knelt down in family prayer, as was our custom; father's prayer seemed more real to me that night than ever before, especially in the words, "Lord, hasten the time when these children shall be their own free men and women."

My faith in father's prayer made me think that the Lord would answer him at the farthest in two or three weeks, but it was fully six years before it came, and father had been dead two years before the war.

After prayer we all went to bed; next morning father went to his work in the barn-yard, mother to hers in the field, and I to mine among the horses; before I started, however, father charged me carefully to keep his advice, as he said that would be the easiest way for me to get along.

But in spite of father's advice, I had made up my mind not to submit to the treatment of Mr. Young as before, seeing that it did not help me any. Things went smoothly for a while, until he called me to him, and ordered me to bring him a switch. I told him that I would bring him no more switches for him to whip me with, but that he must get them himself. After repeating the command very impatiently, and I refusing, he called to another boy named Hardy, who brought the switch, and then taking me into the stall he whipped me unmercifully.

After that he made me run back and forth every morning from a half to three quarters of an hour about two hundred and fifty yards, and every now and then he would run after me, and whip me to make me run faster. Besides that, when I was put upon a horse, if it threw me he would whip me, if it were five times a day. So I did not gain anything by refusing to bring switches for him to whip me with.

One very cold morning in the month of March, I came from home without washing my face, and Mr. Young made two of the slave boys take me down to a pond where the horses and mules used to drink; they threw me into the water and rubbed my face with sand until it bled, then I was made to run all the way to the stable, which was about a quarter of a mile. This cruel treatment soon hardened me so that I did not care for him at all.

A short time afterwards I was sent with the other boys about four or five miles from home, up the public road, to practice the horse, and they gave me a very wild animal to ride, which threw me very often. Mr. Young did not go with us, but sent a colored groom every morning, who was very faithful to every task allotted him; he was instructed to whip me every time the horse threw me while away from home. I got many little floggings by the colored groom, as the horse threw me, a great many times, but the floggings I got from him were very feeble compared with those of the white man; hence I was better content to go away with the colored groom than to be at home where I should have worse punishment.

But the time was coming when they ceased to whip me for being thrown by horses. One day, as I was riding along the road, the horse that I was upon darted at the sight of a bird, which flew across the way, throwing me upon a pile of brush. The horse stepped on my cheek, and the head of a nail in his shoe went through my left cheek and broke a tooth, but it was done so quickly that I hardly felt it. It happened that he did not step on me with his whole weight, if he had my jaw would have been broken. When I got up the colored groom was standing by me, but he could not whip me when he saw the blood flowing from my mouth, so he took me down to the creek, which was but a short distance from the place, and washed me, and then taking me home, sent for a doctor, who dressed the wound.

When Mr. Young saw my condition, he asked how it was done, and upon being told he said it ought to have killed me. After the doctor had dressed my face, of course I went home, thinking they would allow me to stay until I got well, but I had no sooner arrived than the groom sent for me; I did not answer, as my jaw pained me very much. When he found that I did not come, he came after me himself, and said if I did not come to the stable right away, he would whip me, so I went with him. He did not whip me while I was in that condition, but he would not let me lie down, so I suffered very much from exposure.

When mother came that night from the farm and saw my condition, she was overcome with grief; she said to father, "this wound is enough to kill the child, and that merciless man will not let him lie down until he gets well: this is too hard." Father said to her, "I know it is very hard, but what can we do? For if we try to keep this boy in the house it will cause us trouble." Mother said, "I wish they would take him out of the world, then he would be out of pain, and we should not have to fret about him, for he would be in heaven." Then she took hold of me and said, "Does it hurt you, son?" meaning my face, and I said, "Yes, mamma," and she shed tears; but she had no little toys to give me to comfort me; she could only promise me such as she had, which were eggs and chickens.

Father did not show his grief for me as mother did, but he tried to comfort mother all he could, and at times would say to me, "Never mind, my son, you will be a man bye and bye," but he did not know what was passing through my mind at that time. Though I was very small I thought that if, while a boy, my treatment was so severe, it would be much worse when I became a man, and having had a chance to see how men were being punished, it was a very poor consolation to me.

Finally the time came for us to go to bed, and we all knelt in family prayer. Father thanked God for having saved me from a worse injury, and then he prayed for mother's comfort, and also for the time which he predicted would come, that is, the time of freedom, when I and the rest of the children would be our own masters and mistresses; then he commended us to God, and we all went to bed. The next morning I went to my work with a great deal of pain. They did not send me up the road with the horses in that condition, but I had to ride the old horses to water, and work around the stable until I was well enough to go with the other boys. But I am happy to say that from the time I got hurt by that horse I was never thrown except through carelessness, neither was I afraid of a horse after that.

Notwithstanding father and mother fretted very much about me, they were proud of my success as a rider, but my hardships did not end here.

A short time after, I was taken to Columbia and Charleston, S.C., where they used to have the races. That year Col. Singleton won a large sum of money by the well-known horse, Capt. Miner, and that was the same season that I rode my trial race. The next year, before the time of racing, Col. Singleton died at his summer seat. After master's death, mistress sold all the race horses, and that put an end to sporting horses in that family.

I said that Boney Young, Col. Singleton's groom, had a brother by the name of Charles, who trained horses for the colonel's brother, John Singleton, Boney was a better trainer, but Charles was a better man to the negroes. It was against the law for a slave to buy spirituous liquors without a ticket, but Charles used to give the boys tickets to buy rum and whiskey with. He also allowed them to steal the neighbor's cows and hogs.

I remember that on one occasion his boys killed a cow belonging to a man by the name of Le Brun; soon after the meat was brought to the stable, Le Brun rode up on horseback with a loaded shot gun and threatened to shoot the party with whom the beef was found. Of course the negroes' apartments were searched; but as that had been anticipated, Mr. Young had made them put the meat in his apartment, and, as it was against the law of South Carolina for a white man to search another's house, or any apartment, without very strong evidence, the meat was not found. Before searching among the negroes, Mr. Young said to Le Brun, "You may search, but you won't find your beef here, for my boys don't steal." Le Brun answered, "Mr. Young, your word might be true, sir, but I would trust a nigger with money a great deal sooner than I would with cows and hogs." Mr. Young answered, "That might be true, but you won't find your beef here."

After their rooms and clothes had been searched, blood was found under some of their finger nails, which increased Le Brun's suspicion that they were of the party who stole his cow; but Mr. Young answered, "That blood is from rabbits my boys caught today." Mr. Le Brun tried to scare one of the boys, to make him say it was the blood of his cow. Mr. Young said, "Mr. Le Brun, you have searched and did not find your beef, as I told you that you would not; also I told you that the blood under their finger nails is from rabbits caught today. You will have to take my word, sir, without going to further trouble; furthermore, these boys belong to Mr. Singleton, and if you want to take further steps you will have to see him."

Finding that he was not allowed to do as he wanted to, Mr. Le Brun made great oaths and threats as he mounted his horse to leave, that he would shoot the very first one of those boys he should catch near his cattle. He and Mr. Young never did agree after that.

But poor Mr. Young, as good as he was to the negroes, was an enemy to himself, for he was a very hard drinker. People who knew him before I did said they never had seen him drink tea, coffee, or water, but rather rum and whiskey; he drank so hard that he used to go into a crazy fit; he finally put an end to his life by cutting his throat with a razor, at a place called O'Handly's race course, about three miles from Columbia, S.C. This was done just a few days before one of the great races.

Boney Young drank, too, but not so hard as Charles. He lived until just after the late war, and, while walking one day through one of the streets of the above named city, dropped dead, with what was supposed to have been heart disease.

Boney had a mulatto woman, named Moriah, who had been originally brought from Virginia by negro traders, but had been sold to several different masters later. The trouble was that she was very beautiful, and wherever she was sold her mistresses became jealous of her, so that she changed owners very often. She was finally sold to Boney Young, who had no wife; and she lived with him until freed by the emancipation proclamation. She had two daughters; the elder's name was Annie, but we used to call her sissie; the younger's name was Josephine. Annie looked just like her father, Boney Young, while Josephine looked enough like Charles to have been his daughter. It was easy enough to tell that the mother had sprung from the negro race, but the girls could pass for white. Their mother, Moriah, died in Columbia some time after the war. Annie went off and was married to a white man, but I don't know what became of Josephine.

A short time before master's death he stood security for a northern man, who was cashier of one of the largest banks in the city of Charleston. This man ran away with a large sum of money, leaving the colonel embarrassed, which fact made him very fretful and peevish. He had been none too good before to his slaves, and that made him worse, as you knew that the slave holders would revenge themselves on the slaves whenever they became angry. I had seen master whip his slaves a great many times, but never so severely as he did that spring before he died.

One day, before he went to his summer seat, he called a man to him, stripped and whipped him so that the blood ran from his body like water thrown upon him in cupfuls, and when the man stepped from the place where he had been tied, the blood ran out of his shoes. He said to the man, "You will remember me now, sir, as long as you live." The man answered, "Yes, master, I will."

Master went away that spring for the last time; he never returned alive; he died at his summer seat. When they brought his remains home all of the slaves were allowed to stop at home that day to see the last of him, and to lament with mistress. After all the slaves who cared to do so had seen his face, they gathered in groups around mistress to comfort her; they shed false tears, saying, "Never mind, missis, massa gone home to heaven." While some were saying this, others said, "Thank God, massa gone home to hell." Of course the most of them were glad that he was dead; but they were gathered there for the express purpose of comforting mistress. But after master's death mistress was a great deal worse than he had been.

When the master died there was a great change of things on the plantation; the creditors came in for settlement, so all of the fine horses, and some others, such as carriage horses, and a few mules also, were sold. The slaves whom master had bought himself had to be sold, but those who had been born on the plantation, given to him by his father, old Col. Dick Singleton, could not be sold until the grandchildren were of age.

As I have stated, my hardships and trials did not end with the race horses; you will now see them in another form.

After all the fine horses had been sold, mistress ordered the men and boys who were taking care of the horses to be put into the field, and I was among them, though small; but I had become so attached to the horses that they could get no work out of me, so they began to whip me, but every time they whipped me I would leave the field and run home to the barnyard.

Finally mistress engaged a very bad man as overseer, in place of old Ben Usome, whose name was William Turner. Two or three days after his arrival he took me into the field and whipped me until I was sick, so I went home.

I went to mistress and told her that the overseer had whipped me; she asked if I had done the work that he had given me. I told her that master had promised me that, when I got too heavy to ride race horses, he would send me to learn the carpenter's trade; she asked me if, in case she put me to a trade, I would work, and I told her I would. So she consented.

But the overseer did not like the idea of having me work at the trade which was my choice. He said to mistress, "That is the worst thing you can do, madam, to allow a negro to have his choice about what he shall do. I have had some experience as an overseer for many years, and I think I am able to give a correct statement about the nature of negroes in general. I know a gentleman who allowed his negroes to have their own way about things on his plantation, and the result was that they got as high as their master. Besides that, madam, their influence rapidly spreads among the neighbors, and if such should be allowed, South Carolina would have all masters and mistresses, and no servants; and, as I have said, I know somewhat about the nature of negroes; I notice, madam, that this boy will put you to a great deal of trouble unless you begin to subdue him now while he is young. A very few years' delay will enable him to have a great influence among his fellow negroes, for that boy can read very well now, and you know, madam, it is against the law for a negro to get an education, and if you allow him to work at the carpenter's trade it will thus afford him the opportunity of acquiring a better education, because he will not be directly under the eye of one who will see that he makes no further advancement."

Then mistress asked me, "Can you read, Jacob?" I did not want her to know that I had taken notice of what they were saying, so I answered, "I don't know, ma'am." The overseer said, "He does not know what is meant, madam, but I can make him understand me." Then he took a newspaper from his pocket and said to me, "Can you say these words?" I took the paper and began to read, then he took it from me.

Mistress asked when I had learned to read and who had taught me. The overseer did not know, but said he would find out from me. Turning to me he took the paper from his pocket again, and said, "Jacob, who told you to say words in the book?" I answered, "Nobody, sir; I said them myself." He repeated the question three or four times, and I gave the same answer every time. Then mistress said, "I think it would be better to put him to trade than to have him in the field, because he will be away from his fellow-negroes, and will be less liable to influence them if we can manage to keep him away." The overseer said, "That might be true, madam, but if we can manage to keep him from gaining any more education he will eventually lose what little he has; and now, madam, if you will allow me to take him in hand, I will bring him out all right without injuring him." Just at this juncture a carriage drove up to the gate, and I ran as usual to open it, the overseer went about his business, and mistress went to speak to the persons in the carriage. I never had a chance to hear their conclusion.

A few days after the conversation between the overseer and mistress, I was informed by one of the slaves, who was a carpenter, that she had ordered that I should go to work at the trade with him. This gave me great joy, as I was very anxious to know what they had decided to do with me. I went to my new trade with great delight, and soon began to imagine what a famous carpenter I should make, and what I should say and do when I had learned the trade. Everything seemed to run smoothly with me for about two months, when suddenly I was told one morning that I must go into the field to drop cotton seed, but I did not heed the call, as mistress was not at home, and I knew she had just put me to the trade, also that the overseer was trying to get mistress' consent to have me work out in the field.

The next morning the overseer came into the carpenter's shop and said, "Did I not order ye into the field, sir?" I answered, "Yes, sir." "Well, why did ye not go?" I answered, "Mistress has put me here to learn the trade." He said, "I will give ye trade." So he stripped me and gave me a severe whipping, and told me that that was the kind of trade I needed, and said he would give me many of them. The next day I went into the field, and he put me to drop cotton seed, as I was too small to do anything else. I would have made further resistance, but mistress was very far away from home, and I had already learned the lesson that father and mother could render me no help, so I thought submission to him the easiest for me.

When I had got through with the cotton seed, in about three weeks, I went back to the carpenter's shop to work; so he came there and gave me another severe whipping, and said to me, "Ye want to learn the carpenter's trade, but I will have ye to the trade of the field." But that was the last whipping he gave me, and the last of his whip.

A few days after my last whipping the slaves were ordered down into the swamp across the river to clear up new grounds, while the already cleared lands were too wet from rain that had fallen that night. Of course I was among them to do my part; that is, while the men quartered up dry trees, which had been already felled in the winter, and rolled the logs together, the women, boys and girls piled the brushes on the logs and burned them.

We had to cross the river in a flat boat, which was too small to carry over all the slaves at once, so they had to make several trips.

Mr. Turner, the overseer, went across in the first flat; he did not ride down to the work place, but went on foot, while his horse, which was trained to stand alone without being hitched, was left at the landing place. My cousin and I crossed in the last boat. When we had got across we lingered behind the crowd at the landing; when they all were gone we went near the horse and saw the whip with which I was whipped a few days before fastened to the saddle. I said to him, "Here is the whip old Turner whipped me with the other day." He said, "It ought to be put where he will never get it to whip anybody with again." I answered my cousin, "If you will keep the secret I will put it where old Bill, as we used to call Mr. Turner, will never use it any more." He agreed to keep the secret, and then asked me how I would put the whip away. I told him if he would find me a string and a piece of iron I would show him how. He ran down to the swamp barn, which was a short distance from the margin of the river, and soon returned with the string and iron exactly suited for the work. I tied the iron to the whip, went into the flat boat, and threw it as far as I could into the river. My cousin and I watched it until it went out of sight under water; then, as guilty boys generally do after mischievous deeds, we dashed off in a run, hard as we could, among the other negroes, and acted as harmless as possible. Mr. Turner made several inquiries, but never learned what had become of his whip.

A short time after this, in the time of the war, in the year 1863, when a man was going round to the different plantations gathering slaves from their masters to carry off to work on fortifications and to wait on officers, there were ten slaves sent from Mrs. Singleton's plantation, and I was among them. They carried us to Sullivan's Island at Charleston, S.C., and I was there all of that year. I thanked God that it afforded me a better chance for an education than I had had at home, and so I was glad to be on the island. Though I had no one to teach me, as I was thrown among those of my fellow negroes who were fully as lame as I was in letters, yet I felt greatly relieved from being under the eye of the overseer, whose intention was to keep me from further advancement. The year after I had gone home I was sent back to Fort Sumter—in the year 1864. I carried my spelling book with me, and, although the northerners were firing upon us, I tried to keep up my study.

In July of the same year I was wounded by the Union soldiers, on a Wednesday evening. I was taken to the city of Charleston, to Dr. Regg's hospital, and there I stayed until I got well enough to travel, when I was sent to Columbia, where I was when the hour of liberty was proclaimed to me, in 1865. This was the year of jubilee, the year which my father had spoken of in the dark days of slavery, when he and mother sat up late talking of it. He said to mother, "The time will come when this boy and the rest of the children will be their own masters and mistresses." He died six years before that day came, but mother is still enjoying liberty with her children.

And no doubt my readers would like to know how I was wounded in the war. We were obliged to do our work in the night, as they were firing on us in the day, and on a Wednesday night, just as we went out, we heard the cry of the watchman. "Look out." There was a little lime house near the southwest corner of the fort, and some twelve or thirteen of us ran into it, and all were killed but two; a shell came down on the lime house and burst, and a piece cut my face open. But as it was not my time to die, I lived to enjoy freedom.

I said that when I got so I could travel I was sent from Dr. Ragg's hospital in Charleston to Col. Singleton's plantation near Columbia, in the last part of the year 1864. I did not do any work during the remainder of that year, because I was unwell from my wound received in the fort.

About that time Gen. Sherman came through Georgia with his hundred thousand men, and camped at Columbia, S.C. The slave holders were very uneasy as to how they should save other valuables, as they saw that slavery was a hopeless case. Mistress had some of her horses, mules, cows and hogs carried down into the swamp, while the others which were left on the plantation were divided out to the negroes for safe keeping, as she had heard that the Yankees would not take anything belonging to the slaves. A little pig of about fifty or sixty pounds was given to me for safe keeping. A few of the old horses and mules were taken from the plantation by the Union soldiers, but they did not trouble anything else.

After Columbia had been burned, and things had somewhat quieted, along in the year 1865, the negroes were asked to give up the cows and hogs given them for safe keeping; all the rest gave up theirs, but mine was not found. No doubt but my readers want to know what had become of it. Well, I will tell you. You all know that Christmas was a great day with both masters and slaves in the South, but the Christmas of 1864 was the greatest which had ever come to the slaves, for, although the proclamation did not reach us until 1865, we felt that the chains which had bound us so long were well nigh broken.

So I killed the pig that Christmas, gathered all of my associates, and had a great feast, after which we danced the whole week. Mother would not let me have my feast in her cabin, because she was afraid that the white people would charge her with advising me to kill the pig, so I had it in one of the other slave's cabins.

When the overseer asked me for the pig given me, I told him that I killed it for my Christmas feast. Mistress said to me, "Jacob, why did you not ask me for the pig if you wanted it, rather than take it without permission?" I answered, "I would have asked, but thought, as I had it in hand, it wasn't any use asking for it." The overseer wanted to whip me for it, but as Uncle Sam had already broken the right arm of slavery, through the voice of the proclamation of 1863, he was powerless.

When the yoke had been taken from my neck I went to school in Columbia, S.C., awhile, then to Charleston. Afterward I came to Worcester, Mass., in February, 1869. I studied quite a while in the evening schools at Worcester, and also a while in the academy of the same place. During that time I was licensed a local preacher of the African Methodist Episcopal church, and sometime later was ordained deacon at Newport, RI.

A short time after my ordination I was sent to Salem, Mass., where I have remained, carrying on religious work among my people, trying in my feeble way to preach that gospel which our blessed Savior intended for the redemption of all mankind, when he proclaimed, "Go ye into all the world and preach the gospel." In the meantime I have been striking steady blows for the improvement of my education, in preparing myself for a field of work among my more unfortunate brethren in the South.

I must say that I have been surrounded by many good friends, including the clergy, since I have been in Salem, whose aid has enabled me to serve a short term in the Wesleyan school at Wilbraham, Mass., also to begin a course of theological studies at Talladega college in Alabama, which I am endeavoring to complete by the sale of this publication.

CHAPTER II—SKETCHES

The Sale of My Two Sisters

I have stated that my father had fifteen children—four boys and three girls by his first wife, and six boys and two girls by his second. Their names are as follows: Toney, Azerine, Duke and Dezine, of the girls, Violet, Priscilla and Lydia; those of the second wife as follows: Footy, Embrus, Caleb, Mitchell, Cuffee, and Jacob, who is the author, and the girls, Catherine and Retta.

As I have said, old Col. Dick Singleton had two sons and two daughters, and each had a plantation. Their names were John, Matt, Marianna and Angelico. They were very agreeable together, so that if one wanted negro help from another's plantation, he or she could have it, especially in cotton picking time.

John Singleton had a place about twenty miles from master's, and master used to send him slaves to pick cotton. At one time my master, Col. M. R. Singleton, sent my two sisters, Violet and Priscilla, to his brother John, and while they were there they married two of the men on his place. By mutual consent master allowed them to remain on his brother's place. But some time after this John Singleton had some of his property destroyed by water, as is often the case in the South at the time of May freshets, what is known in the North as high tides.

One of these freshets swept away John Singleton's slave houses, his barns, with horses, mules and cows. These caused his death by a broken heart, and since he owed a great deal of money his slaves had to be sold. A Mr. Manning bought a portion of them, and Charles Login the rest. These two men were known as the greatest slave traders in the South. My sisters were among the number that Mr. Manning bought.

He was to take them into the state of Louisiana for sale, but some of the men did not want to go with him, and he put those in prison until he was ready to start. My sisters' husbands were among the prisoners in the Sumterville jail, which was about twenty-five or thirty miles across the river from master's place. Those who did not show any unwillingness to go were allowed to visit their relatives and friends for the last time.

So my sisters, with the rest of their unfortunate companions, came to master's place to visit us. When the day came for them to leave, some, who seemed to have been willing to go at first, refused, and were handcuffed together and guarded on their way to the cars by white men. The women and children were driven to the depot in crowds, like so many cattle, and the sight of them caused great excitement among master's negroes. Imagine a mass of uneducated people shedding tears and yelling at the top of their voices in anguish.

The victims were to take the cars at a station called Clarkson turnout, which was about four miles from master's place. The excitement was so great that the overseer and driver could not control the relatives and friends of those that were going away, as a large crowd of both old and young went down to the depot to see them off. Louisiana was considered by the slaves a place of slaughter, so those who were going did not expect to see their friends again. While passing along many of the negroes left their masters' fields and joined us as we marched to the cars; some were yelling and wringing their hands, while others were singing little hymns that they had been accustomed to for the consolation of those that were going away, such as

> "When we all meet in heaven,
> There is no parting there;
> When we all meet in heaven,
> There is parting no more."

We arrived at the depot and had to wait for the cars to bring the others from the Sumterville jail, but they soon came in sight, and when the noise of the cars had died away, we heard wailing and shrieks from those in the cars. While some were weeping, others were fiddling, picking banjo, and dancing as they used to do in their cabins on the plantations. Those who were so merry had very bad masters, and even though they stood a chance of being sold to one as bad or even worse, yet they were glad to be rid of the one they knew.

While the cars were at the depot a large crowd of white people gathered, laughing and talking about the prospect of negro traffic; but when the cars began to start, and the conductor cried out, "All who are going on this train must get on board without delay," the colored people cried out with one voice as though the heavens and earth were coming together, and it was so pitiful that those hard-hearted white men, who had been accustomed to driving slaves all their lives, shed tears like children. As the cars moved away we heard the weeping and wailing from the slaves as far as human voice could be heard; and from that time to the present I have neither seen nor heard from my two sisters, nor any of those who left Clarkson depot on that memorable day.

(Several subsections featuring sketches about slave life and culture more generally and not reflecting Stroyer's personal story have been excised here. - The Editor)

CHAPTER III
My Experience in the Civil War

My knowledge of the Civil War, extends from the time when the first gun was fired on Fort Sumter in April, 1861, to the close of the War.

While the slaves were not pressed into the Confederate service as soldiers, yet they were used in all the slave-holding states at war points, not only to build fortifications, but also to work on vessels used in the war.

The slaves were gathered in each state, anywhere from 6000 to 8000 or more, from different plantations, carried to some centre and sent to various war points in the state.

It would be impossible to describe the intense excitement which prevailed among the Confederates in their united efforts to raise troops to meet the Union forces. They were loud in their expressions of the certainty of victory.

Many of the poor white men were encouraged by the promise of from three to five negroes to each man who would serve in the Confederate service, when the Confederate government should have gained the victory.

On the other hand, the negroes were threatened with an increase of the galling yoke of slavery. These threats were made with significant expressions, and the strongest assumption that the negro was the direct cause of the war.

How Slaves Were Gathered and Carried to War Points

No sooner had the war commenced in the spring of 1861, than the slaves were gathered from the various plantations, and shipped by freight cars, or boats, to some centre, and apportioned out and sent to work at different war points. I do not know just how many slaves the Confederate Government required each master to furnish for its service, but I know that 15 of the 465 slaves on my master's, Col. M. R. Singleton's, plantation, were sent to work on fortifications each year during the war.

The war had been going on two years before my turn came. In the summer of 1863 with thousands of other negroes, gathered from the various parts of the state, I was freighted to the city of Charleston, South Carolina, and the group in which my lot fell was sent to Sullivan's Island. We were taken on a boat from the city of Charleston, and landed in a little village, situated nearly opposite Fort Sumter, on this island. Leaving behind us Fort Moultrie, Fort Beauregard, and several small batteries, we marched down the white sandy beach of the island, below Fort Marshall, to the very extreme point, where a little inlet of water divides Sullivan's from Long Island, and here we were quartered under Capt. Charles Haskell.

From this point on the island, turning our faces northward, with Morris Island northwest of us, and looking directly north out into the channel, we saw a number of Union gun boats, like a flock of black sheep feeding on a plain of grass; while the men pacing their decks looked like faithful shepherds watching the flock. While we negroes remained upon Sullivan's Island, we watched every movement of the Union fleet, with hearts of joy to think that they were a part of the means by which the liberty of four and one-half millions of slaves was to be effected in accordance with the Emancipation Proclamation made the January preceding. We kept such close watch upon them that some one among us, whether it was night or day, would be sure to see the discharge of a shot from the gun boat before the sound of the report was heard. During that summer there was no engagement between the Union fleet and the Confederates at that point in South Carolina. The Union gun boats, however, fired occasional shots over us, six miles, into the city of Charleston. They also fired a few shells into a marsh between Sullivan's Island and Mount Pleasant, but with no damage to us.

What Work the Negroes did on the Island

After we had reached the island, our company was divided. One part was quartered at one end of the Island, around Fort Moultrie, and we were quartered at the other end, at Fort Marshall. Our work was to repair forts, build batteries, mount guns, and arrange them. While the men were engaged at such work, the boys of my age, namely, thirteen, and some older, waited on officers and carried water for the men at work, and in general acted as messengers between different points on the island.

Engagement on Long Island

Though there was no fighting on Sullivan's Island during my stay there, Confederate soldiers at times crossed the inlet from Sullivan's to Long Island, in the night and engaged in skirmishes with Union soldiers, who had entered the upper end of that island and camped there. Whether these Confederate scouts were ever successful in routing the Union forces on the island or not I have never learned, but I know that they were several times repulsed with considerable loss.

Negroes Escape

The way the Confederates came to the knowledge that Union soldiers were on Long Island was that the group of negroes who preceded us on Sullivan's Island had found out that Union soldiers were camping on the upper end of Long Island. So one night quite a number of them escaped by swimming across the inlet that divides Sullivan's Island and Long Island, and succeeded in reaching the Union line.

The next day it was discovered that they had swam across the inlet, and the following night they were pursued by a number of Confederate scouts who crossed in a flat boat. Instead of the capture of the negroes, who would have been victims of the most cruel death, the Confederate scouts were met by soldiers from the Union line, and after a hot engagement they were repulsed, as they usually were.

Building a Battery on Long Island

Finally the Confederates took a large number of the group of which I was a member from Sullivan's to the south shore of Long Island and there built a battery, and mounted several small field guns upon it. As they were afraid of being discovered in the daytime we were obliged to work on the battery nights and were taken back to Sullivan's in the morning, until the work was completed.

We were guarded by Confederate soldiers while building the battery, as, without a guard it would have been easy for any of us to have reached the Union line on the north end of Long Island. Sullivan's Island was about five miles long.

A Negro Servant Murdered

One of the most heartless deeds committed while I was on Sullivan's Island, was that of the murder of a negro boy by his master, a Confederate officer to whom the boy had been a body servant. What the rank of this officer was I am not sure, but I think he was a Major, and that he was from the state of Georgia. It was a common thing for southern men to carry dirks, especially during the war. This officer had one, and for something the boy displeased him in, he drew the knife and made a fatal stab between the boy's collar bone and left shoulder. As the victim fell at the brutal master's feet, we negroes who had witnessed the fiendish and cowardly act upon a helpless member of our race, expected an immediate interference from the hand of justice in some form or other. But we looked and waited in vain, for the horrible deed did not seem to have changed the manner of those in authority in the least, but they rather treated it as coolly as though nothing had happened. Finding that the Confederates failed to lay the hand of justice upon the officer, we, with our vague ideas of moral justice, and with our extreme confidence that God would somehow do more for the oppressed negroes than he would ordinarily for any other people, anxiously waited a short time for some token of Divine vengeance, but as we found that no such token as we desired, in the heat of our passion, came, we finally concluded to wait God's way and time, as to how, and when this, as every other wrong act, should be visited with his unfailing justice.

But aside from this case we fared better on these fortifications than we had at home on the plantations. This was the case at least with those of us who were on Sullivan's Island. Our work in general on the fortifications was not hard, we had a great deal of spare time, and although we knew that our work in the Confederate service was against our liberty, yet we were delighted to be in military service.

We felt an exalted pride that, having spent a little time at these war points, we had gained some knowledge which would put us beyond our fellow negroes at home on the plantations, while they would increase our pride by crediting us with far more knowledge than it was possible for us to have gained.

Our daily rations from the Commissary was a quart of rice or hard-tack, and a half pound of salt pork or corn-beef.

The change from the cabins and from the labor on the old plantations so filled our cup of joy that we were sorry when the two months of our stay on the island was ended.

At the end of about two months, I, with the rest of my fellow negroes of that group, was sent back to the plantation again, while others took our places.

My Experience in Fort Sumter

In the summer of 1864, when I was in my fourteenth year, another call was made for negro laborers for the Confederate government, and fifteen from our plantation, including myself, with thousands from other plantations, were sent down to Charleston again.

There the negroes were apportioned in groups to be sent to the different fortifications. My lot fell among the group of three hundred and sixty, who were assigned to Fort Sumter. I shall never forget with what care they had to move in carrying us in a steamer from the government wharf in Charleston to John's island wharf, on account of the network of torpedo mines in Charleston Harbor.

From John's island wharf they carried us in rowboats to Fort Sumter, and, as those boats could not carry many, it took all night to convey us with other freightage to Fort Sumter.

The steamer which carried us from Charleston to John's island wharf had to run at night. Indeed every move the Confederates made about there near the close of the war had to be made at night because the Yankees on gunboats outside the channel and those on Morris island kept so close a watch it was very dangerous to convey us from John's island wharf to Fort Sumter because the oars dipping into the salt water at night made sparks like fire, and thus the Yankees on Morris island were able to see us. Indeed their shots oftentimes took effect.

Many of the negroes were killed. Of the fifteen from our plantation, one boy of about my age was struck by a parrot shell while climbing from the boat into the fort. We were told of the perils we were to meet, both before and after we reached our destination. For one of the most disheartening things was the sad report of the survivors of those whose places we were to fill. As the rowboats left them on John's island wharf and as we

were about to embark they told us of the great danger to which we would
be exposed,—of the liability of some of us being killed before we reached
the fort, which proved true, and of how fast their comrades were killed
in Fort Sumter. A number, it was said, died from fright before reaching
Sumter.

The Officers and Quarters

The officers who were then in command of the fort were Capt. J. C. Mitchell
and Major John Johnson. The name of the overseer in charge of the
negroes in the fort was Deburgh,—whether that was his right name I can
not say.

Deburgh was a foreigner by birth. He was one of the most cruel men I
ever knew. As he and his atrocious deeds will come up later in this history,
I will say no more of him here.

Condition of the Fort

Fort Sumter, which previous to this, had not only been silenced by the
Union forces, but also partly demolished, had but one gun mounted on it,
on the west side. That cannon we used to call the "Sundown Gun," because
it was fired every evening as the sun went down,—as well as at sunrise. On
this west side the Confederate officers and soldiers were sheltered in the
bomb-proof safe during bombardment. On the east side of the fort, facing Morris island, opposite Fort Wagner, there was another apartment
called the "Rat-hole" in which we negroes were quartered.

What the Negroes did in Fort Sumter

Fort Sumter had been so badly damaged by the Union forces in 1863, that
unless something had been done upon the top, the continued bombardment which it suffered up to the close of the war, would have rendered it
uninhabitable.

The fort was being fired upon every five minutes with mortar and parrot shells by the Yankees from Morris Island.

The principal work of the negroes was to secure the top and other parts
against the damage from the Union guns.

Large timbers were put on the rampart of the fort, and boards laid on
them, then baskets, without bottoms, about two feet wide, and four feet
high, were put close together on the rampart, and filled with sand by the
negroes.

The work could only be done at night, because, besides the bombardment from Fort Wagner which was about a mile or little less from us, there

were also sharp-shooters there who picked men off whenever they showed their heads on the rampart.

The mortar and parrot shells rained alternately upon Fort Sumter every five minutes, day and night, but the sharp-shooters could only fire by day-light.

The negroes were principally exposed to the bombardment. The only time the few Confederate soldiers were exposed to danger was while they were putting the Chevaldefrise on the parapet at night.

The "Chevaldefrise" is a piece of timber with wooden spikes pointed with iron, and used for defense on fortifications.

In the late war between the Spaniards and the Americans, the former used barbed wire for the same purpose.

If my readers could have been in Fort Sumter in the summer of 1864, they would have heard the sentinel cry, every five minutes, "Look out! Mortar!" Then they would have seen the negroes running about in the fort yard in a confused state, seeking places of safety from the missile sure to bring death to one or more of them. Another five minutes, and again the cry of the sentinel, "Look out," means a parrot shell, which is far more deadly than is the mortar because it comes so quickly that one has no chance to seek a place of safety.

The next moment the survivors of us, expecting that it would be our turn next, would be picking up, here and there, parts of the severed bodies of our fellow negroes; many of those bodies so mutilated as not to be recognizable.

Deburgh, The Overseer

Deburgh, the overseer, of whom I have spoken, was a small man, of light complexion, and very light hair.

If my readers could have been in Fort Sumter in July, 1864, they would have seen Deburgh with a small bar of iron or a piece of shell in his hand, forcing the surviving portion of the negroes back into line and adding to these, other negroes kept in the Rat-hole as reserves to fill the places of those who were killed and wounded.

They would also have heard him swearing at the top of his voice, while forcing the negroes to rearrange themselves in line from the base of the fort to the top.

This arrangement of the negroes, enabled them to sling to each other the bags of sand which was put in the baskets on the top of the fort. My readers ask, what was the sand put on the fort for? It was to smother the fuses of such shells as reached the ramparts before bursting.

After the bombardment of Fort Sumter in 1863, by the Union forces, its top of fourteen or sixteen feet in thickness, built of New Hampshire granite, was left bare. From that time all through 1864, the shells were so aimed as to burst right over the fort; and it was pieces of these shells which flew in every direction that were so destructive.

The fuses of many of these shells fired on Fort Sumter did not burn in time to cause the shells to burst before falling. Now as the shells fell on the rampart of the fort instead of falling and bursting on the stone, they buried themselves harmlessly in the sand, which put out the fuse and also kept them from bursting.

But while the destruction of life was lessened by the sand, it was fully made up by the hand of that brute, the overseer. God only knows how many negroes he killed in Fort Sumter under the shadow of night. Every one he reached, while forcing the slaves back into working position after they had been scattered by the shells, he would strike on the head with the piece of iron he carried in his hand, and, as his victim fell, would cry out to some other negro, "Put that fellow in his box," meaning his coffin.

Whether the superior officers in Fort Sumter knew that Deburgh was killing the negroes off almost as fast as the shells from Fort Wagner, or whether they did not know, and did not care, I never have learned. But I have every reason to believe that one of them at least, namely, Major John Johnson, would not have allowed such a wholesale slaughter, had he known. On the other hand I believe that Capt. J. C. Mitchell was not only mean enough to have allowed it, but that he was fully as heartless himself.

Whatever became of Deburgh, whether he was killed in Fort Sumter or not, I never knew.

Our Superior Officers

The two officers in command of Fort Sumter in July of 1864 were Capt. J. C. Mitchell, and Major John Johnson.

Major Johnson was as kind, gentle, and humane to the negroes as could have been expected.

On the other hand, the actions of Capt. Mitchell were harsh and very cruel. He had a bitter hatred toward the Yankees, and during the rain of shells on Fort Sumter, he sought every opportunity to expose the negroes to as much danger as he dared.

I remember that one night Capt. Mitchell ordered us outside of Fort Sumter to a projection of the stone-bed upon which the Fort was built, right in front of Fort Wagner. At that place we were in far greater danger from the deadly missiles of the Union forces than we were exposed to on the inside of Sumter, and I could see no other reasons for his ordering us outside of the fort that night than that we might be killed off faster.

It seems that during the incessant firing on Fort Sumter the officers held a consultation as to whether it was not best to evacuate the fort.

It was at this time that it was rumored,—a rumor that we had every reason to believe,—that Capt. Mitchell plotted to lock us negroes up in our quarters in Sumter, known as the Rat-hole; and put powder to it and arrange it so that both the negroes and the Yankees should be blown up, when the latter should have taken possession after the evacuation of the fort by the Confederates.

But we learned that Major John Johnson, who has since become an Episcopal minister, in Charleston, S.C., wholly refused to agree with Capt. Mitchell in such a barbarous and cowardly act, and, as though Providence were watching over the innocent and oppressed negroes, and over the Yankees as well, because they were fighting in a righteous cause, Capt. Mitchell's career and further chances of carrying out his cruel intentions were cut short. He was mortally wounded by the sharp-shooters of Fort Wagner, on the 14th of July, 1864, and died four hours afterwards.

Our Rations in Sumter

The working forces of negroes in Sumter with the exception of the boys who carried messages to the different parts of the fort day and night, were locked up days, and turned out nights, to work. We drew our rations of hard-tack and salt pork twice a day; mornings when we ceased work and turned in for the day, and again, between three and four o'clock in the afternoon, so as to have supper eaten in time to go to work at dark.

We often ate our salt pork raw with the hard-tack, as there were no special means of cooking in the negroes' apartment. We were not only in danger, while at work, from the continued rain of shells, but oftentimes when we were put in line to draw our rations some of us were killed or wounded.

I cannot say how they got fresh water in Fort Sumter, as I do not remember seeing any brought there in boats, neither did I notice any conveniences there for the catching of rain water.

The water we negroes used was kept in large hogsheads with coal tar in them; I do not know what the tar was put in the water for unless it was for our health. The "rat-hole" into which we were locked, was like a sweat box; it was so hot and close, that, although we were exposed to death by shells when we were turned out to work, we were glad to get into the fresh air.

We had little cups in which they used to give us whiskey mornings when we went in, and again when we were going out to work at night.

I don't know how many of the forty survivors of the three hundred and sixty of us who were carried into the Fort in the summer of 1864 besides myself are still alive. But if there are any with the keen tenderness of a negro, they cannot help joining me in an undying sense of gratitude to Major John Johnson, not only for his kind and gentle dealings with us which meant so much to a negro in the days of slavery, but also for his humane protection, which saved us from some of the danger from shells to which we were exposed in Sumter.

A short time after Capt. J. C. Mitchell had been killed, Major Johnson was dangerously wounded in the head by a piece of shell.

My Last Night in Fort Sumter and the Glorious End of the War

During the time we spent in Fort Sumter we had not seen a clear day or night. In harmony with the continual danger by which we were surrounded, the very atmosphere wore the pall of death; for it was always rainy and cloudy. The mutilated bodies of the negroes, mingled with the black mud and water in the fort yard, added to the awfulness of the scene. Pieces of bombshells and other pieces of iron, and also large southern pine timbers were scattered all over the yard of the fort. There was also a little lime house in the middle of the yard, into which we were warned not to go when seeking places of safety from the deadly missiles at the cry of the sentinel.

The orders were that we should get as near the centre of the fort yard as possible and lie down. The reason for this was that the shells which were fired upon Sumter were so measured that they would burst in the air, and the pieces would generally fly toward the sides of the fort. But the orders were not strictly carried out, because, at the warning cries of the sentinel, we became confused. That night, at the cry of the sentinel, I ran and lay down on one of the large southern pine timbers, and several of my fellow negroes followed and piled in upon me. Their weight was so heavy that I cried out as for life. The sense of that crush I feel at certain times even now.

At the next report of a shell I ran toward the lime house, but some one tripped me up, and, by the time I had got to my feet again, twelve or thirteen others were crowded into it. Another negro and I reached the doorway, but we were not more than there before a mortar shell came crushing down upon the little lime house, and all within were so mangled that their bodies were not recognizable.

Only we two were saved. My companion had one of his legs broken, and a piece of shell had wounded me over my right eye and cut open my under lip. At the moment I was wounded I was not unconscious, but I did not know what had hurt me. I became almost blind from the effect of my wounds, but not directly after I was wounded, and I felt no pain for a day or so. With other wounded I was taken to the bombproof in the fort. I shall never forget this first and last visit to the hospital department. To witness the rough handling of the wounded patients, to see them thrown on a table as one would a piece of beef, and to see the doctor use his knife and saw, cutting off a leg, or arm, and sometimes both, with as much indifference as if he were simply cutting up beef, and to hear the doctor say, of almost every other one of these victims, after a leg or an arm was amputated, "Put that fellow in his box," meaning his coffin, was an awful experience. After the surgeon had asked to whom I belonged, he dressed my wounds.

My readers will remember that I stated that no big boat could run to Fort Sumter at that time, on account of the bombardment. We had to be conveyed back to John's Island wharf in rowboats, which was the nearest distance a steamer could go to Fort Sumter.

As one of those rowboats was pushed out to take the dead and wounded from the fort, and as the four men were put into the boat, which was generally done before they put in the latter, fortunately, just before the wounded were put in, a Parrott shell was fired into it from Fort Wagner by the Union forces, which sunk both the boat and the coffins, with their remains.

My readers would ask how the Confederates disposed of the negroes who were killed in Fort Sumter. Those who were not too badly mutilated were sent over to the city of Charleston and were buried in a place which was set apart to bury the negroes. But others, who were so badly cut up by shells, were put into boxes, with pieces of iron in them, and carried out a little away from Sumter and thrown overboard.

I was then taken to John's Island wharf, and from there to the city of Charleston in a steamer, and carried to Doctor Rag's hospital, where I stopped until September. Then I was sent back home to my master's plantation. Quoting the exact words of Major John Johnson, a Confederate officer under whom I was a part of the time at the above-named place, I would say: "July 7th, Fort Sumter's third great bombardment, lasting sixty days and nights, with a total of 14,666 rounds fired at the fort, with eighty-one casualties."

What Took Place After

I said that after I got well enough to travel I was sent back home to my master's plantation, about a hundred miles from the city of Charleston, in central South Carolina. This was in September of 1864, and I, with the rest of my fellow-negroes on this extensive plantation, and with other slaves all over the South, were held in suspense waiting the final outcome of the Emancipation Proclamation, issued January, 1863, but as the war continued, it had not taken effect until the spring of 1865.

Here I had less work than before the war, for the nearer the war approached its close the less the slaves had to do, as the masters were at the end of their wits what to do. In the latter part of 1864 Gen. Sherman, with his army of a hundred thousand men and almost as many stragglers, covered the space of about sixty miles in width while marching from Georgia through South Carolina. The army camped around Columbia, the capital of South Carolina, for a short time. Early in the spring of 1865 the commissary building first took fire, which soon spread to such extent that the whole city of Columbia was consumed; just a few houses on the suburbs were left.

The commissary building was set on fire by one of the two parties, but it was never fully settled whether it was done by Gen. Sherman's men or by the Confederates, who might have, as surmised by some, as they had to evacuate the city, set it on fire to keep Gen. Sherman's men from getting the food. After this Columbia was occupied by a portion of Sherman's men, while the others marched on toward North Carolina.

The Glorious End

In closing this brief sketch of my experiences in the war, I would ask my readers to go back of the war a little with me. I want to show them a few of the dark pictures of the slave system. Hark! I hear the clanking of the ploughman's chains in the fields; I hear the tramping of the feet of the hoe-hands. I hear the coarse and harsh voice of the negro driver and the shrill voice of the white overseer swearing at the slaves. I hear the swash of the lash upon the backs of the unfortunates; I hear them crying for mercy from the merciless. Amidst these cruelties I hear the fathers and mothers pour out their souls in prayer,—"O, Lord, how long!" and their cries not only awaken the sympathy of their white brothers and sisters of the North, but also mightily trouble the slave masters of the South.

The firing on Fort Sumter, in April of 1861, brought hope to the slaves that the long looked for year of jubilee was near at hand. And though the

South won victory after victory, and the Union reeled to and fro like a drunken man, the negroes never lost hope, but faithfully supported the Union cause with their prayers.

Thank God, where Christianity exists slavery cannot exist.

At last came freedom. And what joy it brought! I am now standing, in imagination, on a high place just outside the city of Columbia, in the spring of 1865. The stars and stripes float in the air. The sun is just making its appearance from behind the hills, and throwing its beautiful light upon green bush and tree. The mocking birds and jay birds sing this morning more sweetly than ever before. Beneath the flag of liberty there is congregated a perfect network of the emancipated slaves from the different plantations, their swarthy faces, from a distance, looking like the smooth water of a black sea. Their voices, like distant thunder, rend the air,—

"Old master gone away, and the darkies all at home,
There must be now the kingdom come and the year of jubilee."

The old men and women, bent over by reason of age and servitude, bound from their staves, praising God for deliverance.

Life on the Old Plantation in Ante-Bellum Days, or a Story Based on Facts by the Reverend I. E. Lowery

With Brief Sketches of the Author by
the Late Rev. J. Wofford White of the South Carolina
Conference, Methodist Episcopal Church (1911)

—ﷺ—

Introduction

SUSANNA ASHTON AND E. LANGSTON CULLER

Just a few short years after the Civil War, Rev. I. E. Lowery, a nineteen-year-old former slave, became the first student to be admitted to Claflin University in Orangeburg, South Carolina, in the year 1869.* Moreover, as the first student at Claflin, he was also the very first student enrolled at a black university in the entire state. Young Irving Lowery embodied all the hope that the ideals of Reconstruction portended for African Americans in South Carolina: if a former slave could become a college man and follow his calling to both religious and civic leadership, he might help rebuild all that was the best in the South. Despite the hardships Lowery encountered throughout his life, his narrative is marked by an almost disconcerting optimism. The product of a Reconstruction-era education, Lowery's memoir is marked by a relentlessly positive perspective constructed quite consciously as an agenda of uplift and inspiration. Yet, despite the tone of optimism that characterizes

---

*As stated in Blinzy I. Gore, *On a Hilltop High: The Origin and History of Claflin College to 1984*, "A former Baker Theological Institute matriculant, Irving Lowery, is credited with having been the first student to enroll at Claflin University" (Spartanburg, S.C.: Reprint Company, 1993), 53.

this narrative, Lowery's story nonetheless reveals much about the uneasy relations between blacks and whites in the immediate and later years following the Civil War. His story demonstrates just how much was at stake in maintaining such optimism and not falling into fatalistic despair.

The purpose of his narrative is clearly stated: he "felt it to be his mission to write of the better side" of slavery. Lowery admits, "I cannot express the pleasure I have had in sitting down, and recalling the incidents of my childhood and youth." While this observation may seem surprising coming from someone who had been enslaved, his descriptions of his upbringing seem to justify such nostalgia.

Lowery's description of the Frierson plantation on Pudden Swamp is vivid and even graceful. He wistfully recalls the old plantation to be much like a paradise, where the slaves, as well as the whites, "got their portion" of its making. Lowery's Pudden Swamp was an "old farm house, where the white folks lived, nestled in the midst of a clump of stately old water oaks." To emphasize his notion that the Friersons treated their slaves well and had nothing to hide, he adds, "On most plantations in those days the 'negro quarters' was located in the rear, or at least some distance from the white folks' house. But not so in this case, for these were located in front, but a little distance from the house and from the avenue." Lowery's paradise includes fields of orchards bursting with fruit and a smokehouse full of meats, a place in which neither the "white folks" nor the slaves wanted for anything. Lowery portrays Pudden Swamp as almost entirely self-sufficient and likens its barns to "one of Pharaoh's barns in Egypt at the end of the seven years of plenty."

As a boy, Lowery was responsible for a few simple chores, such as blowing the horn to wake the slaves in the morning and fetching the mail, but his overall duties, as he recalls them, appear to have been minimal. As Lowery matured, his master did not fail to notice the talent of his young slave. According to Rev. J. Wofford White, who wrote the section of the narrative titled "Brief Sketches of the Author," Lowery's life was so simple and he was such a favorite on the plantation that Frierson even purchased a pony for his "exclusive use to ride for mail and do errands."

Lowery's narrative is initially shaped by the mediation of the aforementioned Reverend White, a childhood companion, close friend, and fellow black man whom Lowery describes as "born and reared in the same neighborhood with myself."* White's initial "Brief Sketches of the Author" section

---

*Reverend White's "Brief Sketches of the Author" were written and published in a Boston newspaper, the *Christian Witness,* twenty years before Lowery's narrative was published. For more information on the Reverend White, see Thomas J. Lothrop,

of the narrative sets out the basic facts of Lowery's life, especially those involving his later career and achievements, and was evidently composed in intimate consultation with Lowery—even to the point of conspiring to both reveal and mask Lowery's identity (a complicated narrative stance that will be discussed below). The basic facts as outlined by White and Lowery were as follows. He was born as a slave in Sumter County, South Carolina, on September 16, 1850.* His parents were also born slaves, but his father's hard work allowed him to purchase his own freedom and that of Lowery's grandmother. An achievement almost as significant as his own freedom was Lowery's father's purchase of "an excellent farm," which allowed the family to achieve some stability and independence.

Lowery became acquainted with religion through his mother, and his love for Christianity grew with age. As the Reverend White observed, "To her the children are indebted for all the home training they received that pertains to the Christian life." As a boy, Lowery worked as a house slave performing the modest duties mentioned earlier, such as making fires and fetching the mail. His master was Jack Frierson, whom Lowery thought of as a good, God-fearing man. After the Emancipation Proclamation in 1863, Lowery signed a contract to stay with his master one year. However, that year was cut short when he was whipped by Frierson's son, Adolphus. As a result, Lowery made his first public address, a complaint to the provost marshal in Sumter County. Lowery, who learned "from the white folks . . . that the slaves were all free, and that the country had been put under military government," was outraged by the injustice of the young man they still called "Mas Dolphus." Lowery, along with another boy, immediately set out for Sumter to speak to the provost marshal, a Union soldier "who heard and settled difficulties between the freedmen and their former owners." Much to Lowery's surprise, "they met a crowd of other colored people there, who, like themselves, had had difficulties with their former owners, and came from all parts of the country, seeking redress." When young Lowery's turn finally came, he gave a heartfelt account of the wrongs that he and his fellow freedmen had

---

A Memorial Souvenir of the Reverend J. Wofford White, Pastor of Wesley, M.E. Church, Charleston, S.C. Who Fell Asleep, January 7, 1890, Aged 33 Years (Charleston, S.C.: Walker, Evans, and Cogswell, 1890).

*For more information about the history of Sumter County, see Anne King Gregorie, *History of Sumter County, South Carolina* (Sumter, S.C.: Library Board of Sumter County, 1954); and http://www.sumtercountysc.org/history.htm.

endured on the Frierson plantation. In response, the provost marshal wrote a note releasing Lowery from his contract with the Friersons and into the custody of his father, "telling him that his son was now free, and that he must take care of him, and not allow him to return to the old plantation." Thus, Lowery entered into his father's custody and worked on the family farm.

At the age of sixteen, in the year 1866, he began to attend the first free school for Negroes in Sumter County, and a year later he joined the Methodist Episcopal Church. In 1868 Lowery became licensed to "exhort" and was advised by his superiors to attend Baker's Institute in Charleston, South Carolina.* He remained there until 1869, when he registered at the newly established Claflin University. After a year and a half of studies at Claflin he was stationed to preach in Cheraw, South Carolina, where he worked for two years. After an interlude preaching in Columbia he made his way north to study in Wilbraham, Massachusetts, at Wesleyan Academy, a Methodist school with an antislavery tradition.† Unfortunately, his health soon broke down, and he was obliged to return to South Carolina. During the 1870s and 1880s his career continued to take him along an itinerant path; during these years he either taught school or ministered throughout the state in places as disparate as Summerville, Greenville, Charleston, and Aiken.

Lowery's narrative speaks in general terms and with few personal references about his memories of the slave experience, perhaps assuming that the sketches written by White laid out many of the necessary details already. Perhaps, too, he was avoiding any appearance of egotism that might not reflect a properly humble stance of a good Methodist. Nonetheless, in the preface that preceded both the sketches of White and his narrative proper, Lowery instructs his readers to read the initial "Brief Sketches of the Author" (which depict Lowery's achievements from the point of view of a close

---

*"Baker's Institute" refers to the former Baker Biblical Institute in Charleston, South Carolina. It was founded by the Methodist Episcopal Church's S.C. Mission Conference of 1866 for the education of African American ministers. In 1870 Baker Biblical Institute merged with Claflin University. For more information, visit http://www.claflin.edu/AboutUs/ClaflinHistory.html.

†Wesleyan Academy was founded in 1817 in New Market, New Hampshire. In 1812 the academy moved to Wilbraham, Massachusetts, where Lowery attended in 1863. It became known as Wilbraham Academy in 1912 and merged with Monson Academy in 1971. It is currently known as Wilbraham and Monson Academy. For more information, visit http://www.wmacademy.org/.

friend) and "compare them with [Lowery's own] Chapter XI, entitled 'Little Jimmie, the Mail Boy,' and note the similarity of characters."

With this remark, Lowery highlights perhaps the most remarkable characteristic of his narrative, which is the curious displacement suggested in a series of stories he tells about the aforementioned character named "Little Jimmie." The Reverend White includes facts about Lowery's childhood that indeed share obvious similarities to those of Little Jimmie, such as his advantageous position as a house slave, his ownership of a small pony for his own personal use, his interest in Christianity, and his first public address to the provost marshal, among others. It appears that Little Jimmie has a history precisely parallel to Lowery's own. In his own narrative proper, though, Lowery allows the reader to speculate about the association between his and Little Jimmie's identities until, in the last chapter of his narrative, he identifies Jimmie as "Jimmie, the mail boy, (now the Rev.—)." It is uncertain what Lowery's motivations were for this coy play on his identity throughout his text, but it has the unmistakable effect of playing off the full title of his narrative: *Life on the Old Plantation in Ante-Bellum Days, or a Story Based on Facts.* Just how much of the narrative is fact is unclear, but the careful invocation of both truth and perhaps slightly veiled fiction has an especial resonance within the context of an uplift narrative composed to downplay, if not deny, the continuing hardships of the African American experience.

It is not difficult to see why Lowery feels nostalgic when recalling his youth. There are, of course, some moments, whether by accident or art, when Lowery's text reveals an occasional undertone of bitterness or pain or when anecdotes seemingly shared for their charm actually reveal hints of the desperate circumstances in which they occurred. For example, it is tempting to speculate about the origins not only of his birth but also of his parents' births in order to make sense of what seems to be such incredible and seemingly inexplicable favoritism of Lowery by his master. The only information given about his parents' origins is vague, and it is almost certain that they were born on Pudden Swamp plantation. Lowery also identifies them as Jimmie's parents and the characters of Uncle Tom and Aunt Namie, both of whom were mulattoes. Little Jimmie, who may be a composite stand-in for Lowery, identifies himself as "not a mulatto in the strict sense of that word." However, Lowery never reveals more about the circumstances of his parents' births or his own possible white relations and merely reflects gratefully upon his good fortune to be so favored by the Friersons.

Also, when Lowery makes such observations as "[the slaves] more or less completed their tasks before night, and by working after night they were enabled to do almost as much for themselves as they did for the white folks during the day," it is almost impossible to discern either a genuine or a sarcastic tone. Often, Lowery's optimistic portrayal of slavery presents itself as a barrier between what time has erased or made unclear and what may have really taken place. Another curious element of the narrative is the untarnished description Lowery gives of his master, John Frierson. Lowery goes to great lengths to establish Frierson as a morally upright, devout Christian in thought and practice, a man who "regarded the voice of conscience as the voice of God, and to the warnings and mandates of that voice he was always true." According to Lowery, Frierson often served as a protective guardian to "free colored people" and "never failed to respond to the call of distress." However, when Lowery is whipped by Frierson's son Adolphus, Lowery's heroic master is nowhere to be found. In fact, nothing is mentioned about the elder Frierson's reaction to his son's violent outburst. The absence of any reaction seems odd, especially because Frierson tells all of his slaves earlier in the narrative, "I declare unto you that I have not been cruel to any of you . . . and did not allow anybody else to do it—not even my own sons, Mack, Rush, nor Adolphus." After Lowery's nostalgic recollections of his old master, nothing else is mentioned of him except that he died during the spring of 1866, after he "went out into the field to view his growing crop, and fell with a paralytic stroke."

The mysterious elements of Lowery's narrative serve to make it more intriguing. Lowery's life began as enslaved and yet eased by a "lively, sunshiny, and frank disposition, which never failed to win friends for him." It was his character that earned him a spot as a "general favorite on the plantation among both the white folks and the slaves." After slavery, Lowery used his strengths to earn his education and begin his career as a Methodist preacher, a calling he realized as a teenager. Later in life, as he sat down to write his narrative, it is apparent that, for one reason or another, he felt compelled to write of the "better side" of slavery. Judging from the contents of his narrative, he wanted to honor the slaves and their former masters as well.

Lowery's narrative, *Life on the Old Plantation in Ante-Bellum Days, or a Story Based on Facts,* was first published in Columbia, South Carolina, by The State Co., Printers. The State Co. was founded in 1891 as part of South Carolina's largest newspaper. The company is now owned by one of the nation's largest commercial printing and graphics communications companies, R. R. Donnelly. Although State Printing is now corporately owned, it continues to operate in downtown Columbia. More recently, in 2006, Lowery's narrative was reprinted by Gamecock City Printing, Inc., located in Sumter, South Carolina. Gamecock City Printing was established in 1995 by Doug Foxworth, a Sumter native and former high school printing and graphic arts teacher, and Scott Johnson, one of Foxworth's former students.

The sections in Lowery's narrative titled "Brief Sketches of the Author" were written by Lowery's close friend Rev. J. Wofford White, then a pastor of Wesley M.E. Church in Charleston, South Carolina. Like Lowery, White was also a member of the South Carolina Conference of the Methodist Episcopal Church. White was quoted in Philip S. Foner's 1974 book, *Organized Labor and the Black Worker,* and portrayed as a supporter of black laborers' rights.

—∿—

"Backward, turn backward, O Time in your flight; Make me a child again just for tonight."

MEMORIES.
O mystic Land of Smiles and Tears,
O Land that Was and Is,
Alone—unchanging with the years—
The Land of Memories.
—John Trotwood Moore.

PREFACE

I have no apology to make, and no excuse to offer for writing this book— "Life on the Old Plantation in Ante-Bellum Days." It is not the result of vanity, neither is it a desire for notoriety, that prompted me to write it. No, my reasons are higher, and my purposes are nobler. My only desire has been to do good. The religious element runs through the entire story.

It has been a work of faith and a labor of love to me. I cannot express the pleasure I have had in sitting down, and recalling the incidents of my childhood and youth. In doing so, it has enabled me to live my life over again. I only hope that the reader will experience something of the same pleasure in reading the book that I have had in writing it.

The "Brief Sketches of the Author" were written just twenty years ago by the late Rev. J. Wofford White. He was a colored man, and a close friend of mine, and was born and reared in the same neighborhood with myself. These sketches were printed in *The Christian Witness,* a Boston (Mass.) newspaper, and were clipped and carefully pasted in my scrapbook. I republish them in this connection without changing a single word. I would ask the reader to peruse them carefully, and compare them with Chapter

XI, entitled "Little Jimmie, the Mail Boy," and note the similarity of characters.

I have written this book because there is no other work in existence just like it. No author, white or colored, so far as I know, has traversed, or attempted to traverse, the literary path which I presume to have trodden in writing this book. We are now about forty-five years away from the last days of slavery and the first days of freedom, and the people who have any personal knowledge of those days are rapidly crossing the mystic river, and entering the land that knows no shadows; and soon, there will not be one left to tell the story. And it is the author's thought that a record of the better life of those days should be left for the good of the future generations of this beautiful southland. Others have written of the evil side of those days, but the author felt it to be his mission to write of the better side.

Before the war, the relation that existed between the master and his slaves was, in most cases, one of tenderness and affection. There was a mutual attachment between them, which has commanded the admiration of the world. But since the war, an estrangement between the colored and the white races has sprung up, which has resulted in a feeling of intense bitterness and alienation. But I am glad to say that things are now taking a turn for the better. I can see signs of a better day ahead; and if this book should, in any way, contribute to, and help on this much desired day, the author will be satisfied.

I conclude this preface with the following clipping:

WANT TO HONOR OLD SLAVES.

An appeal to erect a monument to the former slaves of the South was issued in New Orleans a few days ago from the headquarters of the United Confederate Veterans by Gen. George W. Gordon, commander-in-chief of the veterans.

The appeal is in the form of a general order, which quotes the resolutions favoring such a monument adopted at the Birmingham reunion in 1908, and adds:

"Only those familiar with the beautiful patriarchal life on the Southern plantations previous to 1865 know of the devotions of the slaves to their owners and the children of the family. They were raised more like members of a large household.

"The children of the owners and the slaves associated most intimately together, and enjoyed alike the pleasure of the home, all receiving the care and attention of the heads of the family, who had a feeling of tender affections for these departments."

The devotion of these slaves during war time in caring for the planta-tions, in sharing dangers at the front and nursing the wounded is noted, and the order concludes with an appeal to the U.C.V., the U.D.C., the U.S.C.V., and the C.S.M.A., to see "that some evidence is given to the world of their appreciation of the faithfulness and affection of this devoted people."

I. E. LOWERY.
Columbia, S.C., September 13, 1910.

BRIEF SKETCHES OF THE AUTHOR.
I.
By the Late Rev. J. Wofford White.

When one has accomplished something of good for his fellowman, and performed work worthy of praise, people become interested not only in what he has done, but also in the history of the person himself. As ful-some praise is invidious, and heartless flattery no less damaging than unjust, we shall not make the mistake of committing the blunder of doing either, but shall state the facts as they exist.

The Rev. Irving E. Lowery, A.M., was born in the County of Sumter, State of South Carolina, September 16th, 1850, and is, therefore, 37 years old. His parents were born slaves; it was in this condition, too, that he came into this world. His father lives today [He has since died—THE AUTHOR] at the ripe age of almost four-score years. He has been known always as a man of integrity, strict honesty, and possessed of much energy and industry, and withal a man of much natural ability. Long before the war, by economy and frugality, he had saved enough in hard-earned wages to purchase his own freedom. He succeeded also in purchasing the free-dom of his mother, and when Abraham Lincoln issued the famous Eman-cipation Proclamation he was making herculean efforts to purchase his wife. Under the new order of things, by dint of perseverance and hard labor by night as well as day, he managed with shrewdness to secure an excellent farm, and although today the hoar-frost of seventy-eight win-ters is clearly observable, he superintends his business, is observant of passing events, and takes a lively interest in the questions of the day. The mother has been noted always for her modesty, piety, and Christ-like demeanor. To her the children are indebted for all the home training they received that pertains to the Christian life.

Years ago, when the subject of these sketches was a mere boy, this pious mother, without a dream of freedom, with faith in the God she served, prayed that He would call one of her sons to be a preacher of the Gospel, which then meant to be an exhorter or class-leader. "Only this and nothing more." Wonderful as mysterious are the ways of God! Long years afterward that mother's prayers were signally answered in a way wonderful to speak of—a way she could not have appreciated at the time the prayers were offered. It is an example worthy of being followed by all Christian parents, who should unfalteringly commit their children by faith and prayer to the Lord. After they are dead, in answer to the prayers on behalf of their children, God will in some way bring about the desired results. How these prayers were answered will be related further on.

Brother Lowery had better advantages than most of the boys on the plantation. Being of a lively, quick and sprightly disposition, his owner took him "into the house" when he was quite young. In the same room, on a little pallet, he slept with his master and wife. He made the fires in the early winter mornings, blew the signal at the break of day for the feeding of the horses and beginning the preparations for the labor of the day. As the master was a Methodist of the old-fashioned type common "in ye olden time," there was a family altar in that house, and this little slave boy was one who bowed at it in devotion. A little pony for his exclusive use to ride for mail and do errands, was furnished him. In going to the county-seat on business, or when visiting alone or with his family, this boy was invariably the companion of his master; thus he saw more than the other boys, came in contact with more people, obtained a better knowledge of men and things, and as a result, he became more observant, more inquisitive, and more intelligent. Thus, even in a condition of abject thralldom, God was making the wrath of men to praise Him by causing them thus to sow the seeds of usefulness in the heart of one whom He determined, in answer to the prayers of a pious mother, to lead into paths of holiness, usefulness and peace, and to become a preacher of the Gospel of our Lord and Savior Jesus Christ. As to church privileges, he had but few, although the best of such as were allowed slaves. Anon he was permitted to go to public service at the church, but more frequently the slaves were gathered together in old master's yard, and some exhorter or leader was allowed to come, under the surveillance of a white man, lest something insurrectionary be said—and conduct a service of prayer and praise.

As this was the limit of their liberty to worship, it is not to be wondered at that they entered into their services with a zeal and fervency, and to this day it is said of the negro that they pray more, and naturally sing better, than any other race. We say nothing of slavery, since it is accursed of God and man, but even with the best possible circumstances under such a condition and environment, no one could become efficient and useful in the highest sense of the term. That system had no elements to draw out the best in any one, be he master or slave. It was calculated to bring out the worst in both, and develop it to an unlimited degree. This proved to be the invariable result. True, many were saved, and we know of many good people that lived in those days, but it must be remembered that God's love is so far-reaching that it accomplishes what is impossible to man. Of itself, what did slavery do for any? What did it do for our brother? Absolutely nothing. Dear readers, when the morning of January first, 1863, dawned upon this fair but then blighted land, and the first ray of hope—the Proclamation of Emancipation—burst forth from a leaden sky, he who has ere this become a familiar name in your household, had not learned his alphabet, was in blissful ignorance of his high calling, had dreamed naught else than a life of slavery; in this condition because of his training from infancy, he was contented to live, and worse than all, he had not tasted of Jesus's blood that purifies our sinful hearts.

BRIEF SKETCHES OF THE AUTHOR.

II.

More than two years passed after that immortal document had been made public. Not till the South had stacked arms at Appomattox, and agents of the Government sent to every plantation to effect a legal contract between master and slaves, did the great mass of negroes learn that they were indeed freed men. When this was thoroughly understood, old men and women jumped for joy, young men and maidens clapped their hands and shouted. The old masters submitted, apparently, to the new order of things. When the agent came around, Brother Lowery was then a boy in his teens, and he signed the contract to remain that year.

He continued, till one day he was approached by his old master's son with a whip in one hand and a gun in the other. Without any provocation, he began to thrash the servants unmercifully. Seeing that his turn would soon come, he said to a companion, older than himself, "I will not stand this; I will go to Sumter and complain to the Provost Marshal." He leaped over the fence, and into the dense forest ran, followed by the friend referred to. Night was fast approaching; they wandered and traveled through swamps, and waded branches, till, after a ramble of fifteen miles, they got to the railroad that runs by the county-seat. Here they stopped to rest, as it was late at night, with the damp earth for a bed and the heavens for a covering. When the sun arose they aroused themselves, and shivering with cold, affrighted and hungry, they hurried toward their destination, about twenty miles away. They reached the place, inquired their way to the proper office, and were ushered into the presence of the Provost Marshal. Their complaint in simple language was made.

This was Brother Lowery's first public address, which was a statement of the grievances he had been made to suffer. After he had finished the reaction came, and the untutored youth melted into tears. The redress he sought was granted in part. A writ from this office turned him over to the custody of his father. With him, on a rented farm, he labored. At the end of that year the family was all reunited. In the year 1866, through the philanthropy of an educational society of New England, a free school, the first ever opened in that community for negroes, began its session. At the age of sixteen he was entered by his father and began the arduous task of mastering the alphabet after the manner pursued by teachers in ye olden time. He readily took to learning, and very soon was reading. His hunger for knowledge became intense. His father, according to his training, thought that work stood first in importance, and schooling was something to attend when farm work was over. This doctrine was very distasteful to one who had begun to drink from the fount of knowledge, so he ran away from his father, hired his time to work on the railroad; but the father, with an eye to business, waited patiently till the month was ended, was promptly on hand when the pay-train arrived and claimed the wages of his son—he being a minor. When the youth realized that thus it would be at the end of each succeeding month, he willingly returned to the home of his father.

The father, recognizing the exceeding anxiousness of the son to become educated, concluded to send him to school. As this stage marks the most important change in his life, pardon a little digression.

In 1865 the Rev. Timothy W. Lewis was sent to South Carolina to reorganize the Methodist Episcopal Church. He was soon strengthened by the Rev. A. Webster, D. D., recently deceased. Baker's Institute was established in Charleston for the training of young men for the ministry. One of the first to enter it was a brother full of zeal and the Holy Ghost. This brother belonged to the same community wherein lived Brother Lowery, and was widely known for his piety, having managed, with great secrecy, to obtain a fair knowledge of English branches. He spent one year at this institute. As the field was white and but few laborers, he was sent out to gather the people and assist in the organization of the church. This brother swayed great influence over the old, and especially the young. Among the young men who frequented the church under his ministry was the subject of our sketch.

Just about the time his father concluded to give every available advantage to enable him to prosecute his studies, he was happily converted under the pastorale of the sainted Joseph White, the brother referred to above. He joined the Methodist Episcopal Church in the year 1867. His conversion was sound and thorough, and although he hesitated to obey, he felt the irresistible call of God to preach the gospel of His Son. Thus the mother's prayers offered years before, when her son was a boy, were most singularly answered in the conversion of this son, and his being called to the ministry. He was licensed to exhort in the year 1868, and as the way was opened, he was directed by his pastor to Baker's Institute, which he entered and remained two years—1868 and 1869. He was the first student that registered at Claflin University. This was October, 1869.

There he continued till the latter part of 1870. In December of that year he was made a local preacher, joined the South Carolina Conference, was ordained deacon by Bishop Simpson and stationed by him at Cheraw. He remained there two years; he was then, at the beginning of 1873, sent to Columbia, where he remained till August. He then went to Wilbraham, Mass., to complete education in the Wesleyan Academy, then under the presidency of Rev. Dr. Cooke. In the spring of 1874 he completely broke down in health and was forced to return home for the year. Influences, strong and powerful, were brought forward to induce him to enter politics. He was offered the nomination for School Commissioner, then equivalent to an election. Although the temptation was seductive, the inducements great and offers flattering, he turned neither to the right nor the left. He commanded Satan to get behind him, and he was obeyed, for the weakest Christian is stronger than the devil, because God dwelleth in him. Until the meeting of the Conference in January, 1875, he taught school in Sumter and was principal of the high school. It was here that he met the young lady who afterward became his wife. She is of noble and pious parentage, well educated, and, from peculiar advantages, was reared in the best colored society and influences in Charleston. It is a blessed union to both, and much of Brother Lowery's success in the ministry is due to the industry, energy and helpfulness of his wife. Five children enliven the interest of their home life, and they are carefully instructed in the way of life by their parents. Theirs is a model, Christian home, where the family Bible occupies a conspicuous place, and wherein is an altar erected to the Lord of Hosts, around which, twice a day—morning and evening—the family gather for worship, prayer and praise.

BRIEF SKETCHES OF THE AUTHOR.

III.

Rev. I. E. Lowery commenced again his active work in the ministry in the year 1875, soon after his return from Wesleyan Academy. He was appointed to Summerville by Bishop Wiley, an appointment high in grade, both because of the intelligence of the local membership and of its proximity to Charleston, many of whose best citizens, both white and colored, own homes and spend the summer there. With satisfaction to the people he remained there two years, and was by Bishop Harris appointed to the station of Greenville, with a membership of about 700, whose acquirements socially, intellectually and religiously are equal to that of any membership of any community or city in the State.

Soon after this young brother's arrival at his new field of labor he discovered that the people he was to serve were not only religious, but were Christians of a very pronounced and advanced type, many of whom were blessed with the grace of sanctification. Such openly professed, and, better still, lived it.

The Rev. True Whittier is one of the noble band of Christian missionaries that came to the South after the war. He was zealous for the Master. He preached sanctification all over the upper part of the State, where he served as presiding elder, and as a result numbers sought till they found full peace and cleansing of heart. Greenville, of which we now write, was the principal hot-bed of this phase of Christian experience. Many here had enjoyed this fullness long before Brother Whittier's time, but they did not proclaim it as a distinct blessing. It is possible that they knew it not. He preached it, it was believed and many experienced it. This was the condition of the church when Brother Lowery took charge. He had not up to this time given much thought to this subject. Now he was made to face it. What could he do with a membership largely in advance of him in Christian experience? You can imagine the answer to such an inquiry more easily than it can be given. What did he do? He did what all ought to do who have not yet received it. Confessed his lack in that experience, earnestly solicited the prayers of the faithful, sought by meditation, prayer and faith until he found to his joy the blessed experience of sanctification, a second, separate and distinctly different blessing to that experienced in regeneration. He began then to preach as never before. His pulpit efforts were filled with a holy unction. Hitherto he had with all faithfulness preached the gospel, but now he preached a full gospel. While he does not make the subject a specialty, yet he hesitates not in claiming it as his own experience, and proclaiming the necessity of this experience not only to complete that of all Christians, but until it is sought and found the whole duty is not performed, requirements of spiritual life are not met, the danger line still in sight, and indeed not passed; for sanctification means, if anything, not only the pardon of sins, assurance and the other divine evidences of acceptance; it includes also the idea of the change in our nature of a proneness, inclination or natural bent to do evil, to a proneness or natural bent in us to do that only which pleases God. From the time of his experience of sanctification he has been, and is today, a different preacher altogether. The change is almost as marked between sanctification and regeneration as that between the highest type of moral living and regeneration. For three full years to an ever-increasing congregation and membership, he acceptably served the church at Greenville. It was with greatest reluctance that the people gave him up.

By Bishop Simpson, in the year 1880, he was appointed to Wesley, one of the three important stations in the city of Charleston. Under him the membership grew rapidly. Here he remained three years, full of labors for the Master, and when he was moved by expiration of the time-limit, he carried with him the good wishes of the membership of the church he had served so faithfully and well. Recently he visited Charleston, and as an illustration of the hold he has on the people, the church was crowded to overflowing to hear his sermons, and by careful computation 1,200 came to hear his lecture, "The Twenty Years' Progress of the Colored Race." Bishop Merrill then appointed him to Cheraw, his first appointment—an illustration of the theory of the eternal cycle that brings things back to the same condition of former times. The people were jubilant over the appointment. They received their old pastor with open hearts. Here he remained three years. Here he was again wonderfully blessed of the Lord. The charge prospered beyond that of any administration since he had left there years before. Here he and his family were bereaved of the favorite of the house—a bright 2-year-old boy—who departed this life and took up residence in Zion, city of our God. How this bereavement tried their souls! Other than prayerful meditation and resignation, two incidents were providentially sent as solaces. One in the person of the minister who conducted the burial services, who selected as a text these beautiful words, "My Beloved is Gone Down Into His Garden to Gather Lilies"—*Song of Solomon*. Such suggestive words were to them fraught with the fragrance of heaven. Ever after, in thinking of their little boy, these words loom uppermost in their minds. The other was from the pen of Bishop Foster, while on the Red Sea, homeward bound. When as a picture there loomed up before him all of his life's work and experience as a minister, he portrayed in graphic style his trials, struggles and the loss of a child, the first of that kind experienced by the young itinerant (himself), etc., which was almost an exact representation of the feelings and experiences of this family. To them this article was a message of condolence divinely sent. After serving a full Methodistic term here, he was appointed by Bishop Andrews to his present place of labor, Aiken, S.C., which, because of the peculiar circumstances surrounding it, is the most important appointment, in the Conference at the present time.

Brother Lowery is tall and of commanding appearance. Suave in manner, quiet in disposition and devotional. His sermons are models of pulpit preparation. His style is more of the exposito-textual than that of the topical. He throws his whole soul into the delivery of a sermon, and not infrequently somebody is either converted or so deeply impressed that conversion follows as a result of his powerful appeals.

In recent years he has developed taste of a literary nature. His papers in the columns of *The Witness* are widely read, and the readers of that journal have formed their own opinions as to their merits.

Twice has he been named as anniversary orator at Claflin University, and twice he has honored the occasion by efforts that surpassed even the expectations of his friends. He never sought nor desired it, yet the university has honored itself by conferring the degree A.M. upon him. If a degree is a recognition of worth, then it has been worthily bestowed in this instance. He is, however, that same modest, unassuming preacher of the gospel.

As a writer, he is painstaking, careful, scrutinizing. As a student, he is methodical, discriminating, industrious. As a preacher, he is forcible, logical, convincing. As a worker, he is indefatigable, energetic, pushing. As a financier, he is successful and skillful. As a Christian, he is sympathetic, consistent and spiritually-minded. God helping, we predict for him a career of usefulness to the church, his fellow men and the cause of Christ.

CHAPTER I.

The Old Plantation.

At a point about eight miles southeast of Mayesville, S.C., and about the same distance southwest of Lynchburg, is a settlement known as "Shiloh." There was a church located there which was called "the Shiloh Church"; hence the settlement took its name from the church. It was a Methodist

Church, and belonged to that denomination known as the Methodist Episcopal Church, South. Not far from the church was a store owned by a man whose name was Chris. Player. Mr. Player kept the post office, and here the planters for miles around got their mail. It was a convenient place for a church and also for the store and post office, for they were located near where the public road forked at two places.

Just about two miles from this church, due north across the swamp, called Pudden Swamp, was the plantation which forms the scene of my story. I do not know the number of acres this farm contained (that is a matter of little consequence anyway), but suffice it to say that it was a good sized plantation.

But how shall I begin to describe this wonderful old plantation? As I write the scene comes fresh before my vision. I imagine I can see the old farm house, where the white folks lived, nestled in the midst of a clump of stately old water oaks. There was a front and back piazza and there was a brick chimney at each end. It was a one-story building, with an ell running back, in which was located the dining room. About thirty feet east of the building was the kitchen, and about the same distance in the rear of the dining room stood the smoke-house and the store-room. That smoke-house was never without meat and lard, and that storeroom contained barrels of flour, barrels of sugar, barrels of molasses and sacks of coffee from one year to another. And the corn, oh, there was no end to that. There were several barns, some big and some little, but when the corn was gathered and the "corn-shucking" was over and the crop was housed, the barns were full to overflowing. They would remind one of Pharaoh's barns in Egypt at the end of the seven years of plenty. There was very little cotton raised on that plantation in those days. Four or six bales were considered a good crop. But the corn, peas, potatoes, hogs, cattle, sheep and goats, there was no end to these. It was a rare thing to buy anything to eat on that plantation save sugar and coffee. Shoes were bought, but the clothing for the white folks and the slaves was made at home. It was the good old "homespun." On rainy days, when it was too wet to do outdoor work, the men and boys got out corn, as they said in plantation language, for the mill, while the women and girls carded and spun cotton and wool. A task of so many hanks of yarn was given them for a day's work, which was a reasonable task, and when it was finished they carded and spun for themselves. They more or less completed their tasks before night, and by working after night they were enabled to do almost as much for themselves as they did for the white folks during the day. The weaving was almost invariably done by the young white ladies, or by some one of the servant girls who was taught especially to do it. Thus everybody on the place was kept well clothed, both the white folks and the slaves. That which the slave women carded and spun at night was their own, and they usually hired their young missus, or some other white woman of the neighborhood, to weave it into cloth for them, and thus they always had good, clean clothing for Sunday wear, so that they could go to "meetin'" without embarrassment.

On the east side of the white folks' house was the orchard. It occupied a space of about five or six acres and contained a large number of fruit trees of every description. There could be found the apple in variety, the peach, the pear, the apricot and the plum. On the west side was a large vegetable garden, which contained, in addition to the supply of vegetables for the table, several varieties of grapes. The arbors built for these grapes were large, strong and, well cared for. And the slaves got their portion of all these delicious fruits. Of course, they were not allowed to steal them (but this does not signify that they never resorted to this method of obtaining fruit), but they could, and did, get fruit by asking for it.

At some distance in the rear of the white folks' house stood the barns and other outhouses, and a little to the east of these was the large horse and cow lot and the stables. In front was a beautiful avenue skirted on each side with lovely oaks of different varieties. And, strange to say, about three hundred yards in front of the white folks' house, and to the east of this beautiful avenue, was located the "negro quarters." On most plantations in those days the "negro quarters" was located in the rear, or at least some distance from the white folks' house. But not so in this case, for these were located in front, but a little distance from the house and from the avenue. But there is another thing that goes to show that the owners and managers of this plantation were people of education, culture and refinement, and that was even the fields were given names. At some distance eastward from the "big house" was a large field called "Sykes field." In the midst of this field stood a large and beautiful walnut tree. It was customary to plant wheat, oats or rye in this field, and when the crop was harvested, which usually took place in June, the field was then made a pasture. Every field of the plantation had a good fence around it, and after the crops were taken off the horses, cattle and sheep were turned in. It was a charming sight to see these creatures during the early morning grazing in different parts of the "Sykes field," and when the sun waxed hot they would gather themselves together and lie down under this tree and rest. And in the cool of the afternoon they would start out again. This was repeated day by day during the summer season. Still east of the "Sykes field," and across the swamp, were two large fields called the upper and lower "Forks." North of these was another called the "Island field." Then there were the "New Ground field," the "Gin House field," the "Middle field," the "Graveyard field" and the "West field." It was necessary that these fields should all have names so that it could be ascertained where the hands were working, or where the horses or cows were being pastured. There were six horses and two mules on the place, and they too all had names. There was "Old Reuben," "Old Gray," "Old Lep," "Fannie," "John" and "Charlie." John and Charlie were young horses raised on the place. The mules were "Jack" and "Ginnie." Jack was a noble fellow, but Ginnie was as wicked as she could be. She had as many devils in her as did Mary Magdalene before she met Christ. Ginnie did very well when hitched to the wagon with Jack or some other horse by her side, but under the saddle she would not carry double to save your life. And pull a plow, that depended on the state of her mind. If she felt like it she would do it, but if she did not she would kick things to pieces in a jiffy. When that mule was foaled she was as good as it is possible for a mule to be, but the negro who plowed her spoilt her. And if Ginnie had been granted the gift of speech as was the good fortune of Balaam's ass, she doubtless would have said to that negro and to the rest of mankind in the language of Shakespeare: "Villainous company hath been the spoil of me."

It will be noticed that the word "old" precedes the names of these horses. This does not signify that they were naturally old, but it was simply a designation given to them by the slaves, and the white folks accepted it and so styled the horses also. The slaves were adepts at giving nicknames to animals, to each other and even to the white folks. But the white folks seldom caught on to the nicknames given to them.

I cannot close this chapter without speaking of the adjoining plantations. To the north was Mr. Isaac Keels and his father, Mr. Billie Keels; east was Mr. Alex. Lemons; south was Mr. Chris. Player, and west was Mr. Fullwood and Mr. Jack Player. The latter was a brother of Mr. Chris. Player. These all were slaveholders, but none of them were cruel to their slaves. They knew that the slaves were valuable property, and, therefore, took good care of them. Mr. Fullwood died, leaving a widow and a number of small children, and the estate could not be settled-up until the youngest child became of age. This made it necessary to put the plantation in the hands of an overseer, and that overseer was Mr. Rance Player, a brother of Mr. Chris. Player and Jack Player. He was pretty strict in his discipline, but not cruel. Such things as bloodhounds and nigger traders were scarce in that community. I will not say that they were never seen, but they were

scarce. It was a rare thing for slaves to be bought and sold in that neighborhood.

I quote a couple of verses from "Lyrics of Love," by Rev. Charles
Roundtree Dinkins, a negro poet. The book was published by *The State
Publishing Company of Columbia, S.C.*:

> "Give me the farm, where grows the corn,
> Shouting with tassel gold unworn,
> While breezes roll;
> Where smiles the fleecy staple, white,
> Like snowy fields of Eden bright Around the soul.

> "Give me the farm—the cabin dear,
> With the fireplace so spacious there—
> Full five feet wide—
> With the backlog just burning down,
> Potatoes sweet and 'possum brown
> Right by my side."

CHAPTER II.

The Proprietor of the Old Plantation.

The owner of this farm was a remarkable character. His name was Mr.
John Frierson, but he was called by his intimate friends "Jack Frierson."
There was another John Frierson, who lived in the upper part of Sumter
County, but this one was sometimes alluded to as "John Frierson on Pud-
den Swamp," to distinguish him from the other Mr. John Frierson. His
age I do not know, but he lived to be quite an old man.

He was a Christian and was, perhaps, the leading man in the Shiloh
Methodist Church. I am told that he was educated for the Christian ministry in early life, but he never entered that holy calling. But he became
a class leader, and this was the only sacred office he would accept, and
he filled it well and to the satisfaction of the ministers and the members
of the Shiloh Church. It was said that he was the best educated man in all
that region of country. He was a very fine elocutionist and one of the best
readers that ever opened a book or held a newspaper. During the exciting
times that led up to the War Between the States, and during the four years
of that bloody struggle, the white neighbors—and many of them were men
and women of wealth and intelligence—used to come to the home of Mr.

Frierson to hear him read the papers and to discuss with him the news and the burning questions of that day.

Mr. Frierson was married three times. By his first wife there was born but one child—a boy—whom he named Mack; by his second wife there were born five children—three girls and two boys, and by his last wife there was no issue. The children by his second wife were named as follows: Mary Ann, Isabella, Rush, Adolphus and Janie. I have given them in the order of their birth, as I remember it. These all grew up to manhood and womanhood. The following lived to be married off: Mack, Isabella, Adolphus and Janie.

Mr. Mack married a lady from Chesterfield County whose maiden name was Miss Martha Garland. Her father's name was Mr. Jesse Garland. He was a farmer, owned a few slaves, but his daughter—Miss Martha—was handsome and considered a belle in society. Miss Isabella married Mr. Ransom Garland, the brother of Miss Martha. Mr. Adolphus married the daughter of Mr Billie Keels, known as "Little Billie Keels." Miss Janie married a Mr. Kirby and afterwards settled in Columbia, S.C., as I have been informed. I also learned that she has some sons, and possibly grandsons living there now, and are merchants in that city. Miss Mary Ann never married, but lived to be a very pious and happy old maid. She became housekeeper for her father after the death of her mother and until he married again, which was his third and last marriage. Her own mother was a very devout Christian, and spared no pains in training up her children in the way they should go, so that when they became old they did not depart from it.

Mr. Rush grew up to a beautiful young manhood and became quite a favorite among the young ladies of the community, but the war broke out and there was a call for volunteers, and he was among the first to enter the Confederate army. His leaving the old plantation to go to the front was a sad occasion. Well do I remember the morning. The handsome young soldier in a beautiful new uniform of gray with shining buttons bade the family and servants good-bye, never to return. In less than two years he fell on one of the battlefields of Virginia, and sacrificed his life for the cause that is so dear to every Southern white man. When the news of his death reached the old plantation there was mourning and weeping among the white folks and the slaves. He was a good young man and was much beloved by all. His body was never brought home but was buried in that far-off land along with his comrades in battle. But he was a Christian, having been brought up in a religious atmosphere and by devout parents, and on the other side of the mystic river he has met them, where peace forever abides and where happiness is the lot of all such.

> "Asleep in Jesus! far from thee
> Thy kindred and their graves may be;
> But thine is still a blessed sleep,
> From which none ever wakes to weep."

Mr. Mack, the oldest son, was also a devout young man. Like Jacob of old, he was a man of prayer. There was a place in the thicket in the rear of the lot where he resorted for private communion with his Maker every evening at twilight. When the day's work was done, and when the horses and mules were stabled and fed, he would steal away to his sacred retreat and pour out his soul in prayer. Many were the times when the writer of these lines, then a boy of twelve, stood in the road just a short distance away from his place of prayer when the stars were being revealed in the heavens and the crimson gradually fading away from the sunset skies and listened alternately to the plaintive sounds of the whippoorwill and the audible voice of prayer, which was tremulous with emotion and frequently accompanied with tears. The scene was awe-inspiring to the inquiring mind and to the reverent soul, such as mine was at that time. I must confess that I scarcely knew what it all meant. But I sure did love to hear Mr. Mack pray and the whippoorwill hello. But, thank God, I have lived long enough to know what prayer means.

But let us consider our subject a little further. Mr. Frierson invariably observed family worship twice a day—morning and evening. The Scriptures were read in course at each service. Singing was usually omitted except on special occasions when perhaps there was a minister present, one who could sing. But he was never in such a hurry that he did not have time for family devotions. It mattered not in what season of the year and how busy they might be in the farm, his prayers he would say. And it was always a treat to hear that man read his Bible and then to take the different members of his family to a throne of grace. And his slaves were not forgotten during these warm, fervent and eloquent intercessory prayers.

Mr. Frierson always looked carefully after the morals of his slaves. I have already stated that he did not allow them to steal if he could possibly prevent it. He did everything he could to teach them to be truthful, to be honest, and to be morally upright. He had it understood on his plantation that there should be no little bastard slaves there. He gave it out that they were not wanted. When the boys and girls reached a marriageable age he advised them to marry, but marry some one on the plantation, and he would see to it that they should not be separated. But if they married some one from the adjoining plantations, they might be separated eventually by the "nigger traders," as they were called in that day and time. But Mr. Frierson was never known to separate a man and his wife by sale or by trading. Nor was he ever known to separate mother and child. He did not believe in this kind of business.

Mr. Frierson was a good man and taught both his children and servants to fear God and keep His commandments. The Lord said of Abraham, "For I know him that he will command his children and his household after him, and they shall keep the way of the Lord, to do justice and judgment." These words may fitly be applied to our subject—Mr. Frierson—for he certainly emulated the example of the Father of the faithful.

There were some free colored people in the neighborhood. Some of these were free-born, but others bought their freedom. But all of them, according to the then existing laws, had to have some white man to be their guardian. That is, some white man to look after their interest to see that they got their rights, and to protect them, if necessary. And Mr. Frierson was chosen by some of these free colored people as their guardian. He was a kind-hearted man and never failed to respond to the call of distress. It mattered not whether it came from the poor slave or from the more fortunate freeman or from the oppressed white brother, he had an ear to hear the call, a heart to respond and hands to help. As Alfred Tennyson said of the Duke of Wellington, so I say of our subject: "The path of duty was the way to glory."

He seemed not to care what men thought of him, but his whole aim was to please his Maker. He regarded the voice of conscience as the voice of God, and to the warnings and mandates of that voice he was always true. He was greatly beloved by all his neighbors. His children, his slaves and all his white associates loved and admired him. And when time shall be lost in the brilliant dawn of eternity's morning, many shall rise up and call him blessed.

> "Asleep! asleep! when soft and low
> The patient watchers come and go,
> Their loving vigil keeping;
> When from the dear eyes fades the light,
> And the glad spirit takes its flight,
> We speak of death as 'sleeping.'

> "Or when, as dies the orb of day,
> The aged Christian sinks away,

And the lone mourner weepeth;
When thus the pilgrim goes to rest,
With meek hands folded on his breast,
And his last sigh a prayer confessed—
We say of such, 'He sleepeth.'"
LUCY A. BENNETT.

CHAPTER III.

Granny, the Cook, On the Old Plantation.

The number that constituted the body of slaves on this plantation was not very large, but they were a fine-looking set of human beings. They were warmly clad, well fed and humanely treated. And, as forty-two years have passed since "the breaking up of the old plantation," it is hardly possible that the writer should remember the name of every slave born and raised on that place. And yet he can recall the most of them and the image of their person still yet lingers in his memory.

Here they are: There were Uncle Fridie and Aunt Nancy, his wife; Uncle Isom and Aunt Tena, his spouse. There were two young women on the plantation—Namie and Peggie—who, after marriage, became very fruitful. Namie married a man by the name of Tom, and Peggie a man by the name of Sam. Tom belonged to a Mr. Durant, and Sam to a Mr. Singletary. Namie became the mother of some nine children and Peggie some twelve or thirteen. Namie's children were Melton, Sam, Nellie, Tom, Kellie, Jimmie, Vinie, Martha and Joe. Peggie's were Prince, Caroline, Sydney, Mary, Henry, Elizabeth, Aleck, Sammie and four or five others whose names I cannot now recall. Nearly all of these grew up to manhood and womanhood and married off, and themselves became fathers and mothers. And when the Emancipation Proclamation was issued by Mr. Lincoln, there were perhaps forty or fifty slaves on this plantation.

But one of the most important characters among them all was Granny, the cook. She was slightly lame in one leg. When she was a little girl she and other children were playing in a bed of deep sand. She ran and jumped into the sand, and as her feet sunk into it she suddenly turned around and this twisted her leg at the knee. The injury at first did not seem to be serious and no doctor was called, but her leg grew crooked and she became lame for life. Because of this lameness she was favored to the extent that she was not made a field hand, but was kept about the house and taught to cook. And right well did she learn her trade; for she became one of the most expert cooks in all that region of country. And she took special pride in her profession, especially when company came to visit the white folks. All they had to do was to give Granny the materials and tell her what to do with them, and it was done. She always carefully followed the instructions given by Mrs. Frierson or Miss Mary Ann, and all was right. When that breakfast, that dinner or that supper was sent into the dining room, especially when company was "in the house," if the reader had been privileged to look upon it or to sniff its delicious odor, he would have thought that there was a Parisian caterer who presided over that kitchen.

Mr. Frierson's house was the preacher's home. Like the Shunammite of old, he set apart a room in his house and denominated it the "Prophet's chamber." He never forgot to entertain strangers, knowing that thereby some had entertained angels unawares. Among the preachers who served the Lynchburg circuit were: Rev. L. M. Little, Rev. M. A. Connolly, Rev. W. L. Pegues, Rev. W. W. Mood, Rev. P. F. Kistler, and Rev. F. Auld. These were all members of the South Carolina Conference of the M. E. Church, South. There were two eminent local preachers who preached acceptably to the people, namely: The DuRant Plantation house near Lynchburg. Rev. Jesse Smith and Rev. William Smith. These two ministers were brothers, and the latter, Rev. William Smith, was the father of three distinguished Carolinians, namely: the late Bishop A. Coke Smith, Rev. Charles B. Smith, and the Hon. E. D. Smith. But whenever these ministers would preach at the Shiloh church they would invariably come to Mr. Frierson's either for dinner or to pass the night. And when Granny, the cook, was notified that the pastor was coming, she would be delighted and made extensive preparations in the kitchen and did her best. All of Mr. Frierson's guests soon learned who the cook was, and seldom failed to give expressions of satisfaction when they left the dining room. Because of Granny's skill, Mr. Frierson did not have much trouble in persuading his pastors and friends to accept the hospitality of his home.

Granny could not be excelled in making and baking bread. Her biscuits, her light bread and her johnnie cakes were, to use a modern expression, "just out of sight." Reader, do you know what a "johnnie cake" is? I am afraid that you don't. If you have never inhaled the odor nor tasted a johnnie cake I am sure I shall have some difficulty in making you understand what it is. It was not baked in an oven nor in a stove, but before the fire.

A board was made out of oak, hickory or ash wood. It was about six inches wide and twelve inches long, and highly polished. The ingredients of the johnnie cake were: corn meal and sweet potatoes for flour, butter for lard and pure sweet milk for water. I think eggs were also used and some other seasoning, which I cannot now recall. These things were carefully mixed in and then the dough was spread out over the johnnie cake board and placed on the hearth before an oak fire. The board was slightly tilted so as to throw the cake squarely before the fire. It would soon "brown," as they said, and when Granny pronounced it done, the very sight, to say nothing of the odor, would make anybody's mouth water. Oh, how those preachers did like johnnie cake! Sometimes they would send for Granny to come into "the house" and shake her hand and congratulate this dusky queen of the kitchen.

It is said that women have a horror for snakes, and it is true. Ever since Mother Eve was beguiled by a serpent, all of her daughters—it matters not what their color may be, whether white, black or brown—have an awful dread of snakes. This intense hatred of the serpent tribe on the part of the women is of divine origin. In the Book it is written: "I will put enmity between thee and the woman and between thy seed and her seed; it shall bruise thy head and thou shalt bruise his heel." Thus spake the Lord to the serpent in the Garden of Eden.

But I want to tell the reader a story about Granny and the snake. The kitchen where Granny did the cooking was a small board building that set some distance from the dining room. It was about fifteen feet wide by twenty feet long. It had two doors—the doors being in the sides and opposite each other—and two windows. The building was unceiled. It was a mere shell. There was not even a loft overhead. This made a den for rats, and in consequence of this, a place for snakes. The rats came in search of food and the snake came in search of rats.

One evening just about dark Granny was getting supper, and while stooping down at the fireplace a great big chicken snake was chasing a rat on the plate above. They turned the corner and while passing over the fireplace where Granny was stooping, the snake fell full length across her neck and instantly wrapped itself around her neck. It is needless to say that Granny alarmed the place. She hollered, she screamed; the dogs barked and the children cried. The white folks and the colored folks all came running to see what was the matter. Granny left the kitchen and took the yard, and the yard was a very large one, too. Doubtless the snake would have fled from fright, but Granny clutched it with both hands—one hand on each side of her neck. The men folks could not catch her to release her from the snake until she fainted, then they killed the snake and Granny soon came to. She was not bitten but greatly frightened. The white women had to finish getting the supper, while Granny tried to get herself together again, which she eventually succeeded in doing. But this was an experience which Granny never forgot. In subsequent years she used to sit down with a dozen or more children at her feet and relate to them, in graphic language, her experience with that old chicken snake. And oh, how the little ones used to ply her with questions! But she answered all of them to their satisfaction.

But Granny was great along other lines and for other things than that of cooking. It has already been stated that when Mr. Frierson lost his first wife she left a little motherless baby behind. It was a little boy, and his name was Mack. But Granny came to the child's rescue and acted a mother's part. She raised him. She prepared his food and fed him. She bathed him, dressed him, took him on her lap, tied his shoes, combed his hair and taught him his prayers. He slept in Granny's own bed with his lily white arms around her black neck. Little Mack loved Granny and Granny loved little Mack. And when he became a man he always entertained a high regard for her, and loved her to the end.

Granny, though she was black, considered herself the mistress on that plantation. She thought that her color was no fault of hers, but circumstances (part of the time Mr. Frierson having no wife) and efficiency, made her head of the household. When Granny gave orders those orders had to be obeyed. White and colored respected and obeyed her.

Granny took great delight in caring for the chickens and the turkeys. She also gave the pigs about the yard some attention. All the waste from the kitchen was carefully saved for them. She saw that the cows were milked regularly. She kept the milk piggins and pans clean and nice, and did the churning herself. Consequently Mr. Frierson always had a plenty of fatted fowls for his table and a pig to roast whenever he felt like it. He also had an abundance of nice milk and butter. Granny took special pride in providing these things, and her master felt grateful to her for it.

Granny lived to see Emancipation, and after becoming free was taken by her son-in-law to his own hired home where she was tenderly cared for until the angels came and escorted her soul home to that "happy land far, far away." She lived the life of the righteous, and died in the Christian faith.

CHAPTER IV.
A 'Possum Hunt on the Old Plantation.

There was a good supply of fresh water fish in Pudden Swamp in ante-bellum days. The varieties known and caught in those days were suckers, pikes, jacks, perches and catfish. But the slaves hadn't much time for fishing;

they had to work during the day. But they were very fond of hunting coons and 'possums, and even this pastime had to be gratified at night.

The flesh of these animals, when properly prepared, makes a very savory and palatable dish. The method of cooking the 'possum or coon was this: They first parboiled it whole and then roasted or baked it brown. Sweet potatoes were also boiled and skinned and roasted around it. The slaves were very fond of such dishes.

As has already been remarked, the young men had a natural fondness for hunting. Like the sporting men of all races, there were some slaves who possessed a natural fondness for the chase.

There were four dogs belonging to the white folks and perhaps one or two belonging to the slaves. These were all trained by the slaves. There was old Sumter, named for General Sumter of Revolutionary fame, and old Bull, Rip and Tiz. The last two were full-blood fox hounds, male and female. Better 'possum and coon dogs never entered the woods. Then there was old Toler. He was half bull and belonged to Tom. He was the fighter. When the other dogs failed he would swing to a 'possum or coon to the last. A 'possum was not much at fighting, unless he was caught in his den, then it took all the dogs to bring him out, and often all failed but old Toler. He would bring him out or die. Consequently the boys seldom left him behind. His presence was necessary to do the fighting.

'Possums usually inhabit the woodland and coons the swamps. The boys thought that they would like to have a 'possum for their Sunday morning's breakfast, and yet they had been told by Uncle Fridie and Uncle Isom not to go hunting on Saturday night, for, as the holy Sabbath began at midnight and as they had no way of telling when midnight came, they would be likely to hunt on Sunday. They owned no watches, but were told that when the seven stars reached a point directly overhead that it was midnight. Such was the case at that season of the year.

After supper the boys started out. The only things necessary to achieve a successful hunt was the dogs and two or three good, sharp axes with which to cut down the trees when the dogs would tree the game. They first went to the woods for a 'possum hunt, but, after wandering away for two miles, the dogs failed to strike a trail. They then concluded to go to the swamp (Pudden Swamp), for a coon hunt. Away they went, holding in their hands bright pitch pine torches. Now and then they would give to the dogs a keen coon hunters' whoop, but there came no response from them. On they went in the dark and dense swamp, whooping up the dogs. Presently the clear, full yelp of old Bull was heard. Sydney said, "It is a rabbit, for old Bull likes to run rabbits." "Wait and see," said Tom. Sam, who was the oldest in the crowd, and who had more experience in the hunting business than all the others, said: "I am waiting on old Tiz, for she never runs rabbits at night. If she barks then I will know it's a coon." Again the boys whooped to the dogs. Just then a long, rolling bark was heard, such as a full-blood fox hound would make when it strikes a warm trail. Sam said: "Boys, it is old Tiz, and I believe it is a coon. Come on." The torch-bearers snuffed their torches and quickened their steps. Again the boys whooped. By this time all four of the dogs, as the hunters used to say, were speaking. Old Bull, old Sumter, Rip and Tiz. The sound of their barking and yelping was like different voices singing the four parts of music. There was the soprano, alto, tenor and bass. Again the boys whooped. On they went trying to keep up with the dogs. The fellows got lively as they thought of the fun just ahead of them, when they would have the pleasure of witnessing a great coon-dog fight. But all of a sudden every dog ceased barking and the hunters stopped. They did not know what to make of it. Again they whooped, but there was no response on the part of the dogs. They listened in silent wonder. Presently the dogs came in, one by one, with their tails drooping between their hind legs. The boys noticed that their bristles were all upturned and they whined at their feet. The hunters became frightened and they began to think. Tom said, "Boys, perhaps it is after midnight and we are hunting on Sunday." Instantly all eyes were upturned as they peered into the heavens looking for the seven stars, and to their surprise the seven stars had passed the zenith and swung far over into the western sky. Then they remembered what Uncle Fridie and Uncle Isom had told them about hunting on Sunday. Immediately they all concluded that God was angry with them for desecrating His holy day, and allowed the devil to come after them. It is needless to say that they left the swamp unceremoniously, for such was the case. They ran nearly every step of the way home, and when they got their breath they awoke the whole negro quarters and related their wonderful but very unpleasant experience. All the slaves believed that it was the devil sent after those wicked boys, but when the white folks heard of it they said it was a bear, for Mr. Adolphus saw one just a few days before while squirrel hunting in that region. But the slaves all held to their belief and still contended that it was the devil and that he came in the form of a big black bear. Suffice it to say that it cured the boys, and from that time on there was no more 'possum and coon hunting by the slaves on Saturday night in all that part of the country.

CHAPTER V.

A Wedding on the Old Plantation.

The slave young men and young women were like the young people of all other races, they fell in love and they married. Their love affairs, their courtship and their marriage were of the simplest form. They could not read nor write, therefore notes and letters did not figure in their love experiences. But they loved all the same. Cupid managed to kindle the divine spark in their breasts, and he had a way to fan it to a flame.

Love, as every one who has loved knows, has a language peculiarly its own. And it is not a language of words, but rather a language like that of free masonry. It is a language of grips, of signs and of symbols. When two young slaves fell in love with each other the young man would make it known on his part by a gentle pressure of the young woman's hand as they shook hands. Or he would give her a peculiar or affectionate smile and accompany his action with a loving gift. And in the majority of cases the gift consisted in the most beautiful red apple that he could secure from the orchard. The girl would rarely eat the apple until the Sabbath was passed and until it had become mellow. The presentation would likely be made on the Sabbath as they went or returned from church, and the girl invariably carried the apple in her hand or wrapped it in her handkerchief. As she gazed upon its beauty and inhaled its fragrance, she would be reminded of the tender love of her sweetheart.

When the young man became satisfied that he had won the heart of his girl, he then proceeded gently and modestly to ask her to become his wife. This was called among the slaves "popping the question." Having secured her consent, he next secured the consent of her parents, if she had any, and the consent of his master and her master, if she lived on another plantation. This ended it. He was considered married, and he took her to be his wife. This was the usual way. There was no religious wedding ceremony and no marriage supper.

But there were a few isolated cases where the slaves were allowed to marry in due form and were given a wedding supper. These were the more prominent or favorite slaves, such as butlers, coachmen, nurses, chambermaids or cooks, sometimes enjoyed this privilege. Sam, the foreman on Mr. Frierson's plantation, was granted such a favor. He married a girl whose name was Bettie. She belonged to Mr. Isaac Keels, who owned the adjoining plantation just north of Mr. Frierson's.

The time was Saturday night and the occasion was a great one. Careful and elaborate preparations were made. The Friersons on Sam's side, and the Keelses on Bettie's side, co-operated to make the wedding a success. Also the relatives of the bride and the groom came forward to render assistance.

There were six bridesmaids and six groomsmen. The bridesmaids were all dressed in white and the groomsmen in black. Most of these costumes were borrowed—some from the white folks and some from the colored. The marriage feast was a bountiful affair. A good size shote, the gift of Mr. Frierson, was nicely barbecued. Uncle Tom, the father of the groom, was an expert at barbecuing. He did a lot of it for the white folks, especially on occasions of general musters, weddings, picnics, etc. Dozens of chickens were roasted, potted and fried. An abundance of sweet potato custards, apple pies and cakes were baked, and several large pots of rice were boiled. Every plantation within a radius of five miles was represented at that wedding. The marriage took place at the bride's home, or I might say in the negro quarters on Mr. Isaac Keels' place. Several white folks were present, especially of the Friersons and the Keelses. Uncle John Woods, an ante-bellum negro preacher, was engaged to perform the marriage ceremony. He was a very intelligent old man. He could read well and talk fluently. He was considered a great preacher by the slaves, and many of the devout white folks were fond of hearing him. He wore black pants and a black shad-belly or pigeon-tail coat and white vest. It was a secondhand outfit, and was the gift of his old master, Mr. Woods. He also wore a black silk beaver hat that looked rather seedy because of its extreme age and exposure to the elements. He wore a stiff standing white collar that spanned his neck and touched his ear on each side and a white tie. But, withal, he had the appearance of a distinguished negro clergyman of ante-bellum days.

The marriage ceremony took place in the yard. At some distance in front of the door of the two-room cabin was placed a small table with a clean white cloth over it and on which were two brass candlesticks. In these burned two tallow dips or candles. Behind this table stood the preacher. Near him sat Jerry Goodman in a chair with a fiddle who played the wedding march. The waiters, as they were called, filed out in couples, a man and a woman walking together. The groom and his bride followed in the rear, with the bride gracefully leaning upon the arm of her beloved. As now, so then, everybody tried to gain a view of the pair. Perfect silence reigned while Uncle John read in a full, clear voice the Methodist marriage ceremony. At the end the preacher was the first to kiss the bride, the groom the second, then followed kisses from all the bridesmaids and groomsmen. This was the custom in ante-bellum days among the slaves.

The next thing in order was the supper. Two tables had been built on different sides of the yard, one for the white folks and the other for the colored. The table for the white folks was about twelve feet long and three feet wide; the one for the colored was about twenty feet long and three wide. Clean white cloths were spread over these tables and plates were placed thereon as close as persons could stand. Food was put upon these tables until, if they were things of life, they would literally have groaned under the burdens of good things. Uncle John was placed at the head of the colored people's table with the groom and his bride on the right and the groomsmen and bridesmaids on each side down the line. He asked the divine blessing, or said the grace, for both tables. There were several tables full of the guests, but as the food supply was ample, all had enough. The whole scene was a picturesque one, and it was made more so by the glare of the big bonfire that was kept burning in the yard.

After supper the fiddle struck up, with the nimble fingers of Jerry Goodman on the bow, and the dancing began and continued until a very late hour of the night. Early in the next week Sam, the groom, settled the marriage fee by giving the preacher, Uncle John Woods, a peck of clean-beat rice. Thus ended the wedding festivities on the old plantation.

CHAPTER VI.

Christmas on the Old Plantation.

Not many of the slaves knew the historical significance of Christmas. They could not read nor write, hence their knowledge of the important events of history, even those of sacred history, was exceedingly limited. Most they knew about Christmas was that it meant a good time for every-body. It was the custom on the plantations in that region of the country to kill the fattening hogs just before Christmas so that all, white folks and slaves, might have plenty of fresh meat to eat during this joyous season. This gave rise to the expression, which originated among the slaves, "a hog-killing time." Backbones, spare-ribs and rice were a favorite dish about Christmas time.

There is another thing to be considered about the way and manner in which Christmas was observed on the old plantation in ante-bellum days, and that is this: Three days were usually given to the slaves for Christmas. The day before, generally called "Christmas Eve," and the day after; hence the slaves thought all three days were Christmas. They frequently referred to Christmas Eve as "the first day of Christmas," to Christmas itself as "the second day of Christmas," and the day after as "the third or last day of Christmas." And this thought and this manner of expression have been brought over into freedom. Among the country colored people we frequently hear similar expressions used even at this day and time in speaking of Christmas.

On some plantations it was the custom to have all the slaves repair in a body to the white folks' house on Christmas morning and receive a dram as "a Christmas present." Old and young, male and female, came forward for the "Christmas dram." It was certainly a lively time with the slaves on the old plantation. Those who came early to the yard would have to wait until all came. And while they waited they would whistle, jig or dance, or

> "They sat and sung
> Their slender ditties when the trees were bare."

But this was not the case on Mr. Frierson's plantation. He was a Christian man, and, therefore, believed in and practiced the principles of temperance. He, nor a single member of his family were ever known to indulge in strong drink. Such a thing as whiskey was unknown on that plantation. But it was freely used on some of the adjoining plantations. On some of these there were drunkards to be found both among the white folks and among the slaves. But not so on Mr. Frierson's place. It was a plantation where sobriety was strictly taught and practiced by the white folks, and consequently, the slaves were greatly benefited.

But Christmas was observed on Mr. Frierson's place in a way that was highly enjoyable to all. It was the custom on all the plantations around to give at the beginning of the winter each male among the slaves a new outfit, consisting of shoes, pants, coat and a cap. The women and girls got shoes and dresses. Mr. Frierson made it a point to give out these on Christmas morning.

On or about a month before Christmas the right foot of each slave, male and female, was measured and Mr. Frierson would get in his buggy and drive to Sumter, the County seat and Sam would bring the two-horse wagon. The purpose was to buy shoes for the slaves. The town was only about twenty miles away, and by starting before day they could and did make the trip in a day and do all their trading, too. The topic of conversation during that day among the slaves while they worked was the trip of the old boss and Sam to Sumter. As the sun went down and the time drew near for them to return, the slaves would listen for the rumbling of the wagon wheels and the sound of horses' hoofs. That night their slumbers were filled with dreams and visions of new suits, new shoes, new caps and new dresses. But these things were not given out until Christmas morning. And while this glad day was perhaps only a month off, yet the month seemed longer, the days seemed longer and the nights seemed longer than at any other season of the year. This was naturally and literally true of the nights, but it was not true of the days nor the month, but so it seemed to the slaves. The anxiety, the longing and the solicitude for the dawn of Christmas morning is indescribable. The thought of old Santa Claus among enlightened people never could produce such a feeling as that which animated the breasts of these poor, ignorant slaves.

But Christmas came. The sun arose without a cloud to obscure his brightness. Breakfast is over and all hands repair to the "house." Presently the yard is full of darkies with smiling faces and joyous hearts. And there are as many piles on that long front piazza of the white folks house as there are hands on that place. In each pile there are shoes, a suit or dress, and a cap. On each pile there is a tag with the name of the person written on it for whom it is designed. Now, imagine, if you can, the exquisite joy that thrilled each heart as his or her name was called. And as each person filed out of that gate on their return to the negro quarters they seemed to be as happy as angels. And it is needless to say that the white folks enjoyed the distribution of the winter's outfit on Christmas morning as much as the slaves, for such undoubtedly was the case. Everybody felt that this was a better way than having a dram on Christmas morning. Such was Christmas on the old plantation in ante-bellum days.

CHAPTER VII.
Sunday on the Old Plantation.

Sunday was always a welcome day on the old plantation, not only by the slaves, but also by the white folks. It came in all right to break the monotony of plantation life. The older and more serious ones went to "meetin'" or visited the sick, or made social calls, while the youngsters met other youngsters from the adjoining plantations and spent the day in wrestling, jumping, boxing, running foot races and sometimes fighting. In the summer season they would sometimes roam through the fields from plantation to plantation in search of watermelons and fruits. They would plunge into the dark and dense swamp in search of wild muscadine grapes or through the fields for blackberries, or the pine woods for huckleberries.

On some of the nearby plantations the younger slaves were made to do light work on Sunday, such as minding the birds and crows from the corn, rice and potatoes. When these plants were coming up the crows and rice birds were very destructive. They would pull them up, and often the whole crop would have to be carefully replanted. But Mr. Frierson, who planted the same kinds of stuff as was planted on the other plantations, did not put any of his slaves on guard in the fields on Sunday, and yet he always made good crops and had an abundance. He was a God-fearing man, and held that the Sabbath was a day of rest for man and beast. He kept the day as sacred and required all his slaves, as nearly as possible, to do the same.

The Shiloh Methodist Church, to which Mr. Frierson and his family belonged, formed a part of the circuit known as the "Lynchburg Circuit." The parsonage was located at Lynchburg, a little cross-roads village about eight miles away. The minister was accustomed to preach in the Methodist Church at Lynchburg Sunday morning at 11 o'clock and at Shiloh in the afternoon at 3:30 o'clock the same day. His appointment at the Shiloh Church was once a month, but to keep the slaves—and especially the younger ones—out of mischief, Mr. Frierson had preaching in his yard under the stately old water oaks on the regular preaching day at Shiloh. This service was conducted by some one of the old ante-bellum negro preachers. There was also a Sunday school conducted at the Shiloh Church in the afternoon just before preaching. All this was done for the spiritual and moral uplift of the slaves as well as to keep them out of devilment, and from desecrating God's holy day.

But the service conducted in Mr. Frierson's yard at 11 o'clock on the preaching day at Shiloh was the center of attraction in all that region of country. The more pious from the adjacent plantations, both white and colored, came in large numbers. The services invariably were conducted by antebellum negro preachers. These preachers were: Uncle John Woods, Uncle Daniel Gass, Uncle Daniel Hand, and Uncle Joseph White. Some of these lived just a few miles away, others again lived a considerable distance. One, Uncle Daniel Hand, lived across the Lynches River, over in Darlington, the adjoining county. They all had their day, and they seldom failed to meet it. Of course, they had to get the consent of their masters to come, and they invariably brought a ticket from their masters for their protection. If they lived far away their masters would let them have a mule to ride; or if it happened to be in the work season and the mules were busy, the master's saddle horse or buggy horse was given instead. But Uncle John Woods lived the nearest, and therefore was oftenest there.

Mr. Frierson's front yard was a large one, and as has been stated heretofore several times, it was well shaded with large and beautiful water oaks. Under these oaks Mr. Frierson had very comfortable seats placed. There was a seating capacity for possibly 250 or 300 people. They were arranged so that the audience would face the east and present a side view to the white folks, who sat in the long front piazza. At the east end of these seats, fronting the audience, stood a small table with a clean, white cloth thrown over it. On this table was placed a pitcher of fresh water and a tumbler, a Bible and a hymn book, and behind it a chair. All this for the use and convenience of the speaker, who was always a colored man. No white preacher was ever known to stand behind that table, though some of them very much desired to do so. That long piazza was usually filled with devout white worshippers, and the seats below with zealous and enthusiastic colored Christians.

The scene presented a very unique appearance. Those who had religion in that day and time had what is now called "the old time religion." Sometimes when the old preacher would warm up to his subject and grow loud, if not eloquent, the audience would break forth in shouts of joy and praise. (While some colored sister would be jumping out in the audience, some of the white ladies were known to act in a similar manner in the piazza. In those days both the white folks and the colored folks had good religion. The singing by the colored folks on such occasions was an important feature of the worship. It was not done by notes nor always by words, but it was from the heart, and the melody seldom failed to stir the soul. Rev. Dinkins, the negro poet quoted previously, describes it thus:

> "Give me the farm when Sunday comes,
> When all the girls and all the chums
> Meet at the spring,
> When long-eared mules, ox-carts in droves,
> Come sailing through the woods and groves,
> Oh, how we sing!

> "The preacher reads the hymn divine,
> And we remember not a line,
> But sing right on;
> When with the text we start to shout,
> Forgetting shame, or pride, or doubt,
> To heaven most gone."

Uncle John Woods was a good preacher, considering his chances, and had an excellent command of good English. He was a man of deep piety, and had the love and respect of both white and colored. The author herewith reproduces, from memory, one of his sermons preached in Mr. Frierson's yard.

A SERMON ON THE OLD PLANTATION.
By Uncle John Woods.

Text—"The men of Nineveh shall rise in judgment with this
generation and shall condemn it because they repented at the
preaching of Jonas; and, behold, a greater than Jonas is here."
—Matt. xii:41.

Brothers and Sisters: These words, which I have taken for a text, were
spoken by our Lord, Jesus Christ. He spoke them to the people of His day
and time, but He commanded His servant, St. Matthew, to write them
down in a book so that all the people in all the ages might have them and
take warning. So I bring them to you today, and you will do well to listen
and to take heed.

St. Matthew was a servant, brothers and sisters, and he was a good servant and obeyed Christ, his Master. Christ called him and he came and
followed Christ. Christ commanded him to write the gospel and he wrote
it. So Christ wants you and me to obey Him in all things. He says, "Repent,
for the kingdom of heaven is at hand." Christ wants us to hear His voice
and obey His words. And if we don't obey Him he will punish us, for He
says in another place: "He that knows his Master's will and does it not
shall be beaten with many stripes." Many of us know, in a two-fold sense,
what this means. But all who are not Christians will learn to their sorrow
one of these days what it means in a spiritual sense. Christ is our Master,
we are His servants, and if we don't obey Him and repent, He will certainly apply the lash, and apply it severely, too.

But let us consider Jonah. He is the man referred to in the text. Let me
read it again; perhaps you have forgotten it: "The men of Ninevah shall
rise in judgment with this generation and shall condemn it, because they
repented at the preaching of Jonah; and, behold, a greater than Jonah is
here." Jonah was called just like Matthew. Matthew was called to be an
apostle and to write a book, and he obeyed. Jonah was called to be a
prophet. He was sent to preach repentance to the people of Ninevah, but
he refused to go. It is hard to tell, brothers and sisters, what were his
reasons for not obeying God and going to preach to these people. But I
remember that Jonah was a Jew, and, according to his raising and training, he did not want to have anything to do with the people of another
nation. He did not wish to associate with them, he did not wish to eat with
them, nor sleep in their houses, nor to preach the word of God to them. I
can't say Jonah was a wicked man, neither can I say he was a bad man, for

I don't believe that God would call a wicked or a bad man to preach His word to the people, no, not even to the heathen.

Now, what did Jonah do? Let us see. He ran away, or, at least, he tried to run away from God. He thought he would go down to Joppa, buy a ticket for Tarshish and take shipping for that place, as though there was no God in Joppa, Tarshish or on the sea. My friends, I fear we sometimes make the same mistake. We do wrong and then try to run away from God. We try to hide from His presence. Adam and Eve, in the Garden of Eden, tried the same trick, but it would not work. They sinned against God. They disobeyed Him and ate the forbidden fruit, and when they found that God was displeased and angry with them, they hid themselves among the bushes of the garden. But God came down and sought them and found them. Right there in the garden the judgment was set; the guilty pair was convicted and the awful sentence was pronounced. In great shame and disgrace they were driven from that holy place out into a world of sin, sorrow and misery. If a man breaks God's holy law and sins against Him, though he may run away and hide, God will find him and punish him. The Bible says, "Be sure your sins will find you out."

But Jonah came to Joppa, and, after paying his fare, he went aboard that ship. He did not feel good. He did not feel like a man taking a pleasure trip, nor like a man going off on business. He did not sit down on deck and converse with the other passengers. No, under the burden of his terrible guilt he went down into the hold of the ship among the freight and went fast to sleep. He went to sleep! Sleep is all right when it is taken in the right place, at the right time and under the right circumstances. Otherwise it is wrong, it is out of place. Hence you see, brothers and sisters, it is possible for a man to sleep with a great burden of guilt upon him, and when he is in great and fearful danger. Jonah was asleep, but God was wide awake with His eyes on him. Jonah thought he was hiding, but God saw him.

By and by I hear loud thunders begin to roll. I see dark clouds coming up. The lightnings flash and play upon the bosom of these black clouds. The sea roars and the waves rise like mountains. The ship pitches and rocks and the shipmaster and his crew become afraid. They threw some of the freight overboard and every man prayed to his god, and yet the storm was not abated. It still raged. Then they thought that they would cast lots to see on whose account this terrible storm had come upon them. They felt that somebody was guilty and they desired to find the guilty man. And when the lot was cast it fell upon Jonah. He was the guilty man. Then the shipmaster went down in the hold and found Jonah fast asleep. How that man could sleep in the midst of such a storm is a mystery to me! I cannot understand it. But every sinner is doing the same thing. He is dead asleep in his sins while the storm of God's wrath is raging all around him.

The shipmaster said to Jonah: "What meanest thou, O sleeper? arise, call upon thy God, if so be that God will think upon us, that we perish not." When Jonah was awakened, the shipmaster, his crew and the passengers all gathered around him and asked him what was his occupation, what was his country and what was his nation. And Jonah answered and said: "I am a Hebrew and I fear Jehovah, the God of heaven, who hath made the sea and the dry land." He then confessed his guilt. He told them that he was trying to run away from God, and begged them to throw him into the sea. They did so. But God had sent a great fish to swallow up Jonah. And Jonah was three days and nights in the belly of the fish. Then God told the fish to cast Jonah out on land, and the fish did so. And when Jonah got free from the fish he went to Nineveh and preached repentance to the people, and the whole city was converted and spared. Now, Jesus says in my text: "The men of Nineveh shall rise in judgment with this generation and shall condemn it, because they repented at the preaching of Jonah; and, behold, a greater than Jonah is here."

Christ declares here in this text that He is greater than Jonah. And so He is. This does not need any argument to prove it. You all believe that Christ is greater than Jonah. Jonah was a man, Christ was God. Jonah was guilty of the sins of disobedience and anger, Christ yielded perfect obedience to God and was without sin. Therefore He is greater than Jonah. But the people of Ninevah repented at the preaching of Jonah, while Christ, who is greater than Jonah, came from heaven to earth to preach to sinners, and they will not hear nor repent. Therefore the people of Nineveh shall rise up in the judgment and condemn them.

My friends, there is going to be a judgment. God has appointed a day when He is going to judge the world. All the good angels will be there. All the devils in hell and out of hell will be there. All the good people saved in heaven will be there, and all the bad people lost in hell will be there. And you, my friends, all will be there, and I will be there. And if you don't repent the men of Nineveh will come forth as witnesses against you. They shall condemn you, because they repented at the preaching of Jonah, and behold a greater than Jonah is here, and that greater one is Christ.

May the Lord help you all to get ready for that awful day, for it will surely come!

This sermon, of which the above sketch is a mere outline, was delivered with great energy and power, and it produced a deep impression upon the entire audience.

CHAPTER VIII.
A Funeral on the Old Plantation.

It may appear strange to the reader, but it is true, nevertheless, that in some way or other the slaves very often connected sickness and death with voodooism or conjuration. This belief and practice of voodooism and conjuration originated in Africa, and was brought over to America when the native African was brought here and made a slave. The idea is deeply rooted in the negro thought and life. Its history runs back perhaps four thousand years among the native tribes of that Dark Continent.

I quote from the University Encyclopedia: "Voodoo, a name given by the negroes of the West Indies and the United States to superstitious rites and beliefs brought with them from Africa, and to the sorcerer who practiced these rites.

"In the Southern States of the Union there was at one time a widespread and deep-rooted belief in the power of these sorcerers. As the negroes advance in education the belief is dying away. At one time, however, despite all efforts of religious teachers to banish the mastery of this belief from the minds of the slaves, the voodoo 'doctor' was an almost omnipotent individual in the estimation of his fellows. No slave could, under any pretext, be persuaded to expose himself to the vengeance or wrath of one of these conjurers. In some cases there was a reasonable foundation for these fears, for in not a few instances has it been proven that some of the voodoos were skillful poisoners, and while the great mass of their professed art was a rank imposture, still they possessed enough of devilish skill to render them objects of wholesome dread.

"Their methods were as varied and variable as the winds. Anything that was mysterious or likely to impress the ignorant mind with a feeling of terror was eagerly seized on and improved by them to their own advantage. Their services were more often invoked in destructive than in curative offices. If a negro desired to destroy an enemy he sought the aid of the voodoo, who, in many cases, would undertake to remove the obnoxious one, and the removal was generally accomplished through the medium of poison. No doubt exists that in many cases the victim of a voodoo died from sheer fright, for whenever a negro had reason to think that he was possessed by the spell of the voodoo, he at once gave up all hope, thus hastening the accomplishment of the end toward which the energies of the sorcerer were directed. Their incantations and spell-workings were always conducted with the greatest secrecy, no one being allowed to witness the more occult and potent portion of their ritual. They were frequently employed by dusky swains to gain for them the affections of their hard-hearted inamoratas, and love powders and other accessories for 'tricking' constituted their stock in trade, and in some instances yielded them no insignificant revenue. The field in which voodooism flourished best was the far South, among the rice, cotton and sugar plantations, where the negroes were not brought into contact so closely with their masters as they were further North."

The above quotation is a correct presentation of the conditions as they existed on the Frierson plantation, as well as on every plantation in the Southern States. What was true of one as regards voodooism and conjuration, was true of all of them.

Well, there was a girl on the Frierson plantation by the name of Mary. She was a black girl of medium size, but rather good looking. She was quite a favorite among the young men of the place and neighborhood. Several, so to speak, were cutting after her. Mary was a daughter of Aunt Peggie and Uncle Sam. But it came to pass that she took sick, and after a lingering illness of possibly four or six months' duration, she died, leaving behind her a little infant. During the entire period of her sickness it was whispered around on the plantation, also on the adjoining plantations, that Mary had been conjured. Of course, this meant that she had been poisoned. There was a woman who lived on a plantation not far away, whose name was Epsey. This woman was said to have been Mary's rival in a love scrape, and therefore was accused of being the one who administered the dose. Some conjurer of the neighborhood prepared the dose for her, so it was said. This thing—Mary's sickness and death, and the talk of her being conjured—stirred the negroes on all the plantations for miles around.

But the white folks took no stock in all these rumors and gossip. They knew that Mary was sick, therefore they sent for Dr. Adolphus Higgins Frierson. He was a brother of the proprietor of the old plantation, and was a graduate of a medical college in Philadelphia, Pa. He was a learned man and a very competent physician. He was the family physician for the white folks, and also attended the slaves.

Dr. Frierson treated Mary, but the slaves did not think that he understood the case perfectly well. He said Mary had been "hurt" or "conjured," and that he alone could cure her. So they treated her secretly at the same time that Dr. Frierson was treating her. But it came to pass that Mary died and her funeral was the largest ever held in all that region of the country.

Death always made a very profound impression upon the slaves. They could not understand it. Their dead was invariably buried at night or on the Sabbath, at which time the slaves from the adjoining plantations attended in large numbers. Mary's funeral took place at night.

The coffin, a rough home-made affair, was placed upon a cart, which was drawn by old Gray, and the multitude formed in a line in the rear, marching two deep. The procession was something like a quarter of a mile long. Perhaps every fifteenth person down the line carried an uplifted torch. As the procession moved slowly toward "the lonesome graveyard" down by the side of the swamp, they sung the well-known hymn of Dr. Isaac Watts:

> "When I can read my title clear
> To mansions in the skies,
> I bid farewell to every fear
> And wipe my weeping eyes."

Mary's baby was taken to the graveyard by its grandmother, and before the corpse was deposited in the earth, the baby was passed from one person to another across the coffin. The slaves believed that if this was not done it would be impossible to raise the infant. The mother's spirit would come back for her baby and take it to herself. This belief is held by many of the descendants of these slaves, who practice the same thing at the present day.

After this performance the corpse was lowered into the grave and covered, each person throwing a handful of dirt into the grave as a last and farewell act of kindness to the dead, and while this was being done the leader announced that other hymn of Dr. Watts:

> "Hark! from the tombs a doleful sound
> My ears, attend the cry;
> Ye living men, come view the ground
> Where you must shortly lie."

These hymns were sung with a spirit and pathos which were sufficient to move the heart of a savage. A prayer was offered, the doxology sung and the benediction was pronounced. This concluded the services at the grave. No burial or committal service was read, for it was only now and then that one could be found among the slaves who could read well enough to do it. At a subsequent time, when all the relatives and friends could be brought together, a big funeral sermon was preached by some one of the ante-bellum negro preachers. And this practice has been brought over into the land of freedom, and is still observed in some places and by some colored people at the present day.

CHAPTER IX.
A Log-Rolling on the Old Plantation.

The slaveholders of ante-bellum days had some customs that were very convenient, and, at the same time, very helpful to each other. There were no markets and butchers in the country, where they could get fresh meats: hence they formed a market among themselves, and each man was his own butcher. That is, a number of them formed themselves into a club, one of which killed a fat young beef every Saturday, and a choice piece was taken to each member of the club. Thus they were supplied with nice fresh beef every week. This beef was not sold, but was distributed around among the members of the club as a sort of an exchange arrangement. When a member of the club killed, he put the whole beef into the wagon (except his own choice or piece) and sent it round to each member of the club, and they made their own selection. When the club was formed, each member subscribed to, or promised to take so many pounds each week, and it was done. This arrangement obtained all through the country, and it worked very nicely. There was another arrangement, which was formed by the planters for mutual helpfulness: namely, the log-rolling. A day was set on which the log-rolling was to take place, and then invitations were sent out to the neighboring planters, and each sent a hand. This work was returned when the others had their log-rolling. A log-rolling always meant a good dinner of the best, and lots of fun, as well as a testing of manhood. This testing of manhood was something that everybody was interested in. The masters were concerned, and consequently they selected and sent to the log-rolling their ablest-bodied men; the slave women were concerned: for they wanted their husbands and sweethearts to be considered the best men of the community. Then, too, the men took great pride in the development of their muscles. They took delight in rolling up their shirt sleeves, and displaying the largeness of their arms. In some cases, their muscles presented the appearance of John L. Sullivan—the American pugilist.

The woodlands of the South were covered with a variety of trees and undergrowth. Among the trees, were to be found the majestic pine, the sturdy oak, the sweet maple, the lovely dogwood, and the fruitful and useful hickory. When a piece of woodland was cleared up, and made ready for planting, it was called "new ground." In clearing up new ground, the undergrowth was grubbed up and burned; the oaks, maples, dogwood, and hickories were cut down, split up, and hauled to the house for firewood;

and the pines were belted or cut round, and left to die. After these pines had died and partially decayed, the winter's storms, from year to year, would blow them down: hence the necessity for the annual log-rolling. These log-rollings usually took place in the spring of the year. They formed an important part of the preparations for the new crop.

On the appointed day, the hands came together at the yard, and all necessary arrangements were made, the most important of which was the pairing or matching of the men for the day's work. In doing this, regard was had to the height and weight of the men. They were to lift in pairs; therefore, it was necessary that they should be as nearly the same height and weight as possible. The logs have all been cut about twenty feet in length, and several good, strong hand-sticks have been made. Now, everything is ready, and away to the fields they go. See them as they put six hand-sticks under a great big log. This means twelve men—one at each end of the hand-stick. It is going to be a mighty testing of manhood. Every man is ordered to his place. The captain gives the order, "Ready," and every man bows to his burden, with one hand on the end of the hand-stick, and the other on the log to keep it from rolling. The next command given by the captain is, "Altogether!" and up comes the big log. As they walk and stagger toward the heap, they utter a whoop like what is known as the "Rebel yell." If one fails to lift his part, he is said to have been "pulled down," and therefore becomes the butt of ridicule for the balance of the day. When the women folks learn of his misfortune, they forever scorn him as a weakling.

At 12 o'clock the horn blows for dinner, and they all knock off, and go, and enjoy a good dinner. After a rest, for possibly two hours, they go to the field again, and finish up the work for the day. Such was the log-rolling in the "days before the war."

At a subsequent day the women and children gather up the bark and limbs of these fallen trees and throw or pile them on these log heaps and burn them. When fifty or seventy-five log heaps would be full ablaze in the deepening of the evening twilight, the glare reflected from the heavens made it appear that the world was on fire. To even the benighted and uneducated slave, the sight was magnificent, and one of awe-inspiring beauty.

The custom of log-rolling, under the changed condition of things, may be done away with, but its name still lingers in the thought and language of modern times. It is often heard in gatherings, both religious and political, where everything goes, or is *made* to go *one way*. Such they say is "log-rolling." The idea comes from the fact that in a log-rolling, every man does his part, and every man goes the same way. There is a unity of purpose, and concert of action. *This* is "log-rolling" in modern times.

CHAPTER X.

A Corn-Shucking on the Old Plantation.

All who have the good fortune to have been born and reared in the country can recall with pleasing recollections the joy that welled up in all hearts during the harvest. Rev. Dr. Henry Duncan, an English writer of singular ability, says: "The heart thus opened, is prepared for that social enjoyment which we observe so remarkably diffused over whole bands of reapers engaged in the same toilsome but healthful employment. The emotion spreads from heart to heart, and the animation which prevails while the work proceeds, is not less an indication of gladness than the joke and song with which the welkin resounds during the intervals of rest. Who can view the joy which sparkles in the eye, and bursts from the lips of the reaper while he plies his daily tasks and not acknowledge a beneficent Creator?"

In the Book of Ruth we have a vivid and beautiful picture given us of an oriental harvest. The fields of Boaz teem with plenty. The golden crop yields its stores to replenish his granaries. The voice of the season calls for the reapers. They take down their sickles and whet them until they are keen and bright. Then away to the harvest-field they go, followed by the binders and gleaners; among the latter is the lovely Ruth. With patient industry they ply the sickle from morn till noon, at which time they gather, master, reapers, binders and gleaners, to partake of their bountiful meal. This they do with a beautiful simplicity and with great joy and gladness. And this joy and gladness is not the result of having a plenty to eat and drink, but the responsive gratitude of the finer qualities of the heart for the gracious and lavish gifts of a Divine Providence. This sentiment—joy at the return of the harvest—is characteristic of human nature. This is the testimony of all ages the world over. So it was with the ancient Egyptians, Greeks, and Romans. And so it is with us at the present day. The writer of these pages can remember the time when, even in America, the grain harvest was a time of great rejoicing. Of course this was before reapers or harvesters became so common. The neighbors for miles around used to send each a hand, with the old-fashioned "cradle," to our house, to assist in reaping down the harvest. And when ours was all done, we sent to help each of them. This was the custom in those days. With twenty hands we could reap down nearly a hundred acres in a day. Each reaper had a binder to follow him, and each binder had a little boy to gather up the handfuls as fast as the reaper would let them fall, and hand them to him or her. The writer was one of those little boys. It was fun for us. We always had a plenty to eat and drink of the best the farm afforded. The fun, the sport, and the joy we all had cannot be described. Only those who have had some acquaintance with farm life can imagine how we enjoyed it. What we ate and drank, and the joy the harvest afforded, constituted a considerable portion of our reward for bearing the burden and the heat of the day in the harvest field. This was wheat harvest, which usually occurred in June.

But the corn harvest came in the fall, and the corn-shucking always took place at that season. The fodder was generally pulled or stripped in August and September, and the ears of corn were left on the stock to dry until about the first of November. But now the day has come, and the corn breaking has begun. The hands all go to the field, and they break off the ears and throw them into piles. These piles are made in the middle of the same row about twenty feet apart, and contain the corn of some twelve rows. Two wagons each drawn by a pair of mules or horses, with bodies the same size, are loaded level full of corn. At the barn yard it is thrown into two piles preparatory to the corn-shucking. One load is put on this pile, and the other on that, and so on, until the entire crop is hauled in.

Then the night is set for the corn-shucking: for it was usually had at night, so that the slaves from the adjacent plantations could come and enjoy the sport. Invitations were sent far and near, and they were readily accepted. Great preparations were made in food and drink. The only drink allowed at the corn-shucking was coffee, but it was customary on some of the plantations to have whiskey at corn-shuckings, but Mr. Frierson never allowed it.

It was often the case that from fifty to seventy-five men, beside the women, came to the corn-shucking. All these had to be fed. Great pots of rice, meat, bread and coffee were prepared. It was enough for all who came and took part in the corn-shucking.

When all the invited hands had arrived, the first thing in order was the election of two men to be captains, and these captains selected their companies from the crowd present. It was done alternately, something after the manner of school boys when they make up their sides to play a game of baseball. Captain Number One had the first choice, and then his opponent, and so on, until the two companies were made up. These preliminary matters having been arranged, they then set in to shucking corn.

The reader will remember that there are two piles of corn of equal size, and now there are two companies of shuckers of equal numbers, each company having a captain. It was considered no little honor to be elected captain of a corn-shucking company. His hat or cap was invariably decorated with the inside shucks of a large ear of corn. He was delighted with the office, and everybody—white and colored—did him honor. In the election of these captains, regard was had to their ability to sing: for the captains usually led their company in singing while shucking corn. At a given signal, each captain took his seat on the top of his pile of corn, and his shuckers surrounded it. While they shucked corn they engaged in singing corn-shucking songs. Much of the fun of the occasion depended upon which side should win. It was a race that grew more exciting as the piles of unshucked corn grew less. They shucked, they sang, and they shouted. Then they knew that a bountiful supper awaited them just as soon as the work was done. On they went—a jolly good set, singing, joking and laughing. In the midst of it all, they could sniff the aroma of hot coffee, and the delicious odor of roasted meats and other nice dishes. This, as well as the hope of victory, was quite an inspiration to the boys. Well, the work is done. The last ear of corn has been shucked, and captain number one, with his company, has won. See the boys, as they toss their hats into the air! Hear them shout! The victory is theirs. They are a happy set.

Supper is now ready. Long tables—well laden with good things—have been prepared. Fully two score colored women are there to wait on the table. And they eat, and eat, and drink, to their satisfaction. The supper being over, with the moon shining brightly (moon-light nights were invariably selected for corn-shuckings) the boys spend some time in wrestling, foot racing and jumping before going home. And in all these games they matched one's agility, strength, and manhood against that of his fellow. This is kept up until a late hour of the night, and then they retire to the various plantations whither they belong.

Such was the corn-shucking on the old plantation in ante-bellum days. It was very much enjoyed by both the white folks and the slaves. The incidents and the happenings of a corn-shucking were long talked of on all the plantations represented. Nearly all the plantations had their corn-shuckings, and they certainly kept things lively during this season of the year in those days.

CHAPTER XI.
Little Jimmie, the Mail Boy, On the Old Plantation.

Little Jimmie was, perhaps, the most interesting character on Mr. Frierson's plantation. He was not a mulatto in the strict sense of that word.

Webster, who is an authority on the meaning of words in the English language, says: "A mulatto is the offspring of a negress by a white man, or of a white woman by a negro." Jimmie was the son of Uncle Tom and Aunt Namie. Both of them were mulattoes. Both of their fathers were white and both of their mothers were black.

Jimmie's father—Uncle Tom—was a free man. He was born a slave, but purchased himself and his mother long before the first gun of the Civil War was fired. He was a man of industry, frugality, and wisdom. His wife—Aunt Namie—possessed the same qualities as her husband in an eminent degree, to all of which she added another very desirable quality, and that was a deep and sincere piety. Though a slave, she was one of Zion's noblest daughters.

Jimmie was not like Isaac, a child of promise; nor like Moses, a goodly child; nor like Samuel, a child of desire and prayer; but like the unnamed offspring of David and Bathsheba, he was a child of affliction. According to the testimony of his mother, his father, and his grandmother, he came into the world a sorely afflicted child. They never thought that they would ever succeed in raising the little fellow. But they did all in their power for the child, backed by the efforts of the white folks; and God blessed the means used, and the child lived, and grew to be a bright and active little boy.

Jimmie possessed a lively, sunshiny, and frank disposition, which never failed to win friends for him. Consequently, from his early childhood, he became a general favorite on the plantation among both the white folks and the slaves. Just as soon as he became old enough, his old master took him from his mother to be his waiting-boy. This necessitated his eating at the yard and sleeping in the white folks' house. Family prayers were invariably had, evening and morning, and Jimmie was always called in. The family sat in a semi-circle around the fireside, and Jimmie's little chair formed a part of that semi-circle. The Bible was read in a most impressive manner, and prayer was offered. The memory of those days has always been helpful and a source of inspiration to Jimmie.

But Jimmie had many narrow escapes from death. In the big house, he slept on a pallet before the fire. One night, between midnight and day, his bed took fire. And, strange to say, it burned some considerable time before he realized what was the trouble. It is true, he felt the fire, but, in his sleep, he imagined himself being toasted by a big oak fire on a cold winter's night. However, he awoke, and to his utter astonishment, found his bed to be on fire. He aroused himself and tried to put the fire out, but failed. By this time the large room was filled with smoke, which became stifling. One of the young ladies—Miss Mary Ann—awoke, and asked if his bed was not on fire, and Jimmie told her, "Yes." She told him to take it out into the yard, which he did. He then applied water, and put it out. He sat up the balance of the night, but, like a shipwrecked seaman, he wished for the morning.

When Jimmie was about twelve years of age, he had a narrow escape from death by drowning. It was the custom among the slaves—both men and boys—to go in swimming after dinner. The place was a deep lake on the stream called Pudden Swamp. Up to this time Jimmie had not learned how to swim. The edge of the lake was shallow, but as you advanced toward the center, it became deeper and deeper until it reached perhaps some twelve or fifteen feet. The boys of Jimmie's age and size bathed near the banks, while the men, and those who could swim, plunged into the deep. Once Jimmie ventured too far out, and got into water where he could not touch bottom. Down he went: and when he arose, he screamed. This attracted the attention of all who were in bathing. He sank again, and when he came up the second time, his oldest brother Sam, who was an expert swimmer, caught him and saved him. Thus he was rescued, through the mercy of God, from a watery grave. Had this occurred on an occasion when these men were not present (for the boys often went in swimming without them) Jimmie would certainly have been drowned.

This boy was full of mischief, and reckless daring. He would venture to ride wild horses, unbroken mules, and even untamed steers. Once, while riding the little mule Jack, he was thrown with violence and tremendous force to the ground. It nearly killed him. After lying there awhile, he came to, and got up, but no traces of the little mule could be seen. In after years, Jimmie thought on these narrow escapes from death, and took comfort in the saying of an old writer: "Second causes do not work at pleasure. This is the bridle that God has upon the world." Lack of space prevents the writer from recording, in detail, all the miraculous deliverances from death, which marked the life of this much favored youth.

Jimmie was something of a privileged character on Mr. Frierson's plantation. It is true, he had to work in the field along with the other hands. Sometimes he dropped corn and peas; sometimes he thinned corn and cotton; and sometimes he hoed or plowed. But when Mr. Frierson would go off on business in his buggy, Jimmie had to go along and drive him. When his daughters went to church, or to make social calls, he went to drive them, and to care for the horses. So Jimmie had the privilege of attending all the big meetings, the weddings, and the parties of the white folks. All this proved to be of considerable advantage to him in gaining knowledge and information. Frequently on his return from some of these trips, the slaves would gather around him—old and young—to hear him tell what he saw and heard. And for days these things would be discussed by the body of slaves. This helped also to break the monotony of plantation life.

But as Jimmie grew up to young manhood, he became an expert horseman. There were none on the place, even among those older than he, white or colored, who could surpass him in this particular. His old master—Mr. Frierson—was so well pleased with Jimmie's achievements along this line that he gave him a pony named Charlie. This horse was a chestnut sorrel, with a star in his forehead, and a double mane, or a mane that fell gracefully on both sides of his neck. He was built exactly like a race horse. His body was long and slim, and his legs long and slender. His tail was of medium length, and inclined to be bushy. Jimmie ran many a race with Charlie, and had him so thoroughly trained that no horse or mule on that plantation, or on the adjoining plantations, could run with him. It was Jimmie's duty—in addition to the work he did on the farm—to go twice a week—Wednesdays and Saturdays—to Mr. Chris Player's, two miles away, for the mail, and to bring up the cows and sheep. Hence Jimmie never made a full hand on the farm, but worked when he was not needed for other duties.

But there is another interesting incident in the life of this youth, which the author cannot fail to relate. It occurred when he was about fifteen years of age. In the spring of 1865 the War between the States ended. The result was, all the slaves became free. A contract was signed by master and slaves to remain together the balance of that year and finish the crop.

It was now in the fall of that year, and the crops were being gathered. The children and young folks were sent to the field to pick peas. Jimmie was one of the number. The field was in sight of the white folks' house. From this house the white folks had a splendid view of these youngsters. They worked tolerably well until toward sundown, when they became very playful and frolicsome. From the house, the white folks saw their pranks. But nothing was said, yet they noticed that young "Mas Dolphus" was coming toward them with his double-barrel shotgun on his shoulder. They suspected nothing; but supposed that he was going on a squirrel hunt, as he was wont to do in the cool of the afternoons. As a matter of course, the youngsters all sobered down to work—seeing "Mas Dolphus" coming. And not a word was spoken, until he walked right up to Jimmie, and drew from under his coat a long whip, and began to lay it on him. The young master uttered these awful words as he continued to hit Jimmie: "Run if you dare, and I'll blow your brains out." Of course, the sight of the gun, and the threatening words of the young master had a decided effect in taming this young freedman. He stood and took it as good naturedly as he possibly could. And when he had gone the rounds (for he gave all a little) and left, Jimmie said: "I am not going to take this: for I am going straight to Sumter, and report this fellow to the Yankees." Brave words these! for a boy of fifteen, who was born and bred a slave, and taught nothing but to obey. He left the field immediately, jumped over into the swamp, went around the plantation, entered his mother's house, got his Sunday clothes, and struck out for Sumter, twenty-five miles away. He was followed by a boy called Henry, who was six months his junior, but was somewhat larger in stature. Henry had never been more than five miles from home in his life, and knew nothing but to work. Hence, it will be seen that Jimmie's traveling companion was not calculated to encourage him very much.

From the white folks, Jimmie had learned that the slaves were all free, and that the country had been put under military government. From them he learned that there was a garrison of Union soldiers in the town of Sumter, and that there was a provost marshal there, who heard and settled difficulties between the freedmen and their former owners. It was a knowledge of these things that prompted him to do what he did.

Jimmie and Henry left the old plantation just about dark. They told nobody of their departure, not even their mothers. How it must have pained them, when they discovered, at supper time, that these boys came up missing. Those were critical times. The war had just closed, but the country was still infested with lawless wanderers, who did not hesitate to commit crimes of all kinds. Robberies and murders were quite common. But in the face of all this, they plunged into a long, dark, and dense woods. Jimmie did not know the way to Sumter by the way of the State road, though he had traveled it several times with the white folks. But he knew that the railroad coming from Wilmington, N.C.—which ran within twelve or fifteen miles of Mr. Frierson's place—and going to Kingville, S.C., went by Sumter: for farmers from that section always crossed it near Sumter, going into the town. Now, Jimmie's plan was to get to the railroad, and then following the track in a westward direction, they would be sure to reach Sumter. And, after pursuing their journey through these fifteen miles of black forest, they struck the railroad about 11 o'clock in the night. Jimmie at once suggested to Henry that they camp for the night. It was agreed to. So they crossed the railroad, and went about a hundred yards, raked up some pine straw and oak leaves, and lay down to sleep close by the side of each other. They slept as quietly and as sweetly as two little fawns.

Sometime during the night, Jimmie was aroused by a passing train. As he rose up, and saw its glaring headlight, and heard its thundering noise, which shook the earth beneath him, he was so terribly frightened until he could not call Henry. The next morning he asked Henry if he heard or saw the train in the night, and he said, "No."

They arose betimes, and began their long journey for Sumter. They had no breakfast. In fact they had no supper the night before. They left home so unceremoniously until they forgot to take provisions for the journey. It is needless to say that they left in great haste: for such was the case. They had no money, and knew nobody by the way, and yet they did not steal. They reached Sumter, and found their way to the provost marshal's office before he came down. And, to their surprise, they met a crowd of other colored people there, who, like themselves, had had difficulties with their former owners, and came from all parts of the country, seeking redress. They were heard one at a time. And when these boys' turn came, they entered the office as timidly as a hare. This was their first sight of a Yankee soldier in uniform. There were two of them, but the boys could not remember their names. When Jimmie and Henry were asked in a most tender manner what they wanted, the former's heart was so touched, until he burst into a flood of tears. But when his tears were brushed away, Jimmie rehearsed the whole matter to them. This was his first public speech, and he never forgot it. The officers asked the boys if they had parents, and they told them, "Yes." But Jimmie told them that his father was a free man, and was living on a rented farm to himself. The provost marshal wrote him a note—telling him that his son was now free, and that he must take care of him, and not allow him to return to the old plantation. This was done. Henry was given a letter to Mr. Frierson, which he took back to him, and was not molested.

CHAPTER XII.

A Love Story on the Old Plantation.

This love story is not a tale of fiction, nor is it one of romance, but it is a real story of love based on facts. It contains all the elements necessary to the making of a fascinating novel of two hundred or more printed pages. The characters were both slaves—having been born and reared in that condition. Nevertheless, they were not so lowly as to escape Cupid's notice. He aimed a dart at the heart of each of them, and in each case it struck and stuck fast. The flame that was kindled in these hearts by the son of Mars and Venus was as pure, and burned as fervently as in any human breast.

Jimmie, the bright little mail boy, fell in love with Isabella. This young girl was a beautiful quadroon. She was inclined to be tall, and somewhat slim, and possessed a lovely face. Her skin was fair, her eyes were dark, and her hair was black and fell in curls upon her shoulders. Her teeth were white, and it seemed that nature took special pains in making them in a uniform size, and in adjusting them in such a way that they would be attractive, and an object of admiration to all with whom she came in contact. Her dresses were always neat and clean. They were such as were worn by the nurses and chambermaids of the well-to-do white folks of that day and time. This beautiful girl—Isabella—belonged to Mr. Charles Durant, who lived on Lynches river, about five miles above Lynchburg, on the main road to Bishopville. This put a space of some twelve miles or more between Jimmie and his lover. And while he loved her dearly, yea, with all his heart, yet he could not go to see her. The distance was too great, and he was too shy and young. Therefore he had to wait until the spring season, when the quarterly meeting took place at the Methodist church at Lynchburg, or until the fall, when the annual camp-meeting was held at the old Tabernacle camp ground on Lynches river about four miles below Lynchburg.

As already stated, the Methodist parsonage was located at Lynchburg, and, perhaps, the largest and most important church of the circuit was at this point. And when the quarterly meeting of this church took place, it brought together many people from different parts of the circuit, and among them were the Friersons and the Durants. It was here that Jimmie would have the privilege of meeting his sweetheart—Isabella. She was nurse and waiting maid for the Durants, and was invariably brought along to care for the baby. Jimmie was coachman, and came as driver for the Frierson girls. While the services would be going on in the church, and the minister would be delivering one of his most eloquent discourses to an intensely interested audience, Jimmie and Isabella would be sitting out in the carriage talking love, and making plans which they could never be able to execute. Being slaves—and quite youthful at that—there were insurmountable barriers in the way, which they did not dream of. But it was a great pleasure for them to meet on these big meeting occasions, and look at each other, smile at each other, and tell each other how much each loved the other. One did not doubt the sincerity and genuineness of the other's love. Each felt that their love was reciprocated, and this, in a measure, gave them satisfaction. These quarterly meetings lasted only about two days—Saturday and Sunday—and thus ended the interviews of Jimmie and his beloved Isabella. These meetings usually were held every three months on the charge, but in the Lynchburg church it took place in the spring of the year, and these lovers would meet no more until the fall, when the great Tabernacle camp-meeting came on.

The location of this camp ground has already been mentioned. The annual camp-meeting was a great occasion. Everybody went to camp-meeting—white and colored. Many of the prominent farmers connected with the Lynchburg circuit were tent-holders at this camp ground. Mr. Frierson and Mr. Durant had tents on the same line. These tents were built of pine lumber, and in cottage style. They were built with several rooms, and with front piazzas. They formed a large circle, with the tabernacle, or church, in the center. Elevated scaffolds, about three feet square, with earth thrown up on them, and a bright lightwood blaze burning on the top, constituted the lighting system of the encampment. In addition to these scaffold-lights, there were bonfires built on the ground in front and in the rear of each tent. All culinary work was usually done at this fire in the rear.

When the trumpet would sound, which was a signal for the commencement of the services at the tabernacle, and when the white folks and the more serious servants and slaves would repair thither for worship, Jimmie would go over to Mr. Durant's tent, and spend the evening with his beloved Isabella, or at least until services at the tabernacle were out. This was done each evening, while the camp-meeting lasted, which usually was five or six days. These camp-meetings were great occasions. In fact, they were the biggest occasions that came within the experience of plantation life, and were hugely enjoyed by all, white and colored, old and young, male and female.

The last camp-meeting that Jimmie and Isabella attended was in the fall of 1864. The following year the white people who owned Isabella moved away to parts unknown to Jimmie. Hence he gave up all hope of ever seeing his lover again, and doubtless Isabella did the same. But while the sacred flame of love burned down, it was never completely extinguished.

In the fall of 1865, as has already been stated in a previous chapter, Jimmie left the old plantation, and went to the Yankees at Sumter. The provost marshal returned him to his father, who lived on a rented farm near Lynchburg. Here Jimmie worked on his father's farm during the summer months, and went to school at Lynchburg in the winter. After completing the course in this school, his father sent him to a school of a higher grade at Sumter. About this time Jimmie was converted, and became a Christian. He also felt that he was divinely called to preach the Gospel to his people. Consequently his father sent him to Charleston,

S.C., to study divinity in the Baker Theological Institute, and afterwards to Claflin University at Orangeburg.

In December 1870, at the age of 20, he joined the South Carolina Conference of the Methodist Episcopal Church, and was sent to Cheraw. He arrived at this historic old town on a Saturday night and was met at the station by one of the officers of his church by the name of Johnson. This brother accompanied the young pastor to his own home, where he spent the night.

The next morning, which was the Sabbath, the young preacher repaired to the church in company with Brother Johnson. There was a large congregation present to see, and hear the new preacher. Expectation, born of genuine curiosity, was at its height. This was true of both the people and the preacher.

At the close of the services, the people—both the brothers and the sisters—gathered around the chancel to become acquainted with the new pastor, and to extend to him a warm welcome. Among the sisters who came forward, Jimmie noticed one who exhibited traces of having been a most beautiful woman. She was tall, with fair skin, dark eyes, and straight black hair. But Jimmie also noticed that her teeth had been shattered, and some of the front ones were gone. But he suspicioned and suspected nothing. Jimmie was an innocent and inexperienced young fellow. But this woman, like every other member of her sex, possessed a woman's instinct. While the other folks withdrew from the altar, she still lingered, and once more brought herself face to face with the young stranger.

Then she ventured to say to him: "I think I have met you somewhere before." "I do not remember," said the young pastor. "But where are you from?" said the woman. "Lynchburg is my home," answered the preacher. "Well, please pardon me, were you ever a slave?" asked the fair inquirer. "I was," he replied. "Well, to whom did you belong?" she asked. "I used to belong to the Friersons on Pudden Swamp." "Well, please tell me what might be your first name." "My first name is James, but all my friends call me 'Jimmie.'" "Oh, don't say so!" she said, excitedly, while her beautiful black eyes filled with tears. She then gently dropped her head, and wiped her eyes with a handkerchief that was well saturated with cologne. When she had succeeded in getting her face straight, she looked up and said in a very familiar way, "Jimmie, don't you know me?" He replied, "I can't say that I do." Then came the astounding words, "I am Isabella, that used to belong to Mr. Charles Durant." Jimmie was stricken with dumbness, and when he became able to break the silence, all he could say was: "Well, well, well." It is needless to say that they were glad to see each other: for their joy was inexpressible. For a few moments, while they stood there, they gave a brief account of their whereabouts during the six or seven years since they last met at the old tabernacle camp ground. During this period Isabella had married, and she and her husband both were members of Jimmie's church.

About this time, he met a young woman of education, a successful school teacher, whom he courted and married. She was born of free parents, and reared in one of the large cities of the South. She is a woman of deep piety, and sustains a high moral standard. She is a great church worker, and much of Jimmie's success in the ministry has been attributed to the aid she has given him. She has proved herself to be a helpmeet indeed. Isabella was beautiful, but was not a woman of education, and therefore could not have filled the bill, and God knew it, and, in His wisdom, ordered otherwise. In discussing this matter, Jimmie has often been heard to repeat the lines:

> "In each event of life,
>   how clear Thy ruling hand I see!
>   Each blessing to my soul more dear,
>   Because conferred by thee."

But all through life Isabella continued to show a fondness for Jimmie. Some years after this, she moved away to the Land of Flowers, and, as an evidence of her friendship for him, she shipped him a crate of beautiful Florida oranges. Since that they have lost sight of each other.

N. B.—Since the above chapter was written, Jimmie, in his wanderings, chanced to meet a sister of Isabella, and from her he learned that she (Isabella) moved from Florida to New Jersey, where she died. Thus ended the earthly career of a beautiful woman, and a lovely character. But Jimmie is still alive, and is doing active work as a gospel minister.

CHAPTER XIII.
The Breaking Up of the Old Plantation.

On the morning of April 12th, 1861, the first gun of the great Civil War was fired. It was fired on Fort Sumter from a Confederate battery located in Charleston harbor. It was a terrific bombardment of thirty-four hours' duration. This was the beginning of a struggle which resulted in the emancipation of 4,000,000 of slaves. On the 1st day of January, 1863, President Abraham Lincoln issued his famous Emancipation Proclamation, and it completely swept away the institution of African slavery, which had had an existence on the American continent for two hundred and forty-four years. But this Proclamation did not go into universal effect until General Lee surrendered at Appomattox Courthouse on the 9th of April, 1865.

At this time—April 9th—the farmers in the South had pitched their crops. The corn, the cotton, and the potatoes had been planted, were up, and growing nicely. And now comes the emancipation of all the slaves, and if they all leave the old plantation at once, what would be the result? It meant starvation and death both for the white folks and the newly made freedmen. But the authorities at Washington relieved the situation by advising the landlords and the ex-slaves to enter into contracts to remain together until the following January, to work the crops, and to divide them at the harvest in the fall. This was done.

We come now to the most pathetic part of our story, namely: "The Breaking Up of the Old Plantation." And well do I remember it. I do not remember the day of the week—whether it was Monday, Tuesday, or some other week-day—but most vividly do I remember the scene.

Mr. Frierson—on a certain day—requested all the hands on the plantation to come to the "house." The men, the women, and the children were included in his order. And some of the free colored people of the neighborhood heard of the order, and they also came to see and hear. In those days of excitement, curiosity reached a high degree of feverish expectation and desire for knowledge, for information, and for light. The slaves had heard of the Emancipation Proclamation, which had been issued a little more than two years before, but which had never changed their condition. They had also heard of the surrender of General Lee, which put an end to the war. Mr. Adolphus—a Confederate soldier—had returned home, and there he sat at a small table on the front piazza, writing. The paper which he was writing afterwards proved to be the contract between the landlord and the ex-slaves, which they were called together to sign.

It was a beautiful spring day. There was not a cloud in the heavens to obscure the brightness of the sun. The yard in front of the piazza, and in front of the east end of the same, was crowded with negroes. Their faces were all turned toward Mr. Frierson, who stood on the piazza with the contract in his hand. Their eyes were fixed on him, and their ears were attentive. But before he read the contract, he made to them a speech. He spoke, in part, as follows:

"My Servants: I call you together today, to read this contract to you, and have you all to sign it. This is the order issued by the Government at Washington. The North and the South have been engaged in a four-years' bloody war. As you all know, I have had two sons at the front—your Marse

Rush and your Marse Adolphus. Your Marse Rush was killed in battle by those cruel Yankees, and is buried in an unknown grave in that far off land. Your Marse Adolphus—through a kind Providence—passed through the awful struggle without receiving as much as a scratch, and has been permitted to return home to us again. I know you all are glad, and rejoice with me in his safe return.

"But I must now tell you that you all are no longer my slaves. All the colored people who have been held in the South as slaves are now free. Your freedom is one of the results of the war, which has just closed. I do not know what you all are going to do after this year. I do not know whether you intend to leave me, and go out to seek homes elsewhere, or whether you will remain. But I want to assure you that I will be glad to have you all remain—every one of you.

"There is not one among you that was not born in my house, save four, namely: Uncle Fridie and his wife, and Uncle Isom and his wife. These four came into my possession by inheritance. They were my father's slaves, and when he died, at the division of his estate, they fell to me. I have kept them through all these years, even down to old age. And when they became so old and feeble that they could not work, I have kindly clothed, fed and cared for them. I have made them as comfortable in their declining years as it was possible for me to do.

"Then again, I declare unto you that I have not been cruel to any of you. I have not abused you myself, and did not allow anybody else to do it—not even my own sons, Mack, Rush, nor Adolphus. And all the neighborhood knew that I did not wish to have my negroes imposed upon. The patrols so understood it. And to avoid trouble with them, and to keep them from slashing your backs when they caught you away from the plantation, I always wrote you a ticket or a pass. But some of you have gone off without my knowledge, and without a ticket, and have been caught and whipped, but it was not my fault. I was not to blame for that. You, yourselves, were responsible for it.

"There is another thing which I want to call your attention to. I have never put an overseer over you, neither have I employed a 'nigger driver' on my plantation. I have owned no blood hounds, and have not given any encouragement, nor employment to those who have owned them. I have never separated, by selling nor by buying, a mother and her child; a husband and his wife. Of the truth of this, you will bear me witness. In all these matters, I have the approval of a good conscience.

"And now, I wish to say again, you are no longer my slaves, but you all are now free. And I want to say to you that I bear no ill-will toward you.

You are not responsible for the great change that has come upon us, and for the separation of master and servants. Others are responsible for these things. In the future let us be friends and good neighbors. You all have been taught to work, and to behave yourselves, and I hope you will continue to lead such lives in the future."

At the close of this talk, Mr. Frierson read the contract, in which it was agreed that all the slaves should remain on the plantation until the first day of January, 1866, when the crop would be divided. When he had finished reading, the older heads of these ex-slaves filed in one by one, and touched the pen in the hand of Mr. Adolphus, and made their mark. They then left the yard, and returned to their work.

But what were their feelings? Ah! words are inadequate to describe them. Their joy was unspeakable. But they had good sense. They imagined what were the feelings of the white folks because of the loss of their slaves. They knew that they were chafed in their minds, and that an outward demonstration of joy on their part would be unwise. Therefore their rejoicing was a subdued rejoicing. Though they had been kindly treated, and their relations to, and their attachment for, the white folks had been one of tenderness, yet they welcomed the change, and were glad of the new order of things. But they scarcely knew what it all meant. It was decidedly a new experience to them. They all remained except Jimmie until January.

During the fall the crops were harvested and divided according to the provisions of the contract, and when January came, there was a breaking up, and a separation of the old plantation.

Nearly all the slaves left and went out and made contracts with other landlords. A few remained for one year, and then the last one of them pulled out and made their homes elsewhere. Thus they were all scattered, as it were, by the four winds of the heavens, never to come together again until the judgment.

Sometime during the next spring (1866) Mr. Frierson, the proprietor of the old plantation, went out into the field to view his growing crop, and fell with a paralytic stroke, and died soon after. He was buried at the old family graveyard.

In 1886, just twenty years after the breaking up and separation of the old plantation, Jimmie, the mail boy, (now the Rev.—) returned to Lynchburg to visit his parents—Uncle Tom and Aunt Namie. It was during this visit that Jimmie proposed to his mother that they visit once more the Friersons' at the old plantation on Pudden Swamp. He thought he discovered in himself a sorter hankering desire to revisit the place where he first saw the light, and view once more the scenes of his childhood. He had heard that Mr. Frierson—the old man—had gone to his long home, so had Mr. Adolphus, but the girls were still living, and occupied the old mansion on the Frierson plantation, and Jimmie wanted to see them once more in this life. Hundreds of times Jimmie had driven those girls in the carriage while attending "big meetings," weddings, and while making social calls. In those days these girls were good to Jimmie, and he had not forgotten it. Now, he wants to see them for the last time, so he persuaded his mother to accompany him to the old plantation. This she readily consented to do.

After breakfast one morning Jimmie hitched up his father's horse and buggy and, with his mother, started for Pudden Swamp. They drove up into the yard at the Friersons' just as the old clock in the "house" struck 12, and Jimmie recognized the familiar tones of the old timepiece, and it so filled him with glee that as he alighted from the buggy, he said: "That is the same old clock by which I used to rise at four in the morning, and blow the horn for the boys to come and feed the horses and the mules." And so it was.

But the girls were filled with surprise. They did not recognize Jimmie. They recognized the woman who was with this young stranger. They knew Aunt Namie very well. They had seen her several times since she left the old plantation. This was not the first time that she had visited them, and once or twice the girls had driven up to Lynchburg to see Aunt Namie. These girls loved Aunt Namie, and Aunt Namie loved them, and it was their delight to visit each other, and talk over old times.

When this young stranger helped Aunt Namie from the buggy, the white girls rushed up to her and kindly greeted her. It certainly was a warm meeting. Jimmie then proceeded, as they used to say on Pudden Swamp, "to loose out the horse." And while doing so, he carefully watched the women folks as they embraced each other, but he had nothing to say. But the girls were pondering the expression which they heard this young stranger make as he drove up into the yard: "That is the same old clock by which I used to rise at 4 o'clock in the morning, and blow the horn for the boys to come and feed the horses and the mules." They closely eyed him, but there was nothing about him that would enable them to detect him. He was well dressed, and had an air of refinement about him which they were not accustomed to see about the male darkies on Pudden Swamp, notwithstanding they had been free for upwards of twenty years.

Now, the girls ventured to ask: "But, Aunt Namie, who is this man you have with you?" Aunt Namie replied: "Why, Miss Mary Ann, you don't know who that is?" "No," was the response.

"Why," said Aunt Namie, "that is my little Jimmie, don't you know him." "Aunt Namie," said Miss Mary Ann, "do you mean to say that that is Jimmie, our little mail boy and our coachman?"

"Yes, that is Jimmie." "Come here, Jimmie," said the girls, "give us your hand. How glad we are to see you. How have you been all these years?" This was another glad meeting. The balance of the day was spent as a reunion of the members of a family long separated.

The ladies showed Jimmie where to give the horse water, and where to feed him. Then they invited Aunt Namie and Jimmie into the house. Dinner was about ready, and a side table was set in the dining room for the visitors. It was the same old dining room, and it was a real good old-fashioned farmer's dinner. Aunt Namie and Jimmie enjoyed it immensely.

After dinner, Jimmie left his mother and the girls to spend the after-noon talking about old times, while he alone roamed over that old planta-tion. From field to field he went, without seeming to grow weary, observing and noting every change. He noticed that the fences, the gates, the bars, and the bridges over the ditches were all gone. And in many places the fields had grown up with undergrowth and looked like woods again. "Ah," said Jimmie, "how cruel old Time is. He has laid his decaying hand upon everything on the old plantation. That which he has not destroyed, he has left in a state of decay and ruin. The colored folks are all gone, and only two of the white folks are left to tell the sad story."

But there is one thing that interested Jimmie more than anything else, and that is the spot where he first learned to sin. Jimmie located the place as nearly as possible, owing to the changes which time had wrought in the face of the country. And when he had found it, he knelt down and prayed to the God of heaven, and asked forgiveness for all the sins that he ever had committed on the old plantation, or anywhere else, and then recon-secrated himself anew to God and to His service. Then he arose, and returned to the old mansion, and chatted with the girls until it was time for him and his mother to leave for home.

This last separation was a very sad one, for the reason that they all knew that they would never meet on earth again. And so it came to pass. They have all crossed the mystic river, save Jimmie, and have been gathered to their people on the other side. Tears were shed by all—white folks and colored folks—as they shook hands, and said "Good-bye."

THE END.

Before the War and after the Union: An Autobiography, by Sam Aleckson (1929)

—ɯɯ—

Introduction

Susanna Ashton and Laura V. Bridges

One might think that the hardships of life under slavery would so alienate people from their surroundings that they would cast off any allegiance to the place of their bondage. After all, many enslaved people were certainly haunted by dreams of escaping and leaving their farms, their states, or the United States itself. And yet, as the life of Sam Aleckson illustrates, enslaved people could be just as tied to a sense of place as anyone else. Furthermore, Aleckson's Charleston upbringing in comparative comfort and ease, free from much of the violence and brutality that often characterized the slave experience, allowed him forever to identify himself fondly and firmly with that city.

Although born a slave in 1852, Aleckson had many comforts of a typical white child, or at least that is how he seems to present it. Indeed, he hardly makes reference to his bondage throughout the text, although he certainly tells of hardships other slaves faced. Aleckson's narrative focuses on the events and places that helped shape his character and personality. He opens the first chapter with his devotion to the city he calls home. He introduces charming images of his original owner's house on Guignard Street, including "the 'Four o'clocks,' that grew there in great profusion and various colors," his white playmates, and his faithful dog called Watch. Though he urges that, provided the power, he would have changed his status as a slave, he writes, "but I should not have changed the place; for it is a grand old city, and I have always felt proud of my citizenship."

Aleckson's narrative offers an especially nuanced understanding of slavery in South Carolina, for while he contradicts what we might assume about the demoralizing institution of slavery and fills his memoir with fond memories of friends, family, and religion, he nonetheless makes it clear that "there is nothing good to be said of American slavery." Much of his gentle nostalgia might be attributed simply to the fondness many elderly people have for their youth, no matter what their actual experiences might have been; yet Aleckson always makes sure to temper such wistfulness with the insights he gained over the years. These insights were, literally and figuratively, revelations of experience and survival.

It is not coincidental that at the time of this narrative's composition at the turn of the century he was recovering from a recent illness that had nearly lost him his eyesight. When his doctor declared that Aleckson would be completely blind in six months, Aleckson endeavored to write his narrative as a means of financial supplement in his impending old age and with declining eyesight. When he was "past middle life," he "began to write at night often under poor light, being scarcely able to see the words as I traced them." He wrote against time, fearing blindness, and finished his manuscript only to set it aside as "untoward conditions prevented publication." Although his sight miraculously recovered, the book was not published until 1929, fifteen years after his death. The preface with which he opens his narrative frames his story as inspiring and educational but also as sobering to a later generation perhaps inclined to take its good fortune for granted. He argues that "there are some things that should never be forgotten." Without overplaying the metaphor, he nonetheless used his restored sight to give eyewitness testimony to the slave experience and to analyze from the perspective of an adult much of what he was oblivious to as a boy.

Aleckson's tone is marked by a careful rhetoric of wry reflection invoked to belie any bitterness. For instance, in reference to his service in the Confederate army, he simply writes, "I have never attended any of the Confederate reunions. I suppose they overlooked my name on the army roll!"* When describing his great grandfather's repute as a handsome man, he adds, "fine looking for a Negro I believe is the usual qualification." As these comments illustrate, Aleckson tempered his solemn disgust of slavery with gentle sarcasm, perhaps to make his stories palatable for future generations.

Sam Aleckson's happy childhood is most evident by the circumstances under which he lived—an intact family, devoted and caring mistresses, and so little hard labor that he was permitted the autonomy to participate in hunting and carousing with neighboring white children. He remarks that he

---

*David W. Blight, *Race and Reunion* (Cambridge, Mass.: Belknap Press of Harvard University Press, 2001).

was often even given "pennies, lumps of sugar and horseback rides." Aleckson was raised in close proximity to his mother and father as well as an older brother and two younger sisters. Growing up with his "father's people," he was reared by three white sisters whom Aleckson calls "Misses Jayne's . . . who were, of all slave holders, the very best." These women taught their slaves to read and instilled in each of them the fundamentals of Christianity. Aleckson writes affectionately that "there never was a better ordered establishment, nor were there ever better examples of Christian womanhood than that of the three ladies who presided over it." Just before the Civil War the women freed all of their remaining slaves (having sent some away), few of whom left the plantation.

Like many slaves, Aleckson was victim to the often casual economy of slave labor in which owners not only sold and traded their slaves but also lent them out to extended family members or boarded them elsewhere for a time. His chain of ownership and allegiance is thus a bit unclear as presented in this narrative. At the onset of the Civil War, the Danes, who owned Aleckson's mother, were forced to send their slaves away to work due to their family's increasing financial instability. Aleckson's mother was sent to work for the wealthy Bale family, who lived in the city, and Aleckson was forced to accompany her. Mrs. Bale's son-in-law, Mr. Ward, owned a plantation eighteen to twenty miles outside of Charleston called Pine Top, to which the Bale family retreated each winter.* He weathered the transition between families and allegiances without trauma, and his references thereafter are to the Dane, Bale, and Ward families as his owners and protectors.

Upon arriving at Pine Top, Aleckson found that the plantation, though incomparable to his home on Guignard Street, exceeded his expectations. He emphasizes the quaintness of the slave quarters, which were whitewashed and surrounded by "well-kept little flower beds." He writes, "Anyone visiting the old time plantation must have been impressed by the boundless hospitality of the people. Everybody came to see us." Aleckson found many playmates who taught him how to hunt and build bird traps.

Aleckson did not stay at Pine Top long because of the risk of malaria that ran rampant in the area, so he, his mother, and the Wards traveled back

---

*Col. William Henry Evans, born in 1819, is listed as owner of Pine Top plantation in Chalmers Gaston Davidson, *The Last Foray: The South Carolina Planters of 1860; a Sociological Study* (Columbia: University of South Carolina Press, 1971), 128. However, since Evans's Pine Top plantation was in Darlington, S.C., a town approximately 140 miles from Charleston, it is unlikely that this is the same one Aleckson refers to as "about eighteen or twenty miles from Charleston."

to the city. When Mr. Ward and Mr. Dane (Ward's brother-in-law, who was appointed on his staff) received commissions to serve at "Secessionville," Aleckson took the place of his older brother (who had died of fever) as an "officer's boy" in the Confederate army.* Aleckson's recollections of this period are focused on overheard adult anecdotes and the scarcity of food, concerns not surprising coming from the memories of a child only ten years of age. Yet his stories of how slaves serving with the Confederates were mistreated and unappreciated, such as that of Dick Brown—a black fisherman who was impressed into service for the army and, despite being the most skilled of his team, was deprived of a fair share of food—deserve attention for how poignantly they paint a picture of what life must have been like for slaves forced to experience service for the secessionist forces.

What happened to Aleckson in the years following the Civil War is not entirely clear. He evidently got married and likely furthered his education in some way through contact with northern aid workers, to whom he refers with great fondness. He does, however, spend a great deal of time analyzing the relationship between masters and slaves after emancipation and uses as evidence the way in which Mr. Ward was received with forgiveness and love by his former slaves. Whether this was a nod to the conciliatory racial politics of late nineteenth-century America or a genuine account of a true event, it serves Aleckson as depicting the uneasy but loving connections that could be forged across race and time.

Despite stories of individual reconciliations, for Sam Aleckson and many of his black counterparts, Reconstruction was a bitter time. As he puts it, "The ruinous conditions that followed that period have been oft and repeatedly charged to the Negroes of South Carolina." He mentions the "Black Code," carpetbaggers, Jim Crow laws, and the governorship of Gen. Wade Hampton as evidence of the injustices faced by people of color in the South.† Aleckson found it hard to come to grips with the fact that, despite

---

*The Battle of Secessionville took place in June 1862 on James Island, S.C. It was the first major effort of the Union army to seize Charleston. See Patrick Brennan, *Secessionville: Assault on Charleston* (Cambridge, Mass.: Da Capo Press, 1996). Also see W. Scott Poole, *South Carolina's Civil War: A Narrative History* (Macon, Ga.: Mercer University Press, 2005). Blacks were crucial participants in the war effort, especially those in the city of Charleston. They were often employed for building defensive fortifications and to replace white males in the trenches, according to Bernard E. Powers, Jr., *Black Charlestonians: A Social History, 1822–1885* (Fayetteville: University of Arkansas Press, 1994), 66.

†A Charleston native, Hampton was elected governor of South Carolina in 1876 and 1878. A noted Confederate general, he raised a cavalry army known as "Hampton's

emancipation and a restored Union, the situation for black citizens in South Carolina continued to be one of uncertainty and often disappointment. Thus, while he does not provide details for how precisely it came about, he managed to forge his future elsewhere.

Disillusioned with life in the South, Aleckson moved to Connecticut, which he describes humorously as a "land of pie" (a food eaten so commonly that it was no longer considered a treat), and quickly became attached to the area. However, he still struggled with the fact that there were so few blacks in the area. He wrote dryly: "This, you must know, was utterly unbearable to any man from South Carolina, be he white or black, unless it be our senior senator." When Aleckson explained to his employer that he could not envision a life for his family as such a minority, his employer wrote him a check that covered the cost of the Aleckson family's trip up north, where they settled with him in Springlake, a small town rarely labeled on any current maps of Connecticut, "for it is hidden away between high mountains."* Springlake, Connecticut, became a permanent home for the Aleckson family and held a special place in his heart. By the time he wrote his narrative Aleckson identified with New England just as strongly as he did with the South, yet all the while admitting, "When I am in the South I feel at home."

Despite Aleckson's awareness of his status as a marginalized person in society, he writes, "My fears are for the American nation, for, I feel as an American, and cannot feel otherwise." What is most poignant about his identity, though, may be his unfailing dedication to the South, as illustrated in a poem that he includes in his narrative:

> I love the land where the cotton plant grows,
> The land where there is no ice.
> I love the land where the jasmine blows
> I love the land of rice.

Sam Aleckson's narrative *Before the War and after the Union: An Autobiography* was first published in 1929 by Gold Mind Publishers in Boston. The text here is taken from that edition.

Legion." He was involved in numerous campaigns, such as First Bull Run, Peninsula, Seven Pines, Antietam, Chambersburg, Gettysburg, and Petersburg. See Rod Andrew, Jr., *Wade Hampton: Confederate Warrior to Southern Redeemer* (Chapel Hill: University of North Carolina Press, 2008); and Walter Brian Cisco, *Wade Hampton: Confederate Warrior, Conservative Statesman* (Washington, D.C.: Brassey's, 2004).

*Aleckson inconsistently spells the name of this place as "Spring Lake" and "Springlake" and notes that it is "a historic old town."

—ɯ—

PREFACE

When I began this unpretentious narrative, I was almost sightless. I had just recovered from a severe attack of illness, during which for a time I became totally blind, and after I was better my eyes seemed hopelessly affected. This I endeavored to conceal as I had to earn my bread, but so frequently did I pass my most intimate friends on the street without the slightest show of recognition that I was forced to admit I was almost blind. I was then urged to consult an eminent physician of the town who gave special attention to ailments of the eye, and after a complete examination, he informed me that my eyes were in such condition that glasses would do me no good, and with a show of sincere sympathy said, "I am sorry for you, but within six months you will be totally blind."

Approaching blindness is always appalling, especially to one who is dependent on his labor for a living. "What shall I do when my sight is gone?" This question forced itself upon me night and day. I was then past middle life, and the prospects of a blind and helpless old age stood out before me. My life had not been wholly uneventful; I had been of an observant turn of mind from my youth. What if I could set down the events that had come under my observation in some connected form? Might I not thereby be able to earn something toward my support when I could no longer see!

I was compelled to give up some of my work on account of failing sight, but I was still employed by day. I began to write at night often under poor light, being scarcely able to see the words as I traced them. Thus my ms. was finished. Untoward conditions prevented publication and it has lain hidden away all these years. The motive that first prompted me to undertake the task no longer exists, my sight has been providentially restored, and at the age of seventy-two I find myself in good health and able to earn my living. There are other considerations, however, which actuate me, even at this late day, to present to the reader this crude story.

It is a remarkable fact that very many of the immediate descendants of those who passed through the trying ordeal of American slavery know nothing of the hardships through which their fathers came. Some reason may be found in the fact that those fathers hated to harrow the minds of their children by the recital of their cruel experiences of those dark days. There is, however, a deeper reason. It is found in the religious nature of the Negro and the readiness with which he fell under the influence of Christianity, and the zeal with which he strove to follow the teaching and example of the lowly Nazarene.

If the Negro had emerged from slavery in a sullen and vindictive frame of mind, he would unquestionably have shared the fate of the American Indian, and we would not now be witnessing the marvelous progress he is making, nor his surprising increase in numbers.

While it is sweet to forgive and forget, there are some things that should never be forgotten. If this humble narrative will serve to cause the youth of my people to take a glance backward, the object of the writer will have been attained. As Frederick Douglass has said, "How can we tell the distance we have come except we note the point from which we started?"

CHAPTER I
Geneology

"Breathes there a man with soul so dead"

I was born in Charleston, South Carolina in the year 1852. The place of my birth and the conditions under which I was born are matters over which, of course, I had no control. If I had, I should have altered the conditions, but I should not have changed the place; for it is a grand old city, and I have always felt proud of my citizenship. My father and my grandfather were born there, and there they died—my grandfather at the age of seventy-two, my father at seventy-six. My great grandfather came, or rather was brought, from Africa. It is said that he bore the distinguishing marks of royalty on his person and was a fine looking man—fine looking for a Negro I believe is the usual qualification—at least that is what an old lady once told my own father who had inherited the good looks of his grandsire.

I do not know the name my great grandfather bore in Africa, but when he arrived in this country he was given the name Clement, and when he found he needed a surname—something he was not accustomed to in his native land—he borrowed that of the man who bought him. It is a very good name, and as we have held the same for more than a hundred and fifty years, without change or alteration, I think, therefore, we are legally entitled to it. His descendants up to the close of the Civil War, seemed with rare good fortune under the Providence of God, to have escaped many of the more cruel hardships incident to American slavery.

I may be permitted to add that on the arrival of my progenitor in this country he was not allowed to enter into negotiation with the Indians, and thereby acquire a large tract of land. Instead, an axe was placed in his hands and he therefore became in some sort, a pioneer of American civilization.

My father and my mother were both under the "yoke," but were held by different families. They made their home with my father's people who were, of all slave holders, the very best; and it was here that I spent the first years of my life

My mother went to her work early each morning, and came home after the day's work was done. My brother, older than I, accompanied her, but I being too young to be of practical service, was left to the care of my grandmother—and what a dear old Christian she was! At this time her advanced age and past faithful service rendered her required duties light, so that she had ample time to care for me. Her patient endeavor to impress upon my youthful mind the simple principles of a Christian life shall never be forgotten, and I trust her efforts have not been altogether in vain. She was born in the hands of the family where she passed her entire life; and it would be a revelation to many of the present day to know to what extent her counsel and advice was sought and heeded by the household—white and black.

Our household was large; beside the owners, three maiden ladies (sisters) there were a dozen servants, some like my father, worked out and paid wages, but all:

"Claimed kindred here
And had their claims allowed."

For there never was a better ordered establishment, nor were there ever better examples of Christian womanhood than that of the three ladies who presided over it; and it is especially worthy of note that all the servants who were old enough, could read, and some of them had mastered the three "R's," having been taught by these ladies or their predecessors. Before the beginning of the Civil War these kind ladies liberated all their slaves, and it is no reflection on the Negro that many of the liberated ones refused to leave them. There were many considerations that prompted them to decline their proffered freedom; in some cases husband and wife were not fellow-servants, and one was unwilling to leave the other. All those who accepted their liberty were sent to Liberia. I know of one who returned after the war to visit relatives and friends. He had been quite successful in his new home, and he gave good account of those who had left Charleston with him. Some had died, others were doing well. He found one of the good ladies still living and had the great pleasure of relating his story to her. When, after a brief stay in the city, he took his departure, he carried with him many tokens of remembrance from their kind benefactress for himself and those at home.

CHAPTER II

Childhood

"How dear to my heart are the scenes of my childhood
   When fond recollections present them to view."

Though fifty years of time and more than a thousand miles of space separate me from the home of my birth and early childhood, the old home seems more plain before me now than places I visited but yesterday. It was a grand old house, built of grey brick. There were three spacious piazzas running along the west and south sides of the house. The wide yard was paved with brick. To the west of the paved yard was a large garden in which rarest flowers bloomed; but dearer than all to our youthful hearts were the "Four-o'clocks," that grew there in great profusion and various colors. We made festoons of them, hung them over our heads while we "played house" and made mud pies beneath. We wove garlands and twined them about the neck of dear old "Watch." He was our great Newfoundland. Was there ever such a faithful dog as he? Noble animal, rough and tumble with the boys, gentle with the girls, but kind to all. The bulldog and pug have taken his place now, but surely there never was a safer or kinder friend to children than he. Our "Watch" had never read "The Rights of the Child," but he put his foot, or rather his paw (no small one), down on any of us being punished in his presence. Whenever our parents deemed it incumbent on them to give forcible and painful evidence that they were not amendable to the charge of "sparing the rod and spoiling the child," it was necessary to lock Watch up in the woodshed, and if in their haste this precaution was neglected he would rush in, seize the slipper or strap (they used both in those days) between his teeth and hang on like grim death. After we had escaped to the yard he would run out, lick our faces and seem to say, "I told you I would not allow it. Come, let us have a romp."

There were fruit trees in our garden; peaches, apricots, pomegranate and figs. We loved the figs most, of which there were several varieties. Our especial pride was the large black fig tree. There were six of us, three girls and three boys. Four of us were white and two were Negroes. Did we quarrel and fight? No indeed! Our little misunderstandings were settled long before we came to blows. There was more of the spirit as well as the letter of the little lines:

> "Let dogs delight
> To bark and bite,"

than seems generally the case now. Would there was more of that spirit abroad in the land today then would we hear less of Negro problems, deportations, and the like.

Every morning in season would find us at our favorite fig tree. The boys would climb into its branches while the girls stood below with extended aprons to catch the fruit as we dropped them. Sometimes there came a voice from above in complaining tones—"Now Jennie! I see you eating." "Oh," would be the reply, "That one was all mashed up." "All right, now don't eat till we come down."

Then when we descended we took large green fig leaves, placed them in a basket, laid the most perfect fruit thereon, and one of us would run to the house with it. "Don't eat till I come back." "We won't." When the messenger returned we went to our favorite nook in the garden and after dispatching about a dozen figs apiece we rushed to our breakfast with appetites as unappeased as if we had fasted for a week—And then to school, "But not the Negroes" you say? Yes indeed! The Negroes, too.

The four white children that formed a part of this little band did not live at our house. They were niece and nephew of our good ladies and lived a short distance from us. They came regularly every morning and after-noon, except Sunday, to "play in our yard." They attended a private school, while Jennie and myself, the two Negroes, were taught at home by their aunts for two or three hours each day. One of these kind ladies, usually Miss S—, strove with our obtuseness. We had only one book each, but it was a great book. I thought so then and I think so now. From it, like all great men, we first learned our A B C's, then came A-b-âb B-â, ba and so on to such hard words as ac-com-mo-da-tion, com-pen-sa-tion and the like. From this wonderful book we learned to read, write, and cipher, too. We also got an idea of grammar, of weights and measures, etc. We had slates, for those useful articles had not yet gone out of fashion.

There were pictures in our book illustrating fables that taught good moral lessons, such as that of the man who prayed to Hercules to take his wagon out of the mire; of the two men who stole a piece of meat; of the lazy maids and of the kind-hearted man who took a half frozen serpent into his house. This book was called, "Thomas Dilworth's," and many a slave was severely punished for being found with a copy of it in his hands. When one had succeeded in mastering the contents of this book (which they frequently did), he was considered a prodigy of learning by his fellows. I do not know whether Mr. Dilworth has ever had a monument erected to his memory, but if ever a man deserved one it is he.

This was a Christian household. The Sabbath was strictly observed. Duties were reduced to the barest necessities, and all attended church. There was no cooking. Cold meats, tea and bread served to satisfy our hunger on the Lord's Day. The ladies were Congregationalists and attended the "Circular Church." The servants were left to their own choice in religious matters and were divided in their religious opinions. My grandmother was a Methodist and attended "Old Cumberland." It required something very serious to prevent the dear old lady going to prayer meeting on Sunday mornings. These meetings were held an early hour, but I always went with her. Each one entered the sacred place in solemn silence. When the moment arrived some leader would raise one of those grand old hymns such as—

> "Early my God without delay
> I haste to seek thy face."

for they sorely felt the need of him who "Tempereth the wind to the shorn lamb!" Then at the close they sang—

> "My friends I bid you all farewell
> I leave you in God's care
> And if I never more see you,
> Go on, I'll meet you there."

It not only had reference to the final dissolution, but also to the uncertain temporal condition under which they lived, for, in many instances before the next prayer meeting they were sold, to serve new masters in distant parts. Often without having time to say good-bye to relatives or friends.

When meeting was over they filed out quietly. No buzz of voices we heard until they reached the sidewalk. Then, after a hearty handshake and a word of cheer and hope, they hastened to their duties; many to serve hard and impatient masters. 'Twere well for these that they had been fortified by those few moments of prayer and meditation.

The people showed commendable zeal in attending these meetings. In those early Sunday mornings, men and women might have been seen standing within their gates. They appeared to be listening intently, as if to catch some sound (for they must not be found on the streets after "drum beat" at night or before that hour in the morning). At the first tap they hastened out to their respective places of worship, there to lift up their hearts and voices in prayer and supplication to God.

My mother's people too, were of the "St. Clair" type. On Sundays after Sabbath School I was permitted to visit my mother at their home. They were Mrs. Dane, a widow, and three grown children—a daughter and two sons. The daughter was married. The sons, Thomas and Edward, were unmarried. I always looked forward to these visits with pleasure as I was sure to be regaled with lumps of sugar and pieces of money, by the old lady and the other members of the family. Besides, Mr. Edward (who was a lover of fine horses, and of whom I shall have more to say later), would treat me to a horseback ride around the large lot.

There is nothing good to be said of American Slavery. I know it is sometimes customary to speak of its bright and its dark sides. I am not prepared to admit that it had any bright sides unless it was the Emancipation Proclamation issued by President Abraham Lincoln. There was often a strong manifestation of sympathy, however. A sad incident which occurred in the Dane family when I was about eight years old may serve to illustrate this: It was usual in those days for each member of a family to have his or her own personal attendant. Mr. Thomas Dane, a kind-hearted gentleman of studious habits and quiet demeanor, had as his servant, a woman called Beck. He did not take breakfast with the family. It was his custom to take his morning meal in his own apartment being waited on by her. Like all the good slaveholders the Danes did not ruthlessly sell their slaves. I do not know how it came about that two of Aunt Beck's children had been sold. She had one remaining child at this time. He was well-liked by all on account of his cheerful disposition. I cannot tell the cause of it, but the boy George was sold away from his mother as had been his brother and sister. This was a heavy blow to her. One morning, shortly after the sale of George, Mr. Dane came down to breakfast. Noticing the dejected appearance of his servant, and no doubt, discerning the cause he ventured some pleasant remark, but Aunt Beck's heart was heavy. At last, no longer able to suppress her great grief she began to weep. "My last chile gone now Mas' Thomas," she said.

"I know it Beck," he answered, placing his hand to his head, "But, my God! I could not help it."

He rose from the table and paced the floor. The woman became alarmed at the agitation of her master, and forgetting her sorrow for the moment, said, "I know you couldn't help it Mas' Thomas. Sit down and eat your breakfast."

But, no breakfast for him that morning. Presently he went up to his room. Soon he returned having arranged his toilet with more than usual care. He stepped out into the yard, entered an outer building—in a moment a pistol shot was heard! They rushed to the step, but his life blood was ebbing away. He never spoke again. The grief of the woman was more than he could stand.

I visited the place a few years ago. There were different people there. They knew naught of that sad tragedy, nor did they know that Petigrue, Rutledge, Horry, Pringle and Lowndes were once regular visitors here. The old house and its surroundings are very much as they were fifty years ago. The chimes of St. Michael can still be distinctly heard and the hands on the dial may still be seen from the house.

It is quite different at the place where I was born. There is not a vestige of the old house to be seen, for a great fire since that time swept over this district and destroyed it and nearly every nearby dwelling house. In my childhood we had as near neighbors Pinckney, Legare, and Prescott. There is nothing about the locality now to show that here was once the abode of aristocracy and wealth, for, in no instance have the old families rebuilt their homes here. Very near our house stood a large and quaint old dwelling built before the Revolution. The front door was reached by high flights of steps. I always stood in awe of that house; partly because of the high wall that surrounded it, and partly because once a member of the tribe of "Weary Willies," chanced to pass that way. He sat down on those steps to eat a loaf of bread that had been given him. Whether from hunger or from some other cause (I never knew), he died there with the bread in his hand. As a result, "Go die on Blank's steps" became a phrase of the day. The wall that surrounded that old place was high—higher than any wall appears to me now. It was ornamented on top with glass bottles—broken bottles. The man who broke them seemed to have had murder in his heart. He did not follow any particular line in breaking them, nor did he seem to strive at color effect. There were white, black and brown bottles all broken in a way that was calculated to inflict mortal injury on any who attempted to climb into the enclosure.

But the old house and its high wall too have disappeared. Cotton yards and ware-houses now occupy the site of many an old mansion. Houses have been built on some of the lots, but they are far less pretentious than their predecessors, and are occupied by different people. For—

"Other men our fields will till
And other men our places fill
A hundred years to come"

There were many walls like the one I alluded to in the quaint old city, but they have nearly all disappeared. All the midnight prowler has to do now is to step lightly over artistically trimmed hedges and meander through beautifully laid out walks to the rear of the premises to where the feathery tribe reposes in ornamental structures. But if the glass bottles and high walls are no more, the dim flickering street-lamps have also been replaced by the brilliant electric light, thus enabling the watchful owner to place his "Mustard seed" the more accurately where they would do the most good. Therefore, the "Knight of the feather" may well sigh for the good old "lamp oil" times.

CHAPTER III

The Fickle Maiden

> "We will ring the chorus
> From Atlanta to the sea."

My mother and her children fell to the lot of Edward Dane, brother of Thomas. This young gentleman was of a gay disposition; fond of horses and the sports of the day. Like his brother he was kind and generous. He taught me to ride, and when I could sit my horse well "bare-back" he had a saddle made for me at the then famous "McKinzie's" saddlery, sign of the "White Horse at the corner of Church and Chalmers Street." (Gentlemen had their saddles made to order on those days). I would often accompany him "up the road" on horseback to the Clubhouse, there to exhibit my youthful feats of horsemanship for the divertissement of Mr. Dane and his friends. My horse, Agile, and myself were the best of friends. He never hesitated at a hurdle and we never had a mishap. Possibly Mr. Dane had "views" concerning me for he owned several fast horses, but before I was old enough to be of practical service, "Sherman came marching through Georgia."

Here I shall have to admit that I was a "Sherman Cutloose" (this was a term applied in derision by some of the Negroes who were *free before* the war, —to those who were *freed by* the war). I am persuaded however that all the Negroes in the slave belt, and some of the white men too, were "Cutloose" by General Sherman. But let bygones be bygones. "We are brothers all, at least we would be if it were not for the demagogues and the Apostles of hate.

Mr. Edward Dane was an ardent supporter of the "Code." He was an authority in such matters and could arrange a meeting with all the nice attention to details that characterized gentlemen of the "Old School" in

South Carolina. His deliberation in such matters would have been a keen disappointment to "Mr. Winkle" as there never was any danger of the police or anyone else interfering when he had matters in hand. The police, however, never interfered with gentlemen of the "Old School" in the "Palmetto" state. The following story is told of a well-known gentleman of a past generation:—He was a man of splendid physique and dignified carriage. One morning he entered the Old Charleston Market with a lit cigar between his lips. Soon he was accosted by a policeman, a new recruit from the Emerald Isle. "It be aginst the law to be afther schmokin in the Market, Sor," he said. "The law," said Mr. ____. "I am the law. When you see me you see the law. The law was made for poor white men and Negroes." And he strode on leaving that son of Erin a wiser, if not a better man.

The Danes were society people. In their well-appointed home they kept many servants. Mrs. Dane and her daughter Mrs. Turner were both kind ladies. The old lady had a way of personally looking into matters about the establishment that secured for her a pet name from the servants. Whenever she started on her tour of inspection word would be passed along, "de old Jay comin'." This would send every one to their post of duty. Of course the servants were ignorant of the fact that Mrs. Dane knew anything about the re-christening she had secured at their hands. Judge of their surprise therefore, when that lady presented herself before them and announced, "Yes, here comes the 'Old Jay!'"

They were all assembled in the kitchen for a little chat, and their attitudes and the expressions of bewilderment on their faces would have delighted the heart of an artist. The cook was just about to emphasize a remark he had made by bringing a large spoon which he held above his head down on the dresser, when the sudden appearance of the lady and her words, seemed to arrest the descent. There he stood in open-mouthed amazement. Mrs. Dane surveyed the scene for a moment, then quietly withdrew, a smile of amusement on her face. This incident was long remembered by those present, but any reference to it in his presence was promptly frowned down by the Cook, who felt keenly the ludicrousness of the figure he cut with the uplifted spoon. It was as much as their dinner was worth for any one of them even to raise a spoon above their heads.

Uncle Renty, the cook, particularly disliked these periodical intrusions in his domain. The altogether unnecessary clatter and clashing of pans and kettles whenever the lady made her appearance was only his method of expressing his resentment. This, Mrs. Dane well understood, and never prolonged her stay in the kitchen, for the old man's ability as an artist in his profession was recognized and appreciated. It was said that when the elder Mr. Dane was alive, he frequently began and ended his dinner with one of Uncle Renty's soups. They were simply marvelous, especially his turtle, calf's head and okra soups. How he made them no one knew, nor would they have been any wiser if he had been questioned on the subject. He had several dishes of his own invention to which he had given original names. The other servants had great respect for him; the old, because of his skill, and the young, because of the name of "Old Scarlet" from his fellow-servants. But those who ventured to call him so always took pains to get out of reach. This is how he got the name:—

In those days personal application for work were frequently made from door to door by the "newly arrived." One day an Irish woman applied to Mrs. Dane. She did not need her particularly, but thought she might give the woman work for a day or two as assistant to Uncle Renty, for they were to have a large dinner party:—"Wait a moment," she said. The lady knew the old man well enough to know that diplomacy was required. Going to the kitchen she complimented him on the neat appearance of things. "You are all in readiness for the dinner I see."

"Yes ma'am." (Now the old man had already been apprised of the purport of her visit. He was fully prepared. He was by no means color blind, but was not well posted in the nomenclature of colors.)

"And do you know daddy Renty," continued Mrs. Dane, "I have thought that you might need some additional help in the kitchen for a day or so."

"Everything was all right las time, ain't ee ma'am?"

"Oh yes, certainly. Everything was just splendid," she replied, "But a white woman has applied to me for work and I thought—."

"Mis Charlotte," interrupted Renty, "I don't car if she white as scarlet, ma'am, I doan want um in my kitchen." Argument was useless and so a job had to be found for Bridget in the laundry.

But all of this was before the untimely death of Mr. Thomas Dane, to which I referred in the preceding chapter. That sad event seemed to have been the beginning of trouble for the Dane family. Indeed things were becoming serious for all. The probability of war between the states was manifested more and more daily. There was a growing feeling of unrest everywhere, and it was soon known that this calamity would not be averted.

The very commencement of the war seemed to have brought disaster to the financial prosperity of many, and the Danes were among the earliest to feel its effects. Some of the servants were sent out to work and so it happened that my mother went as cook for a wealthy family in the city.

They were very kind people. Mrs. Bale was a widow with two children. They were both married. Mrs. Ward, the daughter, and her husband lived with her mother. The son, Tom Bale, had establishments of his own.

It was hard for me to leave our dear old home at the Misses Jayne's, my father's people, for there was my good old grandmother, the kind ladies, my playmates and faithful old Watch. But the distance was too far for my mother to walk back and forth (there were no street cars in those days), so we had to make our home at Mrs. Bale's house. I found some consolation however, in our new home. Mrs. Ward had two boys, and they and I soon became good friends. Besides, there were horses there, and Uncle Ben, the coachman, allowed me to ride them to water. There were children living next door too, with whom I became acquainted, and this led to a romantic incident in my life years afterward. When "the Union had come in," I married one of the little girls who lived next door, although I had to go all the way to New York to find her.

Our stay at Mrs. Bale's was very pleasant, circumstances being considered. It was here, however that I witnessed the first instance of cruelty or harshness of an owner to his slave that ever came under my personal observation. Of this I shall have more to say. I missed my weekly visits to the Danes too, for besides the pennies, lumps of sugar and horseback rides, I had many friends there also. Then there was Cora, the daughter of one of the servants, I am still inclined to believe that she was the most beautiful girl I have ever seen. She was endowed with an olive complexion, large black dreamy eyes, raven hair, pearly white teeth and a bewitching smile. Her voice was one of the most unusual voices I have ever heard. Cora used to kiss me and call me her little sweetheart (for though you would not believe it now, then I was a bright-looking little tow-headed chap, and got many a kiss from the "big girls" in the neighborhood, because they said I was so cute.) But that was years and years ago. Cora promised to "wait for me." Of course I believed her. She was eighteen and I was about nine years old, yet I thought that somewhere in the race of life I would overtake her and she would be mine. It never occurred to me that when I had reached eighteen she would be twenty-seven, and the disparity in our ages would be the same. Years afterward I met her. She was married and had several children, while I was just entering into young manhood. How fickle some girls are, eh?

There was a large garden with fig trees and flowers in it at Mrs. Bale's house, but the figs were not as sweet nor were the flowers half as beautiful as those at my old home. There were two dogs not near so clever as our Watch, and the children—well, they had never lived at a home like our old place on Guignard Street. In fact, there never was another home like that, but "Grief sits light on youthful hearts." All my regrets were greatly modified by the prospects of a visit to the country. Such a trip always seems alluring to a city boy. Indeed the country seems to hold out allurements to everyone except those who live there. Mr. Ward owned a plantation to which the family went every winter, and when it became known to me that we were soon to go there, I was all impatience. I plied Uncle Ben with a thousand questions as to how far away it was, what kind of a place, what was to be seen, were there any snakes, did they bite, was there any wild horse running about in the woods, did he think I might catch one? Etc., etc. Now Uncle Ben was a philosopher. He was not given over much to talking. No one but myself would have dared to ask him so many questions. He had taken a fancy to me. Everyone said it was a wonder. He had no children of his own, besides he was inclined to be somewhat of a misanthropist. I would sometimes have to wait indefinitely for an answer to a very simple question. However, by the exercise of patience and discretion I finally got all the information I desired, or thought I did, which amounted to the same thing.

Uncle Ben was epigrammatic as well as philosophical. One night after a very trying day he went to prayer meeting. He was feeling rather blue, and did not intend to take an active part in the exercises. Of course the conductor of the meeting knew nothing of the old man's frame of mind. "Will brudder Ben jine us in prayer?" he asked, but there was no response. "I mean brudder Ben Bale," he said, fearing there might be some misunderstanding. Being thus importuned the old man knelt down and delivered himself as follows:—"A ha'd bone to chaw. A bitter pill to swoller." Bress de Lawd. Amen.

But Christmas was approaching, and Santa Claus was gleefully expected for the good old man was a real personage in those days—not a myth. Oh, but you say it was wrong to deceive the children, as it had a bad effect on them? I don't know, but it seems to me that the children who believed in Santa Claus in those days would at least compare favorably in their love of truth with those of the present day who know, "It is only father and mother." At all events the country was forgotten for a while. It was sometime after holidays that we left for the plantation. There was not a gayer boy than myself when we boarded the train. (This was in the year 1860).

When we arrived at the station there were three teams awaiting us; one for the family, one for the servants, and another for the baggage. Uncle Ben was there, having brought the horses up by road a few days before. I rode on the baggage wagon. As there were only the driver and myself on it

I thought I could ply the former for information without being requested to "Hold my tongue," an operation that I had always found difficult. My companion I found was a well grown boy whose name was Missouri. Why they gave him this name I do not know. Perhaps it was in honor of the "Missouri Compromise." He said his name was the same as that of a great country miles and miles away, that he was called "Zury" for short, that his principal work on the plantation was plowing, and that his mule, Jack, was the best plow animal on the place. He also informed me that there were a large number of children on the plantation whose work was to play, and to keep the rice birds out of the fields. I suppose he was thoroughly dry by the time we got to "Pine Top," but he was a good-natured fellow. We became firm friends. I always rode his mule from the field to the barn. Zury is now living in Charleston, where he is a successful mechanic known as Mr. Ladson.

Anyone visiting the old time plantation must have been impressed by the boundless hospitality of the people. Everybody came to see us. They brought chickens, eggs, potatoes, pumpkins, plums, and other things too numerous to mention. I soon found many play fellows. My especial chums were Joe and Hector, sons of the plantation driver. The boys were somewhat older than myself. They were skilled in woodcraft, and taught me how to make bird traps and soon had me out hunting. One morning early, we started out, taking their dog, Spot, along. When we reached the woods the dog ran ahead briskly, barking as he went. Shortly he began to bark furiously. "Spot, tree," said Joe, and we hastened on. When we got to the dog he was standing by a tall stump, still barking. "Got er rabbit," said Hector.

"Where?" I inquired.

"En de holler," he replied, and thrusting his arm into it he drew out the poor trembling creature by his hind legs.

"Set him down!" I cried.

"Oh no," said he, "Ee might git 'way."

This was just what I wanted, for I pitied the little animal, but the boys were hunters. They were not going to risk losing their game, so they killed the frightened thing without further ceremony, and put him in their bag. We got three rabbits that morning. I did not enjoy the sport, nor did I partake of the rabbit stew they had for dinner. I did enjoy the night hunts however, for coon and possum were our quarry. I went with some of the young men. While the harmless little rabbit will not even defend himself when attacked, the possum is shy and crafty and the coon will fight. One night the dogs tree'd a coon. Now the wily animal usually selects a tree from which he can reach another, but this coon did not have time to "pick and choose." There was no other tree within jumping distance, so he went out on a limb as far away from the body of the tree as possible. And there he sat. As it was a large tree, it was decided that instead of cutting it down, someone should go up and shake the game off of it. Sandy, one of the party, readily volunteered to do so. Reaching the limb on which the coon was "roosting," he went on it so as to give it a vigorous shaking. The limb broke and down came both man and coon. The coon was dispatched while some of the men went to the assistance of Sandy. We thought he was seriously injured. He was stunned for a moment, but as they raised him up he asked, "Did we git um, boys?" The fall of more than twenty feet was broken by the branches beneath him, and thus he soon was all right again.

These hunts were great, but they were nothing compared to the feasts that followed. These were never held on the same night as the hunt, but on the one following. I never took kindly to either the coon or the possum. The former is usually too fat, and the habits of the other do not appeal to me. But the stories told at these feasts! They would make the fortune of a writer if he could reproduce them. They simply cannot be reproduced, that is all. To get the real, genuine, simon pure article, one must be on the ground. And perhaps you think that you have heard good, sound, hearty unadulterated laughter. Well, may be.

You may disfranchise the Negro, you may oppress him, you may deport him, but unless you destroy the disposition to laugh in his nature you can do him no permanent injury. All unconscious to himself, perhaps. It is not solely the meaningless expression of "vacant mind," nor is it simply a ray—It is the beaming light of hope—of faith. God has blessed him thus. He sees light where others see only the blackness of night.

CHAPTER IV

The Lover

"The tide of true love never did run smooth."

Pine Top, Mr. Ward's country seat, was a beautiful plantation about eighteen or twenty miles from Charleston. The house, an old colonial mansion, stood on elevated ground, well back from the main road, and commanded a fine view of the surrounding country. From the main road the house was reached through a wide avenue, lined on either side by giant live oaks, while immediately in front of the house was a large lawn circled by a wide driveway.

From the front door of the house the barns, stables, gin-house, corn mill and Negro quarters, presented the appearance of a thriving little village. The quarters were regularly laid out in streets, and the cabins were all whitewashed. I once read in a newspaper, a letter from a Northern man who visited the South immediately after the war. He took a rather unfavorable view of the prospects of the Negro, for he said, "There was a lamentable absence of flowers about their cabins." I suppose this "Oscar Wilde" thought the conditions under which the people had lived were well calculated to foster love of the beautiful. The poor fellow could not have visited Pine Top however, and·many other places I could name, or he would have been delighted to see the well-kept little flower beds near many of the cabins. And no doubt, he would have said they were just "too, too" for words. He might even have been tempted to enter some of those cabins by their neat and tidy appearances which could be seen through the open doors.

Mr. Ward was what was called a "good master." His people were well-fed, well-housed and not over-worked. There were certain inflexible rules however, governing his plantation of which he allowed not the slightest infraction, for he had his place for the Negro. Of course the Negro could not stand erect in it, but the Negro had no right to stand erect. His place for the Negro was in subjugation and servitude to the white man. That is, to Mr. Ward and his class, for while he maintained that the supremacy of all white men over the Negro was indisputable, and must be recognized, still there was a class of white men that he would have prevented from ever becoming slaveholders.

While I repudiate Mr. Ward's views I am bound to believe that there is something in blood. In those parts of the South where aristocratic influence is dominant, opposition to the advancement and progress of the Negro is far less than where the contrary is true. Eliminating the Negro altogether, in some of the southern states the "bottom rail" has gotten on top with a vengeance, and where such is the case, it is very bad for the "enclosure."

One evening Mr. Ward sat in his library before a blazing wood fire. He was the picture of contentment; and why should he be otherwise? He had a beautiful wife, two fine boys, hundreds of acres of land and numerous slaves to work them. Furthermore, he had just dined on wild duck. Now I would not tax the credulity of the reader by an exact statement as to how long those ducks had been allowed to hang up after being shot before they were considered "ripe," but, they had reached a stage that would hardly have been appreciated by a man of less "refined" taste than his, for Mr.

Ward was a lover of "high game." The aroma that arose from those "birds" during their preparation for the table would not have tempted the appetite of an ordinary man, even if he were very hungry.

Mrs. Ward had joined her husband for a little chat when Jake, the waiting boy, entered.—(Jake was the assistant and understudy of Uncle Sempie, the veteran butler. Uncle Sempie always retired after dinner, leaving Jake to attend to the later wants of his master.) "Mingo, fum Mr. Hudson place wan ter see yo, sah," he said.

"All right, let him in," said Mr. Ward.

Presently Jake returned ushering in a very young Negro who appeared to be laboring under some embarrassment. As he entered he said, "Ebenin sah, ebenin ma'am."

"Good evening," replied the lady and gentleman.

"Are you Mingo from Mr. Hudson?" asked Mr. Ward.

"Yees, sah."

"How are your master and mistress?"

"Dey berry well, sah."

"Well, Mingo, what can I do for you?"

The young fellow hesitated as if he did not know exactly how to proceed. Both the lady and gentleman looked at him attentively. He was becomingly attired, had a pleasant face and was evidently a favored servant. At last he mustered enough courage to say, "I come sah ter ax yo p'mission ter cum see Dolly. Dolly is the darter ob Uncle Josh and Ant Peggy, sah," he added.

Mr. and Mrs. Ward strove hard to suppress their mirth as they saw the poor fellow was about to collapse. "Oh," said the lady smiling, "So you would a-courting go, eh?"

"Yees, ma'am," recovering himself a little.

Mr. Ward cleared his throat. "Well Mingo," he asked, "Have you got your master's consent?"

"Oh yees sah."

"And you and Dolly understand each other?"

"Yees, sah."

"Are Josh and Peggy willing to have you for a son-in-law?"

"Oh yees, sah. I don ax dem."

"I suppose you behave yourself. I am very particular concerning this matter."

"I know dat, suh. Mas Jeem kin tell yo about me, sah."

"Well, I guess it is all right. Of course I shall inquire about you. Have you got your ticket?"

Here Mingo produced the desired article. Mr. Ward read it, his brows contracting a little. "This is all right," he said, returning the paper, "Except that it does not say where you are to go. Now I never allow anyone on my place with such a ticket. The next time you visit Dolly you must have a different 'ticket.' Ask your master to give you one stating plainly that you are to visit my plantation. Do you understand?"

"Yees, sah."

"Well Mingo, I wish you good luck!" said Mrs. Ward.

"Tankee ma'am, tankee sah," and he bowed himself off.

The "ticket" referred to was simply a permit showing that the slave had his or her master's consent to be absent from home. In some instances their destination was mentioned; in others it merely stated that "A—has my permission to be absent on such a date, or between given dates." Mr. Ward never refused his people "leave of absence," but in every case their destination was clearly set forth. It would not be safe for them to be found "off the coast."

Now I would not insinuate that Mingo was a fickle lover. It is just possible that he wished to visit some of the other girls in the neighborhood simply for the purpose of convincing himself by actual comparison of the superior charms of his own Dolly. His was a monthly "ticket," and under these circumstances we must excuse him for not wishing to have it changed. In fact he determined not to do so. He did not even acquaint Dolly with Mr. Ward's instruction. Possibly he feared that she might have agreed with that gentleman—from different motives of course.

It was the custom of the owner of "Pine Top" during his stay on the plantation to visit the "Quarters," ostensibly to see how his people were getting on, and incidentally, to note that things were as they should be on the place. Mingo was aware of this so he thought that on his future visits to his sweetheart all he had to do was "to lay low" until Mr. Ward had made his rounds. In this he was successful for a time but—

"The best laid plans of mice and men, gang aft agley."

Besides, young love is ever impatient.

One night he took his stand in his usual place of concealment. It had been raining and the weather was decidedly cold. He had waited long after the usual time for the gentleman's visits. "Spec de old feller ain't comin out tonight," he said to himself.

Mingo did not know Mr. Ward. The people on Pine Top expected their master at any hour, and were not surprised to have him present himself at their doors when *he* thought they were not looking for him. He would sometimes even partake of roast possum or coon. Unaware of these habits Mingo hastened to meet the warm welcome that awaited him at Dolly's cabin. He was destined to receive a warmer welcome than the one he anticipated.

Uncle Josh and Aunt Peggy sat by the fire. *Perhaps* they were asleep. Dolly and Mingo were sitting at a small table as far away from the old folks as they possibly could get. "I bin ober to Cedar Hill las nite," he began, "An I see'd the new-gal dey got. I tink she is —."

"I see'd her," interrupted Dolly, "An I tink she's just horred."

And Mingo deeming discretion the better part of valor said, "I tink so too."

Just then there was a loud rap on the door and Mr. Ward entered! Sometimes the very means we use to conceal our fears serve but to make them plain. The moment Mingo sighted Mr. Ward he became alarmed, but he must appear collected.

"Ebenin sah. Cole nite, sah. How is Missus and de chillum?"

Immediately Mr. Ward knew "the lay of the land." "Oh they are all well. How are all at Laurel Grove?" he asked smoothly.

"Berry well, sah, all berry well."

Mr. Ward turned to speak to the old people, taking good care to place himself between Mingo and the door. When he started to leave the house he seemed to remember something. "Oh, by the way Mingo, did you have your ticket changed?"

"Mas Jeems, he bin gon ter town, sah, an Miss Liza say wait til he cum back."

"Ah, then you had it changed when he came back, did you?" Mr. Ward spoke very deliberately.

"When he git back I so busy I forgot, but I hab um fix sho fore I cum er gen, sah."

It was a cool night, but there were signs of perspiration on Mingo's face as he spoke. "I am afraid to trust your memory, Mingo," he said. Then he stepped to the door placing the silver mounted cow's horn which he always carried about the plantation, to his lips, blowing a loud blast.

THE DRIVER

Uncle Joe, as he was called by the Negroes, and Daddy Joe as he was called by the white folks, was Mr. Ward's driver. He was a plantation Negro, the son of a plantation Negro, but he would not have answered to any of the descriptions usually given to the "plantation Negro." He did not have a receding forehead, a protruding jaw, nor bandy legs. In fact, he bore a striking resemblance to a well formed man. He had a thoughtful expression, and although he was rarely seen to smile, he had a pleasant countenance. He was not harsh with those over whom he had been placed. "Boy, doan lemme put me han on yo," was sufficient to bring the most refractory into line, and this was not a mere figure of speech, for when his hand did drop on the shoulder of some erring culprit it came down with a force; the effects of which was felt for a long time after, for he was a man of unusual strength.

But Uncle Joe could laugh, and when he was engaged in relating some particularly ludicrous adventure of Brer Rabbit and Brer Wolf, to his two boys Joe and Hector, at night when the day's work was done, his sonorous voice could be heard throughout the Quarters.

This night the old man had removed the tension from the boys' minds by completing a Jack O'Lantern story begun on the night before. The story was as follows:

"Wonce der was er man. He lib on won plantation en his wife an chillun dey lib on er noder, seben mile off. Von nite de man tink he go see dem, so he ketch er fat 'possum. He put de possum en some oder tings een er bag en start. Wen he git good way on de road he see er brite light. (Dem Jack O'Lantin always lookin out fur trabblers). De lite blin de man an he los de road. Fus ting he kno he fine de man heself een a swamp. Den de jack O'Lantin laf en say, "Now I hab dat bag." De lite gon out wuick en de man cudent see he han befo he face."

Here the old man pleaded weariness and sent the boys to bed, promising to finish the story the next night, for though Uncle Joe had never written a continued story he understood the art of creating a demand for the next number. All the following day the boys talked about the probable fate of the luckless traveler. "I bet," said Joe, "Dat Jack Lantin tak de man bag, den kill um."

"He doan hab ter kill um he self. All he hab ter do es to tak way he bag en lebe um een de dak, en sum ob dem bad wile varmint wat be een de swomp eat um up," answered Hector.

But to their great relief their father had skillfully extricated the poor fellow from his perilous position, bag and all, with no greater misfortune than the loss of his hat which was brushed off by the low hanging branches. His shoes came off in the soft mud of the place. These he did not stop to hunt for as he was glad to get out alive. The boys, thus satisfied went willingly to bed, while Uncle Joe settled himself for a quick nod by the fire. Aunt Binah, his wife, busied herself cleaning up supper dishes. As she went about her work she hummed an old plantation hymn; the humming grew louder as she continued, and soon she began to sing—"I run from Pharo, lem me go."

This seemed to arouse her husband, for he commenced to beat time with his foot. When she reached the chorus he joined in and their strong voices blended harmoniously.

> "De hebben bells er ringin, I kno de road
> De hebben bells er ringin, I kno de road
> De hebben bells er ringin, I kno de road,
> King Jesus sittin by de watah side."

"Hush," said Aunt Binah, "Tink I yer de hon." They both listened attentively. Yes, there was another blast. "Wonder wha dat debble wan wid me now," said Uncle Joe. He slipped on his shoes, got his hat and coat, (meanwhile his wife had lighted his lantern), and hurried out. As he stepped outside a third blast assailed his ears; this to direct him, as Mr. Ward had seen the light.

"Um soun like he ober to Josh house. Wonder wha da him now?" he said to himself, hastening along.

"Ah Joe," said Mr. Ward as the driver reached Josh's cabin, "Mingo has forgotten my orders. Take him over to the barn and give him twenty lashes."

"Cum on boy," said Uncle Joe, not unkindly, yet in a tone that indicated there was to be no hanging back. Under these circumstances Mingo must be excused for not having lingered to say "Good night." In fact, "his heart was too full for utterance." And so the line of march was taken up in silence, Uncle Joe leading with his lantern, Mingo next, Mr. Ward bringing up the rear. When the humiliating performance was over, the party broke up. Mr. Ward returned to the house whistling softly: —

"From Greenland's icy mountains."

Uncle Joe, wending his way back to his cabin, sang in a low voice, "There's rest for the weary."

Poor Mingo neither sang nor whistled. As he painfully took the shortest cut for the main road he conso'ed himself with the thought that—"Faint heart never won fair lady." He did not put it just in that way. What he really did say to himself was, "Well, sum time man hab ter go tru heap to git wife."

Did he win his Dolly finally? We shall see.

CHAPTER V

The Hunting Season at Pine Top

"The Old Flag never touched the ground."

The Color Sergeant At Barrery Wagener

Gay hunting parties composed of friends from the city and ladies and gentlemen from the surrounding plantations often assembled at Pine Top. Many amusing tales were told there of the "Stag Fright" and blunders of amateur sportsmen on their first deer hunt. There was a Mr. Brabham, a carpenter, who being placed at a "stand" for the first time, and told not to let the deer pass him, waited in breathless anxiety. Soon a magnificent buck came bounding towards him almost within arms' reach. Throwing up his arms wildly, his gun held aloft, he exclaimed, "I wish I had my hatchet!" while the terrified animal sped on to be brought down by a more collected hunter on the next stand.

This year however, the festivities were cut short, for Mr. Ward was often called to the city as indeed were many of the other gentlemen who were accustomed to join the gay throng at Pine Top. It was soon known that they were attending Mass Meetings and Conventions. Sometimes Mr. Ward would be absent several days. There were strange whisperings among the Negroes. "Dat ting comin," they said mysteriously to each other, "Pray my brudder, pray my sister." I listened with wonderment, but was taught to say nothing.

Uncle August was Mr. Ward's right hand man. He was equally at home in the fields or in the house, and could always be depended on in an emergency. He was full of humor, a born mimic, and could set those about him in gales of laughter, without seeming to try. Mrs. Ward frequently conversed with him when he was engaged in some task under her directions about the house, or grounds. One day while he was moving some pieces of furniture from one room to another the lady said, "Daddy August, do you know there is going to be war?"

"War! ma'am, Wey, ma'am." Anyone who saw and heard the old man would have been ready to affirm most positively that this was the very first intimation he had had of the impending conflict.

His mistress certainly thought so.

"Why here," she replied.

"On dis plantation, ma'am?"

"Oh no, I don't mean that exactly, but you see, the Yankees are determined to take our Negroes from us, and we are equally determined that they shall never, never do so. Why Daddy August, don't we treat you all well?"

"Ob cose yo does, ma'am. Wha dey bodder deyself bout we fer?"

"That's just it; they are simply jealous to see us getting along so well, and they want to take our Negroes and put them at all kinds of hard work, like horses and mules. They are sending emissaries among our Negroes to make them dissatisfied."

"Wha dem is, Miss Em'ly?" (Of course he had not the slightest idea what an emissary was!)

"Oh they are men who will try to sneak around and talk to the Negroes."

"Wha dey gwine say?"

"Well, they will tell the Negroes that they are their best friends, and so on, just for the purpose of deceiving them you know."

For a second there was a twinkle in Uncle August's eyes which Mrs. Ward did not observe. "Mis Em'ly," he asked with a startled expression on his face, "Wha dem embissary look lak."

"Oh they will be in disguise, you know, but they try to look like our own people. Why?"

"Well yo kno, toder day wen I bin gon ober ter Mr. Hudsin, ma'am? Wen I coming back an git mos to de big gate, I see er strange man comin' up de road. Time as I see um I tink bout dem "Kidnabber" cause you kno dey car off Mr. Hudsin Tom."

"Now Daddy August," interrupted Mrs. Ward, "I don't believe any kidnapper carried off that boy. I think he just ran away."

"Wha he hab ter run away fer, Mis Em'ly? I sho Mr. Hudsin es er good man!"

The aforementioned Tom was at this very moment on the way to freedom by means of the "Underground Railroad," and this Uncle August knew very well.

"Enyhow I fraid dem kidnabber so I mak hase git inside de gate. Wen he git ter de gate he call ter me "Cum yer. I wanter tell you somting."

I say, "Cum een, sah."

He say, "No, yo cum yer."

I say, "I see Mas Henry cummin an I ain't ga time. (You kno Mas' Henry gon ter town dat day). Time as I say dat he hurry way."

"I see yo ergan," he say. Den I say ter maself I know dat da "kidnabber."

"Did you see him again?" asked Mrs. Ward quietly, but she did not succeed in hiding her alarm from the old man. He knew what effect his story (and it was a great big one), would have.

"No, ma'am!" he answered, "An I doan wanter see um gan noder."

Mrs. Ward determined to acquaint her husband with what she had heard, as soon as possible. Therefore, when Mr. Ward returned from the city that evening, she informed him privately of what August had told her. He was even more disturbed than she was. "And," she added, "Daddy August is frightened half to death."

They both concluded that the stranger was a Yankee spy. "It will not be good for him if I find him prowling about here," said Mr. Ward, "I shall question August further about it."

He found an opportunity that evening, without appearing to attach any importance to the incident, to question the old man closely. However, August had nothing to add to what he had told Mrs. Ward. He considered it was already a sufficient "whopper."

But Mr. Ward was uneasy. He told Uncle Joe to have two horses saddled, and they rode over to Mr. Hudson's. He did not acquaint the driver of the object of the visit, but that was not necessary as August and Joe had already had a hearty laugh over the hoax. From Mr. Hudson's they went to Mr. Benton's. To each of these gentlemen Mr. Ward related what he had heard. Neither of them had seen or heard of any stranger in the neighborhood. They both promised to look out, and if such was found it would not be their fault if he did not account of himself. But the mysterious man was never found of course.

Some days after the incident just related Mrs. Ward was superintending some work which Uncle August was doing in the garden; setting out plants and the like, for it was now early spring. A team drove up to the house and the men proceeded to unload a tall pole. "Wha dey gwine do out dey, Mis Em'ly?" asked the old man innocently.

"Why they are going to set up a flagpole. You see we are to have a government of our own so we must have a flag of our own; the Confederate flag. It is going to be a very pretty one, too."

"No priteer dan de old flags upstars."

"Oh yes, a great deal prettier," but the lady was thinking of the old flag her father and grandfather had fought under."

The old man glanced at her. "Well," said he, "It hab ter be berry puty ter beat de old flag." There was more in his words than he meant his mistress to understand.

"Daddy August," said Mrs. Ward, as though not wishing to speak anymore about flags, "We will put that right here," (alluding to a plant the old man held in his hands).

August did as directed, but he was not quite through yet. Presently he said, "Mis Em'ly, wha yo gwine do wid de old flag? Yo pa and yo granpa use ter tink er heap ob dat one."

"Burn it up!" replied Mrs. Ward in rather a vehement tone.

Uncle August knew he had said enough.

It was now about the middle of April 1861. Important matters seemed to require Mr. Ward's attention in the city, and much of his time was spent there. One evening Mrs. Ward told Uncle Ben he must meet Mr. Ward at the station the following day with a pair of horses. He usually used a single horse and a dog cart for this purpose. "Sumting up," said the old coachman to himself.

Mr. Ward had not been home for near two weeks. The Negroes on the plantation knew war was approaching, for though they could not read the newspapers, it is remarkable how well posted they were in regard to the trend of events. They knew also that their master's long absence was to be accounted for in the coming conflict. His return therefore, was anxiously awaited by them; as they hoped to gain some information as to how matters actually stood.

The next morning Uncle Ben had his team in tip top shape, and himself rigged up with his regulation coachman's outfit, including his shiny silk hat. He carried Jake along to open the gates. "I kno wha he want," he had said, "But wait little bit." And he drove away.

As they left the station Mr. Ward said, "Save your horses Ben," but when they swung into the plantation avenue he told the coachman to "let them go."

Uncle Ben pulled up his lines, drew the whip lightly across his horses and said, "Git out."

Tom and Jerry responded and they came up the "home stretch" in fine style. The whole family stood on the front porch waving their handkerchiefs. Mr. Ward waved his in return. As Uncle Ben drew up at the stepping stone, Mr. Ward sprang out, ran up the steps, embraced his wife and children, and kissed his mother-in-law, (a thing which I believe men seldom do). "We have taken the fort," he said, and they entered the house.

CHAPTER VI

The Beginning of the End

That night conflicting emotions governed those who lived on "Pine Top" plantation. In the big house there was gladness and rejoicing, while at the

Quarters there was groaning and lamentation. The Negro believed that as long as Major Anderson held Fort Sumter their prospects were at least hopeful; but when Sumter fell, they felt that their hopes were all in vain. Though the future looked dark, there were two on the place who never gave up; Uncle Ben and Aunt Lucy. You are acquainted with the old man already. Aunt Lucy was the plantation nurse. Years of hard and faithful toil in the fields had gained for her respite from active labor. It was her sole duty now to take care of the young children of the women who had to go into the rice and cotton fields, and those mothers were glad indeed to have such a kind Christian woman as she was to look after their little ones while they were at work. The old woman, though well on in years, was still hale and hearty. "Min, wha I tell yo. De Master gwine bring we out," were her words of encouragement to those who were ready to despair. Uncle Ben's words were, "Dem buckra kin laf now, but wait tel bime by."

Between the "big house" and the Quarters there was a spring from which the people got their drinking water. Every afternoon a long line of children might have been seen with "piggins" on their heads, taking in the supply for the night. On the evening of Mr. Ward's return, the children did not appear. In their stead, and at a later hour, their parents came. It was noticeable too, that they lingered at the spring, being concealed from view by the trees that grew about it. The reason of all this was that arrangement had been made with Jake that as soon as possible after dinner, he was to run down and tell them any news he might gather during that meal. Jake, as a possible gatherer of news! Why that was absurd! He was spry enough about the house and dining-room, but otherwise he was as dense as a block of stone. At least, that was what his master would have said of him. This density on the part of the Negro was, in fact, a weapon of defense—the only one he had. Do you think Captain Small could have run the Planter out of Charleston harbor if it was thought he had sense enough to do so? No, indeed! He never would have had the chance.

I said Jake was to run down. That was a mistake. He was much too wise for that. After dinner was over he sauntered down the back steps as soon as he could. Upon reaching the ground, he thrust his hands into his pockets, and walked slowly toward the spring, whistling, "Way Down Upon the Swanee River," as though he didn't have an idea in his head. "He comin' now," said Aunt Lucy, "Well mi son, wha he say," as the boy drew near.

"Well, ma'am, dey tak de fote. We done now," was heard on all sides.

"Wait, chilun, hope pray," was the old woman's encouraging words as she proceeded to question the boy further. "Wha dey do wid Majer Ande'son?"

"Dey le him go."

"Wha dey say bout him?"

"O he say de Majer es er brave man. He mak er speech befo he cum out. He say, (and Jake drew himself up to imitate the Major) "Genlemen, if I had food fer my men, an ambunachun I be dam if I wud le yo cum en dose gates!"

"Amen, bress de Lawd!" cried the old woman.

"O Aunt Lucy!" said Manda, the housemaid, abashed at the old woman's endorsement of the somewhat impious remarks of the gallant Major.

"Hole yo tong yo braze piece. Go on Jake mi son."

But the boy had little more to tell and so the people went sadly back to their cabins. Aunt Lucy's parting words were, "Hope chilun, pray chilun."

The next day Mr. Ward gave Uncle Sempie orders to prepare for a large dinner party that would be given by him in a few days. This was to be another addition to the long list of similar functions that had taken place at Pine Top under the supervision of the old butler. Among them there was one to which the old man often referred with special pride. It was the great dinner given by Mrs. Ward's grandfather, (for Pine Top had been the home of the Bale's for generations) in honor of the Hon. John C. Calhoun.

When the day for Mr. Ward's great dinner came, the guests began to arrive early; some on horseback, others in carriages, the coachmen vying with each other in the style in which they came up the avenue, and pulled up at the stepping stone. There were distinguished ladies and gentlemen. There were horses that had records, and some of the coachmen had records, too. York, Mr. Boyleston's coachman, was one of these. His horses always showed the best of care and his stables were models of neatness and appointment. He had three well grown stable boys under him who were kept at rubbing and polishing constantly. The boys slept at the stable while York occupied a neat little cabin on a hill a short distance away. Seen early in the mornings coming down to look after his stock, with a cigar in his mouth, he might easily have been taken for Mr. Boyleston himself. As he neared the stable he would say, "Ahem!" and each boy popped his head out and would say, "Sah." Upon entering he went through a minute inspection, and it was for their best interest if everything was found in perfect order. York had the record of having once knocked his master down.

The circumstances which led to this daring performance were these: Mr. Boyleston took great pride in his horses. His stock was always of the finest strain, and it may be added that he appreciated his coachman's ability as a whip and manager. His special pride was a span of dark gray trotters of undoubted pedigree. For these he had bought an expensive pair of blankets. "Now, York," he had said, "These blankets have cost me a great deal of money. Be very careful with them. Never allow the horses to wear them at night."

York took as much pride in those beautiful coverings for his horses as did his master. He never permitted the boys to touch them, but each morning after the finishing touches to the animals, he adjusted them with his own hands. One morning he led the horses out on to the floor of the barn, hitched them, and threw the blankets lightly over them, while he took another horse outside to water. Unfortunately he had tied the animals too closely together. They began biting at each other as horses are wont to do. One of them got his teeth into the blanket of the other, pulled it down on the floor, and together they trampled it under hoofs. The boys were at work at a distant part of the place therefore could not see what was going on. When York returned he was dismayed at the sight. The once beautiful blanket now stained and torn, lay under the feet of the horses! He picked it up, but there was nothing he could do to repair the damage. He placed it on the horse as best he could. To add to his confusion he saw Mr. Boyleston coming down to the stables for his usual morning inspection. The coachman walked to the further end of the barn, pretending to be engaged at some work, while his heart beat almost loud enough to be heard.

"York," called out Mr. Boyleston as soon as he entered and his eyes fell on the damaged blanket, "Did I not tell you never to let the horses wear their blankets at night?"

"I dident, sah, de—."

"You are a —— liar, sir—."

Out flew York's right arm before he knew it, and down went his master. He walked out into the lot, folded his arms, and stood facing the door. Mr. Boyleston got up. As he came to the door York said, "Shoot me down, sah." His master drew his revolver. "Fire, sah, I'se ready," and York stood unflinchingly.

Mr. Boyleston put up his pistol. "Come here to me, York," he said.

"No, sah."

"May I come to you?"

"Yees, sah! I wudent ham a hair on yo head."

"York," said Mr. Boyleston walking out to his coachman, "How came that blanket to be in such a condition?"

York gave his master a straight account of the whole occurrence. "Here is my hand; I was wrong," was Mr. Boyleston's magnanimous answer, "Do not mention this to anyone."

There were not many masters like this one.

Mr. Ward's dinner was a grand affair, and no one rejoiced at its success more than old Uncle Sempie. After dinner the party went out on the lawn where a stand had been erected. Amid cheers the new flag was raised and many gentlemen made speeches which all seemed to be aimed at the "White House." I did not know where that was, but Uncle Ben said it was where "dem buckra wud nebah git." Later I learned that the White House was at Washington, and sure enough they never got there.

Mr. Ward now deemed it necessary to have the plantation carefully guarded at night. For this purpose he chose two young Negroes, brothers, Titus and Pompey. The confidence the southern white had in the Negro, and the fidelity of the latter to the trust reposed in them speaks volumes. Here was this master perfectly satisfied to place the safety of himself and family in the hands of these men, on whom, at that moment, he was seeking to rivet the chains of slavery forever. The men were to relieve each other, and at stated intervals, if things were all right, they were to come under Mr. Ward's window and sing out, "All is well!" If things were otherwise, they were to pull a knob which would ring a bell in their master's room.

Titus was noted for his prodigious strength, and an equally enormous appetite. He created great amusement one night during his watch by standing under the window and shouting, "All is well and I'se hungry!" Mr. Ward took the hint and thereafter the men were each provided with a large "hoe cake," lined with fat bacon every night before going on duty.

The time drew near for our return to the city. We must not remain on the plantation after the tenth of May, for those not acclimated are liable to contract malarial fever. Soon we bid farewell to the old place and to the many kind friends we had met there. The kind-hearted people loaded us with simple gifts. My stay in the country had been most pleasant.

CHAPTER VII

In Town Again

"Mischief, thou art afoot."

On arriving in Charleston we found great excitement there. Men were going about the streets wearing blue cockades on the lapels of their coats. These were the "minute men," and the refrain was frequently heard,

> "Blue cockade and rusty gun
> We'll make those Yankees run like fun."

Soldiers on parade often passed by our house, and we ran to see them. One day a troop of horses went by. The ladies waved their handkerchiefs and the officers saluted. I heard they were on their way to the "Front." I wanted very much to know where that was, therefore, when Uncle Ben and I went to the stable I asked, "Uncle Ben, where's the 'Front?'"

The old man made me no immediate reply. In fact, he never did. Knowing he heard me I waited patiently. Presently he looked up:—"De front, boy, es de place weh dem young buckra gwine ketch de debble," he said, and resumed his work.

Mr. Ward had received a commission in the army with headquarters at Secessionville. It chanced that Mr. Edward Dane was appointed on his staff, and he took my brother, several years older than myself, into the army with him. But the dear boy contracted fever and died. Later, the command was removed to another point in the harbor, and for a short time I took my brother's place as officer's boy! And here I must admit I wore the "gray." I have never attended any of the Confederate reunions. I suppose they overlooked my name on the army roll! I carried a knapsack, too. My uniform consisted of a confederate gray jacket, blue pants, and a Beauregard cap. My knapsack was somewhat smaller than the regulation article, and was covered with glazed leather. It usually contained clothes going to or from the washerwoman in the city. I had a day in the city every week and thus had ample time to do my shopping which usually consisted of five molasses groundnut cakes, at one dollar each! They were not quite as large as those you get for a penny now, either. Once I went to buy a pair of shoes and the storekeeper charged me seventy dollars for them. I tried several other stores and finally got a pair for sixty-five dollars. Talk about little things being high now, why then most things were literally "out of sight"—especially things to eat.

In the early part of our day on the Island things were reasonably plentiful. The real business of the struggle had not yet begun, and General Ward still had cattle at Pine Top. It was his custom to occasionally have a lamb or a "Harry Dick" dressed on the plantation and shipped down to the Island. On these he regaled himself and brother officers. And, "Hereby hangs a tale," from which we get another glimpse of the general's limitation for the Negro.

General Ward had a boat's crew of six men. With one exception they were detailed soldiers—up country men—who had little knowledge of the management of boats. The exception was Dick Brown, a Negro fisherman. As is well known the fishermen in and around Charleston have no superiors in the handling of small craft on the river, or in the open sea.

Dick pulled the stroke oar, acted as coach, and when the wind was fair, he sailed the boat. Relying on Dick's skill and knowledge the general had never missed a trip on account of weather. On one occasion he presented his crew with a side of meat and they appointed one of their number who had had some experience as a butcher, to cut up and share it. The general chanced to pass by while the sharing was in progress. "Ah boys," said he, "Sharing up?"

"Yes sir," replied the butcher, "There are six of us and I am trying to divide as equally as possible."

"Oh well now, I certainly want Dick to have a portion, but I did not expect him to share equally with you white men; a Negro must never share equally with a white man, you know." Where was Dick while this was going on? He stood among the speakers together with Jake, the general's boy and I, for Mr. Ward would never think of being so "unjust" to a Negro as to speak behind his back.

There are two of us alive today. I don't know where General Ward is, but I do know that he is dead. Shot did sometimes fall thick and fast on the Island, but *then*, the general, had the benefit of the sea breeze!

The command was soon ordered to Virginia, and I, being too young to be taken along, was given an indefinite furlough.

During the latter part of my stay on the Island things were tight. As for provisions, well, there weren't any to speak of. Ground-seed corn and hominy with an occasional piece of bacon, was considered very acceptable. Those advocates of "plain food" should have been with us. Nothing could have been more plain than our fare. I don't believe it was unhealthy either, although I have had no desire to try it again. "Pie" is good enough for me. For coffee we had parched grist steeped and sweetened with molasses, "Mule Blood" brand. I went over from the Island in Mr. Ward's boat every Saturday. There were steamers that ran regularly to our Island, ("The Planter," of heroic memory was one of these), but they only crossed at night so as to avoid "salutes" from the blockading fleet. Most of the officers of our command kept row boats in which they could reach the city at their pleasure. Our landing place at first was Market Dock, but when General Gilmore began to raise the temperature in the lower part of the city, we moved our moorings further uptown; for it would have been rather unpleasant to be standing on a wharf and have a shell come whistling by taking one's head off. Furthermore, the head might roll overboard, or else the kind comrade who picked it up might, in his haste, be apt to clap it on again upside down, or backside front; and like the lady who did not receive an invitation to the "pink tea," one would never feel the same again.

"The Old Coffee" and "DeKalb" belonged to our fleet. Captain Christian of the "Coffee" was one of the most popular seamen at the port of Charleston—"as jolly an old sea dog as ever drank grog." I always returned to the Island at night by steamer. Several times, random shots fell near us but we were never hit, and soon got used to them. When one came skipping toward us we simply said, "Shoo fly." At this time I was about ten years old, and rather small for my age. I shall never forget the peals of laughter that greeted my first appearance at headquarters. I boarded the Old Coffee at "Market Dock" and was met on the other side by Mr. Dane who took me up to the place. Then I was taken into a large room in which were General Ward, Captain Parker, Lieutenant Tompson and Jenks. "What in thunder are you going to do with that boy!" they cried in unison.

"This boy is all right Jim," said Mr. Dane looking at Lieutenant Tompson, "He can ride." The laugh was now turned on the lieutenant who, as I afterwards learned, had been thrown from his horse a few days before.

My duties were very light. If any of the old soldiers are now living who were on that Island at that time, (1862–63), remember seeing an officer splendidly mounted, followed by a mite of a Negro boy also mounted, galloping over the Island, the boy was myself. Those who remained at home in the South had many privations to bear, of which I got my full share. Things that we consider common necessities now, were luxuries then. The people who sometimes clamor for war have no conception of what it really is. But let us not dwell on these harrowing times of the past. May we never see the likes again!

CHAPTER VIII
A Turkey Stew

Turkeys and even chickens were very scarce on our Island. It is remarkable how quickly these creatures disappear from the neighborhood of a soldier's camp during war times, especially when rations are scant. I suppose they become alarmed and fly away. Some people may be of a contrary opinion, but we will let that pass.

Adjoining our Quarters there lived an Irishman who owned some turkeys. Besides these there was not so much as a turkey feather for miles around. At this time one of these festive birds was worth his weight in gold. But, there was not gold in circulation hence the amount of confederate money it would have taken to buy one would have equaled the turkey himself—at least in bulk. When Mr. O'Flanagan wanted to buy a piece of real estate, or make some similar investment, he just sold one of his turkeys to some young officer who was willing to part with a small fortune. For these and other reasons you may be sure that Pat kept watchful eyes on his flock.

One afternoon one of these turkeys, without the fear of consequences, flew over into our yard. We had a dog that would "fetch," therefore, Jake quietly remarked, "Sic um, Bull." In less than no time Bull had that turkey by the neck, and in equally short order, Jake had that bird in a bag.

The fence between the lots was a high one. Those on the other side could not see what was going on in our yard, but they heard the dog chasing the turkey. Therefore, it was not long before Mr. O'Flanagan presented himself to the sentinel at the gate. "I wud loike to go in an git me turkey," he said.

Now the soldier had seen what was going on, and with visions of a midnight roast before him, had become a party to the transaction. With a view of allowing Jake time to "cover his tracks" he resorted to "dilatory" measures. "What kind of a turkey was it," he asked with an innocent look on his face, and when he could think of no other questions to ask he told the man he would have to see one of the officers. "There is General Ward coming up the street now," he said, and Pat hastened to meet the general.

"Yr haner, one av me turkeys flyed over de fince an oi belave some wan was afther sittin the dorg on im."

We have already seen that General Ward was a strict disciplinarian even in civil life. He was no less so as a military man therefore he told the Irishman to go in and look for his property, and if he found that any damage had been done to it, he should have ample satisfaction, as he never allowed any crooked proceeding about his headquarters.

In Pat went. He searched in all the out-buildings, high and low without success. He went to the kitchen where Jake was busy getting the general's supper. "The Giaral sa'd oi cud luk fer me turkey. De dorg—"

"Dog nebbah bring no tukey een yer," said Jake, "Yo ken look, doe."

But the search revealed no trace of the missing bird and Mr. Patrick O'Flanagan left muttering "imprecations not loud but deep."

Does the devil take care of his own? I don't know, but during the hunt in the kitchen Jake's heart was in his mouth, for the turkey was hanging peacefully in a bag behind the door where he might easily have been seen if Pat had only looked there.

I do not know whatever became of it. It was never cooked in that kitchen. Jake became alarmed and took it away under cover of night.

Many a story is told about the camp fire, and many a dainty bite goes round that never came from the commissary.

CHAPTER IX
Tom Bale

"If thine enemy hunger, feed him."

In a previous chapter I promised to say something further about Mr. Tom Bale. It was his habit to spend a week or more with his mother every year, and during our stay at Mrs. Bale's, and after our return from Pine Top he made one of his yearly visits, bringing his wife and child, nurse, coachman, and three horses.

It is said that no man is wholly bad. If this is true why the young man of whom we are going to speak must have had his redeeming qualities. But they were never manifested in the treatment of his slaves. He was a very young man. His father had died when the son had barely reached his majority, and he was left in sole control of the large plantation on which were more than four hundred Negroes. It was said, he had from his youth exhibited an ugly disposition, and this early elevation to power did not tend to improve his character. In many instances where the master was harsh, the mistress was considerate; while in others the reverse was true. In either of these cases the servants had a chance, but where both were alike inconsiderate, the fate of the slave was hard indeed . . . . Young Mrs. Bale was hard to please.

Some say that even the devil is not as black as he is painted. I never could endorse that statement. I have always thought he was as black as it was possible to paint him, and a great deal blacker. At any rate I am free to say there was not one, single, mitigating feature in the treatment of those unfortunate creatures who had to serve Tom Bale; they all suffered. A doubled share seemed to fall to the lot of "London," the coachman. To say that this poor fellow had a hard time would convey but a faint idea of his condition. He was competent, faithful and submissive, but these qualities did not secure for him the slightest consideration. Frequently, after going over the cushions, etc., with her handkerchief, his mistress would send the carriage back to the stable as being "Absolutely too dusty to ride in." The slightest complaint from Mrs. Bale exasperated his master against him and he was often severely punished even though he had done all in his power to have everything in perfect order. His patient fortitude under cruel treatment was indeed wonderful. Despite the terrible hardships he had to endure, he managed to extract some pleasure from his occupation. He loved his horses and often spoke of them in terms of endearment. "Dem boys nebber mak me shame yit," he would say in speaking of them, "Wen I say cum Dandy, cum Spug, de Negger dat pick me up got ter know ha be bout."

London and I were the best of friends, and so as to be on hand each morning when he went to the stable I was permitted to occupy a cot in his room, for I liked to go with him. He went much earlier than Uncle Ben. The poor fellow was glad to have me with him at night. It was a relief to him to have someone to talk to. He would tell me about the fine horses he had handled, and others he had known: Of Old Tar River, Bonnet so Blue and Clara Fisher. When he was seated on his box flourishing he whip with the easy grace of the experienced southern coachman, one would not think his life was the terrible grind it really was.

One morning at a very early hour I heard Tom Bale calling from the yard, "London, London!" I tried to rouse the sleeping man without success. Presently I heard the heavy tread of his master coming upstairs.— And London slept!—The balmy air of that spring morning was seductive. The night had been rather warm and London was not encumbered with any superfluous clothing. Now London was very careful with his whips. They were not allowed to lay about carelessly, but were suspended from a rack of polished wood, made for the purpose, and hung against the wall in his room. There was one gold mounted, one mounted with silver, and one was adorned with carved ivory, one had a dainty little red ribbon bow on it, while the two others were decorated respectively with white and yellow.

Bale pushed open the door and strode into the room. He looked at the sleeping coachman a moment, then, with a muttered imprecation, took down one of those whips; I don't know which. I heard the "swish" through the air, for by that time I had covered my head. London thus rudely awakened sprang from the bed. Blow after blow descended upon him until the blood started. "Now," said the tyrant fairly exhausted, "Go down and hitch up my horse! I told you to have my buggy ready early this morning." The abused and bleeding Negro hastened to obey.

Tom Bale had intended that morning to drive up alone to one of his plantations twenty miles from the city. He had hitched a fast young horse to a light buggy. The mistreated London who had handled this animal from a colt had once ventured to warn his master about driving him with an open bridle. In truth, he tried to prevent Bale from possibly having his neck broken. That b—— d——, the bully had replied, "I want his head to show. He has the finest head in South Carolina."

But that morning it appears retributive justice was at his heels, for, late that afternoon the horse reached the plantation with a part of the harness clinging to him; clearly evident a runaway. As you probably know this created no small stir in the place. A searching party was sent out immediately. "Here Ceasar, you take Sancho and two or three other. Hasten out, take lanterns with you. I will follow with a team," and Jim Black, the overseer, hurried away to the barn.

It was remarkable how much time Ceasar managed to consume in getting ready though apparently using all possible expedition. At last they were off. "Cum on boys," he said as they got out into the main road and he started on a brisk run in the direction in which it was least likely to find the missing man. They had gone nearly a quarter of a mile before Black drove out. He yelled at them to come back. Their confusion was so very evident that he simply abused them roundly as a pack of blockheads, and sent them down the road toward the city.

They hunted some miles before any trace of Tom Bale was discovered. At last they found a piece of leather—some part of the harness. It was now quite dark. Lanterns and torches were lighted. A little further on they came to a place where the vehicle had evidently left the road. A few hundred yards out in the pine woods the upset buggy was seen, and nearby lay the young man, pale and unconscious. Even Ceasar felt pity for him.

He was lifted into the wagon in which the overseer had thoughtfully placed a small mattress. He had also dispatched a messenger on horseback who met them on their way back. Upon a hasty examination the physician found that Bale had one leg broken and his shoulders severely bruised. It was weeks before he could be removed to the city, and months after the accident before he was able to get about.

This summary visitation of Providence, should, it would seem, have cured this rash young man; but it did not. At this time the war is on and Tom Bale is impatiently awaiting his physician's permission to join his regiment at the front. The newspapers are giving glowing accounts of Confederate victories. The white people are exultingly jubilant, and the Negroes correspondingly sad and depressed, for though they cannot read the newspapers they are well posted as to the news that comes in.

One morning Mr. Thomas Bale was seated on his piazza in Charleston, reading. The reports of Confederate success pleased him. London, with his heart bowed down was sweeping the sidewalk in front of the house when a fellow sufferer passing by stopped to exchange the usual morning greeting.—"Mornin' brudder Lon'on."

"Mornin' mi brudder."

"How yo gittin on?"

"O mi brudder, ha'd time, an wus cumin," was London's sad reply.

Out flew his master, and with the heavy cane he had carried since his accident he felled the poor slave to the earth. "Say better times are coming, you rascal," he stormed, re-entering the house.

And what did this much abused Negro do? The war being over Tom Bale returned to his home broken in health and fortune; for despite his injured leg he had gone into the war and remained until the end came. At this time many of the men who were engaged in the southern side during the war, not knowing what would be their fate under the new order of things, were hastening out of the country. Bale was among these. He was forced to leave his family inadequately provided for. However, he was still a young man and hoped to retrieve his fortune in a foreign land, or at least to remain away until things were settled.

It was a terrible blow to his young wife with two children to be so suddenly reduced from affluence to poverty. . . . But, there was a friend at hand—London. He had secured a situation as teamster with a wholesale house that had resumed business in the city; and every Saturday evening found him at the door of the house in which Mrs. Bale lived with packages of tea, coffee, sugar, butter, etc., such as she had been accustomed to and could no longer afford to buy; bought with his own money, from the same exclusive establishment where she formerly dealt. Occasionally when passing that way with his truck he would leave a ham at the door. This continued until the death of the lady. Tom Bale never returned. It was said he fell a victim to malaria and died in a far away land.

It is but a few years since London went to his reward. He became a deacon in his church before he died, and on many a Thursday night meeting he would stand and sing:—

> "What troubles have we seen
> What conflicts have we passed!
> But out of all the Lord
> Has brought us by his love.
> And still he doth his grace
> Afford, and hides our lives above."

while tears of gratitude rolled down his cheeks. He had lived to dwell "under his own vine and fig tree, with none to molest or make him afraid."

CHAPTER X
Silla—The Maid

"As we forgive those who trespass against us."

It is more pleasant to me than otherwise that I have no other similar instance of cruelty to relate, coming under my own observation like that of Tom Bale's. Although the following may not be called cruel, still it is not devoid of severity and harshness.

Among our neighbors there was a family whose servants had rather a hard time of it. This family was very religious but not liberal minded. All their servants had to attend the family church.

One of the ladies had a maid whose lot was hard indeed. She was only allowed to wear such dresses as her mistress prescribed, and these were always made of the coarsest material after an original design. She was never permitted to wear a bonnet, but must have her head tied with a bandanna. No idea of economy prompted the mistress. There were those mean enough to say that it was done because Silla was very pretty and the lady was so plain.

Now the maid was fond of dress. She also had strong religious sentiments. She was also an expert needle-woman, and her brother who "hired his time" and "worked out," furnished her with material which she fashioned to suit herself—working at night and at odd times. Sometimes on Sundays she managed to attend to church of her choice, arrayed in such garments as she desired, being careful however, to leave the house after the family had gone, and to return before their arrival. But she came to grief at last.

It was during a season of great excitement in religious circles in the city. The Baptists were making heavy inroads on the Methodist Camp, and the latter found it necessary to bring out their heavy artillery. Many eminent Divines noted for their piety, learning and eloquence had been invited by the Methodist clergy to assist in calming the fears of their flocks. Silla was a strong Methodist, therefore when it was announced that on a certain Sunday a Reverend Gentleman of matchless eloquence would preach, she determined to hear him. It was said that this particular sermon had the effect of sending the wavering ones back to their ranks; for, after an impassioned appeal to his hearers to stand firm, he closed his eloquent discourse as follows:—

"Let others glory in the water
I glory in the blood."

I need not tell you that on that Sunday Silla appeared in a beautiful dress made in the latest style, a rich mantilla, and a bonnet that was not inexpensive. Altogether she presented a very enviable appearance.

When she was ready to start out Aunt Cinda, the old nurse, said to her, "Now gal, yo luk berry nice indeed, but doan le dem tings tun yo hed so de buckra git home fo yo."

"O no ma'am, Aunt Cinda, I'll be in time."

But alas! What with a word of greeting here, and a word of congratulation there, after service, the time slipped by. As Silla sped homeward she became aware of the fact that she was late. She quickened her pace, but "Time lost can never be regained." Miss Octavia had reached home before she got there.

On reaching the house the lady had immediately called for her maid, and was quite surprised to find that she had not yet returned from church. Therefore, she took her seat on the piazza which commanded a full view of the servants' entrance, determined to ascertain from Silla as soon as she came in, the meaning of her tardiness. The lady was not in a pleasant frame of mind either, as she was quite thirsty and wanted a drink of water.

As Silla timidly opened the gate and put her head in she would have withdrawn it, but . . . "Walk in here, madam!" came from her mistress in tones that were not to be misunderstood,

"Where have you been?"

"To church, ma'am."

"What church, pray?"

"Methodist, ma'am."

"And who gave you those horrid things you have on?"

"Bobber Jim, ma'am."

"He did, eh! Come right in here."

Silla's heart sank within her as she meekly obeyed. Miss Octavia followed her servant into the house. "Get me some old newspapers," she said. "Place them in that grate. Take off that hat and lay it on the paper. Now get a match and set the fire." And the poor girl stood there and saw her beautiful bonnet go up in smoke.

"Now madam, go and take off those things and never let me see you with them on again!"

Silla served Miss Octavia for a long time after the war. The lady is dead now, but the maid is still living in Charleston, South Carolina.

CHAPTER XI

The Appraisement

"He will give His angels charge concerning thee."

While we were at Mrs. Bale's and before I went "into camp," I had the following sad experience:—Up to this event it had never dawned upon me that my condition was not as good as that of any boy in the country. With kind parents, two sweet little sisters, an affectionate brother, gentle companions to play with, and every boyish wish gratified, the improbability of my succession to the presidential chair never occurred to me. But now I was made to feel that life was not all "one pleasant dream."

One day my mother received a message calling her down to the Dane's. When she returned she seemed very sad, and upon my father's arrival home I saw them in earnest conversation. Before I went to bed that night my mother told me that I would have to go with her to the Dane's on the next day. "The Old Jay wants to see you," she said.

I was greatly pleased at this for it was a long time since I had been there. When we arrived the next day I found all the servants arrayed as if for some holiday occasion and I also found that they were to be "praised." However, I couldn't understand why persons dressed up as they were, and who had been brought together for commendation, should look so sad. I did not know what I had done deserving of special mention, but I did remember that sometime before my horse ran away with me through the crowded streets, and that I had managed to keep my seat. I finally brought the animal to a stand without any damage. Therefore, I thought I would receive a gold medal, or perhaps "four pence" in money. But to be certain, I would ask Cora what it all meant.

I found her seated alone on a bench in the yard looking more beautiful than ever. "Cora," said I, "What is all of this about?" . . . Instead of answering my question she began to cry and she took hold of me and hugged and kissed me right there in the yard, before all those people!! My, didn't I blush!

The fact was, kind reader, as you have already surmised, the "Estate" was to be sold, and the people had been brought together for "appraisement."

Several gentlemen came out into the yard. The people stood up, and the gentlemen went among them asking questions. One of them placed his hand on my head . . . "Well, my boy," said he, "What can you do?"

"I can ride, Sir," I answered, whereupon my mother gave me a gentle nudge which meant, "Hush." She then explained to him that my brother and I were not to be sold for she had earnestly requested Mr. Dane not to "sell" us. She knew that we should receive good treatment as long as we were in his hands, and that if we went with her, the Negro Traders would soon separate us. With many protestations Mr. Dane had promised her that he would not sell us even if he had to go barefoot. He kept his word, but my mother and two little sisters went and for four years, we neither saw nor heard of each other. When "the cruel war was over" we were brought together again, and you may know there was a happy meeting for—"He had given his angels charge concerning us."—We were all there to greet the gallant Major Anderson when he returned to raise the "Old Flag" over Fort Sumter.

> "'Twas the star spangled banner
> And long may it wave,
> O'er the land of the free
> And the home of the brave."

The war was ended. The Union had come. Soon the schools were thrown open, and under the leadership of the enthusiastic Redpart, and that noble band of pioneer men and women from the North, the children flocked to them. Surely there must be a future for a people so eager to learn as is the Negro, and though we are not yet out of the woods,

"We are coming, Father Abraham
Full many a million strong."

CHAPTER XII

The Big Fire

"Hear the loud alarum bell."

On the night of December 11th, 1861, our dear old home on Guignard street was destroyed by fire. This was the greatest conflagration that has happened in Charleston during my lifetime.

It broke out at, or near the corner of East Bay and Hasel Streets, and swept in a direction across the city to the very edge of Ashley River, at the other side of town; licking up nearly everything in its patch. When the alarm was given Ward 3, we hurried out from Mrs. Bate's where we were living at that time. Not very far away from the old place, looking in that direction, we saw the flames leaping up, and hastened on. The sparks seemed to rain down from the heavens as we ran. When we reached there, we found the engines pouring streams of water on the house, while there was a long line of men reaching from the well in the yard, up the back stairs to the roof of the house, passing buckets of water from one to another.

The devoted ladies stood by encouraging them. "Water! More water!" they cried. But it was all unavailing. The fire soon caught the piazzas, then burst in the windows and doors seeming to say, "Who would stay the 'Fire King?'" Soon the old home together with nearly all of the neighboring houses was a mass of ruin. On swept the flames reaching Broad Street. They raged about the Cathedral. It was thought that owing to the material of which that beautiful structure was built, it would have escaped, but no—under the fierce onslaught of the devouring element, the costly and magnificent edifice melted away; and onward the fire sped, not stopping until it reached the waters of the Ashley River.

I do not know the casualties that attended this distressing event, but the property loss was very great.

CHAPTER XIII

Mr. Ward's Return to Pine Top

"Let us have peace."

It was late in the Fall of 1865 that Mr. Ward was on his way to join his family. As soon as possible after the surrender at Richmond, he had made a hasty visit to Charleston to assure himself of their safety, but had returned to Richmond after a few days stay with them to engage in some clerical work he had previously secured in that city; the compensation for which he found himself sorely in need of at that time. He was now on his way to join them permanently. He had an irresistible impulse however to visit the old plantation. As the train sped on, the desire grew upon him, therefore, when they pulled up at the little station, White House, he got off, determined to walk out to the place. It is worthy of note that this man did not for a moment doubt that he would be kindly received by his former slaves, if any remained there.

Fortunately he met an old friend at the station who gladly provided him with a horse on which he rode out to the plantation, beset by emotions better imagined than described. As he turned from the road into the long avenue a mass of ruins met his eyes. The noble old house had been destroyed by fire! With a sad heart he rode on.

Uncle Joe was at work burning stubble in a nearby field. As he raised his eyes they rested on the lone horseman. "Wonder who da him," he said as he started to meet the stranger, "Um, ee luk like Mass Willum, Lord bless me!"

As the two men drew near each other Mr. Ward leaped from his horse and extending his hand he cried, "Joe!"

They fell on each others necks and wept like children. Oh why did the designing stranger and the native demagogue enter to thwart this auspicious opening of a new era between these men?

After a while they started toward Uncle Joe's cabin. Mr. Ward refused to remount though urged to do so by the old man. As they walked along Mr. Ward inquired about those he had left on the place. Some had gone away. They had sought the city. It were well for many of these if they had remained on the plantation, for the town held many snares and temptations to which they were unaccustomed, and to which they fell a prey. Old Uncle Josh and his wife had gone to Mrs. Ward in Charleston. Uncle Josh was not inclined to leave the plantation, but his wife was anxious to go and see how Mrs. Ward was faring, and if she could be of any help to her. Thus they went.

Mrs. Ward was more than glad to see her old friends. "I thank you very much for coming to me at this time," she said to Aunt —, but I am not able to offer you any wages, for I am without means now."

"I a'int cum fer yo money, Chile," the old woman answered, "Ef yo doan need my sarbis I ken go back."

"Oh you dear old creature, you know how much I need you. I only meant that I cannot pay you anything just now."

And so the old woman took charge, greatly to the relief of Mrs. Ward, also to that of Uncle August who had been constantly with his mistress, and was acting in the capacity of general house servant. The advent of Aunt Peggy allowed him a chance to go out doing odd jobs, thereby earning a few dollars. He steadily refused to accept any work that would take him away permanently from Mrs. Ward. The lady could offer comfortable quarters to Uncle Josh and his wife. The old man soon obtained work in the city and the three servants lived on the premises until they died. It is doubtful if Mrs. Ward ever had any more faithful and truer servants than they were.

Mr. Ward was glad to find that there were still many of his people on the plantation, all of whom seemed glad to see him. Old Aunt Binah, Uncle Joe's wife was dead, and his two boys, now strapping young fellows had gone to the city to work. "Long shore" the old man informed him, also that they had turned out well and came up to see him often.

As they neared the cabin they passed a pen in which were six fine shoats. "Dem b'long to Mingo, sah," said Uncle Joe.

A shade passed over Mr. Ward's face. "Mingo?" he asked.

"Yessah. Mingo mar'ed Dolly, yo kno sah, an ee com ter lib yer wid er. And den wen they gon ter town an my old ooman dead, Dolly un him com lib wid me sah, caise I so lonsum. Mingo is er good christon man sah, an dey berry kine ter me."

The shade on Mr. Ward's face deepened. "Joe," said he, "I treated Mingo harshly once."

"I kno dat, but ee don forgit all bou it, sah."

Mr. Ward sighed as though he wished he could forget also. "Is Lucy still here?" he asked.

"Yee, sah. She es prime es eber."

"Let us go over and see her."

"Praise de Lawd!" cried the old woman as they entered her cabin. Mr. Ward could not speak, but extended his hand.

"Mas Willum, I'se berry glad ter see yer. Si' down. How yer bin all dis time?"

"Well, Ma'am Lucy, I have had some hard raps, but I am thankful to be alive, and to see you all again. A great change has come about."

"Yees sah, God mov een er misterous way."

After a short stay at Aunt Lucy's they visited the other cabins before returning to Uncle Joe's abode. "Sorry de ole ooman ain't yere, sah," said the old man with moistened eyes, as they went in. Dolly, busy with the housework, had noticed Uncle Joe and a white man going to the barn with a horse. They had left the horse there and were next seen coming toward the cabin. With native shyness she drew herself from view, and when she ventured to peep out again, they man had passes her house going in the direction of Aunt Lucy's. "Vonder who dat," she had said, and went on with her work.

Meanwhile Mr. Ward and Uncle Joe had completed their visits and returned. She did not see them until they entered the rear door of the cabin. She was just about to put a large dish into the cupboard when she glanced up. . . . Down went the dish to the floor in a hundred pieces!!! "Don't be frightened, Dolly," said Mr. Ward, smiling and extending his hand. "You got your Mingo after all."

Dolly was speechless for a moment. Then she said, "Ee this you Moas Willum!"

"Yes indeed," replied the gentleman, "and I am truly glad to see you. How are you and your husband?"

"Ve quite well, tankee sah. How yo do?"

"Oh, I feel better now, than I have for many a day," he replied.

The men sat down before the blazing fire and entered into a long and earnest conversation concerning the past, the present and the future. Just before they entered the door, Mr. Ward had noticed a fine possum hanging outside, all cleaned and ready for the oven. He was at the point of express-ing his delight at the sight when he was arrested by the pathetic remarks of Uncle Joe. During a lull in the conversation he turned to Dolly and said, "I see you have a fine possum."

"Yees sah," she answered, "Mingo ketch him las night, and gwine ter hab im for supper. Glad yo cum jest cen time."

"I am glad too," said Mr. Ward laughingly.

Mingo worked at the ferry half a mile away. He was later than usual coming home that evening, and had reached the house without being appraised of Mr. Ward's arrival. When he came in and saw the gentle-man, he stood motionless with astonishment. Mr. Ward got up. Advanc-ing toward the bewildered man with outstretched hand he said, "Mingo, I treated you harshly once. I am ashamed of it, and I wish to ask your pardon."

Mingo grasped his hand. "Doan say nothin bout dat, sah. Ise glad ter see yo—berry glad ter see yo sah. Si down." And the two men had a long talk.

CHAPTER XIV

Roast Possum

"Tun dat possum roun and roun
Tun dat possum roun."

Dolly knew the high estimate Mr. Ward had of old Aunt Lucy's ability as a cook, therefore she requested her to come over that evening. This the old lady readily consented to do, and as she proceeded with her pleasant task, she indulged in many reminiscences of former occasions on which she had officiated to the gastronomic delight of Mr. Ward; and even of old Mr. Bale, Mrs. Ward's father. When everything was ready Dolly brought out a snowy cloth, spread it on the pine table, laid a plate, knife and fork thereon, then she ran down to the spring for some fresh water. Return-ing, she placed a glass of this beside the plate. Meanwhile Aunt Lucy was taking up the supper. On a large dish she gently placed the festive possum done to a turn. Then she carefully arranged some baked sweet potatoes around it. Over all she poured some gravy that had been simmering in a saucepan by the fire. She placed this dish in front of the plate on the table, and flanked it on one side by a dish of rice as white as milk, and on the other by some delicious cornbread. She surveyed the table a moment then announced, "Supper ready."

"Draw up, sah," said Mingo acting as master of ceremonies.

"Surely you are all going to join me!" said Mr. Ward rising.

"No sah," answered Uncle Joe, "It do ve mo good ter see yo eat dan ter eat veself, sah."

Argument was of no avail, therefore Mr. Ward sat down and in a remarkably short space of time that dish of possum and potatoes had very perceptively diminished. After Mr. Ward was through, the table was re-arranged and the others sat down.

The gentleman looked thoughtfully into the fire, and when all had finished he stood up. "Joe, Lucy, Mingo, Dolly," said he, calling each by name, "I can never hope to enjoy another meal such as I have had, as long as I live. His earnestness impressed them all. They made no reply.

Immediately after supper Mingo had excused himself, and was absent for more than an hour. All of those whom Mr. Ward had not seen during the day came in after supper to shake hands with him. Mingo was seen to whisper to two or three of the younger men, and together they went out; seemingly on some mysterious errand.

Some of the older people tarried a while to talk. "Chillun," said Aunt Lucy, "Look at de vonders ob de Master." Then she raised her voice and sang, "And are we yet alive?"

Uncle Joe requested the old woman to pray. They all knelt down while she uttered a prayer of wonderful strength; full of faith and hope. Mr. Ward was asked by the old man to read the 14th chapter of St. John. Uncle Joe, though still vigorous, was quite an old man; therefore, at the conclusion of the reading he sang: —

> "On Jordan's stormy banks I stand
> And cast a wistful eye."

They all felt that he was looking, "For a house not made with hands, but eternal in the heavens." And so he was, for a few months later he passed on to his reward.

They had all joined in the singing and accustomed as was Mr. Ward to hearing them, it seemed as though he was never so impressed as now.

Again and again he requested them to sing, and they responded with such old hymns as: —

> "Roll Jordan, roll
> My bruder, yo aught to bin dere
> To yer wen Jordan roll."

When they rose to leave they sang heartily: —

> "No fearin, no doubtin
> While God's on our side.
> We'll all die er shoutin'
> De Lawd will provide."

Kind reader have you ever heard of those people sing? If a band of these old veterans could be brought together and travel through the country singing their old time songs, I believe it would do more towards settling the so called Negro problem, and allaying the growing unrest caused thereby, than any other single force. The particular ones of whom I write are all, with a single exception, dead; but there are still many of the "Old Timers" living.

Mr. Ward had not expected to stay long, but the hours sped swiftly, and he was forced to spend the night under the roof of old Uncle Joe. Mr. Mingo went to work early the next morning before Mr. Ward was up.

The borrowed horse had been returned by one of the men going to the station, as the gentleman found his stay would be prolonged. Uncle Joe would drive him over to take the train.

After breakfast Uncle Joe went to the barn to "hitch up." When he drove up to the cabin door there was a large homespun sack which seemed to contain something bulky, lying across the rear part of the buggy. "Got quite a load behind you, Joe," remarked Mr. Ward as he stepped in.

"One ob Mingo shoats, sah. Ee kill im las night. Say ee sorry ee didn't hab time to cut up de meat. Yo kin hab dat don wen yo git home. Hang im up in er cool place, sah."

The gentleman made no reply, but there was a strange, far away look in his eyes. As they drove, the old man imparted such bits of information as he thought might be of interest. Finally both became silent. "Joe," at length said Mr. Ward, "You are thoughtful as usual."

"Fine nuff ter tink bout, sah. Member once wen I didn't tink, an ee put de wuk on de plantation bac two days." He laughed loudly as though amused by some recollection. Mr. Ward smilingly asked when this happening had occurred. Then the old man related the circumstances which were as follows: —

Mr. Ward had directed him to have a piece of work done. He had delayed in doing it because there was something about it to which he wished to call his master's attention. However, before he could do so Mr. Ward called him and demanded to know what was the cause of the delay. "I thought sah," began Uncle Joe. "I don't want you to think. Do as I tell you," Mr. Ward had said sternly.

Later the old man's reasons were discovered to be well founded, but his master made no acknowledgment of it. One morning some time after Mr. Ward had said, "Joe, tomorrow morning early, take two double teams and four men, and go over to Mr. Bennett Ward's (a brother of his). There are some things there; furniture, etc., that I wish to have brought here. Make a very early start. I will ride over after you. Wait there until I come."

Now it so happened that on this very day, after Mr. Ward had given his instructions, he received a letter calling him to the city on urgent business. He went down that evening. Naturally he said nothing to Uncle Joe, nor did he change his orders. The old man knew he was gone, also that it was impossible for him to return in time to ride over to his brother's, as it was eight miles across the country. But he was not to think!

By daylight next morning, he with teams and men, was on the road to "Mas' Bennett." On his arrival he told the gentleman the orders he had received from his master. "All right," said he, "Wait." And they waited.

At dinner time Mr. Ward expressed surprise that his brother had not come. At night he felt worried about it. "If he is not here in the morning I shall ride over and see what the matter is," he said.

The next day, when breakfast had been completed, he mounted his horse and rode away, telling Joe to remain there as his brother might come at any moment. He had expected to meet Mr. William on the way, but after riding several miles without doing so, he became quite alarmed and went on to Pine Top. His brother he found, had been called to the city unexpectedly, and had not returned as yet. Mrs. Ward knew that her husband intended to send Joe, but thought he had altered the arrangement when he found that he would be absent. She was just on the verge of sending for Joe to come back.

It was near three o'clock when Mr. Ward got home. His brother was in the act of leaving. "I did tell Joe to go over to your place yesterday, and to wait until I came. I forgot all about it until a few moments ago. When you get home, please see that the wagons are loaded tonight, and let them start back by daylight," said Mr. William Ward.

Not until nine o'clock in the morning of the third day of their absence did they return to Pine Top. Work had been terribly put back on the place. But, Uncle Joe had done as he was told, without thinking.

Mr. Ward remembered facts distinctly. He now learned for the first time the true inwardness of them. "Joe," said he with a smile, "That was not the only mistake I ever made."

They bade each other good-bye at the station. "Remain on the plantation, Joe, and tell all the others to do so until we can see what is to be done," said Mr. Ward as he boarded the train. They never met again!

Mr. Ward entered the ministry and labored for some years on the coast among his own people, in the vicinity where he once had his military headquarters. Was the inspiration furnished by that memorable visit to the old plantation? Who can tell?

CHAPTER XV
After De Union

"Universal Suffrage say to all, Be ye tranquil."

Reconstruction times were now at hand. The ruinous conditions that followed that period have been oft and repeatedly charged to the Negroes of South Carolina. Is this just? Is it true? I say, No! I was but a boy then. I remember going with my father who was one of a delegation of men selected for the purpose of calling on some gentlemen of Charleston. These gentlemen, although they had been slaveholders, were always kindly disposed toward the Negro. I understand that the purpose of the visits was to secure the good offices of these gentlemen in framing new laws for the government of the state.

The first one they called on came out and stood uncovered on the doorsteps, while the spokesman of the Negroes explained the object of the visit. The venerable gentleman thanked the delegates for this expression of their confidence, and promised to do all in his power to bring about peace and tranquility to the state and people.

They made other visits with like results. "Bless be the man who ne'er consents by ill advice to walk," is as applicable to a state of community as to an individual. Ill advice seemed to have ruled the first attempt at legislation in South Carolina after the war; for the outcome of it was the enactment of the Negroes in the state worse if possible, than it was under slavery. These laws were very appropriately called, "The Black Code." It is strange that we do not hear much of that code now. Possibly somebody is ashamed of it.

That was the entering wedge. It opened the door to the designing stranger, and made subsequent conditions possible. It was not the work of the Negroes, but it opened the way for, and brought about, what is called the "Carpet Bag" era, of which nothing good can be said. It was "Bad," very "Bad."

But the state was finally wrested from the hands of the despoiler. The gallant Hampton came to the rescue. About this time men who had found things under the corrupt Carpet Bag System, "as sweet as a daisy in a cow's mouth," awoke to the discovery that the "Civilization of the Cavalier and the Roundhead was imperiled." This discovery it was said, was hastened by the thought that their own heads were no less so. In fact, in Charleston today, a highly respected gentleman and citizen is living, who in a public speech said in effect, "Let us not blame the Negroes; they have been but dupes. Let us rather ornament the lamp posts of the city with the suspended bodies of the rascals who have used them for their own selfish purposes."

At that time I was a young man in the employment of one of the oldest business firms in Charleston. One day one of my employers called me into his private office. (This gentleman was one of the most conscientious men I have ever known. He had been very kind to me, as indeed were all the members of the firm. In all my varied experiences I have never with kinder treatment than I received at their hands). After telling me of the deplorable condition in which the state then was, he asked me to support General Wade Hampton for governor, in the coming election. I told him that while I realized the truth of what he had said, I could not vote for Hampton! Also, that in consequence of the chaotic conditions in the state I had determined not to vote at all. He then asked me if I would go to hear General Hampton, (the general was to speak especially to the Negroes of Charleston). This I readily consented to do.

I do not remember the date of this meeting. It was however, a short time before the election which took place on the seventh day of November, 1876. At the appointed time the Academy of Music was crowded with the Negroes of the city. I could only get standing room. We, the Negroes, could sit in any part of the place we desired then.

General Wade Hampton rose to speak—a splendid man, a perfect specimen of manhood and vigor. The hardships of the war through which he had passed seemed to have had but little effect upon him. He was a fluent speaker. In a forceful manner he told of the sad condition in which the affairs of the state then stood. Our only desire he said, was to save our dear old state from utter ruin. Then, raising his right hand to heaven he said these very words as near as I can recollect, "If I am elected governor, I swear to God that not one right or privilege that you now enjoy shall be taken from you!"

I believe, in fact I know he was sincere, and while I did not vote for him I honored his sincerity. But he had made pledges for his people which they failed to keep. The immediate result of his election was the passing of restrictive measures aimed exclusively at the Negro. The brave old general lived to see the day when he, like his pledges, was laid aside—a soldier and a gentleman. It was well for him that he was bred in the school of the solider; well for him that he was truly brave, else he could not have stood up against it.

"He was a man take him in all for all"
and I fear, we in South Carolina,
"May not look upon his like again."

But the end is not yet, for we hear of other oppressive measures, such as disfranchisement and the like. While this is true it is equally true that the Negro has many friends among the southern white people. Such offensive measures as the "Jim Crow Car," are not the works of the better element of the southern people. Many Negroes owe their success in business enterprises and other efforts they have put forward for their advancement, directly to the aid and encouragement they have received from those who formerly held them in bondage.

If there is a Negro problem before the American people, it is one of the greatest propositions that has ever confronted them. If either of the measures yet proposed could be carried out it would not settle the Negro question, for I hear of no plan yet to remove the Negro from the face of the earth. Though, perhaps even this would find many advocates. If there is a Negro problem, a great principle is involved in its settlement. There is no question of the power of the white people of America to dispose of it in any way they may choose, but, to "settle it," requires the exercise of justice and equity.

To many this problem seems more imaginary than real, and the measures thus far proposed for its settlement seem impractical to say the least of them. One-sided settlements are hardly ever satisfactory or conclusive.

If this is a real vital question it effects the Negro as well as the white man, and the simple principles of humanity and "fair play" would seem to call for the consideration and the interest of both.

Why not call the brains of the Negro into the council for its consideration? There is plenty of it among the men of large caliber, many whose names are frequently before the public, and others whose names are seldom heard. I believe they would convince the country, and the world that this "Great Lion" is no more formidable than those which "Pilgram" saw.

When a boy I knew a man whom I greatly disliked. I did not know anything wrong about him, but there was something about his looks that repulsed me. I never cared to meet him. Some time afterwards I learned something of his history. He had been shipwrecked once. Together with some others he got into a small boat. As they pulled off from the sinking vessel a strong swimmer reached the boat and tried to climb in. This man violently struck the hands of the swimmer away, and the poor fellow sank beneath the waves. He justified himself on the ground that there was already a sufficient number in the boat, and if the swimmer had not been prevented from entering the boat, the lives of these would have been endangered. Perhaps he was right, but I was more afraid of him than ever, for I could not think of him as other than a murderer.

Those who would drive the Negro away from this country for which he has fought and bled, I regard as worse than this man; for, we are all ready in the boat, and they seek to cast us into the sea.

CHAPTER XVI

In the Land of the Puritans

"'Tis a very good land I tell you,
'Tis a very fine land indeed."

For years I had desired to visit "away down cast." I wanted to see more of those people from whom sprung the liberty-loving men and women, who did so much for the amelioration of the condition of the race. I had all ready witnessed the practical working of their christian charity, and the zeal through the labor of that gallant band, who immediately after the war came down to the south with the bible in one hand, and the primer in the other; for the purpose of enlightening and elevating a benighted people.

They have nearly all passed away, for it is more than forty years since, but there remains as monuments to their philanthropy, the schools and colleges they established throughout the southland.

With the view therefore, of becoming better acquainted with these people, I availed myself of the first opportunity that presented itself. Before this I had visited some of their large cities, but the population of cities do not afford the opportunity of gaining such clear insight of a people as the country does. For, in the cities they are on "dress parade," but in the country they are "at home" so to speak, therefore, I wished to visit the rural or semi-rural parts of the country.

It is a "far cry" from the land of cotton and of rice to the land of pie and of beans. Yet, within four days after leaving my home in South Carolina, I found myself among the hills and mountains of one of the eastern states, and I seemed to have landed in the very heart of the "pie belt," as the following story will show.

Soon after my arrival I entered the services of a gentleman, and was assigned to duty at some distance from his residence. It was too far away for me to return to the house for dinner, so I provided with an ample "dinner pail" which the cook arranged for me each morning before I left the house. The first day when I opened my pail at noon, I found some delicious bread and butter, a generous slice of cake, a piece of pie, and a bottle of rich milk. You may be sure I enjoyed this very much indeed. On the second day there were cake, bread, and pie, and on the third day pie, bread, and cake.

Now, I had thought I was somewhat partial to pie, having been accustomed to an occasional bite of that delicacy at home, but this was "too much." There were more than a dozen men engaged at the place, and I discovered that each one of them was as abundantly supplied with pie as myself. At this time there was a dear relative of mine engaged with the same family. She saw how things were going with me, and one night when I returned from work, she surprised me with a dish of rice and tomatoes cooked in southern style. It was a revelation to the cook to see rice served in this manner, but it must have been a far greater revelation to her to see how I devoured it. Soon my relative returned to her home in the south, and once more I found myself eating pie every day like a native.

The country was beautiful. It was in the famed Connecticut valley. The coloring of the landscape was all that could be desired, but there was a lamentable lack of color in the population. This, you must know, was utterly unbearable to any man from South Carolina, be he white or black, unless it be our senior senator. Therefore, I went to my employer and told him if the situation in this respect could not be changed, I could not remain in that part of the United States. "You see sir," said I, "I have a wife and ten children, and ——."

The gentleman leaped making a complete revolution in the air. "Ten children!" he exclaimed, "Where? What in the world!"

Here he seemed to recover his equilibrium. He had four or five children himself. I then explained to him that it was not my purpose to bring all of our children to Spring Lake, that there were ten children in our family, but five of them were at home, while the other five were doing well for themselves in another part of the States; that it was my intention to have my wife bring the five that were at home as far as New York, leave four of them there, and she and the youngest join me at Spring Lake for the present. This arrangement suited him, and he promptly handed me a check covering the amount of their passage.

Before leaving home I had arranged with my wife that if I found my situation satisfactory, I would send for her, and that the arrangement for the children indicated above, would be carried out. Consequently, it was with a light heart I wrote as follows:—

"Dear H.

I enclose check for — dollars. Come on north. Leave Tom, Dick, Harry and Betsy Ann with G—— in New York, and you and Matilda Jane join me at Sorwind.

Your devoted husband."

But at the last moment our plans miscarried; and my wife found it necessary to bring all of the children with her.

The arrival of seven Afro-Americans created some excitement in the little town. I took my family to the Spring Lake Hotel and registered:—Mr. Sam Aleckson, wife and children, South Carolina. The next morning I explained the situation to my employer. He very readily, and with great kindness, placed at our disposal a neatly furnished cottage which he owned. How shall we ever thank the kind hearted Miss M—— who came personally to see that we were comfortably situated, and not in need of anything?

We began housekeeping under very favorable conditions. There was a large apple orchard around the house, and the children were as happy as larks. They had never before seen such an abundance of this delicious fruit. But our troubles were not yet over, as will hereafter appear.

We were quite comfortably situated. I had forgotten all about "pie," and we had resumed our old bill-of-fare: hominy, meat, bread, and tea or coffee for breakfast; meat, rice, and some vegetable for dinner, and bread, butter and tea for supper. One day a kind neighbor stepped in to see my wife. "I have just finished baking," she said, "I have made eight pies, a big pan of doughnuts, some cookies, and a cake. What kind of pie did you have for dinner?"

"Well er, oh, we didn't have any pie today."

"Good land, Mrs. Aleckson! No pie? What do you give those children to eat? Why, why!"

When I got home I found my wife looking worried. "What's troubling you?" I asked.

"Pie," she replied. Then she told me about the visit.

Next day I determined to consult a friend. After telling him my story he looked at me incredulously. "Well, now hain't you been having at least two kinds of pie every day right straight along?" he asked.

"Well no. You see er—er, um—" I began.

"Gosh, man!" he interrupted, "If you are going to stay here you will have to do it."

"Don't you think I might compromise on er, say, one every other day?" I asked helplessly.

"No siree! They might let you off on one each day, but I am not sure of that."

Again kind friends came to the rescue on the next night. When we were about to retire, there was a loud rap on the door. Upon opening it I saw a large delegation of neighbors, headed by our good friend Mrs. B——. It was a surprise party, and they brought us material enough to make pies every day for two months!!!!

CHAPTER XVII
The Town of Springlake

"Maud Miller on a Summer's Day."

I found myself enjoying remarkable prosperity among a kind and hospitable people, who in industry, thrift and economy were unsurpassed.

Near our house there was a large meadow very suggestive of "Maud Miller" and the "Judge." The picture was heightened when I saw a buxom lass at work in the field. However, unlike Maud, she did not handle a rake. The raking is all done now by horse power. Instead she was provided with a fork which she wielded in "tumbling" with as much speed and dexterity as any of the men engaged in the work. She might, too, have proven an acquisition to the household of a judge, as I learned that she was a teacher of the higher branches in a high grade school, and only took this method during vacation to develop health and muscle. I felt sure if she had any rude boys in her class they would get the full benefit of it during the next school term.

The superiority of New England for house cleaning and housekeeping is well known. In house cleaning they excel. This they go about with absolute devotion. The spring house cleaning is scarcely over with when that of Fall begins. Indeed they seem to go about the house continually with hair broom and dustpan in hand. When any stray particle of dust is found, they swoop down upon it like a hawk does on a chicken, and bear it away in triumph to the furnace.

Ours is a great country; great in extent as well as in achievement. But, while many hundreds of miles may separate one community from another, still, through the means of the press and general literature we can readily obtain intelligence of our most distant neighbors. It is remarkable though, notwithstanding these sources of information, how our opinions, formed from what we have read of those at a distance from us, are apt to be altered, or completely changed by actual contact. It is also surprising to what extent people speaking the same language, living under practically the same institutions, and form of government, may differ in forms and customs. Here as elsewhere there are many peculiarities noticeable to the stranger.

Springlake is a historic old town. The public school system is perfect. There is a splendid library which adds greatly to the educational advantages of the place. It boasts of several churches. All the people in Springlake go to church, but I found in traveling through the country, the same falling off in church attendance as is noticeable in other parts of the United States—especially among the men.

When I was a school boy, there was a picture in one of my books that represented a man and woman walking through the forest. The woman held a book in her hand, while the man carried a gun; presumably a safeguard against attacks of wild beasts or savages. Indeed if I remember rightly, there did appear the figure of an Indian peeping stealthily from behind a tree. The picture bore the title, "Going to Church in New England." The date given was sometime in the early settlement of the country. There seemed to be deep snow on the ground.

The devotion evinced by people attending church under such unfavorable conditions attracted my wonder and admiration. This was, no doubt, a faithful representation of that period. But even in the Land of Puritans this good old custom of the fathers seems to be, "More honored in the breach than in the observance."

Somehow mankind seems to require the scourge and the lash. The great religious revival in the far north was preceded by a distressing famine in that country. The earthquake in California set on foot a movement for the abolition of the saloon system. While similar distresses in other parts of this country have caused the "Lion and the Lamb" to lie down together, material prosperity seems to blind men's eyes, and they forget to "Praise God from whom all blessings flow."

Strolling along one day I came upon a neat and substantial edifice. "What church is that?" I asked of an old man who lived nearby.

This ancient was more than eighty years of age. Obligingly he told me the name of the church. "You must have a large congregation."

"No, the number of persons who attended this church when I was young and occupied places reserved for the choir, alone outnumbered the entire congregation that meet here now for worship at irregular intervals," he answered sadly.

There are to be found however, many types of the "Village Preacher,"

> "A man he was to all the country dear,
> And passing rich on forty pounds a year."

for I fell sick, and such a person with his good wife drove six miles, through a snowstorm to bring me words of hope and consolation. In common with those in other parts of our beautiful land, there are many who hope and pray for, and confidently look forward to a great religious revival. To that end let all join, at least reverently in spirit, in the old plantation hymn:—

> "Gib me dat old time religion
> For 'tis good een de time ob trouble,
> 'Tis good wen de doctah gib me ober
> Tis good enuf fer me."

It was summer when I arrived in Springlake, but as I remarked before, summer does not linger here. It was soon haying-time; a very busy season of the year. They had hardly gotten the last load from the meadow before snow came! The snow seemed beautiful—nay, 'tis beautiful. To get the full effects of its beauty you should be in a nice warm room looking out at it through double panes of glass. For, if you have to shovel a half mile through snow three feet deep, you are apt, if you are not a very temperate man, to find yourself using strong and uncomplimentary terms in reference to the poets who sing of its loveliness.

It was my duty to shovel snow; I who had never seen snow more than two or three times in my life before, and at that only an inch or two thick. I had to run the furnace, too. This latter was more to my liking. One day I was sent on an errand during a snowstorm. My way lay down grade, but I went heedlessly on chanting gaily, "Where the snowflakes fall thickest, nothing can freeze."

I had begun to have some misgivings though, for while the flakes were falling thick and fast, I was already half frozen. Some minutes later I knew nothing at all, for down I went, striking my head against a rock. The little Eva of the household was playing out in the storm with the thermometer about twenty degrees below zero, just as happy as are South Carolinian children when they go out gathering jasmines in May. She ran to my assistance, helped me to rise, and led me back to the house. I was stunned and dazed.

When I regained consciousness they were bathing an ugly cut on my head, from which the blood poured profusely. I had relied on Mr. Holmes. I knew he was a humorist, but I confess I had taken him seriously. It cost me about half a gallon of good warm southern blood to discover that he was only joking, for frequently under a very heavy covering of snow, there is a bed of ice as smooth as glass. This is put there by the intelligent New Englander to impart that glad movement to his sleigh, which is so entrancing when he goes out driving with his best girl.

One day when it was very slippery the laundress went out to the clothesline. She was in danger of falling. The chivalry of South Carolina was upon me. I rushed to her assistance, and down I went at her feet. I was in a splendid position to propose, but being already married I refrained. "Arise brave knight," said the lady, "They at the castle doth laugh at us."

My employer was an energetic man. He had built a house on a rock;— rather on the place where a rock used to be. "How are you ever going to build a house on that rock?" he was once asked. Napoleon like—he answered, "There shall be no rock," and straightway began blasting. The result was, a palatial mansion that towers above the surrounding houses, as the owner does above ordinary men in energy and determination. Such a man as he had no time to waste on a "tenderfoot" from South Carolina, therefore, "When the gentle springtime came" he told me I had better return to the sunny south; offering very kindly to arrange for my return passage. But, like the noble Frenchman, I said, "Here I am and here I stay." That is, I declined his offer with thanks.

"What are you going to do?" he asked.

"Work, sir," I replied.

He looked at me with incredulous smile. There was one however, whose kindness I shall never forget. One who had not altogether lost confidence in me, and through whose kind intercession I obtained another situation. By this time I had become "inoculated," and was able to give entire satisfaction to my employers, who were also very kind gentlemen.

The little town of Springlake (you won't find it on a map, for it is hidden away between high mountains), is a most beautiful and a typical New England settlement. Nature has done wonders to beautify the place. Some one has said the Garden of Eden was in the United States. If it were not for the fact that the mercury frequently falls to forty degrees below zero, and that the summer passes like a "watch in the night," I would be inclined to believe that this is the place.

The people of Springlake—well, they are New England people; and that is all that need be said. The women are of course, better than the men, as is the case all over the world.

CHAPTER XVIII

Wrong Impressions

"Twix Twiddledum and Twiddledee."

In many parts of New England a very erroneous impression prevails regarding the attitude of the white people; I mean the white people of the south toward the Negro. The general idea seems to be that the average southern white man sallies forth every morning with a bowie knife between his teeth, and the first Negro he meets, proceeds to lay him open in the back, broil him on a bed of hot coals and thus whet his appetite for breakfast. I found too, that this impression is largely the result of the thoughtlessness and altogether unnecessary talk of many southerners visiting the North, who seem to feel it incumbent on them to disavow the very friendly relations that exist between these two races in many parts of the South, by expressions of indifference, and intolerance, that in many instances are never manifested at home. The northerners do not understand that these expressions are only meant in a sort of "Pickwickian" sense; hence the error.

There is a northern family, a branch of which lives in Dixie, who, before the war were large owners of slaves. Some years after the war, a member of the southern branch visited relatives in the North. In answer to one of the children as to how their slaves had been treated he replied, "Oh we treated them about the same as we did our horses and mules."

Such expressions do no possible good, and are frequently productive of harm. As a matter of fact, the southern family was noted for very humane manner in which they treated their slaves, and some of those old servants as well as the descendants of others, are in the service of the family at this very day.

Again the little girl who had asked this question was asked by one of the servants, how she liked her southern relative. "Not one bit," she replied, "I can never like anyone who speaks of treating people like cattle."

"My father once shot ten of his slaves. Yes sir, shot them down in their tracks because he thought they were planning to run away!" and the young "Munchausen" from the South, looked around with an air of superiority on the Yankee youths to whom he was speaking.

Somehow the impression has gotten abroad that the ordinary form used by the southern white people in addressing a Negro is "nigger." Now, it is well known that this term is never used by the better class, for, "Though I be a native here and to the manner born," I can truthfully say I have never, in a lifetime of fifty years, once had the term applied to me personally; and curiously enough, the only time I ever was offended by it happened in the North. (This of course, was not at Springlake). At this time I was employed at a large store in a country town. One day a farmer came into the store. Now when I was a little boy a kind lady school teacher from New England had given me a little book that contained the picture of the Yankee Overseer on a southern plantation, "Who down in the South became whipper of slaves." Upon seeing this farmer I thought that picture must have been taken from life, for he bore such a remarkable likeness to it.

"Whar's your nigger?" he asked, speaking to one of the clerks, "I got some pertaters I want him to help unload."

I had a good place, but I made up my mind that before I gave him any assistance, I would throw up the job. Therefore I went on with my work, and he got his load off without any help from me.

The term "nigger" is a much controverted one. There is not the slightest doubt that it is offensive to all intelligent, self-respecting Negroes, and is never used by them. This term like any other, without regard to their significance or lack of significance, becomes offensive when applied in derision. And, as has been the case with many other terms, thus applied will lose its offensiveness in proportion, as the object it shall secure the respect of those by whom it is applied.

I can not tell of all I saw and of all I learned in New England: of industry, of economy, of thrift, of wealth, of charity. It is a goodly land, and yet,

> "I love the land where the cotton plant grows,
>   The land where there is no ice.
> I love the land where the jasmine blows
> I love the land of rice."

Both north and south, ours is a great land, and we are justly proud of it. I say "we" and "ours" for I know not what else to say. When I am in the South I feel at home, and as I gaze on the high hills and lofty mountains of New England, I feel as ready to sing "My country 'tis of thee—"as any man in America, for notwithstanding the untoward conditions surrounding my people in many parts of this land, the heart of the Negro is loyal.

"Send him away," say some. "God forbid it!" say I. But, if that sad day should ever come, let the Negro fold his arms. The great fear is that this people are looking in one direction while going in another. The danger is that they may run against a wall.

The financial, the labor, the agricultural, and even the "servant girl" problems have been discussed pro and con very thoroughly. There is one problem, however, that does not seem to receive the attention its gravity demands.

Divorces have reached an alarming proportion in some parts of the United States. It is noteworthy that they so frequently occur where the exes appear to possess in even measure, those qualities that would seem to make them of mutual assistance to each other, and where similar educational advantages should render them mutually agreeable.

The separations too, are often sought on grounds which look ridiculously inadequate. For instance; Because breakfast was not ready promptly at fifty-seven minutes after six o'clock, on the one side, or some equally grave offense on the other side. Were I called upon to say what, in my judgment, are the strongest forces at work to undermine the foundation of this great Republic, I should name, lynching and divorce.

I for one, have no fear for the ultimate fate of the Negro. My fears are for the American nation, for, I feel as an American, and cannot feel otherwise.

Afterword—the
Slave Experience in
South Carolina

—⟋∿⟍—

SUSANNA ASHTON AND COOPER LEIGH HILL

Out of hundreds of published American slave autobiographies, fewer than a dozen address in any detail the slave experience in South Carolina. In light of the fact that slaves comprised over 50 percent of South Carolina's population throughout the nineteenth century, the historical and literary value of the few known extant memoirs is tremendous.* *I Belong to South Carolina* features seven understudied yet significant narratives that need to be understood alongside the handful of better-known South Carolina slave autobiographies as well as within the context of interviews, accounts, and smaller anecdotes that make up the broader corpus of South Carolina slave voices. This afterword seeks to identify some of the South Carolinians who were not included in this collection because their works are readily available elsewhere, because their works are only peripherally about South Carolina, or whose works are otherwise less compelling than the ones included here, and yet whose stories do add a dimension that enriches how we might understand our seven featured stories. In addition, readers are directed to further sources and materials on slave lives in South Carolina more generally.

The narrative likely most associated with South Carolina for both scholarly and lay audiences is the 1836 autobiography of Charles Ball, *Slavery in the United States: A Narrative of the Life and Adventures of Charles*

---

*In 1820 blacks made up 52.8 percent of the South Carolina population; in 1830, 55.6 percent; in 1840, 56.4 percent; in 1850, 58.9 percent; and in 1860, 58.6 percent. See Jullian J. Petty, *The Growth and Distribution of Population in South Carolina* (Columbia: University of South Carolina Press, 1943), 64.

Ball, later published as *Fifty Years in Chains* (1859). This text is not only South Carolina's most well-known slave narrative but also one of the most frequently referenced narratives in studies of slave literature.

While for many slaves South Carolina was their initial point of arrival in the United States, for many others born in the border or northern states, it represented a dreaded destination that signaled a change from the comparatively less severe circumstances of northern enslavement to the more brutal conditions in the Deep South. Ball's narrative paints a picture of how this often horrific relocation worked. Born into slavery in Maryland in 1781, he labored under many different masters until he was sold to traders and forced to march in chains with fifty-one other slaves the entire distance to Columbia, South Carolina.

While Ball never reveals his owner's name or the property he worked on while he was in South Carolina, he describes the plantation and its location in great detail.* His keen observations would aid his escape from South Carolina years later: his recollection of rivers, mountains, and fields he passed on his trek south guided him back north.

Another important slave narrative that has some connections to South Carolina was published by Moses Roper in 1836. Roper's autobiography is of particular significance because it is one of very few direct accounts of slave life from the northwestern counties of South Carolina, a region that was sparsely settled in the eighteenth and nineteenth centuries.† *A Narrative of the Adventures and Escape of Moses Roper* takes place in several states, as he was sold and traded among numerous dealers mostly in North Carolina, but some of his most vivid and brutal memories were of his experiences in South Carolina while enslaved by John Gooch, a cotton

---

*It is commonly believed that Ball belonged to Wade Hampton, a descendant of three generations of influential South Carolina statesmen, war heroes, and slaveholders. See Edward E. Baptist, *Creating an Old South: Middle Florida's Plantation Frontier before the Civil War* (Chapel Hill: University of North Carolina Press, 2002), 82–83; and John W. Blassingame, ed., *Slave Testimony: Two Centuries of Letters, Speeches, Interviews, and Autobiographies* (Baton Rouge: Louisiana State University Press, 1977), xxiii–xxvi. For more information on Wade Hampton and his political and economic influence in South Carolina, see W. Scott Poole, *Never Surrender: Confederate Memory and Conservatism in the South Carolina Upcountry* (Athens: University of Georgia Press, 2004). Also see Cisco, *Wade Hampton.*

†For an unparalleled study of black life in the upstate region of South Carolina, see W. J. Megginson, *African American Life in South Carolina's Upper Piedmont, 1780–1900* (Columbia: University of South Carolina Press, 2006).

planter from the upstate region. For example, Roper reports witnessing an enslaved man being deliberately burned to death by his master during this time in Greenville.* With dogged resilience he repeatedly attempted to escape until he finally managed to flee successfully first to New England in 1834 and later to England. Roper's *Narrative* made an international impact when first published in London in 1836, as it bolstered Britain's support of America's abolitionists. It remains one of the most compelling testaments of bondage from the United States.[†]

The impressive accomplishments of Rev. Alexander Bettis in helping the African American community in Reconstruction-era South Carolina are less dramatic than the stories that Roper was able to tell. Still, they represent an equally important kind of life narrative recounting the experiences of transitional generations that had survived both slavery and Reconstruction-style freedom. Born a slave in 1836 near Trenton, South Carolina, Bettis was spared the more brutal aspects of slavery as a house servant and was entrusted by his owners to oversee the family's business transactions. Despite a South Carolina state law that prohibited the education of slaves, Bettis's mistress taught him to read, although he never learned to write.[‡]

Ordained as a preacher during the Civil War, Bettis organized forty Baptist churches and two of the earliest black Baptist associations in South Carolina. Recognizing that proper schooling was unattainable for black children in the virulent racist atmosphere of the post–Civil War South, in

---

*In an 1836 letter to Thomas Price, Roper describes witnessing a slave burned alive in Greenville, South Carolina. The victim's offense was supposedly preaching to his fellow slaves against his master's orders and attempting escape to avoid the severe whipping he was to receive. See Blassingame, *Slave Testimony*, 24–26.

[†]For an especially insightful reading of Roper's narrative, see William L. Andrews, *To Tell a Free Story: The First Century of Afro-American Autobiography 1760–1865* (Urbana: University of Illinois Press, 1986), 90–96.

[‡]Despite the fact that slave literacy had already been banned in both 1740 and 1800, South Carolina passed some of the most restrictive antiliteracy laws in 1834 out of fear of the growing number of slave rebellions led by literate slaves—in particular, the failed rebellion plotted by Denmark Vesey in Charleston in 1822. See Tom Fox, "From Freedom to Manners: African-American Literacy in Nineteenth Century America," in *Contested Terrain: Diversity, Writing, and Knowledge*, edited by Phyllis Kahaney and Judith Liu (Ann Arbor: University of Michigan Press, 2001), 53. See also Janet Duitsman Cornelius, *When I Can Read My Title Clear: Literacy, Slavery, and Religion in the Antebellum South* (Columbia: University of South Carolina Press, 1991).

1881 he founded Bettis Academy in Edgefield County.* The goal of Bettis Academy was to educate black children based on Christian principles so that they might "command and, ultimately demand, the respect, confidence and esteem of the white people, and in prosperity live at peace among them."† Bettis's memoir, *Brief Sketch of the Life and Labors of Rev. Alexander Bettis: Also an Account of the Founding and Development of the Bettis Academy,* written and published in 1913 by his protégé Alfred W. Nicholson, highlights the principles Bettis sought to instill through church and school. Even though hagiographic to a fault, the narrative nonetheless tells a genuinely moving story of a former slave who grew to be an impressive community leader exemplifying all that was idealized as the self-made man in the mode of Booker T. Washington.‡

The life stories of two other slaves were also linked to South Carolina, albeit in less conspicuous ways. Louisa Picquet, for example, was born around 1828 in Columbia, South Carolina, and was sold as a baby with her mother to a plantation owner in Georgia.** Louisa and her mother were then separated by sale when she was just thirteen years old, and her mother was sent to Texas while Louisa was sent to her new master in New Orleans. Picquet was one-eighth black, or to use the terms of the period,

*For further reading on black academics in post-Reconstruction-era South Carolina, see Adam Fairclough, *A Class of Their Own: Black Teachers in the Segregated South* (Cambridge, Mass.: Harvard University Press, 2007); and George Brown Tindall, *South Carolina Negroes, 1877–1900* (Columbia: University of South Carolina Press, 2002).

†Alfred W. Nicholson, *Brief Sketch of the Life and Labors of Alexander Bettis* (Trenton, S.C.: Alfred W. Nicholson, 1913), 52. Also see Miriam Jean Smith, "The History of Alexander Bettis and the History of Bettis Academy" (M.A. thesis, University of South Carolina, 1951).

‡See Orville Vernon Burton, *In My Father's House Are Many Mansions: Family and Community in Edgefield, South Carolina* (Chapel Hill: University of North Carolina Press, 1985). Also see Burton, "Race and Reconstruction: Edgefield County, South Carolina," *Journal of Social History* 12, no. 1 (1978): 31–56. For further examination of the slave experience in Edgefield County, see Todd Leonard, *Carolina Clay: The Life and Legend of the Slave Potter Dave* (New York: Norton, 2008).

**For recent scholarship on Picquet's narrative, see Gabrielle P. Foreman, "Who's Your Mama? 'White' Mulatta Genealogies, Early Photography, and Anti-Passing Narratives of Slavery and Freedom," *American Literary History* 14, no. 3 (Fall 2002): 505–39. Also see Stephanie Li, "Resistance, Silence, and Placées: Charles Bon's Octoroon Mistress and Louisa Picquet," *American Literature* 79, no. 1 (March 2007): 85–112; Shelli Fowler, "Marking the Body, Demarcating the Body Politic: Issues of Agency and Identity in Louisa Picquet," *CLA Journal* 40, no. 4 (June 1997): 467–79.

an octoroon, and was valued for her light complexion.* She became her master's mistress, bearing him four children. After his death, she was set free and began a search for her mother, which ended with them successfully being reunited. Her memoir was penned in 1861 by a Methodist minister who became fascinated by Picquet's quest to free her mother. While she, not surprising, had very few memories of her experience in South Carolina, her account of displacement and dislocation reminds us again that South Carolina was not only an arrival point for the international slave trade but also a launching point for the domestic slave trade, in both cases dispersing enslaved peoples throughout the United States.

One of the more sensational South Carolina slave stories is *History and Medical Description of the Two-Headed Girl,* an 1869 autobiography of the conjoined twins Millie and Christine McKoy.† Born as slaves in Columbus County, North Carolina, in 1851, the twins had two heads, four arms, and four legs but were joined at the pelvis. By the time they were just three years old, the twins had been medically examined countless times, sold to two different buyers, stolen by a Texan swindler, and displayed at numerous exhibitions, including P. T. Barnum's American Museum in New York

---

*Octoroons and quadroons, or one-quarter blacks, occupied a solitary class in antebellum Louisiana culture. With exceptionally fair features, octoroons and quadroons were generally considered to be part of a separate and higher caste than darker-skinned blacks and mulattoes. However, despite their appearances, caste standing, and often ambiguously free status, they were nonetheless subjected to social exclusions and other racial prejudices. Without a broad social group to mingle with, octoroons and quadroon women often turned to white men for support, ideally by a formal binding, or a "marriage" of sorts. In this contract the man paid a set amount to the woman's parents, and she acquired his last name, as well as the eligibility to inherit property. Despite these privileges, quadroons and octoroons were still shunned by white women in particular and were treated socially as a slave class by all whites. See Karl Bernhard, "Attending a Quadroon's Ball," in *A Documentary History of Slavery in North America,* edited by Willie Lee Rose (Athens and London: University of Georgia Press, 1999), 424. For a broader overview of the topic, see Werner Sollars, *Interracialism: Black-White Intermarriage in American History, Literature and Law* (Oxford and New York: Oxford University Press, 2000). Also see Suzanne Bost, *Mulattas and Mestizas: Representing Mixed Identities in the Americas, 1850–2000* (Athens: University of Georgia Press, 2003).

†The 1869 biography of the twins was published to promote their circus performance and included a medical report verifying their physical condition. A second, undated version of the biography, *A History of the Carolina Twins, Told in Their Own*

City.* After an international custody battle, Millie and Christine were finally reunited with their mother, Monemia, and legal owner, Joseph P. Smith. While the twins continued to tour and perform, they were based in Spartanburg and regularly returned there for many years before, during, and after the Civil War.

Even after emancipation the twins stayed in Spartanburg with the widowed Mrs. Smith to help the family financially, citing their devotion to continue to "contribute to the happiness and comforts of the surviving members of our late master's family."† Eventually Millie and Christine moved back to North Carolina and returned to touring. Now known as "the Two-Headed Nightingale," they became famous globally, performing for audiences across the world.‡

No less exceptional is the life story of the slave Omar Ibn Said, an African captive brought to South Carolina in 1807.** Said was born in

---

Peculiar Way by One of Them, lacks the medical report but is an exact reprint of the autobiographical text. An 1871 version, entitled *Biographical Sketch of Millie-Christine, the Two-Headed Nightingale,* was reprinted for their London tour. This version was altered by their agents to lure the English audience, who changed the title to reference a former beloved performer, Jenny Lind, the Swedish Nightingale, and added (not necessarily factual) Revolutionary War references regarding Millie and Christine's birthplace in North Carolina. See Joanne Martell, *Fearfully and Wonderfully Made* (Winston-Salem, N.C.: John F. Blair, 2000), 158–59, in which Martell refers to the twins as Millie-Christine in her biography, although several variations of this name have been recorded: primarily Millie Chrissie, Chrissie Millie, and Christine Millie. For a comparative study of race and disability as it related to the McKoy twins, see Linda Frost, *Conjoined Twins in Black and White: The Lives of Millie-Christine McKoy and Daisy and Violet Hilton* (Madison: University of Wisconsin Press, 2009).

*Phineas Taylor Barnum (1810–91) became infamous as an entertainer and traveling showman who ushered in an era defined by America's fascination with freak shows and human oddities. See Neil Harris, *Humbug: The Art of P. T. Barnum* (Chicago: University of Chicago Press, 1981). For further reading on race in the era of freak shows in America, see Leonard Cassuto, *The Inhuman Race: The Racial Grotesque in American Literature and Culture* (New York: Columbia University Press, 1997); and Rosemarie Garland Thomson, *Freakery: Cultural Spectacles of the Extraordinary Body* (New York: New York University Press, 1996).

†Millie-Christine McKoy, *History* (Buffalo, N.Y.: Warren, Johnson & Co., 1869), 16.
‡Martell, *Fearfully and Wonderfully Made,* 261.

**Said was one of the last generation of Africans captured for import to the United States before bans on the importation of slaves were passed. The international slave trade was an issue of high debate among the Founding Fathers during

1770 near present-day Senegal to a wealthy family of the Fula tribe. When Said was five years old, his father was killed in a tribal war, after which the young boy was sent to live with his uncle. There he began to study Arabic and the Muslim religion with Muhammadan missionaries.*

Taken captive during a series of tribal wars, Said was sold to an American slave trader and taken across the Atlantic to Charleston in 1807.† Said labored under harsh conditions on a South Carolina rice plantation with a master he describes as a "small, weak and wicked man called Johnson, a complete infidel, who had no fear of God at all."‡ After two years Said ran away, ending up in Fayetteville, North Carolina. There he was discovered

---

the Constitutional Convention of 1787 and throughout the late eighteenth century. Many opponents of slavery saw the banning of the international slave trade as the first step toward the gradual abolishment of all slavery. Yet, ironically, some supporters of slavery saw the abolition of the international slave trade as increasing the value of the people they already held in bondage. Representatives from the lower South, however, were suffering from labor shortages that the domestic trade could not meet—causing their economy to weaken—and they therefore demanded that the capture of African people continue. Thus they forced a constitutional compromise forbidding Congress to outlaw the international slave trade for a twenty-year period. The ban was enacted in 1807 and took effect in 1808. Far from gradual demise, however, slavery thrived in the domestic trade just a decade later with the boom in cotton production throughout the Deep South. See Kolchin, *American Slavery*, 78–80. Alternate spellings of the name Omar Ibn Said are Omar Ibn Seid and Umar Ibn Said.

†Allen D. Austin, *African Muslims in Antebellum America: Transatlantic Stories and Spiritual Struggles* (New York: Routledge, 1997), 133; Tabish Khair, *Other Routes: 1500 Years of African and Asian Travel Writing* (Bloomington: Indiana University Press, 2005), 215–17; George H. Callcott, "Omar Ibn Seid, a Slave Who Wrote an Autobiography in Arabic," *Journal of Negro History* 39 (January 1954): 59.

‡While most scholars agree on the events surrounding Said's sale into slavery, there are other interpretations. Said claims in his autobiography that a large army came to his village, killed many of his people, and captured him. Political tribal wars raging at this time in his homeland coincide with his narrative. However, the University of North Carolina's online database Documenting the American South includes a summary of Said's life that asserts he was sold by his own people to slave traders after being found guilty of an unspecified crime. See Thomas Parramore, "*Omar ibn Said, born 1770?*," edited by William A. Andrews, in *Documenting the American South*, http://docsouth.unc.edu/nc/omarsaid/bio.html.

*Omar Ibn Said, "Autobiography of Omar Ibn Said, Slave in North Carolina," *American Historical Review* 30 (July 1925): 793.

and put in a local jail, where he attracted curiosity by writing pleas in Arabic on the cell walls, begging not to be returned to Charleston. When a South Carolina agent arrived to take Said back to Charleston, Gen. James Owen, an influential figure in North Carolina who was impressed by Said, paid nearly a thousand dollars to purchase him.

Under the ownership of General Owen and his brother John, Said was exempted from hard labor and was even presented with a Bible translated into Arabic after his conversion to Christianity.* In 1831 he composed the only known American slave narrative written in Arabic.† Over the past decade scholars of American slavery have taken a closer look at the Muslim slave experience in the New World and, in particular, how places such as South Carolina were instrumental to that forced transatlantic meshing of religions and cultural identities exemplified by Said's story.‡

The transatlantic nature of slave culture in the Americas can also be seen in the life of David George (circa 1749–1810), a man who escaped slavery during the American Revolution and, like Boston King, was transported first to Nova Scotia and then to Sierra Leone. George's narrative *An Account of the Life of Mr. David George, from Sierra Leone in Africa: Given by Himself in a Conversation with Brother Rippon of London and Brother Pearce of Birmingham* (1793) chronicles his birth in Virginia and his escape to South Carolina, where he hid first with the Creek Indians and later with a Natchez chief, who eventually betrayed him by selling him to

---

*This Bible was likely intended to encourage his conversion to Christianity. Said's autobiography refers to changing over to the language of Christian prayers, but whether or not he fully converted is a matter of controversy. Some scholars challenge the assumption that Said was successfully converted to Christianity. See Richard Brent Turner, *Islam in the African-American Experience* (Bloomington: Indiana University Press, 1997), 38; Geneive Abdo, *Mecca and Main Street: Muslim Life in America after 9/11* (New York: Oxford University Press, 2006), 68–69; Austin, *African Muslims*, 129–33.

†One other African-born Muslim slave in the New World, Abu Bakr as-Siddiq, wrote an autobiography in Arabic, but his narrative concerned his experiences in Jamaica, not the United States. See Austin, *African Muslims*, 129; and Khair, *Other Routes*, 215. Despite its early composition, Said's narrative was first published in English in 1864, while the first authoritative translation of the narrative in its entirety did not appear until July 1925.

‡For further study on Omar Ibn Said and Islam in American slavery, see Austin, *African Muslims*, 129–56; Khair, *Other Routes*, 215–21; Turner, *Islam*, 37–40.

a plantation in Silver Bluff, South Carolina. Converted to the Baptist faith, George took on the leadership of a small black Silver Bluff congregation, and in 1774 or 1775 he helped establish what is generally recognized as the first African American Baptist church. When George's owner abandoned his plantation to flee the British advance, George and fifty other slaves from the Silver Bluff church absconded en masse to the British lines. By 1782 David George was transported out of British-occupied Savannah in thanks for his Loyalist service and settled in Nova Scotia. Like King, George also eventually chose to emigrate from Nova Scotia to Sierra Leone, where he preached until his death in 1810.*

While there are but a few written autobiographies to offer a glimpse into the South Carolina slave experience, other materials such as interviews, petitions, newspaper articles, and letters provide an invaluable source of South Carolina slave voices.† Interviews make up the bulk of these resources, with the earliest systematic documentation of slave interviews beginning before the Civil War.

In 1855 the white journalist and abolitionist Benjamin Drew traveled throughout Canada interviewing slave refugees from the southern states. Drew interviewed over a hundred former slaves who had escaped to Canada, and in 1856 he published a compilation of these brief fugitive stories as *The Refugee; or, The Narratives of Fugitive Slaves in Canada*.‡ Four of the fugitives, Aaron Siddles, Henry Crawhion, William L. Humbert, and Harry Thomas, survived slavery in South Carolina, although only

---

*For more information on David George, see Joanna Brooks and John Saillant, *"Face Zion Forward": First Writers of the Black Atlantic, 1785–1798* (Boston: Northeastern University Press, 2002); for the specific quotations from George's account, see page 180 of that anthology. See also D. Bruce Hindmarsh, *The Evangelical Conversion Narrative* (New York and London: Oxford University Press, 2005), 330–37. Also see Gordon Grant, *From Slavery to Freedom: The Life of David George, Pioneer Black Baptist Minister* (Hansport, Nova Scotia: Lancelot Press, for Acadia Divinity College and the Baptist Historical Committee of the United Baptist Convention of the Atlantic Provinces, 1992).

†Blassingame, *Slave Testimony*, offers numerous examples of South Carolina narratives gathered from varying sources, such as letters, newspaper and magazine interviews, interviews by scholars, and published autobiographies.

‡*The Refugee* was originally published as *A North-Side View of Slavery*. Drew's work was an immediate response to an 1854 proslavery document by the northerner Rev. Nehemiah Adams entitled *A South-Side View of Slavery*. Prior to his return from an extensive tour of the South, Adams had been a major antislavery proponent at the

Crawhion and Thomas describe their experiences in detail. These narrative interviews describe quick use of the lash, among other barbaric punishments, and illustrate how what might seem like vicious pettiness could actually underscore systemic imposition of violent control. Taken by traders to Charleston, Crawhion describes, for example, being "taken up and put in the calaboose," where he received thirty-nine lashes for lighting a cigar in the street.* Harry Thomas sums up his South Carolina experience by bluntly stating that "the treatment there was barbarous," and he tells of an incident in which he was strapped to a pine log for a whipping. *Refugees from Slavery*, like other collections of brief slave interviews concerned with compiling a breadth of data for the abolitionist cause, emphasizes the most sensational aspects of suffering. Nonetheless, the collection provides a devastating glimpse into the South Carolina slave experience and should be considered along with many of the gentler and more nostalgic interviews documented with former slaves from later generations.

Other snippets of information culled from early interviews include accounts compiled by Samuel J. Howe. In 1863, eight years after Drew conducted his Canadian interviews, Howe, also an American abolitionist, traveled to Canada and several southern states and interviewed twenty-eight former slaves. He recorded their stories for entry into the files of the American Freedman's Inquiry Commission (AFIC). Headed by Howe and two other antislavery proponents, this committee was appointed by the government soon after the Emancipation Proclamation to determine how to approach African American policy by researching the conditions of freed blacks throughout the country. Howe's approach was more systematic than Drew's had been. Howe recorded the accounts verbatim, interviewing blacks from the border states, the lowcountry and coastal

---

pulpit and even led a petition opposing the extension of slavery into new territories. His reversal of opinion in *A South-Side View of Slavery,* such as challenging assumptions on the evils of slavery and attacking the veracity of Harriet Beecher Stowe's *Uncle Tom's Cabin,* incited a frantic response from northern abolitionists. In response to the crisis, Drew traveled to Canada to disprove Adams's claims with actual stories from refugees of slavery. He estimated that there were approximately thirty thousand refugees from the southern slave states in Canada at the time. One of the fugitives interviewed by Drew was Harriet Tubman. See Tilden G. Edelstein, introduction to *Refugees from Slavery: Autobiographies of Fugitive Slaves in Canada,* edited by Benjamin Drew (Mineola, N.Y.: Dover Publications, 2004), ix–xi.

*"Calaboose" is a slang term for a jailhouse.

region of South Carolina, and the Deep South. Of the twenty-eight interviews, those of Solomon Bradley, a blacksmith and cook; Robert Smalls, who later became a congressman for South Carolina; and Henry McMillan, a field hand, describe their often horrific experiences as enslaved people in South Carolina.* These chilling interviews paint a graphic portrait of slavery in South Carolina and provide insights not found in later postbellum interviews and autobiographies.†

It was three-quarters of a century before another organized effort to document slaves' stories was undertaken. The Federal Writers' Project *Slave Narrative Collection*, a massive resource of 2,194 slave narratives recorded from 1936 to 1938 and representing seventeen states, became the largest resource of slave interviews ever compiled. The 341 South Carolina narratives make up volume 14, which is organized alphabetically by interviewed former slaves and sectioned into four parts of approximately 100 narratives each. Most of the Works Projects Administration (WPA) narratives are brief accounts, but interviews with former slaves from South Carolina are some of the lengthiest.‡

---

*Robert Smalls (1839–1915) served in the House of Representatives from 1875 to 1879, 1882 to 1883, and 1884 to 1887. Born a slave in Beaufort, S.C., he became famous for piloting a Confederate steamer out of Charleston harbor during the Civil War and delivering it to the Union naval forces. See Philip Dray, *Capitol Men: The Epic Story of Reconstruction through the Lives of the First Black Congressmen* (Boston: Houghton Mifflin, 2008). See also Andrew Billingsley, *Yearning to Breathe Free: Robert Smalls of South Carolina and His Families* (Columbia: University of South Carolina Press, 2007).

†The entire collection of AFIC interviews can be found in Blassingame, *Slave Testimony*.

‡Many scholars have noted some problems in relying on the WPA narratives for insights into the slave experience. Southern blacks during the Depression often lived near or worked as sharecroppers for their former masters and would presumably have been cautious in negative responses, as is evident in the South Carolina stories. The general image drawn by former slaves who spoke with white interviewers, particularly those from South Carolina, was one of a paternalistic system run by generous masters and an overall nostalgic recollection of old plantation days. Those conducted by black interviewers reveal much more regarding punishments and resistance, as well as social and cultural aspects of the slave community. See Blassingame, *Slave Testimony*, liii–lv. Despite these biases and inconsistencies, the WPA interviews remain an invaluable resource in their sheer size and scope. Many of the volumes have recently been published in paperback, including all four parts of volume 14, the *South Carolina Narratives*. Furthermore, the entire collection has been digitized by the Library of Congress and is accessible online. See Blassingame,

As more and more historical periodicals become digitized and searchable, it is quite likely that other South Carolina narratives or interviews may be unearthed. We can only hope that the seven people profiled in this collection and the handful of other voices cited in this afterword are merely the first of many voices to be recovered and that as more are discovered, an even richer and more nuanced portrait of South Carolina history can be painted.

Slave Testimony, li; John W. Blassingame, "Using the Testimony of Ex-Slaves: Approaches and Problems," *Journal of Southern History* 14 (1975): 473–92; Benjamin A. Botkin, ed., *Lay My Burden Down: A Folk History of Slavery* (New York: Dell Publishing, 1989); Charles T. Davis and Henry Louis Gates, Jr., eds., *The Slave's Narrative* (New York: Oxford University Press, 1985); Norman R. Yetman, "The Background of the Slave Narrative Collection," *American Quarterly* 19 (1967): 534–53.

INDEX

ABOUT THE EDITORS

SUSANNA ASHTON is an associate professor and associate chair in the Department of English at Clemson University. She is the author of *Collaborators in Literary America, 1870–1920* and coeditor of *These "Colored" United States: African American Essays from the 1920s*.

ROBYN E. ADAMS is a graduate student in public history at North Carolina State University. DEANNA L. PANETTA is a graduate student in pubic history at the University of North Carolina at Charlotte. E. LANGSTON CULLER is a graduate student in English at the College of Charleston. MAXIMILIEN BLANTON, LAURA V. BRIDGES, and KELLY E. RIDDLE are recent graduates from Clemson University. Cooper Leigh Hill is a graduate student in history at Clemson University.